The Christian Soldier

CLASSIC EXPOSITIONS
FROM D. MARTYN LLOYD-JONES

God's Ultimate Purpose Ephesians 1

Ephesians 1, which sets forth God's glorious plan and destiny for the church, is basic to all New Testament studies.

God's Way of Reconciliation Ephesians 2

These masterful expositions reach the heart of the human problem— our estrangement from God. They drive home the fact that nothing is more relevant today than the message of how God reconciles the world to himself.

The Unsearchable Riches of Christ Ephesians 3

"We can never know too much concerning the great doctrines of the Faith, but if that knowledge does not lead to an ever deeper experience of the love of Christ, it is merely the knowledge that puffeth up." — Lloyd-Jones

Darkness and Light Ephesians 4:17 – 5:17

In his usual incisive fashion Lloyd-Jones explores "How are we to grow up into Christ in all things? How are we to attain to this perfect man? How are we to maintain the unity of the Spirit in the bond of peace?".

Life in the Spirit In Marriage, Home, and Work
Ephesians 5:18 – 6:9

For preachers and teachers, parents and young people, this is an excellent guide for the solid application of the Bible to the perplexities of marriage and family.

The Christian Warfare Ephesians 6:10 – 13

Not only does Lloyd-Jones deal with the character and strategy of the devil in general terms, but he also demonstrates "the wiles of the devil" through discouragement, anxiety, false zeal, lack of assurance, and worldliness.

The Christian Soldier Ephesians 6:10 – 20

What is involved in spiritual warfare? What are the provisions God makes for His servants? Lloyd-Jones answers these questions by examining "the whole armour of God." He explores the general principles of spiritual warfare and the pieces of armour Paul mentions.

The Christian Soldier

An Exposition of Ephesians 6:10 to 20

D. M. LLOYD-JONES

BAKER BOOK HOUSE
Grand Rapids, Michigan

Reprinted 1978 by Baker Books
a division of Baker Book House Company
P.O. Box 6287, Grand Rapids, MI 49516-6287
with permission of the copyright owner

ISBN: 0-8010-5583-0

Tenth printing, May 1995

Printed in the United States of America

Preface

This volume completes the exposition of the Epistle to the Ephesians chapter 6 verses 10–20 which was begun in the volume *The Christian Warfare* (published November 1976), and consists of sermons preached on Sunday mornings in Westminster Chapel.

It needs no introduction; but I would call attention in particular to certain principles which emerge clearly in the text.

The Apostle Paul never stops at mere diagnosis of our ills and problems; but he always starts with them, and reveals their true nature and character, as the previous volume made clear. But, unlike most modern philosophical and sociological writings, the Apostle, as indeed the whole of the Bible, is never content with a mere statement and analysis of the case. There is no lack of diagnosis today; but as Thomas Masaryk, the first President of Czechoslovakia pointed out, 'The philosophers have only interpreted the world in various ways: the point however is to change it'. Where philosophy fails the Gospel succeeds; and in the portion of Scripture dealt with in this volume the Apostle Paul tells us how to fight the good fight of the Faith.

We notice also the contrast between the Apostle's method and that which is becoming increasingly popular – indeed the vogue – at the present time under the name of 'counselling'. There is no admixture here of the psychological and medical with the spiritual. I do not deny that occasionally such elements do enter in; but today they tend to obscure and replace what used to be described as 'spiritual direction'. Much that passes among Christians now as psychological problems is essentially spiritual and due to a lack of spiritual understanding. The Apostle emphasizes that the spiritual warfare must be fought in a spiritual manner; and I have tried to show the way in which the great principles he lays down should be worked out in practice.

I found the preaching of these sermons, and also their preparation for publication, to be most exhilarating. I can but pray that all who read them may have a like experience, and as a result, may be able 'to stand in the evil day' and at all times.

Once more I am deeply grateful to Mrs E. Burney, Mr S. M. Houghton, and my wife for their invaluable help.

London July 1977   D. M. Lloyd-Jones

Contents

THE CHRISTIAN SOLDIER

Ephesians 6:10–20

10 *Finally, my brethren, be strong in the Lord, and in the power of his might.*

11 *Put on the whole armour of God, that ye may be able to stand against the wiles of the devil.*

12 *For we wrestle not against flesh and blood, but against principalities, against powers, against the rulers of the darkness of this world, against spiritual wickedness in high places.*

13 *Wherefore take unto you the whole armour of God, that ye may be able to withstand in the evil day, and having done all, to stand.*

14 *Stand therefore, having your loins girt about with truth, and having on the breastplate of righteousness;*

15 *And your feet shod with the preparation of the gospel of peace;*

16 *Above all, taking the shield of faith, wherewith ye shall be able to quench all the fiery darts of the wicked.*

17 *And take the helmet of salvation, and the sword of the Spirit, which is the word of God:*

18 *Praying always with all prayer and supplication in the Spirit, and watching thereunto with all perseverance and supplication for all saints;*

19 *And for me, that utterance may be given unto me,*

*that I may open my mouth boldly, to make known
the mystery of the gospel,*
20 *For which I am an ambassador in bonds: that
therein I may speak boldly, as I ought to speak.*

I

The Call to Battle

'Finally, my brethren, be strong in the Lord, and in
the power of his might. Put on the whole armour of
God, that ye may be able to stand against the wiles
of the devil.'

Ephesians 6:10–11

There is nothing that is more urgently important for all who
claim the name of Christian, than to grasp and to understand the
teaching of this particular section of Scripture. I say those 'who
claim the name of Christian', because the Apostle's words are
obviously addressed to Christian people, and to Christian people
only. They have no message for those who are not Christians;
indeed nobody else can understand them. The world today
ridicules this kind of statement. It does not believe in a spiritual
realm at all. It is even doubtful about the being of God; it has no
faith in the Lord Jesus Christ; still less, therefore, does it believe
that there are 'principalities and powers, the rulers of the darkness
of this world, spiritual wickedness even in high (or in heavenly)
places'. Such words are meaningless to the world; it has no
appreciation of their value and importance.

But to the Christian the statement is not only full of significance,
it is also full of help and of real encouragement; and, let me repeat,
there is surely no theme that is more urgently important to all
Christians at the present time than just this. I refer, of course, to
the whole state of life, the whole state of the world, and to all the
difficulty of living, and especially living the Christian life in these
confused times in which we find ourselves. Not that I suggest that
life has ever been easy in this world for the Christian. It was not so
for the early Christians. And today, in some respects, the problem
is more acute and more urgent, perhaps, than it has ever been.
There was a time, until comparatively recently, when at least a
man's home was more or less shut off from the world; but now the

world comes into the home in many different ways, not only with the newspapers but with the television and the wireless and other media. Thus the fight of faith becomes particularly difficult and strenuous for the Christian at such a time; and in addition to all this there is the general strain of the times and the anxiety of the hour.

It is because of such considerations that we spent so much time in a previous volume in analysing and considering Paul's great statement. We were occupied there in dealing with 'the wiles of the devil', trying to understand what it means when it says that we are 'wrestling, not against flesh and blood' (in ourselves, or in any other people), but against these spiritual powers and potentates, these principalities, these unseen hordes of wickedness that are at the back of evil, controlling the minds of evil men and all their activities, and that are set against us in order to try to defeat us, to spoil our Christian lives and bring the whole of the Gospel into disrepute. Such occupation on our part was essential. A man who does not understand the nature of the problem he is confronting is a man who is already doomed to failure. Christian people are like first-year college students – they think at first that every subject is quite simple, that there is no difficulty. Well, we know what is likely to happen to such when they face an examination! The first thing you have to do is to understand the nature and the character of your problem. So we have to realize that we are called, in the Christian life, to a battle, not to a life of ease; to a battle, to a warfare, to wrestling, to a struggle. Already we have looked in detail at the varied, almost endless ways in which the devil in his wiliness and subtlety tries to trap and to ensnare, to confuse and to confound the Christian. For the Christian to be forewarned as to the character and strategy of the enemy is absolutely essential, for to be forewarned is to be forearmed, and that in itself is half the battle.

But let us remember that it is only half the battle. Were we to leave it at that we should all undoubtedly be depressed. We would say, 'Life is sufficient enough as it is without your dragging out all these things. You show us that the problem is such that no man is adequate to deal with it. You emphasize that we wrestle against terrible powers and principalities. Who is sufficient for these things? who can stand against such massed hordes of evil, with all their subtlety and malign power?' To consider the problem in isolation, even though absolutely essential, could lead to no result except that we should all feel depressed and completely and entirely hopeless. But, thank God, the Gospel is always realistic. It never hides any of the truth, it never gives a false impression. It is not a true Gospel that gives us the impression that the Christian life is easy, and that there are no problems to be faced. That is not the New Testament teaching. The New Testament is most alarming at first, indeed terrifying, as it shows us the problems by which we are confronted. But follow it – go on! It does not stop halfway, it goes on to this addition, this second half; and here it shows us the way in which, though that is the truth concerning the battle, we can be enabled to wage it, and not only to wage it, but to triumph in it. It shows us that we are meant to be 'more than conquerors'.

So the Apostle goes on to show us this second half; and he does so in his own characteristic manner. He even puts this before he states the problem. He says, 'Be strong in the Lord, and in the power of his might. Put on the whole armour of God, that' (in order that) – then he introduces the problem. Here, I say, is something for which we should thank God always. Here, and here alone, we are told that, despite all that is against us, whether in realms above or in the world in which we live with all its strains and stresses, as Christian people we can be enabled to triumph, to rejoice in the midst of it all, and to know that victory is assured. That is the matter to which we now turn.

What is offered us as we find ourselves, as Christian people, facing all this – this wrestling, this struggling, this combat? You notice that there are just two things. Firstly, 'Be strong in the Lord, and in the power of his might'; secondly, 'Take unto you the whole armour of God'.

As we come to look at these two things there are some preliminary comments that I have to make. The first is that both these are necessary. We are not to take one without the other. The Apostle says both, and we have to do both. We shall have occasion to repeat that constantly as we go along. But notice the order in which he puts them. He does not tell you to put on the armour first, and then to be strong in the Lord. No, it is the other way round: 'Be strong in the Lord, and in the power of his might'; then, 'Take unto you the whole armour of God'. There is a very real significance in the order. I do not stay with it at the moment, but I shall have occasion later to show its significance and the importance of following it as a practical issue.

There is clearly a relationship between the two factors. Let me just hint at what will be developed as we proceed. It is this: that so often people take just one or the other of these factors and therefore make shipwreck of the faith. There are some who say, 'All you need to do is to hand it over to the Lord and rely on His strength'. They never say anything about 'the whole armour of God' – that is left out completely. There are others who put their whole emphasis on the putting on of the armour of God, as if they could wield it themselves. They forget their absolute dependence upon the power of the Lord, and His might and His strength. We see then that there are several interesting matters in the mere presentation of the two things which are essential to a triumphant living of the Christian life.

Let us start, then, with the first – 'Be strong in the Lord, and in the power of his might'. Here is a great order issued by this mighty captain, the Apostle Paul – an order for the day. Here is a word sent out to the Christian army gathered together, with the enemy there in position facing it. Here is the word that comes from this great leader who himself had had long experience in warfare personally, and who, as he reminds us so often, had the care of all the churches upon him, and had seen at first hand the machinations of the evil one against God's people. Here then is a great order for the day – 'Be strong in the Lord, and in the power of his might'. Hold on to this, do not forget it. In the heat and the thick of the battle later on in the day, whatever happens, never forget, never lose sight of, this great guiding and controlling principle.

But what does it mean, and how are we to do it? It is a resounding phrase. To read it, to repeat it, is not enough. We like singing the words of the hymn, 'Put on the Gospel armour'. But what does it mean in practice? Let us investigate the matter. Christianity is not a form of psychology. You do not just walk along the road saying, 'Be strong in the Lord, and in the power of his might', using it as some kind of incantation, or auto-suggestion, repeating the phrases to yourself. That is not Christianity at all! It is true of the cults, of course; it is the psychological method. You repeat the phrases such as, 'Every day, and in every way, I am getting better and better'. You persuade yourself, and you think less and less about your health, and you therefore begin to feel better. Up to a point it works, but only up to a point. But in any case, as I say, it is not the Christian message. So often we are in danger of abusing the Scriptures in this way. We use them as mere phrases in that manner, or light-heartedly we sing our hymns, and we feel better for the time being. But the question is, How do we stand up to temptations when we are in the street outside, and what are we like at home? When you turn Scripture into a drug, into something which gives you a temporary relief without your knowing why or how, the effect does not last. It gives a temporary feeling of exhilaration, but fails you when you are in the struggle and in the heat of the battle.

What, then, is the true application of the Apostle's precept? The first thing to realize is the need to be strong because of the power of the enemy. Never under-estimate that power. The Bible always calls us to face the enemy and to realize that he is, as Peter says, 'as a roaring lion, seeking whom he may devour'. We are told that the archangel Michael dared not speak lightly or loosely to him, and when he debated with him concerning the body of Moses he did not bring any 'railing accusation' against him. All the archangel ventured to say was, 'The Lord rebuke thee' (Jude 9). The enemy is terribly powerful and full of wiles and of subtlety and of guile; he can even 'transform himself into an angel of light' (2 Corinthians 11:14).

Another reason, and a very practical one from the human side, is that if you are to be able to stand, and withstand in the evil day, you need this strength. 'The evil day'! Though the Christian life in one sense is always the same kind of life, there are variations; there are evil days, some days are worse than others; they are exceptionally bad. In general at the present time we are living in a very 'evil' day. It is evil in every respect. I am not only thinking of international tensions; it is an evil day because evil and sin are so powerfully organized, so deeply entrenched; it is an evil day because of the confusion in the Church herself which sometimes seems to deny not only the whole of the Gospel but even belief in the being of God Himself. It is not easy to be a Christian at a time like this when you have men in positions of high authority in the Church talking about 'meeting atheists in heaven'! Christians are being confused by these things, particularly, perhaps, young Christians. The devil is unusually busy and active, creating this uncertainty about the essentials of the faith and producing this utter confusion – 'What is the Gospel? What is not the Gospel?' Undoubtedly we live in a very evil day; and if we are to withstand at such a time as this, there is only one way; and it is the way the Apostle teaches us here. We need this power, and the whole armour of God; and then we shall be able to stand. Thank God that this is so. Though the confusion is terrible, those who believe the truth still can stand. Do not be disheartened, do not be discouraged, do not be misled, do not be put off. You may be standing alone, perhaps, but you can still be enabled to stand though the days are so cruelly evil and vile and foul.

But there are other reasons which should encourage us all to seek this strength and this power. Why should I be 'strong in the Lord, and in the power of his might'? I answer: I wish to be strong in order to avoid personal failure; for I know that, when I do fail and fall into sin, I become miserable and unhappy. This is true of all Christians. So, to save yourself from the misery that is the inevitable consequence of any failure in the Christian life, 'be strong in the Lord, and in the power of his might'.

But I will give you a much higher reason than the fear of personal failure. 'Be strong' because you are who you are, because you are what you are. We are individuals in this matter of salvation but we are not isolated units. We are members severally of the body of Christ; we belong to Him, to God's family. Remember this always, that the Lord Jesus Christ is 'not ashamed to call us brethren' (Hebrews 2:11). Remember also that 'God is not ashamed to be called (your) God' (Hebrews 11:16). The Name of God is upon us, the Name of Christ is upon us. Why should I be strong? Well, for His sake even more than for my own sake. In a sense this is an alarming thought, and yet it is one of the most glorious truths we can ever realize about ourselves – that the reputation, as it were, of Almighty God, Father, Son and Holy Spirit, is in our hands, and any failure in us brings the great and holy Name into disrepute. We are not isolated individuals, we are one in this great and mighty army.

[16]

The world knows how to respond to these appeals, does it not? Nelson knew exactly what he was doing on the morning of Trafalgar: 'England expects that every man this day will do his duty'. Certainly! The name of the country! Multiply that by infinity and see that you and I have no right to be weak because our failure not only involves ourselves. The whole family in heaven and in earth is involved with us. We are representatives.

It is not only that we may live a happier life that I am calling attention to this text. Let us abandon this purely subjective approach, let us learn to look at things from the standpoint of the Church of the living God, this great army with banners; let us think of Him who is the Captain and Leader of our salvation. And let us remember that we belong to Him, and that anything that happens to us inevitably involves Him also.

So finally I put the matter thus. There is no better way of giving a proof of the truth of the Gospel than that we should 'be strong in the Lord, and in the power of his might', than that we should triumph and prevail. To live aright is difficult, and when we see someone who is succeeding, someone who can stand against the enticements and the insinuations of evil, someone who is not carried away off his feet by the popular thing, someone who stands steadfastly for truth and for everything that is worthy, we are greatly encouraged. It undoubtedly has a great effect on those who are looking on. We are all being watched at the present time. The world is most unhappy, men and women do not know what to do, they do not know where to turn. When they see someone who seems to be calm and steadfast, someone who is not utterly bewildered at a time like this, someone who seems to have an insight into it all, and who can see beyond it all, they look and they say, 'What is this? What is that person's secret?' And so you become an evangelist by just standing and being 'strong in the Lord, and in the power of his might'. You are not carried away by the flood, you do not do things because everyone else is doing them, you have principles of your own, and you are ready to stand for them and to suffer for them. That has often been the means, under God's blessing, of awakening others and convicting them of sin, and causing them to begin to enquire after God.

In our daily lives, whatever our earthly calling, we all live in some kind of circle; we are surrounded by people who are blinded by the devil and carried along in evil ways by him at his will (2 Timothy 2:26). You never know when the mere fact that you are just 'standing' – I am not asking you to be priggish, I am not asking you necessarily to talk, but I am just asking you to show that you can stand when everybody else is falling – you never know, I say, when that may arrest attention and open a door of opportunity for the saving Gospel of our Lord Jesus Christ.

There, then, are some reasons and preliminary considerations why we must be strong in the Lord, and in the power of His might.

In the second place, we have to realize our own weakness and our need of help. That is the presupposition behind what the Apostle is saying here. He is not only concerned about this because of the power of the enemy, he is equally concerned because of our own weakness, our own lack of strength; and, again, the best way of realizing this impotency is to understand something of the power of the enemy. There is ample teaching in the Bible to bring you to that knowledge. Go back to the very beginning of the Bible. You find there a man called Adam who was sinless and perfect. But he is confronted by the devil, and the manifestation of 'the wiles of the devil'. Though Adam was perfect, and had lived a life of fellowship and communion with God, he fell; and he fell so easily! The subtlety of the enemy with his insinuation that God was against man, that God was unfair to man, was too much for Adam and he fell. When the devil launches his attack, what is man, even perfect man made in the image of God? Adam fell. And if Adam in that perfect state fell, who are we to stand?

But let us go further. Look at the Old Testament saints, all of them, the patriarchs, the godly kings, and the prophets. They all fell, not one of them could stand up to the devil. He is 'the strong man armed, that keepeth his goods at peace'. All men have failed, they have all 'sinned and come short of the glory of God'; they have succumbed to 'the wiles of the devil'.

This has also been the universal testimony of all Christian saints, the greatest saints of the centuries. It is one of the hallmarks of the true saint, that he never gives the impression that the Christian life is an easy one – never! The man who gives the impression that it is easy has confused something else with Christianity; he has a short-cut which he imagines brings him to a place where every-thing is quite simple. But that is never the Christian way. The greatest saints have always testified to the fierceness of the battle, to their own weakness, to their own inability. They have mourned over this. Let us then pay heed to what this great 'cloud of witnesses' is saying to us today.

But let me commend to you also the study of your own experience. If you feel that you are a very strong Christian, let me ask you why you have failed so much and why you still fail? What happens to your resolutions and resolves? Why do you so often find yourself in the place of repentance? Why are you sometimes attacked with feelings of utter hopelessness and almost despair. To what is it due? It is all due to the plain fact of our weakness, it is because we are insufficient and fallible.

But we must face this honestly. It is not enough just to say in general, 'Yes, I know the enemy is very strong, as you say, and I am weak'. We have got to persuade ourselves of our weakness. This is half the battle. We need to know that we are ill; in other words we need to indulge in a great deal of self-examination. That is why people pay such slight heed to our text; that is why we know so little about what it is to stand, and to be strong in the Lord, and in the power of His might; we have never realized our own need. 'They that are whole have no need of a physician.' That was the chief trouble with the Pharisees. They thought they were right with God; they did not go to the doctor; there was nothing wrong with them. We do not go to the doctor as long as we feel that all is well; we have got to realize that we are 'sick'. But that means examination, self-examination. In that way only shall we discover the elements of weakness that are in us inherently, and that render us so incapable of fighting the battle against sin and Satan.

Another thing we have to realize is that mere principles of morality are not sufficient for us. The world has always been interested in what it calls 'the good life'. Philosophers have always been interested in the subject; they have written about it, talked about it, and argued about it. But the trouble has been that they were never able to practise it. Principles of morality are good as far as they go, but they are not enough; you can read books on ethics and can wax eloquent on these matters, but it is a very different thing to put them into practice. 'To will is present with me, but how to perform that which is good I know not,' said the Apostle. I see that a certain thing is right, but the problem is, 'How am I to do it?' And it is when you really face the problem that you begin to realize the extent of your weakness.

Furthermore, human will-power alone is not enough. Will-power is excellent and we should always be using it; but it is not enough. A desire to live a good life is not enough. Obviously we should all have that desire, but it will not guarantee success. So let me put it thus: Hold on to your principles of morality and ethics, use your will-power to the limit, pay great heed to every noble, uplifting desire that is in you; but realize that these things alone are not enough, that they will never bring you to the desired place. We have got to realize that all our best is totally inadequate, that a spiritual battle must be fought in a spiritual manner. This has been put well in a hymn by Isaac Watts:

> *From Thee, the overflowing spring,*
> *Our souls shall drink a fresh supply,*
> *While such as trust their native strength*
> *Shall melt away, and droop, and die.*

That is true! Remember also the words of another hymn:

> *The arm of flesh will fail you,*
> *You dare not trust your own.*

Here we have the very beginning of an understanding of this whole matter. The problem is not just a problem of moral living. That is the limit of the State's concern with our persons. The State knows nothing about the spiritual background, for it knows nothing about the devil and 'the principalities and powers'. And that is why it continues to believe that education can really solve the problem, and reform persons. That is why it evokes the aid of psychotherapy and various other expedients in prisons. But the more it does so the more the problem seems to increase. It is all due to the fact that men do not realize the spiritual character of the problem.

You and I have to realize that the living of the Christian life does not follow automatically upon conversion. Many a man, having come into the Christian life through regeneration, through a true experience, has then tried to live the Christian life in the old terms. He thinks that he needs this act of God in Christ to save him, but he seems to leave it at that. He feels that henceforward he is going to live the Christian life by his own power; he has a new understanding so now he is going to live this life. But it cannot be done! This is the road along which people 'melt away, and droop, and die', because they are trusting to nothing but their 'native strength'. On the contrary, this is a battle that has to be fought in a spiritual manner and with spiritual understanding.

That leads us to the third general principle. Having realized that I am to be strong and that in and of myself I am essentially weak, because I am still in the flesh, and that it is still true that 'the flesh lusteth against the Spirit, and the Spirit against the flesh, and these are contrary one to the other' – realizing that all that is still true of me, and that I am here in this warfare, and up against this terrible power, what is the next thing? It is to realize that the Lord is strong, that He is mighty, and, as the Old Testament reminds us, that 'The name of the Lord is a strong tower'. His very Name is strong. The Name represents Him, who He is and what He is. And the first thing, therefore, we have to realize is the greatness of His strength. That is what the Apostle is saying to the Ephesians and to us.

Listen to the words; examine them in detail. He says, 'Be strong in the Lord, and in the power of his might'. Do we realize its full significance? What does he mean by 'the power of his might'? The basic thing, obviously, is the 'might'. We are directed to 'the power' of His 'might'. The difference between power and might is that 'might' means power and strength as an enduement; 'might' means inherent power, something a man is given. Think of a very strong, muscular man. The 'might' is that man's inherent muscular strength and power. Power means the manifestation of that might; the might is there as a potential, as something inherent, now manifesting itself, showing its efficacy, showing that it can be effectual. It means this great reserve of strength and power actually in operation, doing something; not the enduement itself but the proof of the fact that you have the enduement.

[21]

So the Apostle uses the two terms, and it is important that we should look at both. He says, 'Be strong in the Lord, and in the might of his strength'; so you start by reminding yourself of His strength. Look at Him, he says, look at His power. You have been looking at the enemy and you have seen his strength; you have looked at yourself and you are trembling in your weakness and in your ineffectiveness; well now, he says, look at Him, 'Be strong in the Lord'.

To be 'strong in the Lord' you must remember 'the might of his power', 'the might of his strength'. Express it whichever way you like, but look at Him and realize all the reserves of strength and power that are in him. That is what these New Testament Epistles are saying almost everywhere. 'In him', says the Apostle Paul to the Colossians, 'dwelleth all the fulness of the Godhead bodily'. It is there in Him. 'In whom', he says again, 'God has hid all the treasures of wisdom and of knowledge'. They are all there. They constitute this 'might', this tremendous inherent strength and power. To be 'strong in the Lord' means meditating about Him and His strength. It is not just a phrase, an incantation, a formula. It means that you sit down and remind yourself of these things, and you look at Him, and you remind yourself of some of the things that are true concerning Him.

Incidentally, that we may do just this is one of the main reasons for reading the Scriptures regularly, and reading the four Gospels in particular. We should not read the Scriptures merely in order that we may say that we have read our daily portion, and so have done our duty. That is no reason for reading the Scriptures. I am not attacking systematic reading; I am a great advocate of systematic reading. All I am saying is that you should be careful that the devil in his wiliness does not come in and make you content with a mere mechanical reading of the Scriptures without really looking at them, and meditating upon them without realizing what they are saying, and without drawing lessons for yourself, and praying about the exercise. It takes time to read Scripture properly. It is very easy to read a number of verses and rush off to catch your bus or train. That is not reading the Scriptures; that may be quite useless. You must stop and look and think. So go back to the Gospels and look at Him and 'the power of his strength'.

Where do I see His strength? I see it in His life. I see Him here in this world in the 'likeness of sinful flesh'. I see Him in the same world as I am in. I see that obviously He knew hunger and thirst and physical weakness and tiredness, that He knew what it was to be disappointed with people. He has gone through it all. And yet what I see, as I look at Him, is that He stands, He always stands. There is never a wavering, still less a failing or a faltering or a falling. He stood, with the world and the flesh and the devil – everything – against Him. He stood. Therefore as I look at His life I see at once One who walked through this world without deviating in any respect. He just went on steadily.

I see even more than that, I see it in all His miracles. I see it especially in the miracles in which He cast out devils. Here is One to whom they were not a problem. Here is One who can command the devils. He can exorcise them. He speaks with power and with authority and the devils have to come cringing to Him, asking Him to spare them, not to cast them into the deep that they might be destroyed. Here is a Master. They come to Him and say, 'We know you are the Holy One of God'. Here is One who, when the devils are operating powerfully, with a word could drive them out. The disciples could not do that. Look at the boy at the foot of the Mount of Transfiguration. The father had brought the boy to the disciples and they had done their best. But they could not help, and the poor boy remained a victim of satan's power. But at a word from our Lord the devil is driven out and the boy is healed and is restored to his father. There we see His power in operation, there we see something of 'the power of his might'. He is the master of 'the principalities and powers, the rulers of the darkness of this world, the spiritual wickedness in high places'.

But we must go still further and observe this 'power of his might' as it is revealed in His own temptation, He was tried directly by the devil himself, not by some of the emissaries, not by one or the other of these principalities or powers, but by the devil himself, with all his wiles. Here the devil himself takes charge of the situation because he realizes that it is the biggest problem he has ever confronted. So he came to our Lord and tempted Him forty days and forty nights in the wilderness and on other occasions; but he was utterly and entirely defeated. With the words of Scripture our Lord repels him, and the devil falls back defeated, waiting for another season. But he completely failed in spite of many efforts.

That is what we must dwell upon, and consider. This is not just a detail or an incident in the life of our Lord which helps you to understand His Person. It does that, of course, and attests His Person; but now, says the Apostle: Make practical use of it. Take it up, take hold of that power yourself. There, you see, He met in single combat the devil with all *his* power in operation, and He easily defeated him, therefore 'Be strong in the Lord, and in the power of his might'. The power was always and already in Him; and when the devil comes He just shows it, He just lets a little of it out, as it were, and the devil is immediately repulsed. Lay hold of that, says the Apostle.

James, in exactly the same way, and grasping this point says, 'Resist the devil and he will flee from you'. That is the way it works out. But it does not work out until you and I are quite certain about Christ's power, and really do know something of 'the power of his might', the inherent power that is in Him. 'In him dwelleth all the fulness of the Godhead bodily'. He is both God and Man. He cannot fail. He did not fail.

Finally, of course, the Lord proves and demonstrates His power on the Cross and in the Resurrection. The Cross seems to be the day of the power of evil. The powers of evil thought that to be the case, as also did the devil and all his hosts. The world, too, had similar thoughts. They riled against Him, they laughed at Him, they jeered, 'Thou savest others, come down, save thyself'. They thought that He could not do so, and that the devil had defeated Him! But what was happening there was that 'He was taking these principalities and powers' (says Paul in Colossians 2:15) 'and putting them to an open shame, triumphing over them in it' (by it). That is, He was triumphing over them when they thought that they had defeated Him. 'Now is the judgment of this world', He says beforehand, looking at the Cross – 'Now is the judgment of this world; now is the prince of this world cast out (cast forth)' (John 12:31). So look at the Cross and meditate upon it. This is the supreme paradox: He appears to be dying in weakness, but do you see the inherent strength there, do you see this might of His, do you see the power of the Godhead there, turning even that into the vanquishing of the devil and the setting of His people free – a glorious victorious triumph? Look at it and see just that!

Then go on and look at the Resurrection. He 'bursts asunder the bands of death', triumphs over the last enemy, and the ultimate effects of sin and evil. He is master completely over all these powers that are set against us, He defeats them all. He rises, He ascends into heaven, 'leading captivity captive'. He is the conqueror over everything that is set against us.

This is not some psychological formula that you and I can apply. But it all comes back to this – to know Him! You will never know power in your life until you know Him. So we must get to know Him. We shall find when we consider the various portions of the 'armour' that they are nearly all directed to that end, to know Him, to know about Him and the truth concerning Him. We start with that here – 'in the Lord' 'and in the power of his might'.

Do we realize something of this? Do we know anything about it? Forget yourself for the time being. Look at Him and realize the truth about Him. Then realize that His power is available for you. That is the key to it all. So we must look at Him objectively as He is portrayed to us, as He reveals Himself to us. Then we must realize that we belong to One who is 'the Lord' and that 'all the fulness of the Godhead' is in Him, that there is invincible might and power in Him, and that it is a might and power that not only remains potential, but also becomes actual. It shows itself, it manifests itself on our behalf, and also in us. So here we begin to look at this saving word that enables us even in this evil day to stand, to withstand, to be strong, to fight the battle of the Lord, and to bring honour and glory to His great and holy Name.

2

God's Battle, not ours

'Finally, my brethren, be strong in the Lord, and in
the power of his might.'

Ephesians 6:10

In our last study we considered something of the content of the
expression 'the power of his might'. The next question that arises
is: How exactly are we related to all this power and might? It is
one thing to remind ourselves of our Lord's almightiness, of the
glorious power that resides in Him, and that He has triumphed
over all; but how is that related to me, how does that help me,
how does that avail me in my own personal problem and conflict
and wrestling with these powers and forces that are set against me?
This is what we must now proceed to consider.

The first thing we must ever remember is that the Lord Jesus
Christ is what the author of the Epistle to the Hebrews calls 'the
Captain of our Salvation'. In the second chapter of that Epistle
verse 10 we read, 'For it became him, for whom are all things,
and by whom are all things, in bringing many sons unto glory,
to make the Captain of their salvation perfect through sufferings'.
We meet the same idea in the second verse of the twelfth chapter
also, where we find, 'Looking unto Jesus the author and finisher
of our faith'. He is a kind of File-Leader, the Originator, the One
who continues to lead – 'the author and the finisher of our faith'.
   That is the first thing we have to realize. In other words, we
must have a true conception of this salvation which we are enjoying. The danger, always, is to look at it in a purely personal and
subjective manner. That, of course, is essential. There are some
people who never realize the personal side, and they are equally

[26]

wrong. But it is wrong to go to either of these extremes. The danger, so often, is that we think of the Christian life as something that we have to do. I am about to emphasize that we have a great deal to do; but before we come to that we must never lose sight of the fact that salvation is primarily of God. It is God's great plan, it is God's scheme. It is something that God is doing. It is something that God has planned and originated. He has initiated the movement and He is carrying it on. This is a fundamental principle of our faith. God is involved in this question of our salvation much more than we are ourselves. We so often tend to think of it as primarily something which we have to do, and that we only turn to God for help occasionally. But that is to put things the wrong way round. Salvation is God's plan and we are simply brought into it.

We are never to forget that we are individual units in a great army. We are not fighting some personal, private war. That is not the position at all. We are simply individual soldiers in a great army which is fighting a great campaign. In other words, the real, the ultimate issue is not so much my fight with the devil, as God's fight with the devil. That is the way to look at it. To look at the matter in this way immediately gives you great strength.

Take the obvious analogy. The private soldier in the ranks or in the trenches during a great battle in a great war is not fighting a private battle, he is not there because he has some personal quarrel. He is just a unit in a great campaign. He does not decide the strategy, he does not even decide the tactics. All that is in other hands. He is in it, he has been called into it, he has been put into his position; but it is not his battle. It is the battle of the King or the Queen or the country, and there is a General commanding and controlling the activities of the army and directing the fight.

Now that is the idea that is taught everywhere in the New Testament; and I know of nothing that is more comforting and solacing, more encouraging and uplifting, than the inward realization of it. If I may borrow a phrase that is used in the Old Testament in connection with King Jehoshaphat: 'The battle is not yours, but the Lord's'. This did not mean that he, Jehoshaphat, had nothing to do; but he was being reminded that what he was involved in was not some purely personal matter, but rather God's. All the battles of Israel, if they could have seen it, were not their

[27]

battles, they were the battles of the Lord. They were involved because they were His people. Their main trouble was that they always tended to forget the Lord and to regard matters as their own battle and their own problem. So they indulged in their politics and in their alliances with Egypt and so on, and found themselves in trouble. If they had only realized that they were fighting the battle of the Lord the entire position would have been transformed. That is the first principle which we must always grasp – 'The Captain of your salvation'; 'the battle is the Lord's'.

Or look at that other astounding phrase used in the tenth verse of the second chapter of the Epistle to the Hebrews: 'It became him' – that is, God – 'in leading many sons unto glory'. It is He who is doing the leading. You and I are not fighting an individual battle trying to get salvation. It is *God* who is bringing us to glory. It is His scheme, it is His plan. It is something that *He* is doing. It is not ours primarily. 'It became him in bringing many sons unto glory, to make the Captain of their salvation' – He was appointed a Leader, a Captain – 'perfect through sufferings'. Take note of the expression, 'It became God'. In other words, this is God's method, this is God's plan.

The moment we realize this truth, the whole position becomes immediately transformed. Think of soldiers in an army fighting in their little sector. They are being hard-pressed and things are going against them. If they think that it is just their own private fight they will soon be defeated. But when they remember that they are only a part of a great and mighty army, and that at the back of it all, and directing it, is the Captain, their Leader, immediately the situation is entirely transformed. In other words we have got to realize as we fight this fight of faith and wrestle with these principalities and powers and face the assaults of the world and the flesh and the devil, that God is involved in it with us. We would never have been in it but for that. The ultimate battle is the battle between God and the devil, between heaven and hell, between light and darkness.

That in turn should make us realize a further truth, that this campaign cannot fail, because God's honour is involved in it. Lift up your minds and your hearts in the thick of the battle and call this to mind. You see the might and the power of the enemy and you are conscious of your own weakness. But say to yourselves,

'This is God's battle, we are given the privilege of being in it and of fighting as individual soldiers, but God's honour is involved in it all. He cannot allow this to fail because His character, His glory, and His honour are involved at every point.' 'Be strong in the Lord'; remember that He is there, and that it is His battle.

This cannot be emphasized too much. It is the theme of the Bible from the beginning of Genesis. God made a perfect world. The devil comes in, the woman and the man listen to him, and fall, and the devil becomes 'the god of this world'. But it is not left at that. God did not turn to the man and to the woman and say, 'Very well, because of your rebellion and your folly and your sin you have brought all this on yourselves. Now get on with it. You have brought it on yourselves, so you will have to fight for the rest of your lives against this evil power that has mastered you'. That is not what He said. He did say that there would be enmity between the seed of the woman and the seed of the serpent. That is the wrestling, the conflict. But He did not stop at that, He gave a promise – 'the seed of the woman shall bruise the serpent's head'. *He* is involved because it is His world and they are His people. He is not going to allow the devil to defeat Him. God cannot allow the Evil One to mar His great work finally. Of course not! So God gives His promise about the seed of the woman that is going to bruise the serpent's head. God is involving Himself in the conflict. The whole movement of salvation is for God's glory; not simply for our deliverance, but for God's glory primarily. Our deliverance is only one expression of this glory and honour for the great Name of God. That is one of the reasons why Paul says, 'Be strong in the Lord'. Let us realize this! Get rid of the notion that it is just a little private battle that you are waging on your own: 'Be strong in the Lord, and in the power of his might'.

But we must go further. That is the starting point, and I am loath to leave it for the reason that I know how ready we are to forget it. We are so subjective, and we live in this unhealthy 'psychological' generation that starts with man and ends with man. Most of our troubles are due to that. We are always looking inwards and pity-ing ourselves and being sorry for ourselves, and looking for something to help us. Get rid of that outlook, forget yourself for a moment; the battle is the Lord's! Salvation is His. It is for the honour of His great and holy Name. But go further and realize that because it is God's battle this almighty power is being exercised on our behalf even when we do not realize it. Things are being done in this great campaign of which we are not aware. We may perhaps be half-asleep at our post, and we do not realize that the great Captain is planning something with respect to us. We are unconscious of it. But that does not matter. Thank God that He does it though we are unconscious of it. We would all be lost were it not for that. He, I say, is exercising this power on our behalf.

The Scriptures are full of this teaching; and what we really need is to know our Scriptures. Later on we shall be reminded that 'The sword of the Spirit is the Word of God'. Exactly! Take Psalm 34, verse 7: 'The angel of the Lord encampeth round about them that fear him, and delivereth them'. You think that you are doing it all yourself; but 'the angel of the Lord' is encamping round about you. He is a very powerful angel. He has great might and power, and he is encamping round about them that fear him. Even when we are asleep he is there, he is always on guard. He is watching because we are God's people, and God's honour is involved in what happens to us.

Listen to Psalm 91: 'He that dwelleth in the secret place of the Most High shall abide under the shadow of the Almighty' (v. 1). What a place to be in! Have you seen little chicks at the approach of danger rushing to the hen? She just spreads her wings and under they go. 'Under the shadow of the Almighty'! That is true of all who are Christians. 'Be strong in the Lord, and in the power of his might'. Do not forget those wings! You shall 'abide under the shadow of the Almighty'.

I am simply selecting certain great words. Note how our Lord states the matter in John 10: 'No man is able to pluck them out of my Father's hand' (v. 29). What a comfort! What a consolation! No man shall be able to pluck them, God's people, Christ's people, out of God's hand. It is strong, it is almighty. Let man, let the devil and hell do what they will, it is impossible. Again, the Apostle Paul says in writing to the Romans, that he is 'persuaded' – he is absolutely certain, there is no doubt about it – 'that neither death, nor life, nor angels, nor principalities, nor powers, nor things present, nor things to come, nor height, nor depth, nor any other creature shall be able to separate us from the love of God which is in Christ Jesus our Lord'. Our foes will try, they will do their utmost, and there will be times when we, in our folly, will begin to think that we have been separated, that we are cut off, and that there is no way of release and no way of escape. But it will never happen. 'Nothing shall be able to separate us from the love of God which is in Christ Jesus our Lord'. Why? For the reason that, if anything could separate us, God would be defeated, and the devil would be triumphant. Such a calamity cannot happen!

To believe in the possibility of 'falling from grace' is to believe in the possible defeat of God by the devil. That is unthinkable and utterly impossible. The final perseverance of the saints is of necessity true in view of the glory and the character and the honour of God Himself. 'Ah but', you say, 'this leads to danger; for a person will say, "I can do what I like".' No! the more you realize this great truth the more careful you will be. This is the truth that makes people keep to the narrow path – the realization that the honour of God is involved, and that I am not fighting my own battle, that if I fail the Name of God Himself is involved in it. So there is no danger of Antinomianism when you truly understand the doctrine. It is the scriptural doctrine.

All this means in practice, of course, that God cares for us, and that His care for us is greater than we will ever realize in this world. Scripture is full of this teaching. Our Lord Himself was constantly teaching it. He said that God cares for the sparrows: 'Are not two sparrows sold for a farthing? Yet not one of them shall fall to the ground without your Father.' Oh how much greater is His concern for you! If God so clothes the lilies, if God is so concerned about the birds of the air, 'how much more' . . . There is no need to go any further. 'How much more' – of course! He has brought us into His plan, He is concerned about us, He is interested in us – 'the very hairs of our head are all numbered'. That shows His care. It is He who is really doing it; and we must never lose sight of this.

Similarly the same Apostle is able to say in the Epistle to the Philippians, chapter 1, verse 6, 'Being confident of this very thing'. Do not forget the context of that statement. Here was the Apostle in prison, and he does not know how much longer he has to live.

He is in the hands of the capricious emperor Nero who may suddenly decide, on a whim, to put him to death. He does not know; he may be killed at any moment. He knows, furthermore, that there were troubles in the churches, even trouble in the church at Philippi. Yet he says, 'Being confident of this very thing, that he which hath begun a good work in you will perform it until the day of Jesus Christ'. Old, ill, in prison, on the verge of death, leaving everything, is he troubled? Not at all; he is confident. Because 'He [God] which hath begun a good work in you will perform it [He will go on with it] until [the end, the consummation] the day of Jesus Christ'.

But this truth is not confined to the teaching of the Apostle Paul. The Apostle Peter says exactly the same thing in his first Epistle chapter 1, verse 5. Referring to the Christians he says: 'Who are kept by the power of God through faith unto salvation ready to be revealed in the last time'. What could be stronger? We are kept by the power of God! 'Be strong in the Lord, and in the power of his might'. Such is the power that is keeping us.

Then one other word, which we so sadly neglect as Christian people – the ministry of the angels! Again go back to the Epistle to the Hebrews. What are these angels? Christ is greater than the angels, but what are the angels? The answer is, 'Are they not all ministering spirits, sent forth to minister for them who shall be heirs of salvation?' That is, for Christian people. We are 'the heirs of salvation'. And the teaching is that God uses these mighty angels whom He has created, in order that they might minister unto us. We are ignorant of this ministry, we forget it; but thank God that makes no difference. He has appointed them to their tasks and they perform them. They do His will, they are ministering spirits; and their work is to minister to us, because we are the heirs of salvation.

Our position is this: we are comparable to the children of some great squire, some lord who has a great estate. He has a son and heir who one day is going to inherit all. But the son is now a babe or but a boy. What does this great man do? He appoints servants who look after this child; he pays them to do so and tells them what to do to protect the child from harm, to prevent his doing things that would injure him, to instruct him and to guide him. That is what the angels do. They are round and about us, though we do not see them. How foolish it is of us to neglect this teaching that is given in the Scriptures! 'In heaven their angels do always behold the face of my Father which is in heaven', says our Lord Himself about little children (Matthew 18:10). It is exactly the same teaching. The reason why we are so often in trouble, and why we become despondent, and why the devil defeats us, is that we forget these things. We forget that we are being 'ministered unto' by these angelic powers, these good angels created by God largely for this purpose.

Such then are some of the ways in which we must realize that this almighty power is working for us. All this, so far, is outside us, round and about us – the angel of the Lord 'encamping', the angels ministering, God exercising this care and this power for our welfare. This is a part of being 'strong in the Lord'. We must realize that this is the way to be strong, to know always what is taking place. We must have confidence in the Author of our salvation, confidence in the One who has initiated the whole campaign and whose Son is involved in it all.

But we can go even further. This power is also working, not only round and about us, but *in* us. And this makes it still more wonderful. This aspect of the matter has already been given a good deal of attention by the Apostle, but it can never be repeated too frequently. Some of the most glorious things in the whole of Scripture are said with respect to this matter. To start with, we would never have been in the Christian life at all were it not that this power of God had begun to work in us. That is stated clearly at the beginning of the second chapter of the Epistle to the Ephesians: 'You hath he quickened, who were dead' – dead! – 'in trespasses and sins'. And in order to impress it upon them he repeats it again in verse 5: 'Even when we were dead in sins, hath [he] quickened us together with Christ, (by grace ye are saved)'. That is the origin of it all. No-one ever becomes a Christian except as the result of the working of the almighty power of God within him. No man, as he is, can decide to accept Christ, for he is 'dead'! spiritually dead! And in addition, and as a result of that, as the Apostle has reminded us in chapter 4, verses 17 and 18: 'This I say therefore, and testify in the Lord, that ye henceforth walk not as other Gentiles walk, in the vanity of their mind, having the understanding darkened, being alienated from the life of God

[33]

through the ignorance that is in them, because of the blindness of their heart'. These words describe man by nature. 'The natural mind is enmity against God; it is not subject to the law of God, neither indeed can be' (Romans 8:7). The natural man can do nothing, he is utterly helpless, spiritually dead. What makes us Christians? He hath 'quickened us'. He has done it by His power, the power of the Spirit. What brings us into salvation is that the Spirit of God begins to work in us and to act upon us, to convict us of sin, to open our eyes. He does it all – 'by grace ye are saved'. It is 'the power of God unto salvation'. And there would be no hope for anyone but for this. It starts in that way by the power of God working in us and bringing us to a knowledge of salvation.

But he does not merely start it, He goes on with the work. This is the ultimate comfort and consolation. Look at the way in which the Apostle puts it in his first chapter. He starts with this great truth in chapter 1. Then, as is so often his habit, he interrupts his line of thought by working out some subsidiary point and then takes up again the original matter. That is exactly what he does in chapters 1 and 2 of this Epistle. Chapter 2 in many ways is a kind of digression to elaborate the point that he hinted at in the first chapter. The Apostle is writing to these Ephesians and he thanks God for them. He tells them that he is praying for them, 'that the God of our Lord Jesus Christ, the Father of glory, may give unto you the spirit of wisdom and revelation in the knowledge of him: The eyes of your understanding being enlightened'. What for? 'That you may know what is the hope of his calling' – what His ultimate purpose for you is – 'and what the riches of the glory of his inheritance in the saints'. Look ahead, he says, look forward, see what *His* inheritance in the saints is, as well as *your* inheritance. But more: 'And what is the exceeding greatness of His power to us-ward who believe'. He says in effect; I am praying that you may have understanding, that you may know the exceeding greatness of this power of God which is working to us-ward who believe – 'according to the working of his mighty power'. Notice how he brings out his adjectives, how he piles one superlative upon another because there is no limit to the power and the might of God. But he adds, What I am praying for, is that you may know that all this great power is working toward you, it is working in you, it is working for your good, if you could but realize it. Now this is what we need to pray for ourselves. We need this enlightenment, we need this understanding. If you only knew God's purpose with respect to yourself, and that He is working in you to bring this to pass, and what His ultimate objective for you is, your whole outlook would be revolutionized.

But the Apostle returns to it again in chapter 3. He is once more praying for them. Look at verse 13, which is an introduction: 'Wherefore I desire that you faint not at my tribulations for you, which is your glory'. These Ephesians, like so many other early Christians, were in grave danger of depending too much upon the Apostle Paul. He had preached the Gospel to them, and they had been converted under his ministry. Now he is in prison and is ill, and is becoming old, and they say, What shall we do if Paul goes? To whom shall we be able to write? from whom shall we get advice and help? If Paul goes, we are undone. Such were their feelings. But he says, 'I desire that you faint not at my tribulations for you, which is your glory. For this cause I bow my knees unto the Father of our Lord Jesus Christ, of whom the whole family in heaven and earth is named, that he would grant you, according to the riches of his glory to be strengthened with might by his Spirit in the inner man'. The power of the Spirit within the inner man! 'The exceeding greatness of his power to us-ward who believe!' It works in the inner man and it strengthens the inner man. You need not faint, says Paul; it matters not what happens to me, the salvation goes on, because it is His power, not mine. I am a mere instrument, just a little servant running here and there to give a message along the trenches. But when I have gone He will carry on His work, He has other servants, He will produce other men. Go on! It is His power you need, and you have got it in the inner man, and I am praying that you may have it more and more.

Then he comes back to his theme again in verse 20: 'Now unto him that is able to do exceeding abundantly above all that we ask or think, according to the power that worketh in us.' It is working in us, and it is a power which is measured in these terms – 'exceeding abundantly'. Work out these words for yourselves! They imply that Paul has come to the limits of language. He was fond of superlatives. You must be when you are talking about God; nothing but superlatives will do. But even they are inadequate. It is all entirely 'above all that we ask or think'. Even imagination fails, everything fails. The theme is altogether above it all. 'According to the power that worketh in us.' It is not only working round and about you, it is working in you. In the believer! 'According to the power that worketh in us.'

But consider also statements found elsewhere in Scripture in order that we may never fall into a fainting, hopeless condition again. I have already quoted from Philippians chapter 2, but let us go back to verses 12 and 13: 'Wherefore, my beloved, as you have always obeyed, not as in my presence only, but now much more in my absence.' It does not matter whether Paul is there or not. They thought it did; but it was not so – 'much more in my absence, work out your own salvation with fear and trembling. For it is God which worketh in you both to will and to do of his good pleasure.' His power is working in us. This is the power that, suddenly, when you are doing something quite different, turns your mind to the Lord; this is the power that works in us and makes us desire to pray. What made you feel that suddenly? You do not know. But the answer is – the Spirit! His is the power that is at work in you; it is there the whole time. Thank God it is! How hopeless we would be but for this! He brings us back, reminds us, calls us to the Word, calls us to prayer, calls us to service, calls us to some duty – 'it is God that worketh in you'. This energy, this power, 'the exceeding greatness of His power to us-ward who believe'!

Another wonderful statement of it is found in Colossians 1:29. Here the Apostle is describing himself as a preacher. 'Whereunto' he says, 'I also labour, striving according to his working.' The Apostle is striving, but he is striving 'according to his working'. You see, he does strive. I shall deal with this question of the balance later on, because so many go wrong there, but I am now emphasizing God's power. 'Whereunto I also labour, striving according to his working, which worketh in me mightily', says the Apostle. What was Paul doing? 'Whom we preach, warning every man, and teaching every man in all wisdom; that we may present every man perfect in Christ Jesus: whereunto [to this end] I also labour, striving according to his working, which worketh in me mightily.' He was aware of the power working within him. There is no higher or more glorious experience than that. You feel that you are just looking on. It is not you; you are being used. It is He who is doing it, and you are almost a spectator.

This is the language the Apostle always uses. In writing to the Thessalonians in his first Epistle, chapter 1, verse 5, he says: 'Our gospel came not unto you in word only, but also in power, and in the Holy Ghost, and in much assurance.' He knew it; he was conscious that the Spirit was working mightily and overwhelmingly in him. And it is the same power that is in us, that is working in us, and working mightily.

The Apostle John has the same teaching in his first Epistle, chapter 4, verses 4–6: 'Ye are of God, little children, and have overcome them' [the antichrists]: Why? 'because greater is he that is in you, than he that is in the world. They are of the world, therefore speak they of the world, and the world heareth them. We are of God: he that knoweth God heareth us; he that is not of God heareth not us. Hereby know we the spirit of truth, and the spirit of error.'

Then in the last chapter of the First Epistle of John, in verses 18 and 19: 'We know that whosoever is born of God sinneth not' – that is to say, he does not go on, he does not habitually sin – 'but he that is begotten of God keepeth himself' – which the authorities tend to agree means that he is kept by God – 'and that wicked one toucheth him not'. The devil can shout at you, he can make you tremble, but he cannot touch you. 'We know that we are of God, and the whole world lieth in the wicked one' – in his embrace and in his clutches. We are not there; we have been taken from him. We are 'of God', and that is why the devil cannot touch us. He can molest us and try to frighten us, but he will never get us back into his embrace again, for that is impossible. 'We are of God', we are 'safe in the arms of Jesus', we are in the arms of God, the everlasting arms are underneath and round about us. 'We are of God, and that evil one toucheth us not.' He will never touch us; he cannot do so. We have been taken out of his realm, 'translated from the kingdom of darkness into the kingdom of God's dear Son'.

Finally, let us look at it thus. This power works in us. But then it is put in another way, for the whole doctrine of the Church is involved in this matter. What is the Church? Let me remind you of the teaching in this Epistle. The Apostle gives us a hint in chapter 1. He talks about this 'power that worketh in us'. It is the power 'which he wrought in Christ, when he raised him from the dead, and set him at his own right hand in the heavenly places, far above all principality, and power, and might, and dominion, and every name that is named, not only in this world, but also in that which is to come: and hath put all things under his feet, and gave him to be the head over all things to the church – [that is where we come in] – which is his body, the fulness of him that filleth all in all'. The Church is the body of Christ, and the Head of the body is Christ Himself.

But let us go to the elaboration of this truth in chapter 4, especially in verses 15 and 16: 'But speaking the truth in love, may grow up into him in all things, which is the head, even Christ: from whom the whole body fitly joined together and compacted by that which every joint supplieth, according to the effectual working in the measure of every part, maketh increase of the body unto the edifying of itself in love.' That means that Christ is the Head and we are the parts, individual parts and portions of the body. But every single part and portion of the body derives its strength and its nutriment from the Head. I am not an isolated unit, I am not just mechanically attached. The blood that supplies the head goes through the little finger, and all the nervous energy and the power comes from the head. We are ultimately related to the Head and to each other through these joints and ligaments and these means of communication. Paul is saying that the power that is in the Head is working also in all the members of the body. The energy in us is His energy. This is the power that worketh in us mightily.

Work it out also in terms of the indwelling of the Holy Spirit. That is why in chapter 5, verse 18, Paul says this to us: 'And be not drunk with wine, wherein is excess; but be filled with the Spirit', with all the power of the blessed Holy Spirit Himself. In addition we have His companionship – 'The grace of the Lord Jesus Christ, the love of God, the fellowship [the communion] of the Holy Spirit'. The Spirit is in us: 'He shall be in you', says Christ in John 14 to the disciples who had become disconsolate because of His departure. 'I will send you another Comforter. He will not only be with you, He will be in you.' And so it is. He is with us and in us – the companionship, the fellowship of the

Holy Spirit working as a power within us. Moreover, as Paul says in Romans 8, verses 25, 26 and 27: the Spirit even 'maketh intercession for us with groanings which cannot be uttered'. When we are so hard pressed that we know not what to pray for as we ought, 'the Spirit himself maketh intercession for us with groanings which cannot be uttered'. He stimulates prayer, causing us to ejaculate some petition, not always understanding what we are saying. But it is He who is doing it, and working in us.

This power of the Lord is not only round and about us, and not only caring for us and planning for us, but it is in us. 'The exceeding greatness of his power to us-ward that believe.' We are wrestling 'not against flesh and blood, but against principalities and powers, against the rulers of the darkness of this world, against spiritual wickedness in high places'; we are fighting and having to stand against the devil. So let us 'Be strong in the Lord, and in the power of his might'. Remember the energy and the power that is working in us, and remember that it is invincible because it is His. Let the devil and all his powers come, we can 'Stand in His great might, with all His strength endued'.

3
Who does the fighting?

'Finally, my brethren, be strong in the Lord, and in
the power of his might.'

Ephesians 6:10

We now come to what in many ways is the crucial point in this
whole discussion, namely, to the practical question: How is all
this related to us in practice, in our day-to-day needs, in our
constant warfare against the world and the flesh and the devil?
This is the question that troubles so many – How is this exhortation of the Apostle to be interpreted precisely and in detail?

Here, unfortunately, I have to start with a negative, because it
is quite clear, surely, that in such a vital matter as this, the enemy
is likely to be particularly anxious to cause confusion. And he has
caused confusion, great confusion; and there are many who are
in great confusion and perplexity at this present time.

There is a popular teaching – it has been popular for about
ninety years – which says that the great trouble with most of us in
the Christian life is that we go on struggling and fighting so
much, and therein lies our error and the great cause of our defeat.
They say 'Why is it that people do not listen to the exhortation
of the Apostle?' He says, 'Be strong in the Lord and in the power
of his might'. That means, they say, that all we really have to do
is to 'Let go and let God' do it for us. That is the phrase which in
so many ways summarizes the teaching that has been so popular.

Another way they have of expressing it is the phrase that has
been repeated so constantly, 'Hand it over to the Lord'. 'It is not
your battle, it is His; hand it over to Him.' Another saying is:
'Let Him do it for you; that is what He is offering to do.' They
say that there is no need for any struggle; that our mistake is
that we have gone on struggling and striving; but that is quite

unnecessary. There is no need to struggle, there is no need to feel any difficulty.

Here is yet another phrase: 'It is quite simple.' All you have to do is to stop struggling and hand it over. And such teachers have used many illustrations in order to show what they mean. Here is one, for instance, which has been very popular. They say that the Christian is like a man in a room. There is brilliant sunshine outside in the street but the room is in semi-darkness. That is because the blinds are drawn, and here is a man fumbling, trying to find his way round the room, looking for things. He cannot see them. What a tragedy! There is all that brilliant sunshine outside, but here is a man in semi-darkness and in trouble and confusion. What is he to do? Well, they say, it is so simple, all he has to do is to let up the blinds and the sunshine will come streaming in, and all his problems will have gone. Quite simple! Why go on struggling?

We must obviously consider this teaching, because it presents itself to us as an exposition of the text with which we are dealing. We are told that what is needed first of all is some sort of crisis in our lives. The defeated Christian has to come to a point of crisis in which he will be ready to admit and to confess defeat. He is hopeless until he does that – and here we are in entire agreement! Then, they say, having realized his defeat, and having confessed it, he must come to this crucial question, Is he ready to surrender himself and this whole battle entirely to the Lord? Is he prepared to surrender, is he prepared to submit, to give up utterly and absolutely? If so, they say, he will pass through a crisis in which he will lose all sense of struggle and strain, and from there will go on to a process. The process amounts to this, that, having passed through this critical experience all this man has to do now is to go on 'abiding in the Lord'. That, to them, means that he has to go on refusing to struggle and to do battle himself and to leave it entirely to the Lord; the Lord will then win the battle for him. The Christian has nothing to do but to 'abide in Christ'; he himself must not struggle at all; it will all be done for him.

Now this is the familiar and popular teaching. Furthermore, it is presented as something that one can do immediately in a meeting. So, often, people are invited to come forward, to take a decision, to decide to accept this offer of victory. They are called either to come forward or to hold up their hands in a meeting, and told that it can all happen in this critical experience. Then they must go on with the process of abiding in the Lord, and they will find that their whole life will be entirely different. The stress and strain will have gone, there will be no more 'struggle'; it will be a life of victory, but on condition that they go on abiding in the Lord.

There are many Christians who are trying to do this, trying to surrender, trying to be willing to surrender, trying to be 'willing to be made willing', as the phrase goes, and thus they may spend months and years in the attempt to do this thing which is recommended to them. Others claim that they have done this, and that in consequence they find that life has become very simple, for all they need to do is to go on looking to the Lord and abiding in Him; and they find that their battles are fought for them.

This teaching obviously demands serious and earnest attention. There are certain considerations, I suggest, which show that this teaching is contrary to the plain teaching of the Scripture itself, and that is the first test we must apply. I mean, for instance, that if this teaching is correct, then the second thing the Apostle tells the Christian to do here is unnecessary, namely, 'Put on the whole armour of God'. He repeats the exhortation in verse 13: 'Wherefore take unto you the whole armour of God', and he then proceeds to take these pieces and portions of the armour one by one, in order that we may know how to use them. My argument is that if the Lord does it all for us and we have nothing to do but to abide in Him and look to Him, then it is needless to tell me to put on this armour. Yet it is obvious that the armour is something that I have to wear and to employ. So the erroneous teaching immediately cuts right out that which the Apostle himself couples with this exhortation to be 'strong in the Lord, and in the power of his might'.

But that is only one objection of many. Look at the matter, in the following way: if the teaching is right which says that we have nothing to do, and that our mistake is that we have been doing so much; that we have but to hand it all over to the Lord, to 'let go and let God', let Him fight our battles for us so that we do not fight them ourselves – I say, if that is true, then it seems to me that all the exhortations in the Scripture, particularly in the Epistles, are not only unnecessary but actually wrong.

What are these exhortations? Here is one for instance in the Epistle of James, chapter 4, verse 7: 'Resist the devil, and he will flee from you.' You have to resist him. It is an exhortation to us to resist the devil. James does not tell us that we must not resist him, that all we have to do is to look to the Lord and He will resist the devil for us. On the contrary, James tells us to resist the devil, and that he will flee from us. It is an exhortation to do something. Then take a parallel in the First Epistle of Peter, in the fifth chapter, where there is a very clear and specific statement made. 'Be sober, be vigilant' – you have to be 'vigilant' – 'because your adversary the devil, as a roaring lion, walketh about seeking whom he may devour: whom resist steadfast in the faith, knowing that the same afflictions are accomplished in your brethren that are in the world' (1 Peter 5:8–9). That is an exhortation to us to 'resist steadfast in the faith'. Here we have two exhortations, without going any further, which come to us and tell us that we have to be vigilant and observant, and that we ourselves have to resist the devil. They urge us to do so with all the care and the energy that we can command.

But there are many others. Take what the Apostle Paul writes in Romans 8:13 about temptations arising in the flesh from within, used by the devil and fomented by the devil. Paul says: 'For if ye live after the flesh, ye shall die: but if ye through the Spirit do mortify the deeds of the body, ye shall live'. Notice that *you* have to do it; you do it 'through the Spirit'. It is not done for you. The teaching is not, 'Leave it to the Lord, look to Him, hand it over; but 'If you through the Spirit do mortify the deeds of the body, you shall live'. In Philippians 2:12 we have exactly the same teaching: 'Work out your own salvation with fear and trembling.' Not 'Hand it over to the Lord'. 'Work (it) out!' You and I are to work out our salvation with fear and trembling. This is an exhortation to Christian people.

It is not surprising, therefore, that people are in a state of confusion. Take, again, those exhortations given to Timothy in Paul's Second Epistle to him. There is a whole series of them. Having started by telling Timothy to 'be strong in the grace that is in Christ Jesus', Paul goes on to give him such detailed instruc-

[43]

tions as, 'Shun profane and vain babblings', 'If a man therefore purge himself from these' – he has to do it, it is not done for him – 'he shall be a vessel unto honour, sanctified, and meet for the Master's use'. 'Flee also youthful lusts.' He does not say, 'Go through this crisis of surrender, hand yourself over to Christ and look to Him, He will fight it for you'. What the Apostle says is, Take to your heels, flee youthful lusts, make no provision for the flesh! Everything he tells us in this connection is also an exhortation to us. He has been telling this young man Timothy precisely the same thing in his First Epistle in chapter 6, in detailed instructions: 'Thou, O man of God, flee these (evil) things; follow after righteousness, godliness, faith, love, patience, meekness.'

These are but random selections. The Epistles are full of this kind of teaching. They address men who had been habitual liars. Do they say, 'Now look here, my friends, do not struggle any longer with this tendency to lying; hand it over to the Lord, He will take it out of you, He will do it for you, all you have to do is to look at Him and to abide in Him'. No, what the Apostle tells such men is that they must not lie any longer, must not do this. Here is a man who has been troubled by the temptation to steal, the tendency to thieve. It seems to be in him and a part of him. What is he to do? Hand it over? No, 'Let him that stole steal no more: but rather let him labour, working with his hands the thing which is good, that he may have to give to him that needeth' (Ephesians 4:28). Then, 'Let no corrupt communication proceed out of your mouth, but that which is good to the use of edifying' (verse 29). You do not hand it over, you have to control yourself, you have to do this. 'Grieve not the holy Spirit of God . . . walk in love, as Christ also hath loved us, and hath given himself for us . . . But fornication, and all uncleanness, or covetousness, let it not be once named among you, as becometh saints; neither filthiness, nor foolish talking, nor jesting, which are not convenient: but rather giving of thanks' (Ephesians 4:30 to 5:5).

Those are some of the detailed instructions. But, above all, this teaching to which I am referring not only makes these exhortations unnecessary and indeed wrong, but this applies particularly to what we may call the military metaphors and similes that are used by the Apostles in order to make us do the things they are urging us to do. Have you noticed the frequency with which they use these military images? It is found in the text we are studying. The Apostle talks about our 'standing' and 'withstanding'. He says, 'Put on the whole armour of God, that ye may be able to stand against the wiles of the devil'. Then he uses this term 'wrestling'. It is a military term. 'We wrestle not against flesh and blood.' You and I have to do the wrestling, we are actively involved in this struggle. Not a word about 'handing it over', but a stern reminder that we are involved in this! Again, he uses the word 'withstand'. In 1 Corinthians 16:13 he says, 'Watch ye' – be on the watch – 'stand fast in the faith, quit you like men, be strong'. That is typical New Testament exhortation. Then take 2 Corinthians 10:3, where we read: 'Though we walk in the flesh, we do not war after the flesh: (for the weapons of our warfare are not carnal, but mighty through God to the pulling down of strongholds).' It is our warfare and we have to wage it in this particular way. We do not do so only in the flesh; but the opposite of that is not to say that you do nothing at all, that you just hand it over.

Look carefully at these military terms. I have already referred to one of them in Timothy 6:12: 'Fight the good fight of faith'. The Apostle is exhorting Timothy. Timothy has to 'fight'. Timothy's trouble was that he lost hope very easily; he became discouraged, and felt that he was weak and could not go on. He was inclined to ask Paul to come to help him, and to lean on Paul. But Paul writes back to him: 'Fight the good fight of faith'. Pull yourself together, says the Apostle. 'Be strong . . . Thou therefore endure hardness as a good soldier of Jesus Christ.' That is the picture. 'No man that warreth entangleth himself with the affairs of this life; that he may please him who hath chosen him to be a soldier' (2 Timothy 2:3-4). The whole picture is in military terms. We are the fighters, soldiers in the army of the living God; and we are not just 'to hand it all over'. We have our part to play, our battles to fight, as participators in a great battle. So the exhortations come to us in this military form.

But not only so. This erroneous teaching, it seems to me, is utterly inconsistent with what the great Apostle says about himself and his own life. Listen to him in 1 Corinthians 9:26 and 27. 'I therefore so run.' He is telling us of the way in which he takes part in this contest. He is using an illustration of a number of men in a race, a marathon race, if you like, in the Olympic Games, in which a number of competitors are running. The point is that they are running, they are not spectators sitting back and watching something being done before them; they are not like the great crowds that sit and watch others running. That is not the picture of Christianity. Paul is running in the race himself, so this is how he puts it: 'I therefore so run, not as uncertainly; so fight I' – he now turns to the image of a man boxing. This is not my interpretation; commentators are agreed about this. He takes an illustration from the boxing ring; he himself is in the ring and he is boxing an antagonist. *He* is doing it: it is not being done for him. He is not looking at somebody in the ring fighting on his behalf; he is in the ring himself. 'So fight I, not as one that beateth the air.' He wants to beat his man, he is hitting the man, not the air. And he says that he does not do these things uncertainly. 'I keep under my body', which being correctly translated means: 'I beat myself, my body, until I am black and blue. I beat my body, I keep under my body.' He is doing it himself, and it is not an easy thing to do. There is a struggle involved here. He is not saying to himself, 'Well now, I have all these problems within me in the flesh, rising up and tempting me and getting me down . . . Ah, I see there is only one thing to do, I need not struggle against these things any longer, all I have to do is to surrender, to hand them over to the Lord and let Him do it for me'. No, no! 'I keep under my body, and bring it into subjection.' He not only keeps it under, he masters it – 'brings it into subjection: lest having preached to others, I myself should be a castaway'. Such is the language which the Apostle Paul uses about himself.

But there is more. In Philippians 3 we have the well-known words, 'Not as though I had already attained' – he has not arrived at the end of his journey. There are certain things he is looking forward to – 'that I might know him, and the power of his resurrection, and the fellowship of his sufferings . . . If by any means I might attain unto the resurrection from among the dead. Not as though I had already attained, either were already prefect'. What then does he do? 'I follow after . . .' Then he goes on to say, 'But this one thing I do, forgetting those things which are behind, and reaching forth unto those things which are before, I press toward the mark'. That is his picture; he is pressing with all his might and main towards the mark – 'for the prize of the high calling of God in Christ Jesus' (Philippians 3:10–14). Then he introduces a word of exhortation in verse 16. 'Nevertheless,' he says, 'whereto we have already attained, let us walk by the same rule, let us mind the same thing'. Look to me, he says, I am your leader, follow me in this matter. 'Let us all be of the same mind', he says, 'let us walk by the same rule, let us mind the same thing.'

Then look at the Apostle at the end of his life. He is facing death, writing his last letter, the Second Epistle to Timothy. He looks back at it all and this is what he says: 'I have fought a good fight.' But according to the teaching we are evaluating he should not have done so. He should have said, 'The Lord has given me continuous victory, I have done nothing. The Lord has sustained me, fought my battles, kept me in peace; I have just been resting in Him and looking to Him and all has been well'. That is not what he says. He says, 'I have fought a good fight, I have finished my course, I have kept the faith'. Note how the Apostle speaks about himself in all the stages of his Christian life. He himself lived the kind of life to which he exhorted all these early Christians and in each case he is calling them to fight and to battle and to press towards the mark, and to exert themselves.

Moreover the ultimate logic of the wrong teaching, surely, is this, that though it sounds wonderful, as if all is going to be done for us, in the end it leaves it all to us, because the crucial point is our 'handing it over' and the 'abiding' in that position. Those who hold to that teaching are compelled to speak thus for this reason: Here is a teaching which tells us that we must 'let go and let God', and 'hand it over to the Lord' and then . . . Ah yes, but you suddenly find yourself falling into sin and you say, 'How is this happening to me? Has the Lord let me down? I had handed it all over to Him; you told me that He would fight the battles. But I have fallen into sin. Has the Lord failed, has the Lord let me down?' Of course they have to say at once, 'No, you must not say that; the Lord can never fail'. Well then, you ask, 'How then have I failed?' 'Ah,' they say, 'you did not go on abiding in the Lord.' So what matters ultimately is what *you* do. It is your abiding in Him that really matters, for the moment you fail to do that, or stop doing so, you fall. You are not being kept; you have to keep yourself in the Lord, you have to keep yourself in this place of abiding. It all comes back to you; you are left where you were at the beginning, which is surely a most serious matter.

Here, then, is a teaching which is self-contradictory, which apparently takes it out of your hands but in the end leaves it all in your hands. It entirely depends upon your maintaining this position of surrender. Furthermore, it always seems to me that there is here an incipient denial of the doctrine of the new-birth. I know that the friends who hold the false teaching believe in the new-birth, but they are inconsistent at this point. They do not see that in their teaching they virtually deny the doctrine of the re-birth, and in this way. The doctrine teaches that a man in the new-birth receives a new disposition, that a new principle of life is put into him that was not there before. 'If any man be in Christ he is a new creature; old things are passed away, behold, all things are become new' (2 Corinthians 5:17). Before conversion a man is 'dead in trespasses and sins'. he is altogether 'without strength'. The Apostle has been reminding the Ephesians of this truth: 'This I say therefore, and testify in the Lord, that ye henceforth walk not as other Gentiles walk, in the vanity of their mind.' He says that they were once like that but that they are no longer in that position. He continues: 'But ye have not so learned Christ; if so be that ye have heard him, and have been taught by him, as the truth is in Jesus: that ye put off concerning the former conversation the old man, which is corrupt according to the deceitful lusts; and be renewed in the spirit of your mind; and that ye put on the new man' (4:17-24).

Before a man becomes a Christian he is the 'old man' only, he has nothing but the evil, sinful, fleshly, carnal nature. But the re-birth means that a new man has come into being, and the new man is one 'which after God is created in righteousness and true holiness'. The Christian is not as he was before; there is a principle of new life in him which is righteous and holy and working in that direction. There is a new power in him. The Apostle says exactly the same thing in the next chapter: 'Ye were sometimes darkness, but now are ye light in the Lord: walk as children of light' (5:8). This is vital and fundamental teaching. But according to the other teaching we remain always the same; there is no strength, no good in us at all, and all we have to do is to rely on the Lord.

You may remember the illustration about a poker that was used by one of the famous teachers of this doctrine of passivity. Look at a poker, he used to say. What do you see about it? Well, it is black, it is rigid, and also cold. Now put that poker into the fire. What happens to it? It becomes hot whereas it was cold, it becomes red whereas it was black, it becomes malleable so that you can bend it, whereas it was formerly rigid. Yes, but only as long as it is kept in the fire! Take it out of the fire, says the illustration, and it reverts to its former condition of being cold and black and rigid.

Now that teaching is surely a denial of the doctrine of the new-birth. It is not true of the Christian. The Christian is a man who has a principle of new life in him, and there is power in that new life because it is a principle of righteousness and of true holiness. Not only so, it is something which can grow, it can develop. But the other teaching does not allow for that. Take the poker out of the fire and it reverts to exactly what it was before.

The same is true of another illustration about the wings you can put on, or the lifebelt you use, to keep you up in water. As long as you are wearing the wings you will go on floating; but get out of the wings, and you will sink to the bottom. There is no room left there, no place at all for growth or development or advance; whereas in the Scripture, according to the doctrine of the new-birth, we should grow. We are born as babes in Christ, then we become little children; then young men and then fathers. 'Grow in grace, and in the knowledge of the Lord.' Obviously! There is new life here, and life is something which grows. I must not be told about myself that I am so utterly hopeless that there is nothing that I can do but rely upon the Lord and His strength. And as I hope to show, what the strength of the Lord does is to feed and to develop this new life that is in me, and to make it stronger and stronger. So it seems to me that at that point, though our friends most certainly believe in the doctrine of regeneration, in this particular aspect of their teaching they are guilty of virtually denying it.

This teaching, moreover, is entirely unlike the whole of biblical teaching concerning sanctification, in that it is passive. The

[49]

biblical teaching is not passive. I have given examples which prove that it is always very active. It would not, and could not, contain exhortations if it was a teaching of passivity. But the Bible is full of exhortations and appeals and arguments and demonstrations and reasonings. As I have pointed out, these New Testament Epistles would never have been necessary at all if that other teaching were right. All the Apostles would have had to say would be this: 'Now then, you have been converted, you have been saved, you have been justified. That is step number one. There is only one other thing for you to do now: Hand it all over to the Lord, He will keep you, He will do everything you need. Do not do anything, do not strive or struggle, hand it over to the Lord, let go and let God'. The New Testament Epistles, with all these involved arguments, reasonings and refutations of error, and exhortations and appeals would be entirely unnecessary. There would only be one thing to say; and, of course, that is what our friends do say: 'You have been converted, very well, take the next step and you will get this other blessing. That is all you have to do – and it is 'quite simple'.

But according to the Bible it is not 'quite simple'. These Epistles are not quite simple. And they are not quite simple because life itself is not simple, because the devil is not simple, and because the Christian life is not simple. That other teaching is too passive. Not only so, it is too mechanical. There is nothing mechanical in the biblical teaching; it deals with life and growth and food and energy. The others just hand over, leave it, that is all, and stay there. No, that is mechanics, not life – a man is not a poker!

But another important objection to it is that it is a short-cut. There is never a short-cut in the spiritual life. That is the characteristic always of the cults. All the cults which are attracting so many people today offer short-cuts. That is their secret. They say, 'It is quite simple; these preachers take you through these Epistles and all this theology and doctrine and argument and difficulty. Do not listen to them. Just believe this teaching we offer you and all will be well with you. It does not matter what you were like when you came into contact with us; you can go out having no problems, no troubles. You will walk with a light step, you will be walking on air. It is all quite simple'. Such is the characteristic teaching of the cults; but it is never the Scripture teaching.

The erroneous teaching also shares another characteristic with the cults, most of which started in the nineteenth century, as did this particular teaching itself. They say, 'What a tragedy that for all those centuries people missed this teaching. Look at the saints, read their lives. See them fasting, sweating, and agonizing in prayer. What a tragedy, what a pity that they had not realized the truth of this essentially simple teaching'! Read Mrs Pearsall Smith on *The Christian's Secret of a Happy Life*, and you will find that she says just that. Read a similar book called *So Great Salvation* and you will find it there. It says, 'Is it not extraordinary that throughout all those centuries people missed it? At last they discovered it last century; it had never been known before. Suddenly the simple solution has been found'. All the cults say exactly that, and I argue that, in and of itself, it is sufficient to prove that this teaching is wrong. All the Patristic Fathers, all the Protestant Reformers, all the mighty men of God, who knew God in such an intimate manner, and who did such exploits for Him, and whom He used so mightily – we are asked to believe that they all had missed the crucial teaching, they all had gone the wrong way, they had misunderstood the Scriptures. Surely that, in and of itself, is enough to make us reject this teaching. An arrogance attaches to it which in itself proclaims that it is not true exposition of Scripture. I speak strongly because I am dealing with the claim that the teaching makes for itself.

The final argument the protagonists of this teaching generally bring at this point is, 'Say what you like about this teaching, but it works. There was I for all those years struggling in vain, and then I met this teaching. I believed it, and immediately I got release. It works, it does it! What do you say to that?' I answer that that is precisely what all the devotees and cults say. 'But how do you explain that?' asks someone. There is no difficulty at all. All these cults and psychological teachings can produce results. Obviously they would not succeed for a day if they could not. People would not rush after them and buy their books and attend their meetings if they did nothing at all. Of course they can produce certain results. We are strange creatures, we can persuade ourselves of many things. There are many ways of getting temporary relief and release. Christian Science, for example, makes many people very happy, but that is far from proving that Christian Science is true. You do not test a teaching by results only; you test every teaching by the Scriptures. If you are going to fall back on the argument that it works, that it has done something for you, well then, I ask what argument have you to give to the devotees of the cults? You have no answer at all. They can repeat everything you say. They can say, 'I used to be a terrible worrier, everything was a burden to me, I could never get rid of it, I could not sleep at night. Fortunately one day a friend said to me, "Come to this Christian Science meeting with me". I went in full of troubles, anxieties, cares; but when I came out they had all gone. I have never had a worry since'. They say such things and they are speaking the truth.

But the vital question is, How has it been done? The test is never the test of the results only. The primary test that should always be applied to any teaching is the test that we have been applying; it is the test of the Scriptures. 'What saith the Word of God?' My desire should not primarily be to be happy, but to be holy; it should be to conform to the Scriptures, it should be to do what God calls upon me and tells me to do. There is no short-cut in the Christian life. You can reject at sight any teaching that tells you that it is quite simple. It is not quite simple. 'We wrestle not against flesh and blood, but against principalities, against powers, against the rulers of the darkness of this world, against spiritual wickedness in high places.' What then are we to do? Well, you need to 'be strong in the Lord, and in the power of his might'; you need to 'Put on the whole armour of God', and attend to each part and portion; you need to fight and to go on fighting, so that at the end of your life, with the great Apostle you will be able to say, 'I have fought a good fight, I have kept the faith, I have finished my course; henceforth there is laid up for me a crown of righteousness'. A victor's crown! The New Testament uses such language. It is you and I who have to do the fighting.

Thus far we have been almost entirely negative; but we have to be negative. There are many people who will not listen to any other teaching because they believe the teaching we have been analysing and rejecting. We have to get rid of that first, and then we can turn to the Scriptures' own teaching, the positive teaching, which shows us how we are to fight and to wrestle, and how we are enabled to do so. It is not done for us, but we are enabled to do it ourselves. 'Be strong in the Lord, and in the power of his might.'

4
Morale

'Finally, my brethren, be strong in the Lord, and in
the power of his might.'

Ephesians 6:10

Having seen the wrongness of any suggestion of passivity in our
interpretation of these exhortations and that our activity is
involved, we are left with this problem: How do we reconcile
our activity with this statement, that we are to be 'strong in the
Lord, and in the power of his might?' How are these statements
which on the surface appear to be irreconcilable to be reconciled?

Surely the answer is that, though it is our activity, the Lord
provides the power for the activity. Paul does not tell us to do
nothing. Indeed he tells us to exert ourselves for all we are
worth, but that the power given to us to do so is His, and from
Him, and that we must learn increasingly how to rely upon that
power.

I start therefore with a proposition – that these two things must
always be taken together. Not that I do nothing and that He does
everything. Not, as others have tended to say, that I do everything. Not, as others have tended to say, that I do everything and
only ask for a little help and encouragement. It is neither of these
alternatives. It is a perfect blending of His power and my activity.
It is my activity in and through the power that He gives me.

Let me adduce a number of Scriptures which prove this, and
show clearly the relationship between these two things – my
activity and His power. There are certain terms used in the
Scriptures which show the perfect blending of the two, and how
the two came together. Take, for instance, the words in Hebrews

2:18. In his second chapter the author explains how, because He was to be the Captain of our salvation, the Lord Jesus Christ took unto Himself human nature. Because the children are of flesh and blood 'he also himself likewise took part of the same'. And in addition to that, having come as a man and in the likeness of sinful flesh, He was Himself subject to temptations. And the reason for this is given: 'For in that he himself hath suffered being tempted, he is able to succour them that are tempted'. He does not take the battle from them. He does not tell them to hand it all over to Him, that because He has been through it He will fight their battles for them. Rather it is, 'He is able to succour them'. He helps them. He does not take it completely out of their hands so that they do nothing but 'abide' and reap the fruits of His victory. On the contrary, He, having gone through all this experience, and having been made perfect in His suffering, and having learned obedience through that which He suffered, is now in the position in which He can succour, and help and aid. He can sustain, He can hold us who are still being tempted. The word 'succour' is enough in and of itself to show the true explanation of the text that we are considering. There the two come together. We are involved in this fight with the devil, and the Lord comes and succours us because of what He Himself has experienced. His sufferings were a part of His preparation for this work. He has been appointed to be a faithful high priest, not only in representing us to God, but also in helping us here on earth. And thus we are told that He 'succours' us; but not that He does it all instead of us. We do not hand it over; we fight and He succours us, He comes to our aid.

There is a like and parallel statement in Romans 8:26 and 27: 'Likewise the Spirit also helpeth our infirmities'. He does not take the problem from us because we are infirm, but 'the Spirit helpeth our infirmities'. 'For we know not what to pray for as we ought: but the Spirit itself maketh intercession for us with groanings which cannot be uttered.' That is exactly the same idea. He does not take it all from us, we do not hand it all over, we do not sit silent while the Spirit prays for us. No, 'He helpeth', He comes to our aid. The term used pictures us as trying to carry a heavy log or a plank, and we are staggering beneath it; but the Spirit comes, He takes up the other end and together we carry it forward. 'Helpeth!' We do not cease to carry, He carries the burden with us, comes to our aid, gives us a helping hand.

That is the terminology of the Scripture. There is nothing in it which tells us to 'hand it over to the Lord' or 'Let go and let God'. It is the exact opposite to this other teaching. That is why I am paying such prolonged attention to it.

Then take another example from 2 Corinthians chapter 12 where the Apostle is describing his rich, wonderful experience when he was lifted up, 'whether in the body, or out of the body, I cannot tell', and he heard things that are 'unspeakable'. Afterwards, he tells us, he was given a 'thorn in the flesh' and he was troubled. He prayed three times to the Lord that it might depart from him. But the reply he received was this: 'And he said to me, My grace is sufficient for thee'. In other words, My grace, the grace that I will give you, will be sufficient for you to go through and do this work you have to do, even though the thorn in the flesh still remains. The thorn was not taken out of him, he still had to struggle with it; but he was given grace, and the grace was sufficient – 'for my strength is made perfect in weakness'. His strength and my weakness come together. I still have to go on in my weakness, but His grace and His strength are sufficient. And the Apostle says: 'Most gladly therefore will I rather glory in my infirmities, that the power of Christ may rest upon me'. The power of Christ rests upon me, and so I am enabled to carry on; this is how His grace is sufficient. 'Therefore I take pleasure in infirmities, in reproaches, in necessities, in persecutions, in distresses for Christ's sake: for when I am weak, then am I strong'. That sounds paradoxical; but it is true – 'when I am weak, then am I strong'. I still have to go on my weakness, doing all He is calling me to do; but He enables me, He energizes me as it were, even in the weakness. I am not a mere passive spectator; I am using all my powers and I am conscious of the hindrance of this thorn in the flesh. But 'when I am weak, then am I strong'. It is the power that He gives me that enables me to continue with my work.

But let us look at what in many ways is the crucial passage in this connection – Philippians 2, verses 12 and 13. Here again we have a blending of the two aspects: 'Wherefore, my beloved, as ye have always obeyed, not as in my presence only, but now much more in my absence, work out your own salvation with fear and trembling'. That exhortation is the exact contradiction of 'Let go and let God', and 'Hand it over to the Lord and He will do it for you'. Here the two sides are brought together. I am to work out my own salvation with fear and trembling, and it is an extremely difficult task. I have to be careful; it involves 'fear and trembling', which is so different from the theory which says, 'Don't be unhappy any longer, there is nothing to fear at all, hand it over to the Lord, He will do it for you; rest in faith, look to Him, abide, you will have no troubles, you will go on rejoicing all the day'. 'Work out your own salvation with fear and trembling', says the Apostle. Who is sufficient for these things? Who can do this? The answer is, 'For it is God that worketh in you both to will and to do'. The two things come together, and are not separated in the false way which that other teaching suggests.

But let us look at further statements in which the Apostle tells us about himself and the way in which he lived the Christian life. Look, for example, at Galatians 2:20: 'I am [have been] crucified with Christ, nevertheless I live'. Observe the way in which Paul seems to be contradicting each statement which he makes. He does so to save us from the very error we are considering. He says, 'I have been crucified with Christ'. To those who hold the wrong teaching that means that he has ceased to do anything, he has handed it all over, he has finished with this life of struggle and of endeavour. He is dead. But immediately he adds, 'nevertheless I live'. Then again, as it were to increase our amazement, 'yet not I, but Christ liveth in me'. 'Ah,' they say, 'there you are after all, you see that is what the Apostle is teaching, "nevertheless I live; yet not I". I have finished, I have handed it all over to the Lord, Christ is now living in me. I am finished, I am no longer living, I am no longer doing anything. It is Christ that is living in me and getting the victory for me, and I am just abiding in this "rest of faith".' But, unfortunately for that teaching, the Apostle continues – 'and the life which I now live in the flesh'. You see he is still there, and says in effect, I am still living, and in the flesh, in this body with all that that involves. 'The life which I now live in the flesh I live by the faith of the Son of God, who loved me, and gave himself for me.' I am living this life in terms of my faith in Him and what He has done for me and what He will yet do.

You cannot get rid of man's activity, all along it is here in these crucial texts. That is how I live, says the Apostle. He will not allow you to leave out either side. To leave out either is wrong. If you say that you have to do it all yourself, you are wrong: if you say that you do nothing and He does everything, you are equally wrong. It is I, living my life in the flesh. It is Christ living in me and thereby enabling me to live this life in the flesh. *I* am living it – 'the life I now live in the flesh I live by the faith of the Son of God'. 'I live.' But Christ also lives in me.

There is an equally clear statement in Philippians 4, verses 11 to 13. The Apostle is in prison, and the Philippians have sent him a gift. In writing to thank them for it he says, 'Not that I speak in respect of want: for I have learned in whatsoever state I am, therewith to be content. I know both how to be abased, and I know how to abound: everywhere and in all things I am instructed both to be full and to be hungry, both to abound and to suffer need'. Then he sums it all up: 'I can do all things through Christ which strengtheneth me'.

In order to bring out this point let me tell you the story of a quaint old preacher preaching on this very text. In order to impress the point upon his congregation he put it like this. He read the words, 'I can do all things' – then stopped abruptly and put a question to the Apostle in these words: 'Don't you think you are saying too much, Paul? Do you really say you can do all things? Is there nothing that you cannot do? Can you really fight these principalities and powers? Are you equal to the devil? Look what he did with all the patriarchs, even men like Abraham, the friend of God. The devil defeated Abraham, and are you claiming that you are superior when you say "I can do all things"?' The old preacher went on in that manner for some time, putting up the difficulties and asking the Apostle questions and suggesting that Paul was going beyond himself. But then he proceeded to read the whole text, 'I can do all things through Christ which strengtheneth me'. 'Oh, I beg your pardon, Paul,' said the old preacher, 'I didn't realize that there were two of you!' He had been giving the impression that there was only one, namely, the

Apostle Paul. Certainly that must be emphasized: 'I', says Paul, 'can do all things'. But he is able to do all things only 'through Christ which strengtheneth me'. Christ is strengthening him, is infusing power into him; but it is Paul who does all things. It is he who knows both how to be abased, and how to abound. Paul has not handed it all over and become a sitting spectator passively 'abiding'. He is involved, he is the one who is doing all these things. But the glory of it is, he says, that I am enabled to do all these things through Christ who – not 'does it all for me', but Christ who – 'strengtheneth me'. It is a kind of blood transfusion, the power is put into him, he is strengthened. The tasks are not taken out of his hands, but he is enabled to do them because he is being strengthened in this way.

Let us glance for a moment at some of the Apostle's experiences which illustrate the truth in a somewhat more objective manner. Paul passed through some very trying experiences. Some of them are recorded in the Book of the Acts of the Apostles. Take, for instance, Acts 18, verses 9 and 10. Paul is being threatened, but this is what I read: 'Then spake the Lord to Paul in the night by a vision, Be not afraid, but speak, and hold not thy peace: for I am with thee, and no man shall set on thee to hurt thee: for I have much people in this city'. That is how the Lord's gift of strength works. The Apostle is made strong by the vision and assurance that are given to him. He still has to go on with his preaching, but he is assured in this special way that he is not left to himself, and that the Lord will be with him to strengthen him.

There is a similar example in Acts 23:11: 'And the night following the Lord stood by him, and said, Be of good cheer, Paul: for as thou hast testified of me in Jerusalem, so must thou bear witness also at Rome'. In this way the Lord speaks to him, manifests Himself to him; and thus he is filled with strength to continue his testimony. Having this assurance he is able to do so. He has to do it, and he will do it the more confidently in the strength of this great power.

But there is also that very dramatic and exciting story in the twenty-seventh chapter of the Book of the Acts of the Apostles in connection with the shipwreck of Paul and his companions on the way to Rome. I pick out particularly verses 23 and 25. The position was becoming quite desperate, they had even thrown the tackling of the ship overboard. 'We cast out with our own hands the tackling of the ship. And when neither sun nor stars in many days appeared, and no small tempest lay on us, all hope that we should be saved was then taken away. But after long abstinence Paul stood forth in the midst of them, and said, Sirs, you should have hearkened unto me, and not have loosed from Crete, and to have gained this harm and loss. And now I exhort you to be of good cheer: for there shall be no loss of any man's life among you, but of the ship.' How was he able to speak with such confidence? There they were, all at their wits' end, captain and mariners and everybody else utterly distraught and desperate, shipwreck expected at any moment – the end, disaster. The Apostle says, 'Be of good cheer!' What enables him to overcome these circumstances in this way? He tells them: 'For there stood by me this night the angel of God, whose I am, and whom I serve, saying, Fear not Paul; thou must be brought before Caesar: and, lo, God hath given thee all them that sail with thee.' Then they proceed to do various things themselves. They do not just let the ship drift, they attend to many necessary things. Thus Paul was made strong by the word that was given to him, and he in turn was able to make his fellow voyagers strong by giving them this assurance. They had given up hope, they were desperate; but as the word of Paul gave them assurance they became capable of dealing with the situation.

But take yet another example from Paul's experience in his very last Epistle. Writing in the Second Epistle to Timothy the Apostle mentions his 'first answer'. He refers to the first occasion on which he appeared before the authorities in connection with his trial. The procedure then was much as it is now; the case would be started, then there would be an adjournment, then another appearance, and so on. 'At my first answer no man stood with me, but all men forsook me: I pray God that it may not be laid to their charge. Notwithstanding, the Lord stood with me, and strengthened me.' Note the sequence of events, always in the same order. What the Lord does is to strengthen us. He does not take the problem out of our hands so that we do nothing. 'The Lord stood with me, and strengthened me; that by me the preaching might be fully known, and that all the Gentiles might hear: and I was delivered out of the mouth of the lion' (2 Timothy 4:16). 'The Lord strengthened me!' He makes us powerful and mighty and strong, and capable of fighting and of wrestling; He does not take the action out of our hands.

Then take this final word, no longer about the great Apostle. It is a most significant word in the Book of Revelation, chapter 12, verse 11, describing how the saints are attacked by the enemy, the old dragon, the serpent, the devil. 'And they overcame him.' *They* overcame him; not 'He was overcome for them' – 'they overcame him by the blood of the Lamb, and by the word of their testimony; and they loved not their lives unto the death'. Could anything be plainer?

How did the saints overcome the devil 'by the blood of the Lamb, and the word of their testimony'? Doubtless it includes the thought that they spoke to the devil. They put into practice the exhortation, 'Resist the devil; and he will flee from you'. How do you do so? 'You cannot touch me any longer. You used to be able to touch me, but you cannot now, the blood of Christ is upon me.' And the mention of the word 'the blood of Christ' always defeats the devil. 'They overcame him by the blood of the Lamb, and the word of their testimony.' They turned upon him and they said: 'You are a defeated foe and we belong to the One who defeated you; we are no longer afraid of you.' That is how it is done! 'They overcame.' They did not just sit back and let Christ overcome them. That is not the teaching of the Scripture. You and I are enabled to do the overcoming by the blood of the Lamb, and by the word of our testimony. There is no 'let go and let God' here. You hold on and you fight. The astounding truth is that we are enabled to conquer the devil, to overcome him, to be more than conquerors over him. We are to resist him, and he will flee from us as long as we do so in this right way.

It is clear then that we are involved; your activity and mine must continue and go on, indeed it must increase. But He will enable us more and more. Now here comes the practical question: 'How does all this,' says someone, 'all that you have been saying, actually work out in practice? What exactly am I to do? I have accepted your argument, I can see that I have to go on, I can see that I shall be enabled to go on, but what do I do in detail and in actual practice?'

The first answer is that we must realize and understand actively all that we have said hitherto on this subject. That is absolutely essential. Let me put the matter in a different way by saying that if you and I are to wrestle triumphantly against the devil and all his powers, the first essential is assurance of salvation. There is no hope for us in this conflict unless we know God's power and God's might. But if we are uncertain about our relationship to Him we cannot stand and withstand in the fight. In other words the key to victory over the devil is assurance of salvation, certainly concerning our relationship to God in Jesus Christ. That is but another way of saying, 'They overcame him by the blood of the Lamb, and by the word of their testimony.' You cannot give a testimony if you do not know your position. It is only one who is certain who can give a testimony, and who can act as a witness. The saints' testimony in the Book of Revelation is that the blood was on them, that they belonged to Christ; they possessed assurance of salvation.

By assurance you are made 'strong in the Lord, and in the power of his might'. How does it work? Take that most interesting and profound psychological remark of Ezra, a man who had to face very great difficulties. Ezra had to face the problem of reconstruction after the destruction of Jerusalem, after the sacking of the city and the carrying away of the people. He was sent back to Jerusalem. Everything was a mass of ruins, a complete chaos. Here was a man facing a tremendous task with enemies all around attacking. Now Ezra makes one of the most profound remarks, from the practical standpoint, in the whole of Scripture. He says: 'The joy of the Lord is your strength.' While you are miserable and unhappy and uncertain, says Ezra, you will never succeed, will be utterly defeated.

This can be illustrated endlessly. We all know this in experience. You are feeling unhappy, miserable, troubled. You wake up in the morning, perhaps, and you find yourself in that condition. Now you know the sort of day you may expect to have. Everything will go wrong. The work which you do day by day will be difficult, full of problems. You begin to wonder whether you are equal to it, whether you should not resign, or go away for a while. Because you are miserable you are full of foreboding. 'All seems yellow to the jaundiced eye.' But, on the contrary, when you are happy your work gives you no trouble. You just run through it, as it were. Everybody knows this experience.

Your personal condition will determine the way you do your work, and your attitude towards your work. A man who has domestic troubles leaves his home having had an argument or a quarrel over certain problems. How can he face his work happily in his office or his factory or profession, whatever it is? He cannot. He is already defeated. But if everything is well and happy at home, everything is well in his work. Do we not all know this kind of thing? 'The joy of the Lord is your strength.'

We had several clear illustrations of this kind of thing during the last war. When things were at their worst the then Prime Minister, Winston Churchill, would speak to the nation on the wireless. That is all he did. He did not change a single fact, but everyone felt very different when he had finished. We felt strong again, we were ready for the battle. He had done nothing but speak, but he had given us assurance, he had made us feel happy. There is nothing to compare with happiness. If you are happy and all is well, you will go through your work easily; its tasks will be surmounted. In a much higher sense 'the joy of the Lord' puts strength into you, puts power into you.

'But,' you may ask, 'how is this possible? The problem is still there, and I am still the same man!' Yes, but you are not a machine. Man is a strange amalgam. He has the same nerves, and the same muscles, and the same brain, he is the same throughout, always! But you have not finished talking about a man when you say that. There is a kind of electricity in man as well. You cannot measure it and we do not know much about it, but it is there; and suddenly when this electricity is generated it charges everything else and you are twice the man you were before. From the strictly materialistic point of view you are the same man, but in practice you are not the same man at all. You are much stronger, everything is keyed up, you are energized, you are ready for anything, and you can do things which you could not possibly have done when you were miserable and doubtful and unhappy.

That is the very thing the Apostle is saying here: 'Be strong in the Lord, and in the power of his might'. 'The joy of the Lord is your strength.' What you have to do is not to 'let go and let God'. What you do is to 'make your calling and election sure', as I am about to explain. As you do this more and more you will find that you are filled with the strength you need,

Or take what Daniel says in chapter 11, verse 32. He puts it thus: 'But the people that do know their God shall be strong and do exploits.' They are not called upon to fold their arms and to look on while the exploits are done for them. The essential factor in the situation is that the people know their God. It is the knowledge of God that makes them strong. It infuses power into them, it keys them up, it makes them capable. This is the secret. Not passivity – quite the reverse! This idea that the Christian just does nothing and sits back passively and all is done is the very antithesis of the biblical teaching which teaches that the Christian is suddenly charged with power and feels himself to be a Colossus, and that there is nothing he cannot do – 'strong in the Lord'. It depends upon the fact that he knows his God, and because he knows Him he is strong, he is able to stand up, he is afraid of nothing, and he can do exploits.

We must grasp this truth; because if we do not, we are already defeated. Let me give another statement of this selfsame thing by this same Apostle Paul. It is found in the twentieth chapter of the Book of the Acts of the Apostles, where Paul says: 'And now, behold, I go bound in the spirit unto Jerusalem, not knowing the things that shall befall me there.' All he knows is, 'that the Holy Ghost witnesseth in every city, saying that bonds and afflictions abide me'. That is his position. It could not be much worse. The devil and all his forces are arrayed against him, and are using communities and individuals, Jews and Romans alike, to provide 'bonds and afflictions' for the Apostle. The Holy Ghost is witnessing this to him in every city; wherever he goes someone or other prophesies to this effect. But listen to what he says: 'But none of these things move me, neither count I my life dear unto myself, so that I might finish my course with joy, and the ministry, which I have received of the Lord Jesus, to testify the gospel of the grace of God.' 'None of these things move me,' says Paul. He is not frightened, he is not alarmed, he is not

daunted, despite the prophecies of trouble. His only complaint
is against his friends who were weeping and hanging round his
neck and pleading with him not to go forward. Don't do it,
says Paul, I am going on. 'None of these things move me.' Why
not? All he desires is 'to finish his course with joy'. He rejoiced
in his ministry, 'the ministry which I have received of the Lord
Jesus, to testify the gospel of the grace of God'. His joy in the
work! His joy in the Lord! He is rejoicing in the fact that he, who
had been 'a blasphemer, and a persecutor, and an injurious
person', was now an evangelist, an Apostle of Christ. His joy in
this was so great that though he knew what was coming he could
still say, 'None of these things move me'. He is 'more than
conqueror', he has overcome them. It is his joy in the ministry
that lifts him up above all his adverse circumstances, and thus
enables him to triumph and prevail.

All this drives us to the conclusion that if we are in any kind of
doubt or uncertainty with regard to our salvation the devil has
already defeated us. We are to be assured of our salvation. The
Scripture emphasizes this constantly; so much of it is devoted to
teaching which brings us certainty and assurance. If you at this
moment are uncertain of your salvation, there is only one reason
for it, and that is that the devil has somehow or other defeated
you. It may be that you have not had the right teaching, but that
is because the devil has been blinding those who have taught you.
It may be that the devil blinds you as you read the Scriptures for
yourself, or he may make you look inwards in too introspective a
manner, and so rob you of your assurance of salvation. So it comes
to this: if the devil has got you down and has defeated you at this
crucial point, he is cutting off the source of supply, the source of
energy and of power and of life. If he has already done so,
obviously he aims at defeating you everywhere else. You are in a
miserable state, you are unhappy, and when the devil comes and
tempts you in the flesh or in the spirit or any other way, he has
little difficulty in defeating you. You are already down in spirit,
and he kicks you on the ground and spits upon you, and so you
feel quite hopeless and helpless. If that is your case, there is only
one way of recovery – you must get up, and you must get
assurance and an absolute certainty with regard to your salvation.
That is what will give backbone to you, and strength and power.

Then, you will be ready for the devil in whatever form or guise he happens to come to you.

I end on this note. As Christians, the first and the greatest thing we have to realize is who we are and what we are. This is the way to defeat the enemy. In other words, we must realize that we are the children of God. The mere realization of the fact that we are the children of God is one of the greatest sources of strength and of power a man can ever have. Let me give two illustrations of this.

I go to the Old Testament again, and to the Book of Ezra. And if this was true of Old Testament saints how much more should it be true of New Testament saints! There is a great story in chapter 8. Ezra had asked the king for a certain number of people and provisions to go back to Jerusalem to start the work of reconstruction. They arrived at a critical point, and Ezra hesitated for a moment. He realized the difficulties, how that there were enemies waiting and ready to attack; and his first instinct was to send a messenger to the king in Babylon and ask him for a troop, a body of soldiers, to accompany them and to defend them and to safeguard them from the attack of the enemy. But he suddenly said to himself, I cannot do that. So instead of sending a messenger to the king to ask for a body of soldiers he says, 'I proclaimed a fast . . . for I was ashamed to require of the king a band of soldiers and horsemen to help us against the enemy in the way' (vv. 21–22). Why was he ashamed? 'Because we had spoken unto the king, saying, The hand of our God is upon all them for good that seek him; but his power and his wrath is against all them that forsake him'. He was on the verge of sending the message asking for this body of soldiers and so on, but suddenly he says, 'I cannot do that, because of what I have already said to the king'. He had told the king that they were going on a hazardous journey. 'Do you think you are wise?' the king asked. 'It is all right', Ezra had said. 'What if the enemies attack you?' asked the king. 'All will be well', Ezra had replied. 'The hand of our God is upon all them for good that seek him.' 'We are the children of God', Ezra had said to the pagan king, 'and our God is almighty'. But then, later, a temporary feeling of fear had arisen, and Ezra almost gave in. But he says, 'I cannot ask for soldiers; I am one of God's people; and I have told the king so, and I have claimed great things in the name of God. Very well, we do not ask for troops, we call a fast instead and get back into contact with God, and then set out'. That knowledge made him strong. He was no longer a defeatist; and he went forward on his way triumphantly.

Now consider Nehemiah who was also engaged in the same work, as we find him mentioned in the Book that bears his name, chapter 6. A critical moment had come in the reconstruction work in Jerusalem. They had started building the wall, but there were enemies looking on and jeering at them, and threatening to come in to destroy it all. They had to work with a trowel in one hand and a sword in the other, and there was a constant watch day and night. The position was really desperate. Then a supposed friend of Nehemiah came to him and said, 'Look here, don't you think that you as the leader in this enterprise ought to take some measures to protect yourself?' 'Come, let us go together into the house of the Lord and find sanctuary; we shall be safe there from the attack of the enemy. You must not stay by the wall. If you are killed all will be lost. Let us go in and there we shall be in safety in the house of God.' Then Nehemiah made this immortal reply: 'Should such a man as I flee?' What saves him is that he knows who he is! 'Should such a man as I flee?' Is he just a great egotist, is he guilty of over-estimating himself? Not at all! 'Should such a man as I flee? And who is there, that, being as I am, would go into the temple to save his life? I will not go in. And lo, I perceived that God had not sent him' – this messenger of woe who was asking him to save his own skin. The man claimed to be speaking in the name of God. Nehemiah knew that that was impossible. Such advice is not characteristic of God, is not consistent with God's way. Nehemiah realizes who he is – God's man! 'Should such a man as I flee?' I who have made statements to the king to whom I was the cup-bearer? Is what is proposed possible? It is impossible! I cannot! I am God's man! 'Should such a man as I flee? Impossible! I cannot! I am God's man!'

The moment he stood on that great fact that he was a man of God, it was given to him to see that God had never sent this messenger at all, but that it was Tobiah and Sanballat, his enemies, who by a ruse and subterfuge had engaged a man to act as traitor in order to defeat Nehemiah. So Nehemiah gets his victory, loses his fear, and is 'more than conqueror'. On what grounds? Simply on the knowledge of the fact that he is a man of God. That is the beginning of 'being strong in the Lord, and in the power of his might'. As you realize who you are and what you are, you are already far on the way to certain victory over the devil and all his forces.

5
Food and Drink

'Finally, my brethren, be strong in the Lord, and in
the power of his might.'

Ephesians 6:10

Having seen the vital importance of the assurance of salvation
and the realization of who we are, and what we are, the next step
in the argument is that there is nothing so strengthening as the
realization of what is awaiting us, and coming to us, as God's
people. This theme is frequently held before us in the Bible. It is
the 'blessed hope' that is offered to all God's people. The biblical
view of life in this world, in the Old Testament as much as in the
New, is that life is a journey and that this is a passing world at
best. The days allotted to a man are 'three score years and ten',
and if he is strong, a little more; but always it is a passing life.
Life is a pilgrimage, life is a journey. That is a fact, of course, of
which everybody is aware. But the man of God, the Christian,
is in this peculiar position, and has this great advantage, that he is
not troubled by that realization. He knows that the real life is the
one which is yet to come, and he keeps his eye upon it. This was
the secret of all the great patriarchs of the Old Testament –
Abraham, and all the others. They went out 'not knowing whither
they went'; but they knew with whom they went. They knew
the ultimate goal. They were 'seeking for a city which hath
foundations, whose builder and maker is God'. Moses was ready
to sacrifice all the prospects that lay before him in Egypt. He
refused to be called the son of Pharaoh's daughter. He put all the
glories of Egypt aside. Why? Because 'he had his eye on the
recompense of the reward'; he knew what was coming. This is a
great principle which is taught everywhere in the Bible, and
particularly, of course, in the New Testament. The Christian is a

man who has his eye on the glory to which he is going. 'Beloved,' says John in his First Epistle, chapter 3, verse 2, 'now are we the sons of God, and it doth not yet appear what we shall be: but we know that, when he shall appear, we shall be like him; for we shall see him as he is.' And then he immediately draws the deduction in verse 3: 'Every man that hath this hope in him purifieth himself, even as he is pure.'

In other words the argument is that as long as we realize this truth, as long as we realize that we are going to glory, as long as we have a right view of life in this world, and realize that the thing that matters ultimately is our arrival there, we must feel that the most urgent thing in life is to purify ourselves, even as the Lord is pure. The man who knows this is always preparing himself. He knows that he is travelling to a glory that is indescribable, to a holiness, to a purity, to a land of light where there is no darkness and no sin at all; he knows that he is destined to see God, to see the Lord Jesus Christ, and to be like Him. A man who has this uppermost in his mind and in his heart, holds a corresponding view of all that the world has to offer him – all its attractions and interests, all the things that it dangles before him, all its glittering prizes. He has a new view of everything. The realization of all this makes the man purify himself, even as Christ is pure. He realizes that he has not much time to prepare himself for eternal glory.

The analogies that suggest themselves to us at this point should be quite obvious. If you have some great honour coming to you, if you are expecting to meet some great personage – a king or a queen or somebody in a very prominent position – you will be preparing for it days and weeks and perhaps months ahead. You will be preparing yourself, preparing your clothes, preparing your deportment, discovering what you have to do, what to say, and especially what not to do. Your whole life will be governed by the expected event, everything else will recede in importance and in significance. The prospect will dominate your life and you will live for it and prepare yourself for it. That is precisely the argument of the New Testament: 'Every man that hath this hope in him, purifieth himself, even as he is pure.' As Christians we do not really belong to this world; we are 'strangers and pilgrims' in it. Such is the biblical argument.

I have often used a simple, almost childlike analogy to bring out this point. It is what parents always tell their children when they send them to a party at Christmas-time or some other time: 'Now remember that you behave yourself.' And for this reason: the children have to remember who they are, that they are the representatives of the whole family. Now that is the kind of argument that should work with the Christian. When he is confronted by the devil, and the principalities and powers, he should not be deluded, or misled. He realizes what is happening. He says, 'I do not belong to you, I am no longer a citizen of your kingdom. I am a member of Christ's kingdom. My citizenship is in heaven and I am preparing myself for heaven'. That confession puts life and vigour and strength into him.

That, then, is another way in which we become 'strong in the Lord, and in the power of his might', namely, the recollection of our relationship to Him, and the realization of the fact that we are going to stand before Him and see Him face to face.

Let us add to that this further consideration, which follows by an inevitable logical necessity, namely, that we remember that God's honour, and the honour of the Lord Jesus Christ, and the honour of the Holy Spirit are, as it were, in our hands. We cannot live to ourselves. We are God's people and we cannot divorce ourselves from the relationship. The whole family is involved in what we are and in what we do. What a difference it would make if we always remembered this! What strength and power it would put into us! You cannot detach yourself, you cannot say you are an isolated individual.

We cannot isolate ourselves, of course, in the natural sphere. A prodigal son may feel that he can, that he has finished with his father and his mother and his brothers and sisters and home. He goes away, he thinks he is an isolated individual, and he is determined no longer to be bound by family ties. Nevertheless, what he does reflects upon the whole family. The whole family has to suffer, the whole family is brought into a kind of disgrace, everybody will be talking about the family. He has besmirched the family name, he is indeed the black sheep in the flock, and he cannot isolate himself. There are certain things we cannot do, and this is one of them. It is exactly the same with the Christian. That is why I sometimes say that there is no such thing as a holiday in the spiritual realm. Our relationship to God and to one another is always with us, and we are always Christians. There must be no kind of false dualism in us, no false dichotomy. We are one, and we are always God's people, God's children; and what we do reflects upon the name of God, and the name of the Lord Jesus Christ. The realization of this is obviously a tremendous source of strength. We are thus conscious of the fact that we are representatives, that we are agents, and that the honour of our family, our country, and all that we belong to, is, as it were, in our hands. There is nothing that is more calculated to strengthen us and to give us vigour and courage and power than just that realization.

We now turn to another aspect of the subject which is still more practical.

We have seen ourselves as children of God, and we have this new life in us. Now the question we want to ask is: How can I keep this life and the power and the vigour that are in this life? Yes, how can I increase it? How can I become yet stronger and stronger in the Lord, and in the power of His might? Let us look at it in the following way. What makes a man a Christian is that a seed of new life is put into him. This is the biblical terminology, as seen for instance in the First Epistle of John, chapter 3 and verse 9: 'Whosoever is born of God doth not commit sin', that is to say, does not practise sin, does not continue habitually in sin. And for this reason: 'for his seed remaineth in him: and he cannot sin' – he cannot go on living in sin – 'because he is born of God'.

The argument is that to be 'born of God' means that a seed, or a principle of eternal life, has been put into us. It is the doctrine, as I was indicating in a previous study, that makes it quite impossible to accept the teaching about 'Let go and let God'. We are told that because this seed of new life is in us we cannot go on in sin. The truth is stated categorically. We are not told that we can do nothing but hand ourselves over to the Lord; we are to realize that He has put a principle of life, a seed, into us, and we cannot go on practising sin because the seed is in us; that is to say, we are born of God. This principle of life that He has put into us has power in it, has strength in it, it changes everything. 'If any man be in Christ, he is a new creature: old things are passed away; behold, all things are become new' (2 Corinthians 5:17).

That other idea that a Christian remains what he always was, but now relies upon the power of the Lord – that idea put in terms of the illustration of the poker – is also a denial of this teaching about the seed. The Christian is not simply a man who has taken a decision, who has decided to follow Christ, and to do this or that. He has done so, but what makes him do so is that this seed of eternal life has been put into him, that he is born of God. There is something new in this man that is bigger than the whole man, this is the new principle that is going to govern the whole of his life. Because it is so, he cannot go on living as he did before. The Bible says that at the first he is but a babe, an infant, in Christ. So the question arises, How can this babe grow, how can this infant develop? Or to put the query in another form – How can this principle of life and of power and vigour be fostered, nurtured, and developed, so that it may become yet stronger and stronger?

The best way of answering that question is to follow the line of the analogy that is suggested by the terminology used in the Scripture itself. What is obviously needed is food and drink. What does the new-born babe need above everything? Food and drink! It needs to be nourished. If the babe is to develop into a child, into an adolescent, into a full-grown man, it must have sustenance. The new-born babe is helpless and weak and cannot do anything for itself. But a day will come when it will have vigour and strength and power, and be able to do things for itself and others. Food and drink produce this change. It is exactly the same in the Christian life; and this is one way in which we become 'strong in the Lord, and in the power of his might'.

As Christians we are given a strength, a power, in the seed of life that is put into us. But the seed has to grow and develop, and we have to take measures to see that the life that God has given us will grow and develop, and become steadily stronger.

To show how this happens we must summarize the teaching that deals with this problem almost everywhere in the Bible. I start with food and drink because they must come first. How do we get them? Our Lord Himself answers in the thirty-fifth verse in the sixth chapter of the Gospel according to St John: 'He that cometh to me shall never hunger; and he that believeth in me shall never thirst'. Food and drink satisfy hunger and thirst. They are to be found in Him, by going to Him, by keeping on going to Him. You do not just go once at the beginning and then rest, you keep on going to Him. 'He that cometh' – that keeps on coming – 'to me shall never hunger, and he that believeth on me' – keeps on believing – 'shall never thirst'. In the same chapter at verse 53 we read: 'Then Jesus said unto them, Verily, verily, I say unto you, Except ye eat the flesh of the Son of man, and drink his blood, ye have no life in you. Whoso eateth my flesh, and drinketh my blood, hath eternal life; and I will raise him up at the last day. For my flesh is meat indeed, and my blood is drink indeed. He that eateth my flesh, and drinketh my blood, dwelleth in me, and I in him'. Then, further, 'As the living Father hath sent me, and I live by [or, because of] the Father: so he that eateth me, even he shall live by me'. There we have profound mystical teaching. Certain of the hearers reacted and said, 'This is an hard saying; who can hear it?' What is He talking about? 'How can this man give us his flesh to eat?' they ask. They stumbled at it. We are told, indeed, that from that time, 'Many of his disciples went back, and walked no more with him' (v. 66). They could not understand the Lord's words and, indeed, resented them.

So these words come to us as a test. Our reaction to these words proclaims exactly what we are, and where we stand. Nothing more glorious, more wonderful, has ever been offered to human beings and yet it is possible for people to reject the message and dislike it heartily. Everybody seemed to be leaving Him, so our Lord turned to the disciples and said, 'Will ye also go away?' Peter, not fully understanding what he was saying, said, 'Lord, to whom shall we go? Thou hast the words of eternal life, and we believe and are sure that thou art that Christ, the Son of the living God'.

What then does it mean? Our Lord says that His words are spirit, not flesh. He is not talking about material things. He is talking in a spiritual manner. He is using an analogy here. What He means, He says, is: The Father hath sent me, and I live because of the Father. I am living by the Father, I am receiving my strength and nourishment and power from the Father. This is a part of what was involved in the Incarnation. Jesus had not ceased to be the Son of God, but He had taken unto Himself human nature. He was now living His life as a man in human nature. He was not living in terms of His Godhead; it was still there, but He was not living by it. He was living a life of utter dependence upon His Father. That is why He prayed as He did regularly. He says, 'I live by the Father', that is, I draw My strength, My nutriment, My everything from Him. And He says that, in the same way, the man who truly 'believes in me is a man who lives because of me'. He puts it in terms of eating His flesh, and drinking His blood; which means really taking Him, believing in Him as He is in all His fulness, and living a life henceforth determined and controlled and governed by this belief in Him, this surrender to Him, this reliance upon Him and the power of His might.

The Lord puts it dramatically in those words in order that we may see that this is something that you and I have to do in a very thorough manner. We do not merely say, 'Yes, I believe in the Lord Jesus Christ. I believed in Him at a given point of time, and I have been a Christian ever since'. True believing leads to 'eating the flesh, and drinking the blood', that is to say, really taking it in, chewing it, masticating it, making it a part of yourself, realizing that He is your Bread of life. 'I am the bread of life', He says. He contrasts Himself with the manna in the wilderness which was but a type and a figure – something given to maintain physical well-being – yet a great type of what He was going to do when He came. 'I am the bread of life . . . if any man eat of this bread', He says, 'he shall never die'. Whosoever eateth of me will never die in this spiritual sense because he is receiving life, he becomes 'a partaker of the divine nature', he is feeding on a heavenly manna. He is eating me, he is living on me, he is living by me, he is living because I am what I am, and have accomplished the work which the Father gave me to do. Jesus expresses it in terms of flesh and blood in order that we may realize what a thorough work this is, that we really have to 'appropriate' Christ. A mere intellectual belief is insufficient. Christ must become our life – our food, our drink, our everything. Such then is the meaning, a part of the meaning at any rate, which can be expanded infinitely, of that most astonishing statement which our Lord makes in John's Gospel, chapter 6.

Let me put it in another way by using the analogy which the Apostle has himself used in this Epistle in chapter 4, and especially in verse 16, where he again reminds us that the Church is the Body of Christ, and that Christ is its Head – 'From whom the whole body fitly joined together and compacted by that which every joint supplieth, according to the effectual working in the measure of every part, maketh increase of the body unto the edifying of itself in love'. This means that everything clearly comes from the head and that what we have to do is to realize our dependence upon the head. All the vital energy comes from Him, comes from the head, the brain. He is the source of all power, of this energy, this nervous energy by which we live and move, our muscular energy, our everything. In order to be 'strong in the Lord, and in the power of his might', I have to realize that Christ is the Head, and that I am a part of Him, and utterly dependent upon Him for this strength and power. I operate as a part of the body with all my might; but the energy, I know, comes from Him, and on it I live. I rely on Him, eating and drinking the flesh and blood of the Son of man. The first and the most important principle is that we must always realize that we draw our life from Him. He has put the seed into us, but all that is necessary to its growth and development still comes from Him. He gives it, and we are to partake of it more and more.

We next move on to something which is still more practical. Christ Himself is our food and drink, but because of our weak condition, we need something to help us to partake of that food, something to give us a greater appetite for it. It is found in this Word, this written Word; that is why it has been given to us. Christ comes to us as food through the Bible. And at the same time it is a tonic. Let me remind you of the statement which the Apostle Paul makes to Timothy who was a very temperamental, unsteady, unstable young man, always ready to be frightened and alarmed. The devil could very easily depress Timothy; he could terrify him and frighten him by reminding him that Paul was an old man who must shortly die. What could they do after Paul's departure? To whom could they then write? Where should they get advice? Paul has to reassure Timothy. He says, 'Thou therefore, my son, be strong in the grace that is in Christ Jesus'. But he does not stop at mere exhortation; he gives him some practical advice as to what he has to do. 'Yea, and all that will live godly in Christ Jesus shall suffer persecution.' Paul tells Timothy not to be depressed by such a development, but to expect it. As they have persecuted me, says Paul, so they would persecute Timothy and all true Christians. And he proceeds to add: 'But evil men and seducers shall wax worse and worse, deceiving, and being deceived. But continue thou in the things which thou hast learned and hast been assured of, knowing of whom thou hast learned them.' That is the way for Timothy to be strong. He must remember the things that he has been taught by Paul and others. 'And that from a child thou hast known the holy scriptures, which are able to make thee wise unto salvation through faith which is in Christ Jesus. All scripture is given by inspiration of God, and is profitable for doctrine, for reproof, for correction, for instruction in righteousness: that the man of God may be perfect, thoroughly furnished unto all good works' (2 Timothy 3:16).

Many other statements in the Scripture point in the same direction. There is a particularly beautiful one in chapter 20 of the Book of the Acts of the Apostles. Paul is giving his last words of advice to the elders of the Church at Ephesus, the very place to which this Epistle we are studying was written. 'Take heed,' he says, 'unto yourselves, and to all the flock, over the which the Holy Ghost hath made you overseers, to feed the church of God, which he hath purchased with his own blood' (v. 28). And again, 'And now, brethren, I commend you to God, and to the word of his grace, which is able to build you up, and to give you an inheritance among all them which are sanctified' (v. 32). This is how a Christian becomes 'strong in the Lord, and in the power of his might'; not by just sitting down and saying, 'I leave it all to the Lord, I hand it over and just keep looking to Him'. You need to be built up, and you can be; the Word has been given in order that we may be built up and made strong.

The texts I have quoted alone prove abundantly that all Scripture has been provided for that reason. Have you ever asked yourself the question, Why did God give us the Bible? What is the purpose and the object of the Bible? This is the answer. It was given to strengthen us, to build us up in our most holy faith. Obviously, therefore, the more we partake of it the stronger we shall be. So if we want to be 'strong in the Lord, and in the power of his might', one of the first things we have to do is to read and to take in and to masticate thoroughly this Book.

Now that does not just mean hurriedly reading your daily portion and rushing off to catch your train. That is not really taking the Bible as food. I am a great believer in systematic Bible reading. People waste a lot of time in opening the Bible at random or reading favourite passages. There is nothing better than to be a systematic reader of the Bible, and to make sure that you go through the whole Bible at least once every year. But the devil can even make a snare of that. You may have your daily portion printed on a card, and the danger is that you become more concerned about reading your daily portion than about what you are reading. And so it does not help you at all. You can so skim through, and skip over, verses that you might as well have been reading a novel. You may have read your daily portion, but have you got the Truth, have you really taken it in? But you must not bolt this food. You have to chew it and to masticate it, so that it may be thoroughly digested and become a part of your constitution and build you up. The Bible gives us knowledge; and knowledge build us up. True understanding, true knowledge, is something that makes us strong and builds us up and establishes us in the faith.

The Scripture commends itself to us in this way. Take the Old Testament for instance. There are many foolish people who say that there is no point in a Christian reading the Old Testament. 'Ah,' they say, 'we have finished with that, we are in the New Testament. Old Testament Jewish history is quite interesting in its way, but it has nothing to give us as Christians.' That is not what the New Testament says about the Old Testament. The Apostle Paul for instance, in 1 Corinthians 10:6, refers to a part of Old Testament history. He reminds us that the children of Israel were led by Moses out of Egypt and that they passed through the Red Sea. 'Now,' he says, 'these things were our examples, to the intent that we should not lust after evil things, as they also lusted.' In other words you can learn much from the children of Israel in the Old Testament. Verse 11 adds: 'Now all these things happened unto them for ensamples: and they are written for our admonition, upon whom the ends of the world are come.' In other words, here is a man in New Testament days confronted by the devil and all his wiles and by principalities and powers. How is he to be made strong? A very good way, says the New Testament, is to read your Old Testament. Not exclusively of course. Read the New as well, but certainly read your Old Testament, because there you will find some very wonderful warnings. The children of Israel were God's people; but look at their history. Look at their shameful behaviour, look at the defeats to which they were subjected. Shame came to them because they did not remember that they were the children of God. They began to rely on themselves, their armies, their own power. They made alliances with Egypt and with Assyria and were defeated; simply because they were fools; they did not realize who they were and did not rely upon the power of the Lord's might. Read their story, says the New Testament, it was written for our learning. Do not make the same mistakes; look at them and take warning.

So as you read your Old Testament you are warned in this way against this very danger. As you see how others have gone astray you are made strong yourself. It is an obvious argument, is it not? A wise man always learns from the mistakes of others who are in the same business, whatever it may be. He sees a man going to disaster, and he asks, 'Well, what exactly did that man do that he should not have done? Where did he go wrong, where did he make a mistake? 'Ah', he says, 'it was at this or that point. Very well, I am going to watch that point'. Now that is wisdom. That is precisely the argument used here: 'These things were our examples.'

Or turn to Paul again in Romans 15:4: 'For whatsoever things were written aforetime were written for our learning, that we through patience and comfort of the Scriptures might have hope.' That is why the early Church decided to incorporate the Old Testament with their new documents. The same God, speaking in both Testaments; the same people of God are the subjects of the record. We can learn, and learn tremendously, from the Old Testament. Let us then make use of it, let us read it, let us take it in; and it will make us strong. As we see the warnings and the dangers we are strengthened, we are on guard, and we are ready to quit ourselves as men. Let us all work out its lessons for ourselves.

When you come to the New Testament the lessons are still

more obvious. Why were these New Testament Epistles written? They were written in order to feed believers who were liable to go wrong though they believed in Christ. Many were going wrong in their doctrine, and because they went wrong in doctrine they went wrong in their lives. 'Evil communications corrupt good manners.' The moment a man begins to play with doctrine and to go wrong, his whole life is sure to follow in the same direction. That is what we are witnessing in the Church and in the world today. The Church first goes wrong in her doctrine; she then goes wrong in her life. It always happens that way.

In the early Church there were many believers who were frightened and alarmed, so men of God were moved by the Spirit of God to write letters to them in order to make them strong, to feed them, to give them understanding. It is only as we have understanding that we can fight. If you come into the Christian life thinking that all you have to do is to take a decision and say you are going to be a Christian; if you suppose that you will never have any more troubles or problems, that you will be perpetually reclining on some bed of ease, and be carried to heaven without doing anything – if you come into the faith with these ideas and think that that is Christianity, you will not have gone very far before you become very miserable and unhappy. You will find yourself failing, you will find things going wrong with you; you will have all kinds of troubles, and you will begin to wonder whether there is anything in Christianity or not. Many have come into such an experience. The answer is to know your New Testament, to know the truth about the Christian life, to realize that 'all that are godly in Christ Jesus must suffer persecution'. Paul had to tell Timothy this truth repeatedly. Timothy complained because he was persecuted, that though he was a preacher and a follower of Paul he was being persecuted, and people were unkind to him, and doing unpleasant things to him. He was trembling and quaking and wondering what the future held for him. And Paul had to tell him, 'All that will live godly in Christ Jesus shall suffer persecution'. It is inevitable. That was the lot of the Master, and He warned His followers to expect the same treatment. 'If they have called the master of the house Beelzebub, how much more shall they call them of his household?'

We also need to be told these things. Being prepared in this way by the teaching, when the trial comes to me I do not quake and begin to run away; I stand and I say, 'I stand as a man of God. This is a proof of my calling. I am suffering persecution because I am a child of God. Very well, I am ready to stand'. Similarly with all the other subtle attacks that come to us as the result of the wiles of the devil.

Every New Testament Epistle was written in order that we might be strengthened for the fight. The more we know, the abler and the stronger we shall be. On the other hand the teaching which tells you that you have nothing to do but to hand it over to the Lord is really saying that all these Epistles are totally unnecessary. But the New Testament says they are essential. It also tells us that different types of teaching are needed at different stages of experience. 'I have fed you with milk,' says Paul to the Corinthians, 'and not with meat, because hitherto you were not able to bear it' (1 Corinthians 3:2). Whatever your condition and state at this moment there is the appropriate food and drink for you in the Word. If you are a new-born babe in Christ there is 'the sincere milk of the word, that ye may grow thereby' (1 Peter 2:2 and 3). That is the purpose of all the Scriptures. There is milk for the babe; but there is stronger food, and we are meant to go on to the stronger food, to the 'strong meat'. Whatever your physical condition, whatever your spiritual condition, you need the appropriate food. You live on milk when you are a babe, but you do not spend the rest of your life on milk. You go on to 'strong meat'. There are different types and grades of food in the physical realm. And it is exactly the same in the Christian life. We must go on, and we shall get stronger and stronger until we develop into adult men. That is why John divides up the Church into 'little children', 'young men', 'fathers' – different grades according to the way in which they have grown and developed.

Prayer, too, comes into view. Prayer is but another way of receiving sustenance and strength and vigour and power. Prayer not only means petitions; prayer means, primarily, communion and fellowship with God. Christ says: 'Behold, I stand at the door and knock: if any man hear my voice, and open the door, I will come in to him, and will sup with him, and he with me.' This is not an evangelistic statement, it is addressed to the Church, to

Christian believers. He is ready to come in and to sup with us. That is the meaning of prayer. It is not just sending up your petitions and taking your requests to God. It means opening the door, and Christ comes in and sits at the other side of the table and has a meal with you and you talk as you are taking the meal. Fellowship and communion! And as you are talking to Him and supping with Him you are receiving strength and power from Him. You are making your requests known unto Him, and He is telling you things about Himself and His concern for you and His care for you. Prayer is communion, having fellowship, having a conversation with God the Father, God the Son, and God the Holy Spirit. That is the way to be strong.

The greatest saints have always been men of prayer, and they have spent much time in prayer. New Testament believers, when in trouble, always turned to God in prayer. And as they did so, they did not start with their difficulty; they began by adoring Him and worshipping Him and praising Him. They always started by realizing His presence and being conscious of His presence. One of the greatest men of prayer of the last century was the saintly George Müller of Bristol. He was an expert in prayer; and he always taught that the first thing to do in prayer is to realize the presence of God. You do not start speaking immediately. You may utter a lot of phrases but you might as well not have done so if you have not realized the presence of God. There must be this fellowship, this communion, this conversation. And the realization that you are in His presence is infinitely more important than anything you may say. As we realize this we are filled with strength and power.

Again a human analogy is obvious. When you are in the presence of any saintly person you always feel better yourself, you always feel stronger. Multiply that by infinity and you will see that the realization of the presence of the Triune God is the greatest possible source of strength and vigour and power.

Lastly we must remember the Sacraments – baptism, and the Lord's Supper – but particularly the latter. The object of the Lord's Supper is to strengthen us, to give us vigour, and power and life. 'We take of Him.' Again we must remember to avoid the error that those Jews fell into who were offended by our Lord's words, and who interpreted them carnally, not spiritually.

We do not believe in transubstantiation, we do not believe in any magic of that type. No, in the Supper it is a spiritual 'taking' of the Lord. He chose to use this simple analogy and it helps us very much. Men eat bread and drink wine, and that is a figure of the way in which 'we take of Him'. We not only remember His death. We start with that; but we remember that He rose again and that He is the Head of the Church, giving us life and power. 'We take of Him'; 'We take of Thee, the living Bread'. We are eating of Christ, we are taking Him in, and we are reminding ourselves that He is our life and our vigour, our power, our all. He will make us strong, and enable us to go back into the battle and to fight as men. Here we find the reason for partaking of the Lord's Supper. There is nothing there that you do not get, in a sense, from the preached Word, but it is another way of receiving it. He appointed the preaching of the Word, He appointed this Sacrament also – the breaking of the bread, the drinking of the wine. And in this way we partake of Him. We feed on the Bread of life. He is the heavenly manna, He is God's food for the soul, and we take of Him. And we go out from the Communion Service with new power, new vigour, 'strong in the Lord, and in the power of his might', God has provided for us abundantly and it is our business to partake freely of what He has provided. That is the way to become 'strong in the Lord, and in the power of his might'.

6

Exercise

'Finally, my brethren, be strong in the Lord, and in
the power of his might.'

Ephesians 6:10

Our last study was concerned with food and drink. The next
thing that is necessary is that we should exercise ourselves. This
is the way to become strong in a physical sense. Food and drink
certainly, but then exercise. This is of vital importance also in the
spiritual life. The same idea is to be found in the twelfth chapter
of the Epistle to the Hebrews: 'Let us run with patience the race
that is set before us' (v. 1). Nothing is more important in such a
race than that we should keep ourselves fit, that we should be
taking exercise. There are many people who are failing in their
spiritual life because they do not take exercise, and many who are
confused.

First, there is nothing more important than that we should take
exercise regularly. We 'run with patience'; that means, go on
with 'patient endurance'. This is one of the great secrets of the
Christian life, the secret of knowing in its fulness the comfort and
the consolation of the Christian teaching. We must take this
exercise regularly.

As we come to look at this in detail let us look first at the spiritual
aspect. Take, for instance, this point as it is to be found in many
other places in the New Testament. Here, I am told to be 'strong
in the Lord', and 'to stand'. In the Epistle to the Hebrews I am
told to 'run with patience the race that is set before me'. Jude
expresses it in his Epistle thus: 'But ye, beloved, building up
yourselves on your most holy faith, praying in the Holy Ghost,

keep yourselves in the love of God, looking for the mercy of our Lord Jesus Christ unto eternal life' (vv. 20, 21). Again, far from doing nothing and 'handing it all over to the Lord', we have to 'keep ourselves in the love of God', we have to 'build ourselves up on our most holy faith', we have to 'pray in the Holy Spirit', and we have to 'look for the mercy of our Lord Jesus Christ unto eternal life'. Nothing is more obvious about the teaching of the New Testament than this, that the Christian life is a life of activity, a life of vigour, a life of exertion. The strength is given to us by the Lord, but we have to act. We have to build ourselves up, we have to 'keep ourselves in the love of God'. And the business of preaching is not just to give a temporary word of comfort which will soon be forgotten; it is so to build us up in the faith that, whatever comes, we will be secure. We always tend to be looking for some magic drug; you take the drug and all is well. We are always expecting something to be done for us suddenly, quickly, while we relax passively. But that is never God's way. We have to 'run a race', we have 'to build ourselves up in our most holy faith', we have to be 'able to withstand all the wiles of the devil' in the most evil day conceivable. And if we are to do these things we have to prepare ourselves.

We are told forcefully in the Epistle to the Hebrews exactly what we have to do. There we have a man writing to a number of Christian people who were in a very dispirited and unhappy condition. They were having great troubles, they were in an 'evil day'. They were being persecuted and misunderstood and tried, their houses had been despoiled and they had been robbed of their goods, simply because they had become Christians. Some of them were in a most unhappy state, almost giving up and giving in, as so many have done in this present century, feeling utterly hopeless. The author writes to them in order to deal with that very condition, and far from merely giving them a little word of comfort and patting them on the back, and saying nice things to them, he says some of the most serious and stern things that can be found in the whole of Scripture. Think of chapters six, ten and twelve, for instance. That is characteristic of the whole of the Epistle; and it is in this way that the Word of God comes to us today. Ours is not a sentimental message, a little general comfort which makes the hearers shed a tear or two and then forget all about it. It is a stern message, it is 'the iron rations for the soul', it is a call to 'be men', to 'run a race', to 'build ourselves up'. Let us consider its programme and method.

The first thing we have to do in this matter of taking exercise in the spiritual sense is to hold on to what we have. The Hebrew Christians were in danger, as the Epistle tells them at the beginning of its second chapter, of 'letting things slip', or of 'slipping away from these things'. 'Therefore,' the author says, 'we ought to give the more earnest heed to the things which we have heard, lest at any time we should let them slip', or 'we should slip away from them', as a ship slipping away from its moorings, or a ring slipping off a finger. That is the kind of analogy which is being used. So the first thing we have to do is to lay hold on these things, to be absolutely certain of them. Never was there a time in which we needed that exhortation more than this present time.

We have got to lay hold especially on the promises. These promises are found, not only in the Scriptures, but also in our great hymns. The comfort and consolation of the Scriptures for the Christian in a world such as this is nothing that this world has to offer, but rather:

> *There is a land of pure delight,*
> *Where saints immortal reign.*

'In the world,' says the Lord Jesus Christ Himself to His own disciples, 'ye shall have tribulation.' 'Ah, but,' people say, 'that is very distressing; I thought Christianity had some hope to offer.' But you have to take Christianity as it is. You may expect to be depressed if you are still looking for anything in this world!

The first thing we have to learn is that this world has no hope to give us at all. Our task in this world is not to fall, to keep on our feet to the end, to withstand in the evil day, and 'having done all things to stand'. If you succeed in doing so it is a victory for God, and for Christ. Everybody else goes down. Our only comfort and hope, the thing we have to lay hold on, is 'a hope set before us'. That is how it is stated in the fifth verse of the second chapter of the Epistle to the Hebrews: 'For unto the angels hath he not put in subjection *the world to come, whereof we speak*'. We 'run the race that is set before us' through this world unto that glory which in the world to come awaits the people of

God. Christian people should always be looking forward. The author of the Epistle to the Hebrews keeps on saying so. Look at the theme again in the sixth chapter: 'We desire that every one of you do show the same diligence to the full assurance of hope unto the end' (v. 11). And again in that same chapter we find: 'That by two immutable things, in which it was impossible for God to lie, we might have a strong consolation, who have fled for refuge to lay hold upon the hope that is set before us.'

The Christian message is not one which lauds or praises the past; it is concerned to make us look to the future. The past only helps us in that it teaches us how to set our hope on things above, and how to run the race that is set before us. These are the things we have to hold on to. If we are uncertain about these things we have no hope at all. If you are in any way looking to this world you must be miserable. or you soon will be. But Christianity says that you must not do so, because this is a doomed world, a sinful world. But there is another world – 'the hope that is set before us'; 'the world to come of which we speak'. That is the world to hold on to, and therefore hold on to all the promises of God with respect to it. It is a part of the Christian's exercise, to lay a firm hold on the world to come. 'Lay hold on eternal life' says Paul in exactly the same way to Timothy. Do not just have your hands on it, but grip it, hold it firm and fast. That is the first great exhortation.

But let me add to this, as the author of the Epistle to the Hebrews adds to it himself. At the end of the fifth chapter he has something further to say to them. He was introducing them to the doctrine of our Lord as High Priest but he says, 'Of whom we have many things to say, and hard to be uttered, seeing ye are dull of hearing. For when for the time ye ought to be teachers, ye have need that one teach you again which be the first principles of the oracles of God; and are become such as have need of milk, and not of strong meat. For every one that useth milk is unskilful in the word of righteousness: for he is a babe. But strong meat belongeth to them that are of full age, even those who by reason of use have their senses exercised to discern both good and evil'. That is a vital statement. It says in effect, You Hebrew Christians are in this unhappy and miserable and dispirited condition simply because you have not been taking exercise. You are flabby and you have not grown. I have strong meat to give you; I have doctrines to put before you which will make you strong and vigorous. An adult man cannot live on milk, he needs strong meat to form his muscles and to give him energy and vigour. He cannot live on milk. he cannot work on milk, he needs this stronger food, 'But,' he continues, 'I cannot give it you because you cannot take it. You are still babes; you are not men. You ought by now to be able to teach other people, but instead of being able to teach other people you are whimpering and crying like children because you are ignorant.'

Does this not come as a rebuke to us? The world around us is completely without hope; and we should be able to give them hope. Are we able to do so? This is the business of Christianity. We are not here to talk politics. Your business and mine is to help our next-door neighbour who, because of the state of the world, is alarmed and terrified, and does not know what to do or where to turn. We ought to be able to teach him. Can we teach him? 'You ought to be teachers,' says the writer of Hebrews, 'but you are in such misery and unhappiness yourselves, and in such uncertainty and doubt, that you cannot teach anybody for you yourselves remain ignorant. I ask a simple question: Are you able to tell your neighbours how to stand, how to look to that glorious future which is coming? Do you know the way of salvation? Are you clear about the first principles of the Gospel of Christ? Can you tell others about it? Can you "give a reason for the hope that is in you"?' – to use the words and the language of the Apostle Peter. If we cannot, there is only one reason for it; we have not been exercising our senses with regard to these things. That is exactly what the author of the Epistle to the Hebrews says, 'But strong meat belongeth to them that are of full age, even those who by reason of use have their senses [their faculties, their understanding] exercised to discern both good and evil'. That means that we have to spend time in understanding and studying these truths, these great doctrines of the Christian faith. It is only as we do so that we shall become strong, and become men, and be able to take the stronger meat, and so grow, and be powerful and able to teach others.

There is no doubt but that the most unhappy and discouraged Christians today are those who do not exercise their senses with respect to this Word of God. We cannot live on snippets in the spiritual realm. We have to get down to these profound truths of the Scripture; we have to make time to read them and to read books about them. The trouble today, as it has been for so many years, is that Christian people have not been reading their Scriptures, not troubling to understand them. They say, 'Oh, I am too busy, I have too many things to do, and life is very harassing at the present time'. But our forefathers, who worked much harder, and for much longer hours, and for much smaller wages, found the time. Those men used to read their Scriptures and study them. They generally bought a Bible which had a commentary at the bottom of each page, and they studied it and spent time with it. They also read other books which helped them to understand the Scriptures. They were 'exercising their senses'; and that is what made them strong. That was the secret of the Protestant martyrs. It was the secret likewise of the Covenanters in Scotland in the seventeenth century. Those men were strong because they knew their Scriptures, and they knew the truth of the Scriptures. They had exercised their senses. They gave time to the exercise; they lived by the Word. And thus they ceased to be babes and became mighty, strong men.

You and I must behave in a like manner. There is no substitute for that. We do not sit back and 'just look to Jesus' to do it all for us. That is a false doctrine: I do not hesitate to use such a term. We must exercise our senses, we must build ourselves up in our most holy faith. It will not happen to us automatically; there are no short-cuts in the Christian life.

If you want to build yourself up, exercise yourself in the Scriptures. All the illustrations I have given really point to the same grand and glorious truth. And as we put this into operation and continue in it, it will not be necessary to be going back always to the first principles. The Christian Church today is tending to live in the realm of first principles only. People seem to think that nothing matters but evangelism, and so the Church herself becomes weaker instead of stronger. The way to evangelize, ultimately, is to build up the Church. If every member of the Christian Church were adult, were strong, were able to take strong meat, and to teach others, you would find that the world would be evangelized in a way we have never known. It is you and I who are to do this. We are not to sit back in crowds and let one or two do everything. We are all meant to be teachers, every one of us; and this is the way in which we become teachers. Never was there such an opportunity for the individual Christian as there is at this moment.

But then the author of the Epistle to the Hebrews goes on to tell his readers something further. In the tenth chapter, in verses 24 and 25 we find: 'And let us consider one another to provoke unto love and to good works: not forsaking the assembling of ourselves together, as the manner of some is; but exhorting one another: and so much the more, as ye see the day approaching.' Do we get the significance of these words? People who only come to the house of God on special occasions, or when they are in some particular need, and never at any other time, know nothing about the Christian life, even if they are Christians at all. The Hebrew Christians were failing, were miserable and unhappy: it was partly because they were not coming together to exercise their spiritual senses together. You must not only take your private exercise; you must also take exercise together. The Church is God's special creation for His people. He has given apostles, evangelists, prophets, teachers, pastors for the edification of His people, to enable them to become strong. That is the meaning and purpose of the ministry. That is my function as a preacher and teacher, I am called to do that. I spend my time studying this Book and trying to expound it. 'But,' you say, 'I can read it for myself.' I know you can; but it is a good thing to have it expounded to you also. There are things here that you have not seen, and it is the function of preaching to call attention to them. That is why you should come and listen to it. We help one another as we talk to one another and discuss these things together. 'The fellowship of the saints.' 'Not forsaking the assembling of yourselves together, as the manner of some is; but exhorting one another: and so much the more as ye see the day approaching.'

The slack Christian is always a miserable Christian – grumbling and complaining, asking why this and why that. The answer to that is to take more exercise, exercise your senses on the Word, come and listen to the exposition of the Word, avail yourself of every opportunity of doing so.

But look at it in this way also: Are you able to help others and to teach others? If not, the reason may well be that you only attend a place of worship once on a Sunday or perhaps still more infrequently. You imagine that is enough. But if so, why do you fail, why are you not successful in helping others? You need all the help you can be given, especially 'as you see the day approaching'. And 'the day' is approaching, and it behoves us to take advantage of everything that God has provided for us. The fellowship of the saints is one of the things that God has provided; so let us make full use of it.

But the author of Hebrews has yet a further exhortation. Having said what we have considered, he writes the eleventh chapter which he sums up at the beginning of chapter twelve, saying, 'Wherefore seeing we also are compassed about with so great a cloud of witnesses, let us lay aside every weight, and the sin which doth so easily beset us'. He has dealt thoroughly with that sin, but now he is talking about this great 'cloud of witnesses'. He has been telling his readers about them in chapter eleven; he has been looking back across history and has been picking out certain men. He has chosen them because of their glorious lives and because of the way in which they triumphed and prevailed. He looks at those giants of the faith one after another as the Bible does frequently. It does so in order to give us encouragement and help. It has been exhorting us to do certain things, to hold on to the truth, and to hold it firmly, and to exercise our senses, to live in the Word and to study it and understand it, to be assembling ourselves together and to help one another. Then, thank God, it gives us this encouragement at the end by urging us to consider the great men of the past, to look at them and see how and why they stand out as spiritual giants. We must go through the whole list and think of men like Abel and Noah and Abraham and Moses and David and Jephthah and all other men great of faith. They all lived in the same world in which you and I are living; the world has always been the same. And their record reads as follows: 'Who through faith subdued kingdoms, wrought righteousness, obtained promises, stopped the mouths of lions, quenched the violence of fire, escaped the edge of the sword, out of weakness were made strong, waxed valiant in fight, turned to flight the armies of the aliens. Women received their dead raised to life again: and others were tortured, not accepting deliverance; that they might obtain a better resurrection: and others had trial of cruel mockings and scourgings, yea, moreover of bonds and imprisonment. They were stoned, they were sawn asunder, were tempted, were slain with the sword: they wandered about in sheepskins and goatskins; being destitute, afflicted, tormented; (of whom the world was not worthy): they wandered in deserts, and in mountains, and in dens and caves of the earth'.

That is the kind of world they lived in. Our world is no worse; but it is as bad. They lived in an evil day, and we live in an evil day. But these men triumphed. They were heroic figures, they were able to stand, and to withstand. Having done everything, they stood as men, and they still stand out in history as giants.

Their secret was that they did the very things these Hebrew Christians had not been doing. They were men who were 'strong in the Lord, and in the power of his might'; they were men who 'exercised their senses' to understand God's truth; they were men who knew how to differentiate between good and evil. Take a man like Moses. Brought up as the son of Pharaoh's daughter, he could have been the heir to the throne. But he put it on one side and did so because he had his eye 'on the recompense of the reward'. That is the secret of all these men; and you and I are to look at them and consider their example.

It is in this way that these men who lived in the past really help us. We see them doing the very thing we are called upon to do. They ran the race, and they triumphed. They built themselves up in their most holy faith. They stood against the wiles of the devil in spite of all their suffering. What magnificent men! Their story is written in order that we might be helped and strengthened. Do you not always feel better as you read about them? It is a very good tonic. When you feel that the fight is too much for you, and all is against you, and when you complain of all that is happening to you, read chapter eleven of the Epistle to the Hebrews. If you do not feel ashamed of yourself at the end, you are a very poor Christian. And if you do not get up and say, 'Yes, they did that in the strength of God, and I am going to do the same. If God enabled them, He will enable me. That is the constant argument of the Scriptures. James quotes the case of Elijah. He says: 'Elijah was a man of like passions with ourselves.' There was nothing peculiar about Elijah that accounts for the things he did; it was God who enabled him. Very well, do the same, says James. And so it is with all of them. The entire Book of Job is a great treatise on this subject. Consider the patience of Job, and how at the end God dealt with him and blessed him.

To read of these men helps us to be strong, and encourages us to go on with the exercises. If we do so we shall become such as they were. Follow them, follow in their train; these are the men we are to imitate and to emulate.

And so we move on to our last principle: 'Wherefore seeing we also are compassed about with so great a cloud of witnesses, let us lay aside every weight, and the sin which doth so easily beset us, and let us run with patience the race that is set before us, looking unto Jesus, the author and finisher of our faith; who for the joy that was set before him endured the cross, despising the shame, and is set down at the right hand of the throne of God. For consider him that endured such contradiction of sinners against himself, lest ye be wearied and faint in your minds. Ye have not yet resisted unto blood, striving against sin.' The Son of God is the ultimate message. 'Looking unto Jesus' who came deliberately into this evil world, this world of wars and sin and shame and unworthiness. He did not belong to it. He came into it deliberately; and He suffered and He endured the contradiction of sinners against Himself. He endured 'even unto blood'. He did so because of 'the joy that was set before him'. He possessed knowledge of where He was going, and of the glory that was to come. He therefore 'endured the cross, despising the shame'.

That is the way to exercise, that is the way to 'run the race' that is set before us, that is the way to build yourself up in your most holy faith! This is the only message for men and women in a world like this today. We cannot change circumstances, but we can triumph in them. We can be 'more than conquerors'; and we become so as we are found 'looking unto Jesus'. Look at Him! Look at the nights He spent in prayer, look at His knowledge of the Word of God, look at the way in which He 'exercised His senses'. And all who follow Him have done the same; they are all imitators of Him.

We must become imitators of Him. We must look beyond men,

we must look to the Son of God and what He has done in order 'to save us out of this present evil world', and to introduce us to the glory that awaits us with God.

Christian people, the world is looking to you for teaching, for instruction, for an example of how to live triumphantly. So exercise your senses, lay hold on these things, look to the great heroes of the faith for inspiration. Above all, 'look unto Jesus the author and the finisher of our faith', and thus you will become 'strong in the Lord, and in the power of his might', and you will be able to withstand in the evil day when it comes. There is only one way to 'stand' at such a time, and that is to know this Truth, and to be strong in it, and so having done all things, to stand.

7
Discipline

'Finally, my brethren, be strong in the Lord, and in
the power of his might.'

Ephesians 6:10

Having looked at the importance in the Christian life of nourishment and exercise, the next step, clearly, is to put our powers into
practice, our purpose being to live the Christian life in its fulness.
We now proceed, therefore, to consider what we have to do in
actual practice; and in applying our principles practically we shall
find that we grow more and more as we do so. 'Practice makes
master.' Quite right! And the more we use our faculties the more
they will be developed. In other words, the best form of exercise,
and in the last analysis the best way of keeping up our strength,
is to be doing our work. Notice the difference between a man who
has to do his work in order to make a livelihood and a wealthy
man who merely does exercises to maintain his health. The
working man does not need to do the exercises because as he
does his work he exercises the whole of his body. The wealthy
man does not work in the same way so he has to spend time doing
exercises in order to keep up his strength. Both are of value. It is
good to take exercise, but, after all, the best form of exercise is to
be doing some work, to be active. We are never in a more
dangerous position and condition than when we are idle. There
are many illustrations of that in the Scriptures. David's greatest
sin, his most terrible fall, in a way resulted from the fact that he
was doing nothing. His armies were fighting great battles, but
he was at home in Jerusalem with very little to do. And it was
because of his idleness that the temptation came and caught him.
Isaac Watts in one of his poems for young people reminds us
of this:

In works of labour or of skill
I would be busy too;
For Satan finds some mischief still
For idle hands to do.

That is very true. When your hands are idle, when you are doing nothing, Satan is ever ready to take advantage of the position and to come and entice you. It is a dangerous state to be in. So the Christian is exhorted in many places in the Scripture to be active in the work of the Lord. In the right way of course! I am not advocating a mere foolish activism, just some bustling about in business without knowing what we are doing. I am talking about living the normal Christian life. This is a distinction that is being forgotten today. People think that being active means doing something outside themselves, as it were, whereas the main activity to which we are always exhorted in the Scripture is the living of the Christian life itself. That is the highest form of activity for those who are not specially called to some peculiar task in connection with the life of the Christian Church.

I know of no more succinct and convenient way of considering this kind of activity, this living of the Christian life in its fulness, to which we are exhorted, than to look at what we find at the beginning of the Second Epistle of Peter in the first chapter, beginning at verse five. Here the Apostle Peter is exhorting the people to whom he was writing to do the very selfsame thing which the Apostle Paul has in mind at the end of this Epistle to the Ephesians. 'And beside this,' says Peter, 'giving all diligence, add to your faith virtue.' But before we come to look at this in detail I want to emphasize once more the element of our activity. We must get a firm hold of this principle. We cannot hope to advance until we see this clearly. Peter does not say, 'Hand it over to the Lord; you have nothing to do. Trust to Him, leave it to Him, He will do it for you'. What he says is, 'Giving all diligence'. It is an exhortation to us. We have to give the matter 'all attention', we have to be constantly at it, we have to apply ourselves to it, to add virtue to virtue (vv. 5, 6, 7). It is not going to be added for us; we have to do it. As a man cannot be strong by merely sitting down and reading books about exercises, so the Christian will never be strong until he does what Peter bids him. He has to do this thing, it is his activity, and it is done as he becomes strong and powerful and mighty in the Lord.

But why are we told to do all this? Peter's answer is, 'If these things be in you and abound' – if you do all these things, in other words if you do add to or furnish your faith with all the additional things which are mentioned – 'they make you that you shall neither be barren nor unfruitful in the knowledge of our Lord Jesus Christ'. Our greatest need is to have this 'knowledge of the Lord'; because the more we know Him, and the more we know about Him, the more we shall know His strength and the power of His might. Then Peter puts the point negatively: 'He that lacketh these things is blind, and cannot see afar off.' Not only so – 'he hath forgotten that he was purged from his old sins'. He does not realize what has happened to him, and he is not really living as a Christian man. 'Wherefore,' he says again, positively, 'the rather, brethren, give diligence to make your calling and election sure.' You do not elect yourself, but what you do affects your assurance of your election; you can as it were make it sure in this way. Then, to drive the duty right home, Peter adds: 'for if you do these things you shall never fall'. But if you do not do them you will fall; the devil will trap you, the principalities and powers, the rulers of the darkness of this world, the wickedness in high places, will entrap you, and before you know where you are you will have fallen. How can people teach a doctrine of passivity in the light of such words?

This is the way to 'stand', says Peter 'if you do these things you shall never fall'. But it is all a question of our activity; that is how this strength and might will grow. Then he sums it up by saying, 'For so an entrance will be ministered unto you abundantly' – you will not barely get in – 'into the everlasting kingdom of our Lord and Saviour Jesus Christ'. You will have an 'abundant' entrance, it will be a glorious entrance, the trumpets will be sounding, there will be great acclamation.

These preliminaries are important. They remind us that we have to act, that we must give 'all diligence'. We are given the power, it belongs to the life that is in us; and therefore the exhortation can be addressed to us. And as we practise these things we shall be filled with yet more and more strength, and we shall become stronger and stronger in the Lord and in the power of His might.

What, then, have we to do? The Apostle Peter says, 'Add to your faith' (v. 5) – and this is an interesting term. It means 'to supplement it', or even better, 'to furnish it out with'. It seems that the word originally came from something that was done in connection with Greek drama. They did not simply have the actual performance of the play itself, they furnished it out, or elaborated, or supplemented, or filled it out, as it were, with a chorus and various other things. Such is the term that is used here by the Apostle Peter – 'furnish it out with'. You have your essential plot or story, the thing itself; but you do not just put it on the stage, you furnish it out, produce it well, make it something fuller, develop it. That is the meaning of the term.

We can divide what we actually have to do in practice as follows. These things, of course, merge one into the other – the exercise and the practical application of the activity. One inevitably leads to the other, so there is a certain amount of overlapping. The first exhortation deals with matters of personal discipline. Peter tells us a number of things. 'Add to your faith virtue.' The meaning of this term virtue has changed. We attach a particular meaning to the term 'virtue' at the present time; but it does not mean that here. The essential meaning of the word is 'vigour', or 'moral energy'. It is a word which describes 'strength of soul'.

It is good, perhaps, to look at this word negatively in order to ascertain its precise meaning. When he says, 'Add to your faith virtue', it is a way of saying, 'Don't be languid', 'Don't be lethargic'. If you approach any task whatsoever in a languid, half-hearted and half-asleep state and condition, you will not only do it very badly, but you will also tire yourself tremendously. The first thing a man has to do is to pull himself together; it is the essence of wisdom in any form of activity. In other words you must not shuffle to your work, or approach it in a lounging, half-hearted manner. This is a theme that could be easily elaborated at the present time. I sometimes wonder whether the whole future of this country of ours is not going to be determined by this very principle. Men do not seem to enjoy work any longer. They shuffle to it, and lounge at it; there is a lack of this vigour, this 'virtue', this energy, this keenness.

The first thing you have to do, says Peter, now that you have faith, is to rouse yourself, to get rid of that languid, lethargic, slack condition. 'Pull yourself together.' It is something that we all have to do. So shake yourself, rouse yourself, say to yourself, 'I have this work to do, and I must be all out in this work'. That is the meaning of the term. Far from relaxing and reclining on a bed of ease, and just reaping the fruits of the victory, you have to pull yourself together. You may wake up in the morning perhaps with a headache, feeling slack and lethargic. Now if you attempt to do your work in that frame of mind you will not only do it very badly but you will be a very tired man at the end. This is a most extraordinary fact. But if on the other hand you rouse yourself, and pull yourself together, you will not only do better work, you will be much less tired at the end.

This seems to be a principle of one's very physical constitution. Your muscles are meant to be taut. Have you ever watched a dog relaxing, completely, lying on the hearth perhaps? Then something happens and immediately he tightens up all his muscles and is ready and straining at the leash. That is the principle, and it is equally true in the Christian life. There are too many languid Christians. Too many of us suffer from what Charles Lamb called 'the mumps and measles of the soul'. We are too sickly, too lethargic; we lounge too much. We must brace ourselves together.

This is something that you can do. You may say, 'I am not feeling well'. But, quite frequently, you are by no means as bad as you think you are. Is not that often the trouble? This is a well-known psychological fact. A great deal of the so-called 'faith healing' of today can be adequately explained in this way. What it does is to bring psychological good to people. We always 'add on' to what we are suffering from; so you can always 'shake' yourself. This, of course, must not be pressed to a ridiculous extreme. When you are really ill you need treatment and you have to be kept in bed. But I am talking about those hypochondriacal conditions, the valetudinarianism from which we all tend to suffer so much. There is only one thing to do in this case, and that is to shake yourself, to pull yourself together. Do not be languid,

[99]

but say to yourself, 'I have this work to do', and soon you will find yourself feeling remarkably well and you will be able to do your work well. 'Add to your faith virtue.'

Do you not find that even as you consider these things you already feel conscious of deriving a strength from the Lord? It is like the order of a great Commander. When he addresses you he puts strength into you. Actually, physically, he has not done anything to you; but he has put a new spirit into you, and you pull yourself together and you feel stronger. 'Add to your faith virtue.'

Peter goes on to speak of knowledge, with which we need not stay because we have already been elaborating it. 'Add to virtue knowledge', 'insight', 'understanding'. The more we know about Christian truth, and the more we understand it, the stronger we shall be.

So we go on to the next addition – 'temperance'. 'Add to knowledge temperance.' Here again is a term which has become somewhat constricted in its meaning and connotation at the present time. People tend to think of temperance only in the matter of alcoholic drinks. That is included of course, but the word has a wider meaning. The Temperance Movement, so-called, is not really a temperance movement because its members generally talk about total abstinence. Temperance in its essence means 'self-control'. How am I to be strong in the Lord? Am I just to wait for something to happen? No, you will become stronger if you control yourself.

This is the principle, in a sense, of the conservation of energy. Many of us are weak because we waste our strength. If we conserved the energy we have we would be much stronger men. We all waste a lot of energy unnecessarily. One of the commonest ways is when we give way and fail to control ourselves. If we cannot control ourselves, what hope have we when we meet the enemy, the devil? Look at the professional sportsmen – footballers and others – and observe the discipline they have to exercise. They are not allowed to smoke, not allowed to drink when a great match is near at hand. They have to live for this match, and to control themselves. They have to refrain from many things which they like to do and which they normally do. They are required to discipline themselves in order that they may do well in the great contest.

This is still more true in the spiritual realm. To fail to control ourselves means a loss of energy. These things can actually be measured. When I say 'self-control' I include controlling one's temper, controlling one's spirit. Have you ever seen a man trembling in a rage? What energy that man is wasting! He is emitting energy at a tremendous rate because he cannot control his temper, and his own spirit. And, of course, he is but as putty in the hands of the devil. When a man cannot control himself how can he possibly deal with the enemy? Discipline is an absolute essential in an army; it is one of the most important things of all. If an army is not disciplined it is already defeated, it becomes a rabble.

The Bible has much of this kind of teaching. It is a major theme in the Book of Proverbs. The wise man in dealing with this matter says: 'He that is slow to anger is better than the mighty' (Proverbs 16:32). What he is saying is that a man who is slow to anger, a man who can control his temper, is a much stronger man in the end than a mighty man who loses his temper. The second man is much mightier by nature, but if he dissipates and wastes his energy by failing to control his own temper he will lose the battle. This first man has nothing like the vital force and capacity, nor the strength of the second, but he controls himself; and a man who can control himself will often beat a man who is very much better at the task, and who has much greater strength, simply because he is reliable and steady. This is something often seen in games. A man may be a brilliant tennis player but if he is erratic and bad-tempered he will probably lose his match, and someone who is not in the same class will beat him simply because he goes on steadily, and can control himself. Brilliance alone will not carry you through to success; you must have discipline as well. This is a most important principle in connection with physical strength. The wise man in the Book of Proverbs was a great observer of life, and he came to this conclusion, that a man who rules his own spirit is mightier than he that takes a city. What energy we often waste spiritually through sheer lack of control!

It is precisely the same with all the other things which tend to master us. Not only temper, but the desires within us, the instincts and all the impulses. They are all quite legitimate in themselves, but if you do not control them you will soon lose your strength. If you eat too much you will soon become lethargic; you will have much less strength though you are taking in so much source of energy. Because you do not use it, it becomes fat, and you are flabby and toneless. Eventually you become more or less useless if you cannot control your appetite. It is the same with all other appetites. It does not matter how great a brain a man has, if he drinks too much his brain will soon fail him. What tragedies there have been along that line! and it is the same with every other instinct that God has given us.

Faith, virtue, knowledge, are meant to contribute to our strength; but if a man does not control himself, it will mean the dissipation and wasting of energy. I could give some notable examples from biography to illustrate what I am saying. Self-control is absolutely essential. This is obvious in every walk of life. If you are in a business and at the head of a number of men, if you really want to get the best out of them, you must control your temper. If you cannot control your temper you will not control your men. They may be afraid of you up to a point, but they will do the minimum, and they will only do so while you are watching them. If you want to win their confidence, and get the best out of them, start by controlling yourself: to control others, control yourself. 'Temperance'! Let us exercise it in every respect all along the line, for all this is as true in the spiritual realm as in every other.

The next step is that we must add 'patience'. The Christian life is a very active life. It takes time and trouble to control oneself and to exercise discipline. Nobody can do it for you, you have to do it yourself patiently. 'Ah, but,' says someone, 'surely there is an experience to be had in which I can get rid of all this effort.' Not according to the Apostle Peter! If there were such a thing he would be saying so. Instead, he urges 'adding', 'giving all diligence'; 'furnishing it out'. When you have added this, go on and add that. Add 'patience'.

'Patience' means what we normally take it to mean, but there is something we can add to common usage. It really means 'patient endurance'. It means 'going on', 'continuing in a patient manner'. This is the normal, biblical meaning of the word. It means that you go steadily on. You do not do things in 'fits and starts'. You will never get strong in that way. The analogies are again obvious. I have known men who have decided now and again that they will go in for physical exercises in order to be strong. They continue for a while and the results seem wonderful; but then they drop it, and they are soon back where they were. Then they take it up again. They never become strong, because they operate by fits and starts. This is profoundly true in the Christian life. You cannot live this life, you cannot be strong or become strong and victorious in this life, by doing things spasmodically.

Or we can put it in this way: do not wait until you are in the mood to do the things: get up and do it. The man who waits for the mood will probably never get it; and so he never does it. It is your duty; it is an exhortation. Do not do things only when you feel like doing them; do them also when you do not feel like doing them. Then you will begin to feel like doing them. This is the way to solve the problem. Do not shiver on the brink; plunge in, get on, and soon you will be enjoying yourself. 'He that regardeth the wind will never reap' because he never sows; he is always hesitating, wondering. It is the same in the Christian life. There is nothing more important than this constant, persistent, continuation, come what may. There will be hindrances, there will be obstacles, there will be disappointments, there will be oppositions and persecutions; but let it make no difference. Go patiently on. This has to be done in all departments of life. Whether you are a student, whether you are in a profession or anything else, keep on; never wait for a mood to come, start doing the work. Pour some water into the pump and be able to get water out of the pump! We have to start ourselves going, and to keep on going. 'Patient endurance!'

Then Peter adds to patience, 'godliness'. Here, we come to a different category. We are, as it were, leaving the realm of purely personal discipline and we are now looking at ourselves in our relationship to God. This is the centre and the key of all. 'Godliness' means 'piety'. It is not a popular word now, but it is a very good word. It means consciousness of walking in the sight of God, and with God. 'Enoch walked with God' – that is godliness. We are told the same about Noah. In other words, these men were conscious of the fact that they were living in the presence of God. They were walking under the eye of God, and they were walking 'with God'. This again is something which we have to do, and we have to remind ourselves of it. We are told this repeatedly in the Scripture, but we have to remind ourselves of it. That is why we have to add 'godliness'. Once more, it is not done to you, you have to add this element of godliness. You have to obey the command that was given to Abraham on one occasion: 'I am the Almighty God; walk before me, and be thou perfect' (Genesis 17:1). That command comes to every one of us. God is saying to us, 'walk before me, and be thou perfect'. In other words, He says, Realise that you are always in my presence, and that you are always doing these things not only for me but as realizing that I am watching you, and taking delight in you.

The Apostle Paul is never tired of telling us this same thing. He says at the end of the second chapter of his Second Epistle to the Corinthians, 'For we are not as many, which corrupt the word of God: but as of sincerity, but as of God, in the sight of God speak we in Christ'. He says a similar thing in chapter 4. He tells them how he is doing his work: we have 'renounced the hidden things of dishonesty, not walking in craftiness, nor handling the word of God deceitfully; but by manifestation of the truth commending ourselves to every man's conscience in the sight of God'. What a word to preachers! That is the only way to preach. You preach to your congregation, of course, but you should not only be seeing the congregation, you should be seeing God also – 'in the sight of God'. What chiefly matters is that God is looking down upon you. Preach as realizing that you are in the sight of God. That is godliness. You do not need to become a monk or a hermit or an anchorite, and to go into a monastery, in order to be godly. To be godly really means that you are always conscious that you are doing everything 'in the sight of God'. And as you do so you will be filled with the strength and power that comes from the Lord. So 'add to patience, godliness'.

Then Peter goes on to talk about our relationship to others: 'add to godliness brotherly kindness'. This explains itself. Be kind to your brother. There are many weak Christians, and one of the chief causes of their weakness is that they do not love their brethren. They waste much of their time and energy in thinking harsh thoughts about other people. This is most enervating; it always drains you of energy. To think unkind thoughts of people always leaves you weaker; whatever it may or may not do to others, it always does you great harm. How can you begin to pray in the Spirit if you have been thinking in that way of others? How can you go out and try to help others if you are condemning some brother? It is impossible. 'We know,' says John, 'that we have passed from death to life, because we love the brethren.' Love is a proof of life. All this failure to love the brethren simply drains us of energy. If you spend your time thinking harsh, unkind, cruel, spiteful thoughts you will become weak yourself; and you will be utterly useless. So if we want to be strong in the Lord, and in the power of His might, let us love the brethren.

There is a difference between loving and liking. We are not told to like everybody; we are not meant to so so because we are all different. There are some people whom you like by nature more than others. But we are commanded to 'love' all, and to be kind to all, to treat them as brethren, whatever way we may react to them in a physical or in a psychological sense. We all know that from experience. If you have been exercising brotherly kindness you feel better, you feel stronger, and you are ready to meet the enemy. Whereas if you are miserable and unhappy and full of spiteful thoughts, the enemy has already more or less defeated you before the contest has even started. The more we exercise brotherly kindness, the more we go about doing good to one another and helping one another, the stronger we ourselves become. This is a great principle in the Christian life. 'It is more blessed to give than to receive.' The more you give the more you will have. The man who sows sparingly also reaps sparingly, but the man who scatters abroad and sows in all waters, as it were, casting his bread upon the waters, will reap abundantly after many days. He is the man who is going to become strong.

'And to brotherly kindness charity.' That means 'love', and it means universal love to all. Again I remind you that it does not mean 'liking'. There are many hateful things about sinners and others, but we are to love them as Christ loved us. So you add to your brotherly kindness this final thing which is the principle of love.

There, then, are those vital elements worked out in practice; and as we practise all these, and all the other New Testament exhortations, we shall become stronger and stronger. 'Practice makes master.' The more we add to our faith these various other qualities the stronger we shall be in the Lord, and in the power of His might. Those are things which we are to go on doing always. We must never relax. We never take a holiday in the spiritual realm; we are always doing these things – eating, drinking, taking exercise, practising, putting it all into practice in these various ways. That is to be our perpetual, constant action.

There is one further matter. How am I to be 'strong in the Lord, and in the power of his might' in the actual battle? I have to do all these things even when for the time being the devil may be leaving me alone; but what have I to do in the actual battle? How can I be strong in the Lord and in the power of His might in the thick and the heat of the battle itself? I mention one thing only for the time being. It is the use of His Name. The use of the Name of the Lord is a tremendous source of strength. Here, again, we find it in the Book of Proverbs, chapter 18, verse 10: 'The name of the Lord is a strong tower' – only His Name, remember! 'The name of the Lord is a strong tower: the righteous runneth into it, and is safe.'

But there are other notable examples of how to use His Name, and the power of His Name. Do you remember the story of Gideon? Gideon was a mere nobody. He came from a very unimportant tribe, and he belonged to one of the smallest families in that tribe. But God called him to stand up and fight against the Midianites; and there were great hosts of them. But God, you remember, would not allow Gideon to have a great army. He leaves him with a mere handful of men – 300 – the rest having been sent away. How did he fight? Did he rely upon his own strength only? No, his battle-cry, was 'The sword of the Lord, and of Gideon'. There is our doctrine, perfectly illustrated. Gideon did not say, 'Men, stand behind me; in the name of Gideon let us attack them. Here is the sword of Gideon, stand behind me'. Neither did he say, 'The sword of the Lord'. Here is the perfect Scriptural teaching – 'The sword of the Lord, and of Gideon'. 'Trust in God and keep your powder dry!' Both trust and powder come in. It is the sword of the Lord – certainly; we are helpless without it. Yes, but it is the sword of the Lord, 'and of Gideon'. And thus they proceeded to the battle and they fought with all their might and main and won a great victory. 'The sword of the Lord, and of Gideon.'

But the greatest example of all in many ways is that of David and Goliath. These Old Testament incidents, in addition to being history, are at the same time perfect parables of the great Scriptural truth that is taught us here, in Ephesians 6, about 'standing against the wiles of the devil', and 'wrestling against principalities and powers'. It is all taught there in that picture of Goliath and David. The conquest is unequal. Look at this giant. He conquers all others, no one can stand up against him. Here on the other hand is David, a mere stripling. He cannot walk in the armour of Saul, he cannot use Saul's sword. He has a sling and a few stones. That is all! But David triumphed, and did so because he faced Goliath in the way of godliness (1 Samuel 17:45). 'Then said David to the Philistine' – who had been ridiculing David and trying to frighten him and harass him, and to beat him before the encounter began – 'Thou comest to me with a sword, and with a spear, and with a shield: but I come to thee in the name of the Lord of hosts, the God of the armies of Israel, whom thou hast defied. This day will the Lord deliver thee into mine hand; and I will smite thee, and take thine head from thee'. Note that David fights 'in the name of the Lord, the God of the armies of Israel'; and the moment he utters 'The name' he is filled with confidence and strength and might and power; and he is given a resounding victory.

Elisha, at the beginning of his career, employed the same principle. Elijah had just gone to heaven, and here is Elisha standing before the River Jordan. He has recently seen how Elijah, by waving his cloak, divided the river: and here he stands facing his moment of great testing. Is he fit and strong enough to follow Elijah as the prophet of God? Notice how he faces his task. He says, 'Where is the Lord God of Elijah?' That should be the battle-cry of the Church of God today, it seems to me, fighting the principalities and powers as we are. In general as well as in particular this is what we should say. We should not be weak and hesitant and frail, and hopeless; we should say 'Where is the Lord God of Elijah? Where is the God of our fathers, where is the God of the Reformers, where is the God of the Puritans, where is the God of the early Methodists? Where is He, the God of revivals? In His Name we can be strong and mighty'.

Turn to the New Testament. Look at Peter and John in the

early days of the Christian Church. They are confronted by a lame man at the Beautiful gate of the temple. What must they do? This is what Peter said: 'Silver and gold have I none, but such as I have give I thee. In the name of Jesus Christ of Nazareth rise up and walk' (Acts 3:6). The Name! The power of the Name! It was Peter and John who actually spoke and acted, but they were enabled to do so because they used the power of the Lord's Name. 'The name of the Lord is a strong tower' – always!

Look at the Apostle Paul writing to that nervous, frightened, young man Timothy. He has already told him to 'endure hardness as a good soldier of Jesus Christ'. He tells Timothy to pull himself together. Now he wants to give him something that will really fill him with power, so he says: 'Remember that Jesus Christ of the seed of David was raised from the dead according to my gospel' (2 Timothy 2:8). Paul says, Why are you hesitant and fearful? 'Remember that Jesus Christ of the seed of David was raised from the dead according to my gospel.' Christ has not only conquered men, He has not only conquered the devil, He has conquered death and the grave, the last enemy. He is all-powerful. Remember that! And while a man remembers it, he is filled with the power of the Lord and the strength of His might. The Name, the recollection of the power and the effect of the Name of the risen Lord works wonders.

And so I read in the Book of Revelation, 'They overcame him [the enemy] by the blood of the Lamb, and by the word of their testimony'. They threatened the devil with Him, and they conquered him by so threatening. This is the only way. Ah, yes, says a man centuries later:

> *How sweet the name of Jesus sounds*
> *In a believer's ear,*
> *It soothes his sorrows, heals his wounds,*
> *And drives away his fear.*

It makes him strong. The very name of Jesus does that. 'How sweet the name of Jesus sounds!' 'It drives away his fear.' Do you know how to use this name? Do you know how to invoke it? Do you know what it is to be strengthened by the very sound of it? Here it is again:

Strong in the Lord of hosts
And in His mighty power,
Who in the strength of Jesus trusts
Is more than conqueror.

The Christian fights, but he trusts in this name, he invokes it and he is made strong by it. And so he is 'more than conqueror'.

I trust we all know how to use the Name of the Lord in this way. This always makes me think of something that I often heard when I was a boy. I had the privilege of being brought up in a village, in a small community where we all knew one another. Sometimes a bully would be threatening a little boy, and the little boy was terrified because he stood no chance at all against the bully. What did the little boy do? Well, this is what I often heard. The little boy knew that he was helpless, that he could do nothing; but he stopped the bully many a time by just saying 'I will tell my father about you', or 'You hit me and I will tell my big brother'. And the bully, though he was a bully, was afraid of the name of the father. And you and I in our weakness and helplessness must threaten the devil with the Name of our Father and our blessed Lord and Saviour. Threaten him! 'Resist the devil, and he will flee from you.' Say to him, 'I know that I alone cannot do anything against you; but if you touch me *He* will avenge me'. Threaten him with the Name of the Lord. It is a strong tower and the righteous runneth into it and is safe. It does not add, in a purely physical and material sense to your strength, but it puts strength into you by putting confidence into you. The very Name, the very word, energizes you; you can threaten the bully that is threatening you, and you can cause him to run away and flee.

This is a principle found everywhere in life. It explains how an ambassador succeeds in doing his work. He is nobody in and of himself, but he speaks for his country, he speaks for his sovereign, he speaks for the powers that are behind him. It is his word, but the power is that of his country. And the other country listens to the word of one man because it knows that he is the representative of this unseen, hidden, mighty power that is behind him.

Here, then, is one of the most excellent ways of standing against the wiles of the devil and being made more than conqueror.

'Strong in the Lord, and in the power of his might.' Knowing the power of His name! 'In the name of Jesus Christ of Nazareth,' say to your enemy, 'leave me. I do not belong to you, I belong to Him, I am covered by Him.' 'They overcame him by the blood of the Lamb, and the word of their testimony.' May God enable us to implement these precious truths so that we 'may be able to stand in the evil day, and having done all, to stand'.

8

The Promises

'Finally, my brethren, be strong in the Lord, and in
the power of his might.'

Ephesians 6:10

The phrase 'Be strong in the Lord, and in the power of his might'
reminds us that additional power can become available to us,
power that we can call upon particularly in times of unusual
stress and difficulty. We are to be strong always, always to be
vigorous, as we live the normal Christian life; but there are special
times and seasons in the Christian life. The Apostle refers to 'the
evil day'. Of course life is always evil, but there are some days
that are worse than others; there are 'evil days'; there are times
when the fight is particularly hot, when the enemy makes an
unusual attack upon us. Life is always a warfare, but there are
times when the devil concentrates and masses his attack upon us.
Now at such times, in addition to what we are always doing,
there are certain other things which we can do. We considered
one of them in our last study – that we can call upon His Name!
   A further reference to that is found in the Epistle of Jude,
verses 8 and 9. Jude is referring to scoffers and others who
claim to be Christian but who do not understand the Christian
life. He says: 'Likewise also these filthy dreamers defile the flesh,
despise dominion, and speak evil of dignities. Yet Michael the
archangel, when contending with the devil he disputed about the
body of Moses, durst not bring against him a railing accusation,
but said, The Lord rebuke thee.' Michael the archangel realized
the nature of the power that was confronting him, and the greatness of that power, so he did not 'speak evil of dignities'. What
he did was to invoke the Name – 'The Lord rebuke thee'. He
threatened the devil in this way and thereby obtained his victory.

There are times when that is the only thing that you and I can do. Confronted by the enemy, and realizing our own weakness, we can threaten him with this Name that is ever victorious, this Name that is above every other name, the Name at which 'every knee shall bow, of things in heaven, and things in earth, and things under the earth'.

We now pass on to consider another source of strength which is still more glorious, namely, the active realization of His nearness and His presence. Here is teaching that is most exalted and yet most comforting for us, something which is taught in the Bible frequently, in the Old Testament and in the New. It is also found, thank God, very prominently in the history of the Church, and in the biographies of men whom God has used notably in the advancement of His kingdom. As they are engaged in this warfare, this wrestling 'not against flesh and blood, but against principalities and powers', they all testify to this fact, that over and above the strength and the power which they have received in general from the Lord, at times they have been aware, in a very unusual way, of His nearness and His presence supporting them, succouring them, and delivering them.

We must look into this because it is one of the most wonderful aspects of Christian truth. I would emphasize that this is not to be thought of as something constant and regular, but rather as something unusual and exceptional. The normal is to be strong in the Lord, and in the power of His might at all times. Feeding ourselves on the Word, engaging in prayer, and exercising and living the Christian life, we are thus strong in this battle against the devil. But there are times when the battle is unusually strenuous and severe; there are particular 'evil days' when all hell seems to be let loose against us, and the devil for some purpose, or rather in his own evil strategy, masses all his forces against us in order to get us down, in order to mar our witness and to bring us into a state of unhappiness and captivity. There are times when the battle is so fierce and so hot and so strong that the Christian feels he is on the point of being overwhelmed. He has been fighting valiantly, he has been striving with might and main, but the enemy has brought up, as it were, all his reserves, and the poor Christian feels that the end has come, that he must give in.

This is found frequently in the biographies, as for example in

John Bunyan's *Pilgrim's Progress*, indeed in almost all his works. He knew about this, and he deals with it in a remarkable manner. But it is found quite generally in the lives of the saints; and the teaching is, that at such a time, and in such a predicament, one is given unusual strength and power from the Lord. This happens in two main ways, and we must look at both. I am emphasizing that it is unusual. It is not the regular and the normal. It can be put into the same category as miracles. Miracles are not constant and usual; they are unusual and exceptional. This kind of experience goes into that category, and you must not expect it to happen every day or many times during a day.

This is something that is given to us when we need it most of all; and it comes in two main ways. The first is that God gives us special grace. The fundamental promise with regard to it is found in Deuteronomy 33:25 where we are told, 'As thy days, so shall they strength be'. This means that we shall always be given the grace and the strength that is adequate to whatever situation we are in. Whatever our 'day' may chance to be, our strength will correspond to it. That was the promise of God to His ancient people, to the Church in the Old Testament. They were travelling on their journey, they had not yet arrived in the promised land; and they were confronted by enemies without and within, and by all the problems that are described in the pages of the Old Testament. But they were given this fundamental promise, that they need not fear, for, whatever the circumstances, God's grace would be sufficient. If the days were particularly bad ones, then they would have extra strength from God. God knows all about us, and God will always provide the particular strength. Nothing could have contributed more to their comfort.

You look to the future and wonder what may happen. Many become dejected as they do so. They read of Christians being persecuted and maligned and arrested, and perhaps subjected to all kinds of tortures – brain-washing and such things. They then say to themselves, 'I could never stand that; it is impossible. I could never do it, I could not stand up to it, I am certain that I would fail'. Now that is wrong; for the promise is, 'As thy days, so shall thy strength be'. It is true that you cannot do it yourself; you cannot do it in cold blood, you cannot do it as you are. But the promise is that if ever you find yourself in such a position you will discover that you are being given this extra grace and power. Whatever you may have to go through you will be enabled to do so. It is a universal promise. 'As thy days, so shall thy strength be.' You may have to look forward, may be compelled to look forward by circumstances, to some great trial that is coming, and you will be tempted to say, 'I do not see how I can go through with it'. Do not say so: that is lack of faith. Listen to the promise of God. Whatever comes to you, you will be given strength. Whatever it may be, 'As thy days, so shall thy strength be'.

But we must add a further teaching. The words form not only a promise of needed help, we are encouraged to ask for it. There is a comforting statement to that effect, in chapter 4 of the Epistle to the Hebrews, verses 14-16. It makes the same point, but states it from the other side: 'Seeing then that we have a great high priest, that is passed into the heavens, Jesus the Son of God, let us hold fast our profession. For we have not an high priest which cannot be touched with the feeling of our infirmities; but was in all points tempted like as we are, yet without sin. Let us therefore come boldly unto the throne of grace, that we may obtain mercy, and find grace to help in time of need.' Note again the expression 'time of need', or 'timely help'. The suggestion is that all times are not the same, and what we stand in need of is 'the grace to help in time of need', just what we need at that point. We need 'timely help'. We are always being helped, we are always being given grace; we could not live for a day without it. But there are times when we need something extra, and our comfort is this, that we have a great high priest there in the presence of God who has been in this world and subjected to all the temptations that we are subject to, One who has met all the trials and the antagonisms and the disappointments of life. Nothing can happen to us which He has not experienced. Go, then, with confidence, with boldness, to the throne of grace. You need mercy, but you need also 'grace to help' in this time of need, in this period of unusual stress and crisis and strain. Ask for it and you will be given it; go to 'the throne of grace' in the name of your great high priest and you will be given 'timely help', you will be given it when you need it, and you will be given the right amount, so that you will be enabled to go through and be made more than conqueror.

This comes from Christ, our 'great high priest', 'touched with the feeling of our infirmities'. 'Be strong in the Lord, and in the power of his might' means that you anticipate difficulties. As you do so, remember that you can turn to Him, and be sure that you will receive what you desire, that He will take you through your particular crisis or problem. That, then, is another aspect of this matter.

We turn now to a third aspect which introduces a term we find in the New Testament with regard to the work of the Holy Spirit. It is the 'anointing'. We are told that we receive 'an anointing of the Holy One'; and this anointing of the Spirit is a very practical matter, and particularly so in this context of the battle of the Christian life. To see what it means consider what we are told about our Lord Himself in Acts 10:38. Peter, preaching to Cornelius and his household, says: 'God anointed Jesus of Nazareth with the Holy Ghost and with power: who went about doing good, and healing all that were oppressed of the devil; for God was with him.' This 'anointing' always leads to power. It is a particular aspect of the work of the Holy Spirit. The Holy Spirit is a seal. He is also 'the earnest of our inheritance'; but there is an anointing aspect of the work of the Holy Spirit in the Christian believer by which he is enabled to do various things.

The best way of looking at this is to take the illustration of what happens in a time of revival. When the Holy Spirit comes in revival there is a great anointing, and it shows itself in many ways. You read of men who had believed the truth, and who were preaching faithfully and regularly, but who were ineffective and lacking in power. Suddenly they are filled with power. They speak with boldness and with power and with great authority. That is the anointing of the Spirit. The same anointing happens in connection with prayer. In a time of revival people have freedom in prayer. You do not have to persuade them to pray; there are no pauses; there is a keenness, and enthusiasm, a power, and a liberty of speech and understanding. That is part of the anointing. You see it, of course, in revival, in an exceptional manner, but it illustrates the point. The power to testify and to speak to others is also always a remarkable feature in connection with revival.

But this anointing is not confined to revival. I use that simply as an illustration. Thank God it is given at other times. Any man

who has ever preached should be able to testify to this. There are
times when, entirely outside his own control, he is given a
special authority, special power, an unction which is unusual.
And there are good reasons for its bestowal. There are circumstances which he himself is not always aware of, which he only
discovers afterwards. Somebody may have come to the congregation who needed a particular message or word, and the preacher,
without knowledge on his part, is guided to say something which
is just appropriate to that particular state and condition. There is,
therefore, this special enduement of power which is called 'the
anointing'. It is something that one should seek and covet, it is
something for which one should be constantly praying.

That same anointing is also given to Christian people in their
'evil day'. At times of unusual stress and crisis and problem and
difficulty they receive an anointing of the Holy Spirit which is
quite unusual; and it enables them to detect and to understand
what is happening. It gives them a spiritual insight which they
normally do not possess. This, of course, is essential in our fight
with the devil. Unless we detect the hand of the devil we shall
attribute his activities to something in ourselves, or we may feel
that God is being unkind to us. But when you have the unction,
the anointing, you realize at once that it is the devil, and you are
enabled to see through his strategy. You see why he is doing it,
you see how he is doing it, you see through all his subtlety.

Not only so, you are 'given' Scriptures. Have you experienced
this? It is a very good test of your state and condition in the
Christian life. Suddenly Scriptures are brought to your mind in
order that you may answer the devil. You recall how our Lord
answered him in His temptations. Every time, in the three
temptations, when the devil comes in his subtlety and makes his
suggestion, our Lord is given the perfect, the appropriate
Scripture. This happened to our Lord immediately after the
'anointing' that Peter was speaking about in the house of
Cornelius. Our Lord was setting out on His public ministry. As
the Son of God, He was always full of the Spirit. But in order to
do His work He needed a special anointing and He received it at
His baptism in the river Jordan by John the Baptist. The Holy
Spirit then descended upon Him, He was given this special power.
He was God; but as man He needed this 'baptism', this 'anointing'

with the Holy Spirit. And now, filled with the Spirit, He is led into the wilderness to be tempted of the devil. The devil comes in his subtlety but our Lord has got the answer, the appropriate Scripture; and the devil is confounded and repulsed.

Now this experience is offered to all God's people; it is something to which they have testified throughout the centuries. They have been aware of something most unusual, they have been lifted up above themselves, Scriptures they had forgotten come back to them, and they know how to apply them. They are given this insight and understanding, with the result that they are able to stand even in this 'evil day'.

These, it seems to me, are the main ways in which we are given this special grace. We do not know what may come to meet us, we do not know what a day may bring forth, nor what, as Christian people, we may have to pass through. Here is comfort. Whatever may happen, remember this, 'Be strong in the Lord, and in the power of his might'. Remember that there are promises and that they are absolutes, that God will fulfil them. There is this special anointing given to enable us to go through and to stand in the evil day.

Now let us look at the second aspect of this matter. Our Lord gives us this special help, not only in what I would call an indirect way, He does so also in a direct manner. He makes His actual presence felt. How much do we know about this? I remind you that this is not usual, not the norm, not the habitual. This is exceptional. What does it mean? Again, let us start in the Old Testament. 'The Lord God', says the psalmist in Psalm 84:11, 'is a sun and shield'. 'The Lord God is a sun', giving life and health and vigour and power. That is the normal, that is constant, that is something that goes on day by day. But He is also a 'shield', a protection. He covers us, as it were, in these unusual times, and shields us and guards us. This means a direct intervention of God on our behalf; and it is interesting to look at some examples of this.

I go for my first illustration to the Book of Joshua. At the end of chapter 5 we find Joshua facing the first big crisis after he had taken over the leadership from Moses. He is standing before

Jericho, a very strongly fortified city. He has all the promises, all
that Moses said to him; but here he faces a tremendous problem.
This is what happened: 'And it came to pass, when Joshua was
by Jericho, that he lifted up his eyes and looked, and behold,
there stood a man over against him with his sword drawn in his
hand: and Joshua went unto him, and said unto him, Art thou
for us, or for our adversaries?' Note the tinge of nervousness
there. 'Art thou for us, or for our adversaries?' 'And he said, Nay;
but as captain of the host of the Lord am I now come. And
Joshua fell on his face to the earth, and did worship, and said
unto him, What saith my Lord unto his servant? And the captain
of the Lord's host said unto Joshua, Loose thy shoe from off thy
foot; for the place whereon thou standest is holy. And Joshua
did so.' What happened there is an intervention. The Lord in the
person of this mighty angel appears to Joshua; it is one of the
theophanies. The Lord Jesus Christ Himself in that particular
form appears to him, to comfort and to strengthen him, and says,
'I am with you, I am Captain of your host and of the battle, do
not be afraid'.

Another illustration is to be found in the Second Book of Kings
in chapter 6, verses 11–17, in the life of the prophet Elisha. A
great attack is being made upon the Israelites by the king of Syria.
But listen to the story. 'Will ye not shew me which of us is for the
king of Israel?' asks the king of Syria: 'One of his servants said,
None, my lord, O king: but Elisha, the prophet that is in Israel,
telleth the king of Israel the words that thou speakest in thy bed-
chamber.' Then says this king: 'Go and spy where he is, that I
may send and fetch him. And it was told him, saying, Behold, he
is in Dothan. Therefore sent he thither horses, and chariots, and
a great host: and they came by night, and compassed the city
about. And when the servant of the man of God' – that is to say,
the servant of Elisha – 'was risen early, and gone forth, behold,
an host compassed the city both with horses and chariots. And his
servant said unto him, Alas, my master! how shall we do?'
The poor servant gets up and sees the place literally surrounded
by soldiers and chariots and horses and he is utterly alarmed and
terrified – 'Alas, my master! how shall we do?' 'And he answered,
Fear not: for they that be with us are more than they that be
with them.'

What Elisha said seemed utterly ridiculous, of course. There they are, the prophet and his servant, virtually alone, surrounded by these troops of the king of Syria – horses and chariots and men, literally surrounding them; but he says: 'Fear not: for they that be with us are more than they that be with them.' 'And Elisha prayed, and said, Lord, I pray thee, open his eyes, that he may see. And the Lord opened the eyes of the young man; and he saw: and, behold, the mountain was full of horses and chariots of fire round about Elisha.'

That is the kind of thing of which I am speaking. The servant could not see them; but Elisha could see them. Elisha was a man of faith, the servant was a young, inexperienced man, ignorant of these things and only seeing the obstacles and the enemy and the difficulty and the trial. So he is alarmed and terrified and full of fear. All is well, says Elisha, for there are more on our side than on their side. But where are they? asks the man, I see nothing. Elisha prayed, 'Lord . . . open his eyes, that he may see'. The result was, 'And the Lord opened the eyes of the young man; and he saw: and, behold, the mountain was full of horses and chariots of fire round about Elisha'. The unseen hosts, the army of the living God, were present to protect God's prophet and to deliver him, as the account goes on to tell us. This is the Scriptural teaching as to what happens to the people of God when they really believe and have faith, and are 'strong in the Lord, and in the power of his might'.

But let us turn to the New Testament. Here is our Lord Himself, Son of God; but He has taken unto Him human nature, and is living His life as a man in this world. Immediately after His temptation in the wilderness we read this: 'Then the devil leaveth him, and, behold, angels came and ministered unto him'. He had passed through a severe trial, a shaking experience, so the angels are sent to minister to Him and to comfort Him immediately after the trial. But He had been helped also *in* the trial as we have already seen.

But then look at Him in the Garden of Gethsemane. Here, perhaps, is His supreme trial. Our Lord is now facing His death. There is only one way to save mankind, and that is to die for them. This is 'the cup' that He must drink. In His agony He goes alone in the Garden and prays. He has taken Peter and James and John with Him up to a certain point. They have left the main body of the disciples, and He says: 'Stay here, while I go and pray over there'. But they all slept. They could not stand the strain; it was too much for them and they were weary and tired and frightened. So He is there alone praying in the Garden, and in such agony that He begins to sweat great drops of blood. But Luke, in his account of this – and he is the only one who records it – says, 'And there appeared an angel unto him from heaven, strengthening him' (22:34). He needed that help, though He was the Son of God. 'Yet learned he obedience', says Hebrews 5:8, 'by the things which he suffered'. As the Son of God He is here fighting the devil and all his forces who are arrayed against Him, urging Him not to go forward, and saying, 'Is God about to forsake you? Is your life about to be lost? Where is the love of God? He cannot allow this to happen to you'. The devil was attacking with all his might and main, and what we are told is that the Lord was given help, the angel was sent to help Him and to strengthen Him. And thus He is enabled to go to the Cross. So, addressing the disciples, as recorded in John 16:32, He says, 'Behold, the hour cometh, yea, is now come, that ye shall be scattered, every man to his own, and shall leave me alone: and yet I am not alone, because the Father is with me'. When all men shall have forsaken Him, saving their lives in their cowardice, He says without fear, 'Yet I am not alone, because the Father is with me'. That was an 'evil day' that the Son of God had to pass through, and suffer; and above all the strength that He had normally, He was given this further strength. The angel strengthened Him in the Garden, He knows that the Father would be with Him.

In the light of His own experience our Lord makes a promise to His people. We are to follow in His footsteps, we are to follow His example; but in addition to that we must listen to His teaching. He has given us a very great promise. It was spoken after His resurrection: 'Lo, I am with you alway, even unto the end of the world' (Matthew 28:20). That is the promise, the basic promise, in this respect.

But if that is the promise, what has happened to it? Has it been fulfilled? Here we have something that should fill us all with great encouragement and with great hope. The Book of the Acts of the Apostles has many illustrations of how this promise was fulfilled. Take Acts 18 concerning the Apostle Paul in Corinth. He had been having a very difficult time there. Persecution broke out, and the Apostle was in danger of being discouraged and downcast. But in verses 9 and 10 we read: 'Then spake the Lord to Paul in the night by a vision, Be not afraid, but speak, and hold not thy peace: For I am with thee, and no man shall set on thee to hurt thee: for I have much people in this city.' Undoubtedly Paul had gone to bed that night wondering what was about to happen; everything was against him, and he might even suffer the loss of his own life. In any case his ministry there would be fruitless. But here the Lord appears to him and speaks to him. We are not surprised to read what follows: 'And he continued there a year and six months, teaching the Word of God among them.' Now that was a special visitation, a special manifestation of the Lord Himself to His tried, harassed, perplexed, tired and discouraged servant. This did not happen to Paul every night, but it happened that night.

Thank God this is real, this is true, this is something which does happen. It does not follow one particular pattern, of course, but when it occurs, it is equally real and authentic.

Take another illustration of the same thing. In Acts 22 the Apostle describes something which happened to him. 'It came to pass,' he says, 'that when I was come again to Jerusalem, even while I prayed in the temple, I was in a trance; And saw him [the Lord] saying unto me, Make haste, and get thee quickly out of Jerusalem'. He was told to stay in Corinth; he is now told to get out of Jerusalem – 'for they will not receive thy testimony concerning me. And I said, Lord, they know that I imprisoned and beat in every synagogue them that believed on thee: And when the blood of thy martyr Stephen was shed, I also was standing by, and consenting unto his death, and kept the raiment of them that slew him. And he said unto me, Depart: for I will send thee far hence unto the Gentiles' (vv. 17–21). Here, again, is a special intervention of the Lord at a moment of great crisis, when the Apostle was in greater danger than he realized. The Lord appears to him in a trance and manifests Himself to him. He tells him to go, urges him to go, and tells him of the greater and wider work which He has for him to do.

But then there is another illustration of special help in the

Second Epistle to Timothy, chapter 4. 'At my first answer' – Paul was on trial – 'no man stood with me, but all men forsook me: I pray God that it may not be laid to their charge. Notwithstanding the Lord stood with me, and strengthened me; that by me the preaching might be fully known, and that all the Gentiles might hear' (vv. 16, 17).

Those are special appearances of the Lord Himself in order to strengthen His servant in an evil day when he was on trial and passing through an unusual crisis. 'The Lord stood with me' – and He appears in different ways! Sometimes He does so indirectly through angels. We have a wonderful illustration of this in Acts 12, concerning Peter in the prison. James, the brother of John, has already been arrested and put to death. Peter is next arrested and King Herod Agrippa I is purposing to kill him. He cannot do so immediately because it happens to be Easter time and the days of unleavened bread, so he determined to put him to death when those days were ended. There is Peter sleeping in the prison the very last night, surely thinking to himself that he was to be killed next morning, feeling that there was nothing at all that could be done to save him. But suddenly 'a light shined in the prison' and an angel smote Peter on the side, and raised him up. Chains fell off, doors opened, gates turned on their hinges, and Peter finds himself following the angel through the main gate and out into the streets of the city, when suddenly the angel vanishes. That is history. The angel appeared in order to release God's servant.

The Apostle Paul had a similar experience in connection with the voyage to Rome and the shipwreck recorded in Acts 27. Everything seems to have come to an end, they have not only thrown some of the cargo overboard, and lightened the ship, they have even thrown the ship's tackle overboard. There was nothing more to be done, they were in a position of utter desperation. Suddenly Paul stands forward, and says: 'And now I exhort you to be of good cheer: for there shall be no loss of any man's life among you, but of the ship. For there stood by me this night the angel of God, whose I am, and whom I serve, saying, Fear not, Paul; thou must be brought before Caesar: and, lo, God hath given thee all them that sail with thee'. The Apostle knew little about navigation by contrast with these people, and yet he is the man who is able to comfort them. He does so because, 'The angel of the Lord stood by me', and he was given the divine message.

Sometimes the Lord's special help comes through visions. Peter had a vision before he admitted the Gentiles into the Church. He would never have done so but for the vision. That was one of the great tests and crises in the life of Peter. He did not believe the Gentiles could become Christians; he was a narrow, rabid, prejudiced Jew. But God gave him a vision. He saw a sheet descending from heaven with all kinds of animals in it; and Peter is taught his lesson through the vision.

These are examples and illustrations of what I mean by the Lord's special help. In unusual times of difficulty He Himself makes His presence known to us. You do not see Him but you know that He is there. This is more than the strength He gives, this is more than the grace He gives; He gives Himself. You are aware that He is by your side, He surrounds you. The same is true concerning angels. Hebrews 1:14 tells us that the angels are 'ministering spirits' sent by God to help us who are 'the heirs of salvation'. You do not see them, but you feel their presence, you know that you are not alone. You are given words, you are given assurance, you are given peace, you are given certainty. This can be illustrated endlessly out of the biographies of God's saints throughout the centuries. And these promises are still true. The testimony of the saints is to this effect: the Lord Jesus Christ does manifest Himself, in moments of extreme agony and crisis, to help us. Many have testified to this immediately before their death – the greatest crisis of all. Suddenly He has appeared to them, and the people standing by the bedside have seen a smile upon their faces. I remember being at the bedside of an old saint, aged 78, who had once been a terrible sinner. I shall never forget it. Suddenly he must have seen the Lord, for he held out his hands and said, 'I am coming, Lord!' This is something that you will find frequently happening in the last moments of the children of God. The Lord has appeared to them, they have seen Him in a vision, they have seen Him in some form that we do not always understand, and they are enabled to go through death triumphantly and gloriously and happily. This is one of the ways in which we are enabled to be 'strong in the Lord, and in the power of his might'.

What have we to do therefore? What we have to do is to believe
this teaching, and to act upon it, and to commit ourselves to Him
and to pray to Him. Many hymns deal with this theme.

> *I need Thee every hour, stay Thou near by.*

Why? – Because,

> *Temptations lose their power when Thou art nigh.*

Do you know anything about that? Listen to other expressions
of faith:

> *Sun of my soul, Thou Saviour dear,*
> *It is not night if Thou be near;*
> *O may no earth-born cloud arise*
> *To hide Thee from Thy servant's eyes.*

> *Abide with me from morn till eve,*
> *For without Thee I cannot live;*
> *Abide with me when night is nigh,*
> *For without Thee I dare not die.*

Here is another –

> *When other helpers fail, and comforts flee,*
> *Help of the helpless, O abide with me!*

> *I need Thy presence every passing hour;*
> *What but Thy grace can foil the tempter's power?*
> *Who like Thyself my guide and stay can be?*
> *Through cloud and sunshine, O abide with me!*

Then the author goes on – his confidence rising –

> *I fear no foe, with Thee at hand to bless;*
> *Ills have no weight, and tears no bitterness.*
> *Where is death's sting? where, grave, thy victory?*
> *I triumph still, if Thou abide with me.*

Listen to another –

> *I shall not fear the battle*
> *If Thou art by my side,*
> *Nor wander from the pathway*
> *If Thou wilt be my guide.*

> *My foes are ever near me,*
> *Around me and within;*
> *But, Jesus, draw Thou nearer,*
> *And shield my soul from sin.*

Here is another prayer –

> *Jesu, Lover of my soul,*
> *Let me to Thy bosom fly,*
> *While the nearer waters roll,*
> *While the tempest still is high.*
> *Hide me, O my Saviour, hide,*
> *Till the storm of life is past;*
> *Safe into the haven guide,*
> *O receive my soul at last!*

The conclusion at which we should arrive is that these promises are as true today as they have ever been. The Lord has not changed, He is still the same, and as He has appeared in this way, and made His presence known and felt and real to His struggling saints at moments of crises in evil days, He will do the same for us. But we must seek to know Him, we must seek the realization of His presence. And the way to do so, as I have been saying, is to take these prayers of saints who have gone before us and who have realized His presence, and appropriate them and plead them at His throne of mercy and grace. We can then be sure not only that we shall have grace to help in time of need, but that we shall have the rich experience of knowing that He is at our side with us, and that He will 'never leave us, nor forsake us'.

9
'Trust in God and. . . .'

'Finally, my brethren, be strong in the Lord, and in the power of his might.'

Ephesians 6:10

We now come to the practical application of what we have been considering. It is all stated perfectly in a well-known hymn by John Newton who puts it thus:

> *Though many foes beset your road,*
> *And feeble is your arm,*
> *Your life is hid with Christ in God,*
> *Beyond the reach of harm.*

> *Weak as you are, you shall not faint,*
> *Or fainting, shall not die;*
> *Jesus, the strength of every saint,*
> *Will aid you from on high.*

There we have an excellent statement of the doctrine we have been elaborating. He goes on:

> *Though unperceived by mortal sense,*
> *Faith sees Him always near,*
> *A guide, a glory, a defence:*
> *Then what have you to fear?*

That is why we should proceed without fear or hesitation; and good old John Newton encourages us further, saying:

> *As surely as He overcame,*
> *And triumphed once for you,*
> *So surely you that love His name*
> *Shall in Him triumph too.*

That then is the doctrine and the teaching. We have seen it clearly taught in the Scriptures, and the hymn from which I quote is a very good summary of it.

But someone may say, 'How am I to know all this in practice? how am I to live in that way?' In the first place we must bear in mind, and keep on holding in mind, the two elements I have been emphasizing all along – God's strength and our activity. These two things are absolutely essential. John Newton does not say in his hymn that God intends to do it all for us, that He will triumph for us. Note his words: 'As surely as He overcame and triumphed once for you.' That is what our Lord did in His death. We can do nothing about our justification, we take no part in justification or in regeneration. We are 'dead in trespasses and sins', we are 'altogether without strength'. That is entirely His work; it is done for us and we but receive it. But when you come to this other matter of sanctification, and fighting in the Christian life, the language changes, because now we have been given new life and strength and power. So John Newton continues: 'As surely as He overcame and triumphed once *for you*, So surely you that love His name shall *in Him* triumph too.' You will triumph he says, because you are 'in Him'. You do so because you have this life from Him, and because you are united to Him. 'Though unperceived by mortal sense faith sees Him always near'. We must hold on to these two elements – the strength and the power that He gives us, and our activity in the might and the strength of that power. There is this essential difference between justification and sanctification. Justification is taken entirely by faith; sanctification is something that we work out by faith, through faith, in the faith which we now have, and in our relationship to Him, and in the possession of the life that He has given us. This is the fundamental doctrine. Many are confused because of failure to understand it. The two aspects, the two activities, must ever be borne in mind.

Let me summarize by reminding you again of another statement of this doctrine which is to be found at the beginning of the Book of Revelation. In chapters 2 and 3 there are seven letters written to seven churches, and in the seven letters you have the same statement repeated. It is this: 'To him that overcometh . . .' Certain promises are made to those who overcome. In the case of

[127]

the first church it is: 'To him that overcometh will I give to eat of the tree of life, which is in the midst of the paradise of God.' It is exactly the same throughout the seven. Look at the last one – To the church of the Laodiceans, chapter 3:21: 'To him that overcometh will I grant to sit with me in my throne, even as I also overcame and am set down with my Father in his throne'. Note that the teaching is that *we* have to overcome; it is not all done for us. We do not just rest in faith, as it were, and look on as He gains the victory for us. The exhortation is that we are to do certain things; we have to repent, we have to regain our first love, we have to do the first works again, we have to watch, we have to be observant, and so on. But we are given the unction, the anointing, the eye salve, the gold, the raiment, everything we need. We are given the possibility of doing it, but we have to do it. It is our activity. There then in the last book of the Bible, in the letters of the risen Lord to His churches, is a wonderful summing-up of this doctrine.

But we must return to the practical matter as to how I apply all this and translate it into daily living and practice. It comes to this: we have to believe the teaching we have considered about the need for the food and drink, the need for prayer and for communion with the Lord; we have to grasp the all-importance of realizing our condition in Him; we have to have assurance of salvation. The situation is hopeless if we fail to do so. We must be certain as to who we are, that we are the children of God; and we have to believe all these 'exceeding great and precious promises'. We cannot fight triumphantly if we are not clear about all these matters.

Then we have to maintain the realization of His grace, and the realization of His nearness and His presence. We have to engage in 'The Practice of the Presence of God'. This takes time. Any teaching which gives the impression that we can suddenly get all this in a meeting is entirely opposed to the New Testament which keeps on telling us to go on with these things, to continue in them, to give diligence to know them. These are its terms, the military terms which are used in the exhortations. They all carry this notion of our continuance in essential activity. You do not 'receive' this as some kind of second blessing in a meeting. There is no such teaching anywhere in the Bible. All the teaching is rather that of 'continuing' and fighting and wrestling. So we go on 'practising the Presence of the Lord', seeking His face, seeking the realization of His nearness, seeking the manifestations of the Son of God. There is a hymn which tells us to 'take time to be holy'; and it does take time. We do not like that, of course. We like the short cuts; hence the cultic teaching is always popular. We like any teaching that seems to offer itself to us in a formula, and suggests that everybody has been wrong in this matter throughout the centuries, but now 'Here it is!', 'This is all you do!' 'Quite simple!' No! 'Take time to be holy'; and it does take time to put these things into practice. Or take again the Scriptural exhortation, 'Grow in grace and in the knowledge of the Lord'. 'Grow!' Growth takes time. You do not suddenly jump up; instead, you develop almost imperceptibly.

As we continue to follow the biblical pattern our confidence will increase. There is no question about this. 'Unto him that hath shall be given, and he shall have more abundance.' The more we know, the more certain we become. Every experience we have of His grace, His nearness, His presence, makes us stronger. We are in a better position than we were; and we go on from week to week, and month to month, and year to year, growing in strength and in an understanding of these things. And as we go on we shall be able to agree, more and more, with John Newton when he tells us that we have 'nothing to fear'. We shall even be able to confirm James' statement, 'Resist the devil, and he will flee from you'.

But there is always the difficulty of the beginning; and this is where many tend to stumble. All I have to say about the beginning is that there is only one way to know these things, and that is, to try them, to practise them, to make a beginning. We have got to act on our faith. There is no point or purpose in reading the doctrine and understanding the teaching if we do nothing about it. We have got to translate it into practice. There is always an element of venture in faith. Faith is entirely different from a mere intellectual assent and belief. Faith is putting what we believe into practice and into operation.

I am tempted to repeat the story that has often been told to illustrate this point. It is the story of the person who was standing on one side of the Niagara Falls and watching a man who could not only walk over the Falls on a tightrope, but who could actually trundle a wheelbarrow across as well. He turned to the man standing by and said: 'Do you believe that I can not only take a wheelbarrow over to the other side but that I can also take it across with a man sitting in it?' 'Yes, I do' said the man. 'Well', he replied, 'take your seat in the barrow.' But the onlooker would not! The story represents the difference between intellectual assent and the true faith. Faith gets into the wheelbarrow! It believes the message to such an extent that it begins to practise it.

Practice is a fundamental principle with regard to faith. There is a very good expression of it in Psalm 34. David has had an experience of the goodness and the grace of God, and he wants everyone to share it. Any man who has had an experience always wants others to have it. He says: 'I want you to rejoice with me, let us tell forth His praise together.' But there were certain people who could not do that and who would not join in. So David begins to appeal to them. 'O taste,' he says, 'taste and see that the Lord is good.' You will never see until you have tasted! He says in effect: 'The trouble is that you people are just standing there. You have your theoretical difficulties. You say, This sounds very wonderful but it is too good to be true.' So he says to them: 'You will remain standing there, and you will be without this knowledge and without this blessing until you actually do something about it. Taste, and then you will see. But you will never see until you taste.'

This is true in the whole of the Christian life. People will persist in standing back and looking on and saying, 'Is what you tell me true? I know it has happened to other people, but can this happen to me?' I believe that this is the very thing the Apostle had in mind as he was writing these words: 'Be strong in the Lord, and in the power of his might'. Many of the early Christians were fearful, timorous, hesitant people, rather like Timothy. That is why they are always being exhorted to venture out, to trust, to try, to 'taste', and being assured that then they will see. So we must not stand by faintheartedly saying: 'How can I? The thing seems too good to be true, it is not for such as I.' The only remedy for this state of things lies in the principle that faith is venturesome. There is always this element of venture;

if we but 'venture on Him' we shall soon discover wonderful things. The answer to the question, 'How I can be enabled to live this sort of life?' is that the enabling is in the command itself. That is the whole secret. 'Be strong!' How can I be strong? You can be strong by obeying the command to be strong! Let me supply certain illustrations to show that the enabling, the power, to do these things is really implicit in, and contained in, the command to do them.

Go back to the Old Testament. We find Moses leading those grumbling, recalcitrant children of Israel. They come to him one day and say: 'There is no water here; have you brought us out of Egypt in order that we may die of thirst here in the wilderness? There is no water; everything is as dry as a bone; what can we do?' And God told Moses to strike a rock, informing him that when he did so water would come pouring out of it. Now there lies the predicament. Moses was a man, and though he was a very good man he knows that if he strikes rocks nothing will happen. He may have struck many a rock but no water had come gushing out. But here he is told that if he strikes a certain rock with his rod water will come gushing out of it. That constitutes the whole predicament of faith. That is exactly the position of all of us as we stand face to face with the command: 'Be strong in the Lord, and in the power of his might'. 'But who am I?' you say. 'I am just a weakling. What is the use of telling me to be strong?' The answer is this. Moses in faith took his rod and he smote, he struck, the rock; and out of it came the water gushing forth. It was not Moses' power, but it was his arm and it was his rod. Moses did not just stand by and see the water gushing out. Moses had to lift up his arm and he had to strike, to smite, that rock. But as he did so the power was given to him, and the water came gushing out of the rock. There you see the two elements in this matter. You see the activity of the man, but you see that the power is given to him by God. It was not Moses – Moses lacked the power to do such things. But Moses was given the power to do them. The two things come together. But the point I am emphasizing now is that Moses, if he had hesitated there, and had done nothing, would not have seen this marvellous miracle; but by acting he discovered that the power was given. He 'tasted' and he 'saw'! That is the way in which it happens.

Take another illustration from the New Testament. There is recorded in three of the Gospels, the case of the man with the withered hand. Our Lord encountered that man on the Sabbath day, and obviously had the intention of healing him. The Pharisees were present, and they began an argument with our Lord as to whether it was right to heal a man on the Sabbath day (Matthew 12:9-14). The material point in the story is this, that our Lord having answered the Pharisees and their foolish objections, said to the man, 'Stretch forth thine hand'. Now here again is the predicament; here is a man with a withered hand, paralysed, possibly it had never developed at all. It was a useless hand, he could do nothing at all with it. Partly because of the disuse and the lack of development, the muscles were flaccid and shrunken and feeble, and had no power and strength in them. Yet the Lord says to that man, 'Stretch forth thine hand'. And what we read is, 'He stretched it forth; and it was restored whole like as the other'. The whole marvel of this story is that when our Lord said to the man, 'Stretch forth thine hand', at the command of our Lord the man did it.

Obviously the man had to make the effort. What happened was not that the man said, 'Well, yes, my hand is withered but I believe that all things are possible with you, and that you can heal my hand and restore it. I believe that you can do it', and suddenly, as he expressed his faith, his hand sprang forward. It is not that. The man did not suddenly find his hand jerking up and stretching forward; it was not done for him. The vital point is that our Lord says to the man who cannot do it, 'Stretch forth thine hand', and as He spoke the power was given to the man. So when he made the effort, to his own amazement and astonishment, for the first time he found that he could stretch forth his hand. The two elements are absolutely necessary; and as you study the miracles you will find that in most of them, these elements are present. Our Lord always calls upon the person to do something. For instance in the case of the woman who was doubled up and bent: 'Stand up', He says, and immediately she straightened. And so with all the others, the lame, the paralysed: 'Take up thy bed and walk'. It all sounds monstrous, the man has not got the power. True, but the power is given in the command; and as he makes his effort he suddenly finds that he can do it. 'Be strong in the Lord, and in the power of his might'; you will never know this until you are practising it.

But there is a still better illustration which brings out still further elements. I hope it is clear that I am not using the miracles in order to teach sanctification. That is always a fallacy. What I am doing is to show how the power 'to do' is given in the commandment. So we come to the famous case of Peter walking upon the water as described in the fourteenth chapter of Matthew's Gospel. The disciples were on their own in a boat and the sea had become boisterous because of a storm. Suddenly our Lord comes walking on the water. They thought at first that it was a ghost, but at last He told them who He was, and they recognized Him. Then Peter did something very characteristic of him. He was impressed by our Lord's ability to walk on the water and he said: 'Command me to walk on the water.' 'Is it possible for me also to do this thing?' And our Lord said to him, 'Come'. Then we read: 'And when Peter was come down out of the ship, he walked on the water, to go to Jesus.' Next we are told that Peter, beginning to see the waves boisterous near him, began to be afraid, and as the result of that he began to sink. Then came the word: 'Immediately Jesus stretched forth his hand, and caught him, and said unto him, 'O thou of little faith, wherefore didst thou doubt?' Again the essential element is that Peter has to make the move: 'When Peter was come down out of the ship.' The thing is not done to Peter or for Peter. Peter, who had never before in his life walked on the waves, believing this word, gets out of the boat and begins to walk on the waves. He has to make the effort, but he is given the power to do so. Then when he doubts he loses the power and begins to sink; but our Lord lays hold upon him.

That is the perfect illustration showing what we have been trying to say, that we are given the power, and that this is a part of the working of God's grace. But in moments of exceptional difficulty and stress, when the battle is unusually hot and strong, and the devil brings out all his forces, the Lord appears and lays hold upon us: we are not allowed to sink. The two elements are there. If Peter had continued practising faith there would have been no need for the Lord to take hold of him, and deliver him; he could have continued walking on the waves. But the emphasis is again upon our effort, our activity. Peter would never have known that it was possible for him to walk on the waves if he had not got out of the boat, if he had not made the effort, if he had not done all that he could, always relying of course upon the power of the Lord to enable him to do so.

Now let us go on to look at the various miracles performed by these same Apostles as recorded in the Book of the Acts of the Apostles. There are some observations which we must make about these miracles. One is that there was never a failure in the apostolic miracles as recorded in the Book of the Acts of the Apostles. Another is that the Apostles did not work miracles every day. Again, they never made preliminary announcements that they were going to do so. That is the way in which they differ from many who claim to be working miracles today, and who claim that they can announce that they intend to do so on such and such a day. The Apostles never spoke in such a manner; and the reason for that is obvious – they never knew beforehand when they were going to work a miracle. It is clear that they were suddenly given the commission and the power. Peter and John seeing a lame man sitting at the Beautiful gate of the temple knew that they had the commission, so Peter says: 'In the name of Jesus Christ of Nazareth rise up and walk.' And the man rose, 'and immediately his feet and ankle bones received strength: and he leaping up stood, and walked, and entered with them into the temple, walking, and leaping, and praising God'. The principle is that with the commission the power is given, in the command there is the enabling.

The same principle holds good in connection with the whole question of preaching. People have held very strange, odd views with regard to preaching. I have actually known men personally who did not hesitate to say that a preacher should never prepare his sermon. They thought that preparation was quite wrong, that it indicated a lack of faith. They sometimes quoted the Psalm which says, 'Open thy mouth wide and I will fill it' (81.10), and argued that all the preacher has to do is to enter the pulpit and open his mouth and start speaking. Another verse they have often misquoted, taking it right out of its context, is Matthew 10:19, where we are told: 'Take no thought how or what ye shall speak: for it shall be given you in that same hour what ye shall speak.' But our Lord is there dealing with His people on trial in law courts during persecution, suddenly arrested and apprehended. 'At such a time,' He said, 'do not be troubled, I will be with you, I will give you words to speak.' He is not talking about a preaching ministry. But they persist, arguing 'It all comes from the Lord, and you must not bring the human element into it; you must not use your own mind, you must not use your own understanding and knowledge. You must rely entirely upon the Spirit'. They argue that Whitefield was quite wrong in using the amazing oratorical powers that had been given to him by God at his natural birth. 'Oratory is all wrong,' they say, 'that is the flesh.' They do not recognize that oratory is a gift of God. 'You have to be entirely passive' they argue. No preparation, no use of your natural faculties!

Such an outlook is utterly unscriptural. In the Scriptures we find that the men whom God used prepared themselves and their matter. Paul spent three years in Arabia obviously working out his new-found faith in terms of the Old Testament. His great experience had suddenly come and had to be reconciled with his knowledge of the Old Testament. He has to prepare his message for Jews and Gentiles, so he spends three years in Arabia.

You will find always that the men whom God has used signally have been those who have studied most, known their Scriptures best, and given time to preparation. You are to do your best and your utmost; but you must not rely upon what you do. You must rely upon the Spirit. In addressing ministers, I sometimes say that the greatest danger threatening a minister who has finished the preparation of his sermons for Sunday – whether by Friday night, or midday Saturday, or Saturday evening – is to say to himself, 'I am ready for Sunday; I have my two sermons'. The danger arises in this way. He must have his two sermons; but if he relies upon his two sermons only he will fail. The man should prepare his two sermons and put all his abilities and knowledge into them; but he should realize that unless the Spirit comes upon them they will be of no avail. The Spirit generally uses a man's best preparation. It is not the Spirit *or* preparation; it is preparation *plus* the unction and the anointing and that which the Holy Spirit alone can supply. The danger always is to go to one or the other of the two extremes. Your effort energized by the Lord, and your relying upon Him! There is no difficulty here, no contradiction!

It is precisely the same in the matter of healing. There are many who get trapped into a difficulty over the question of what is called 'faith healing'. They interpret 'faith healing' to mean that you should never use means at all, you should never make use of any drug or medicament. They claim that that would be lack of faith. 'You have to leave it entirely to the Lord, you have to trust wholly in Him.' And they argue that you cannot exercise faith if you are using means. The answer is to ask the following questions: Who has provided us with the means? Where have these various drugs and medicaments come from? They are found in nature, in flowers, in metals, and various other places. 'God has provided us all things richly to enjoy.' God has provided all these things and, clearly, He would not have provided them unless we are meant to use them. Once again, the danger is to swing from one extreme to the other. There are some who rely upon the means only, and that is the great danger today. Because of all our advances and developments and medical discoveries people think that God is not needed; they trust only to the medicaments and the means. That is wrong. But then these others are equally wrong who say that you do not need means at all.

One of the best illustrations in regard to this matter is an incident in the life of Hudson Taylor, the founder of the China Inland Mission. When he was making his first voyage to China he felt that it would be a lack of faith to make use of 'a swimming-belt' with which, to comply with the earnest wish of his mother, he had provided himself. He felt that he must trust entirely to the Lord to keep him and he would not consider putting it on. In fact he gave it away. But later he came to see that he had been mistaken. It is not a lack of faith to use a lifebelt. Put on your lifebelt but trust in God still. Use the means that are available, but put your confidence in God. Hudson Taylor came to see this later and corrected what had appeared to him in the first instance to be a sheer matter of faith.

A similar illustration belongs to the case of Andrew Murray of South Africa, a well-known holiness teacher. He went through a period where he thought it was lack of faith, indeed a denial of faith, to use means in healing; the sufferer must trust entirely to the Lord. He does not need a doctor, he does not need any medicaments. But Andrew Murray, likewise, as the result of painful experiences, came to see that he was wrong, and later in his life he used both doctors and their medicaments. But there was no lack of faith involved there; the ultimate faith is in God.

The last word on this matter was spoken by Oliver Cromwell: 'Trust in God, and keep your powder dry.' You do not trust in God and do nothing. You have to fight, keep your powder dry, make certain that you can use it in the thick and the heat of the battle. But notice the order of the words: 'Trust in God' precedes 'keep your powder dry'. It is clear as you read the life of Cromwell that his great secret was his trust in God. That was the ultimate thing, but he was wise enough to see that you need means, and that you have to use them. You do not just stand back and wait for it all to be done for you. No, 'Trust in God and keep your powder dry'.

Is not this whole matter very similar to what we often do when we are encouraging a child or someone who is beginning to learn. The beginner, the child, says – 'I cannot do it'. He is nervous, he is frightened, he has never done it before and he says that he cannot do it. Those who are trying to ride a bicycle for the first time may have similar feelings. They keep on saying that they cannot do it. How does one handle such persons? What we have to do, of course, is to reassure them, to make them venture, to show them that it can be done. What we normally do is to hold them, but without their knowing it we hold them less and less tightly, and at the end our hand merely rests on them, it is not holding them at all. On they go, our hand is no longer on them, and they suddenly find they have done 'the impossible'. They have the power within them latently, but they do not believe it, they do not know it; and the only way in which they will ever be able to ride the bicycle or whatever it is, is to make the venture. They have to make the effort, they have to do all they can. 'Stretch forth thine hand'; and as the man did so he found that he had the ability. It was given to him. I have used this multiplicity of illustrations in order to help those who are still timorous, frightened, alarmed. We are not meant to be like that. We are meant to listen to this great exhortation. As you hear it saying, 'Be strong in the Lord, and in the power of his might', do not say, 'But I am weak, I am feeble'. It is because you are weak that you are given the exhortation. You are not being told that you have this 'strength' and 'power' in yourself, and there the matter rests. What you are being told is that you are a child of God, that you have a seed of divine life in you, that you are united and related to Christ the Head, that you are always in that relationship, and that, as you do things in His name, you will find that you are able to do them. You will find that you have the power, the enabling, which is so necessary.

So we find that the whole secret in this matter is to believe that God is speaking to us through these very words. It is not a slogan, it is not just a general statement, it is not merely some kind of caption. It is very practical and it works out in the way I have indicated. The Lord is saying to every one of us in some way or other, 'Stretch forth thine hand'; stop saying that you cannot do it, stop talking about your paralysis, listen to what I am saying. The power is given, do it, go on doing it, keep on doing it. And as we put it into practice we shall find that it is not only true, but infinitely more true than we have ever imagined or thought. 'Taste and see that the Lord is good.' 'Be strong in the Lord, and in the power of his might.' At times you will be amazed at your own strength and power; you will find it difficult to believe that it is really you. Weak, faint, feeble, you will be astonished at yourself, and filled with amazement at the power and the strength and the ability which has been given to you by the Lord.

Whatever may be facing us, whatever may be set against us in particular, you and I have to realize these precious truths – that the power is given, that He is with us, and that 'nothing shall ever be able to separate us from the love of God, which is in Christ Jesus our Lord'.

> *Fight the good fight with all thy might;*
> *Christ is thy strength, and Christ thy right;*
> *Lay hold on life, and it shall be*
> *Thy joy and crown eternally.*

> *Run the straight race through God's good grace,*
> *Lift up thine eyes, and seek His face;*
> *Life with its way before thee lies;*
> *Christ is the way, and Christ the prize.*

Cast care aside; lean on thy guide,
Lean and His mercy will provide;
Lean, and the trusting soul shall prove
Christ is its life, and Christ its love.

Faint not nor fear, His arm is near;
He changeth not, and thou art dear;
Only believe, and thou shalt see
That Christ is all in all to thee.

(John S. B. Monsell)

10

Things to Avoid

'Finally, my brethren, be strong in the Lord, and in
the power of his might.'

Ephesians 6:10

We have been seeing that it is essential to concentrate positively
on the realization of the power that is given to us in our rebirth,
when we receive a seed of life possessing power and vigour. We
must see to it that this grows and develops. We do so by taking
the appropriate spiritual food and drink, praying, taking exercise,
serving the Lord, making ventures of faith, and so on. All along
we have been concentrating on what I may call the positive side
of this teaching. That is, of course, the most essential part of it;
but to make our investigation complete we must add a certain
amount on the negative side, because this too is also absolutely
essential. Let me use the analogy that has been in our minds from
the beginning, the analogy of the growth and development of
the human being in a physical sense. We begin with the helpless
infant, but he is not devoid of strength. He cannot walk, but he
can kick his legs about and move his hands and arms. There is
strength there. These powers have to be developed and fostered
and trained in a positive manner. But we also see, using this same
analogy, that there are certain negative truths which are of vital
importance for us. In other words, if we are to remain healthy and
strong and vigorous and powerful there are certain things which
we must avoid. The fight for health, if one may so call it, has these
two aspects – positive and negative. There is no purpose in trying
to build yourself up if, on the other hand, you are doing certain
things that are bound to sap your energy and your vitality, and
may even rob you of your health altogether. The strongest man
alive if he walks into an infected chamber will probably become

a victim of the disease. So we must avoid, in general, anything that tends to weaken us, to sap our energy, or to rob us of the spiritual health, out of which comes our spiritual energy and vigour. I propose, therefore, at this point, to call attention to certain things we have to avoid.

The first thing we have to avoid is dissipation of energy. However much energy we may have, if we misuse it, dissipate it, throw it away, the result will be that we shall have less of it, and will become less effective and efficient. This is quite obvious in the physical realm. Many a man has become weak who was once strong, simply because he has been over-exerting himself in various ways. He has overstretched and overstrained himself; and the result is that he develops a tired heart (so called), or a weak heart, and eventually loses his health and has to take great care of himself.

This is equally true in the spiritual realm. I sometimes think that it is one of the greatest dangers confronting many evangelical people, particularly, at this present time. I was asked once to address a certain conference of evangelical Christian people, and the theme suggested was this very matter. It was that a number of Christian people in professions, and various other walks of life, were troubled about themselves, that they seemed to have lost the edge of their spiritual life, did not enjoy the Bible as they used to do, did not enjoy praying, and so on, and were generally unhappy about the spiritual state and condition into which they had fallen. There are many in that condition and I have no doubt in asserting, that its commonest cause, in my experience as a pastor, is simply dissipation of energy.

The Apostle Paul writes about his own countrymen as having 'zeal' without 'knowledge' (Romans 10:2). This ailment is not confined to unbelievers, but is quite common among believing people. 'Zeal without knowledge.' That means, partly, thoughtless activity, or what may be described as 'activism'. We are all meant to be active and, as I have pointed out, there is nothing that is so guaranteed to increase our strength as to be active. But you have to know how to be active. There is all the difference in the world between true activity and activism, between healthy activity and a dissipation of energy. The need is for our activity to be thoughtful, disciplined, governed, and directed. One can well understand this danger and how it arises. For all to be 'doing something' happens to be the popular teaching at the present time. 'Give the new convert something to do.' That is the current phrase; and, incidentally, it is quite unscriptural. The Pastoral Epistles teach almost the exact opposite; they warn us not to ordain a novice because he is not yet fit to do certain things; and it is dangerous for him because he may be lifted up with pride, as was the devil. But it is the controlling teaching today: we must all be doing something here, there and everywhere.

This is a very dangerous condition for the soul, because what generally happens is that such people become overtired, and overstrained. The spiritual tone of their lives then suffers. This principle is true in every realm and department of life. Any man who overdoes things – I do not care what he is doing – will soon discover that, first of all, the quality of his work begins to suffer. A man who preaches too much, who works too hard in the ministry, a man who is over active, a man who sings too much – in all cases the first thing to go will be the quality. The general public will not detect it for some time. The critics, however, will recognize it; they will say that the man is being carried along by his past reputation, but that he is not the master he used to be, that the finesse is not there, that he has lost something. It is simply because the man is overworking, is getting tired, and the result is that he is steadily losing something vital.

This is particularly true in the spiritual realm. There are many who, with very good intentions, and feeling that they must be doing something to justify their Christianity, often get into this state because they are afraid of the criticisms of the devotees of this popular teaching at the present time. Many Christians, because of their fear of the glib clichés that are being used so much, feel that they must be always doing something.

This is a very real problem. Some Christian professional men are out at meetings almost every night of the week. That is even wrong from the standpoint of family life; but I am not concerned about that at the moment. I am concerned about the danger to themselves. They find themselves exhausted, with nothing to give in the end; they are just mechanically doing something which is of very little value. I call their fault 'dissipation of energy' – it is unintelligent activity.

Every man has to sit down and plan his life, and decide what he can do and what he cannot do. He must be resolute, and not be governed by 'what people say'. He is the one who is in the best position to know how much he can do, when he is to do it, and where he is to do it. Never allow yourselves to be dictated to by others. Do not allow 'the thing to do' in any realm to determine what you do. We must be in charge of ourselves, otherwise we shall become weary and tired and exhausted simply through dissipating, throwing away, our energy.

There are other ways in which the same fault comes to the surface. Is there not a danger that some of us dissipate a lot of energy in just talking too much? We talk so much that we never stop to think or to meditate. Most of us talk far too much, and so waste a lot of energy. Long-drawn-out conversation can be very exhausting. Through sheer talk there are many who find themselves in spiritual trouble. We must learn to follow the exhortation of the Scriptures. 'Be swift to hear, slow to speak, slow to wrath' (James 1:19). Let us make sure that we do not go through life talking, and never really thinking over and understanding the truth, and thereby failing to grow in grace and in knowledge. We have to discipline ourselves in this matter.

Energy may also be dissipated in mere argument and disputation and wrangling. Many warnings are given to us in the Scripture concerning this. Take 1 Timothy 1:4: 'Neither give heed to fables and endless genealogies, which minister questions, rather than godly edifying which is in faith.' Again in verse 6: '. . . some having swerved, have turned aside unto vain jangling', that is to say, they have spent their lives in arguing and disputing. Turn again to the Second Epistle of Timothy, chapter 2, where there are quite a number of references to these matters. Look at verse 14: 'Of these things put them in remembrance, charging them before the Lord that they strive not about words to no profit, but to the subverting of the hearers.' They were giving the impression that they were very clever; they were arguing and debating. But there was no profit in their talk. However much you may be inclined to argue about truth, if you are not growing spiritually as the result of it, do less of it; perhaps for the time being you had better cut it out altogether and begin to examine your soul. 'No profit, but to the subverting of the hearers.' Then again in verse 16: 'Shun profane and vain babblings: for they will increase unto more ungodliness.' Take note of the outcome of that kind of thing. Verse 23: 'Foolish and unlearned questions avoid, knowing that they do gender strifes.' These are things that we must avoid. Again in Titus 3:9: 'But avoid foolish questions, and genealogies, and contentions, and strivings about the law; for they are unprofitable and vain.' The test of everything must always be whether it is profitable – profitable to our own souls, profitable to the souls of other people. There is much dissipation of energy, sheer waste of energy, in pointless disputations and wranglings. If you are not growing as the result of your activity in that respect you had better start examining yourself again. If you know so much you should be showing it in your life. 'The foundation of God standeth sure, having this seal, The Lord knoweth them that are his.' Yes, 'And, let everyone that nameth the name of Christ depart from iniquity'. Knowledge, contending for the faith, and growth in grace, must always go together.

This theme merits much attention. It is a very difficult matter, because we are told two things in the Scriptures. First of all, we are exhorted to 'contend earnestly for the faith'. That is Jude's exhortation. 'Contend earnestly for the faith which was once [forall] delivered unto the saints.' And there is great need of this at this present time. The Apostle Paul thanks the Philippians that they have stood with him 'in the defence and proclamation of the gospel'. We are called upon to do this; and never more so than at the present time. But we have to keep to a position which is between two extremes. There are some people who never defend the faith at all. They claim that they are just nice, good people, who do not argue, who do not understand, who are not 'controversialists'. That is an unscriptural position to assume for we are meant to contend earnestly for the faith.

That is one Christian duty, but there is also the other. We are never to become guilty of this 'vain disputation', 'vain wrangling'. We must not become such that we are always criticizing and always arguing. That is a bad fault. There is a middle position between the two. 'The servant of the Lord' says the Apostle, 'must not strive' (2 Timothy 2:24). At one and the same time we have to contend for the faith and to refrain from striving. 'Striving' means that your spirit is wrong, and once your spirit becomes wrong your motive becomes wrong. You tend to pride yourself as being 'a defender of the faith', and you lose your spiritual quality. This is a terrible danger, and especially to a preacher. During the course of my ministry I have known men who illustrate this only too perfectly. I can think of two men in particular, who began with powerful ministries under which people were converted and then built up. These two men ended as mere contenders and disputers. They attracted crowds of people to listen to them on Sunday nights – people who enjoy a kind of spiritual dog-fight, wondering who was to 'have it' next, who was to be attacked. There is a mentality that enjoys this type of thing, and the more you give it the more it enjoys it. That is very bad. We must contend, but we must never strive. We must do the one and avoid the other. The moment a man begins to strive he is dissipating his energy. These two men I knew were very able men, and very great preachers; but they ruined their ministries. They began to strive, and the power went; and in the end they became more or less entirely ineffective.

Furthermore I suggest that we must also avoid spending too much time in what I would call 'enervating atmospheres'. It does not matter how strong you may be, if you are in a wrong atmosphere, if there is too much humidity, for instance, you will not feel very strong. It will sap your energy and your vitality. You will feel limp though, naturally, you are a very strong person.

This, again, is as true in the spiritual life as in the natural. There are certain atmospheres which are very enervating. It is possible for us to waste a lot of time through sheer lack of self-discipline; and there is nothing that is more enervating than that. A man can just sit about doing nothing; the more he does so the less he will be able to do. Merely to laze and to be slack through lack of discipline is thoroughly enervating. It does not mean that you are doing bad things of necessity; time can be wasted in doing nothing or in doing things that are hardly worth doing. I remember a man once giving advice to ministers. He was an old man and he was warning ministers especially against the morning newspaper. He said he had discovered in his own ministry that, somehow or other, he seemed to spend most of the morning in going through his newspaper, and then suddenly he would realize about eleven o'clock or half-past eleven that the morning had gone and he had done nothing. That is the kind of thing I mean. It is right that a minister should read a newspaper so that he may know the contemporary situation; but if he wastes all his morning reading the newspaper, he is at fault. I knew another man who had a preaching gift which nevertheless came to nothing because he used to go out every morning and talk to people on the streets of the town. Everyone praised him as an affable, nice man; but he was not doing his work, he was not reading, he was not preparing himself for the ministry. Let us apply all this to ourselves. If you get into this slack condition you can waste your whole life doing nothing. It is utterly profitless and it saps our energy.

Then, to look at the matter from another aspect, we can spend too much time in wrong company. I do not mean of necessity bad company. I am thinking of company that is not really positively helpful in a spiritual sense. Of course I do not mean that we must cut ourselves off altogether from such people, otherwise we should never be able to help them. That is one extreme; the other is this, that you spend too much time with them. I am not suggesting that you should become a monk or a hermit and go out of life. That is wrong, it is not New Testament teaching, it is a false asceticism. But then the other danger is that you spend too much time with them, just talking, not about bad things, but about things that really do not matter very much. This is what is described in the Scriptures as 'the world'. The world is the enemy of the Christian. You do not go out of it, but you must not spend too much time in it. If you spend too much of your time in a worldly atmosphere you will find that the edge of your spiritual life will become dulled. There is nothing wrong inherently in looking at television or listening to the radio, but if you spend too much time in doing so, it is certain that you will not be able to pray so well, and you will lose your taste for the Scriptures.

We have to walk on a knife-edge in these matters; you must not become extreme on one side or the other. But you have to be watchful. And, of course, you can always tell by examining yourself whether your strength is increasing or declining. Do you feel at the present time that there is something lacking spiritually, that you have lost the edge, that you are not enjoying Christian things as you once did, and as you know you should? Well, I just ask you one question, How much time are you spending with these other things, and why do you do so? This is an absolute rule; the atmosphere immediately affects our constitution. So make certain that you are not spending too much of your time in that kind of atmosphere.

But there is something worse than that. The Apostle has already warned us in this Epistle to the Ephesians about what he calls 'foolish talking and jesting'. We are not to be pompous, we are not to take ourselves too seriously; but that is a very different thing from being guilty of 'foolish talking and jesting'. I am often surprised by hearing Christian people indulging in this 'foolish talking and jesting'. Let us make sure that we are not producing a wrong atmosphere by this kind of thing. That type of talk belongs to the world, and does not belong to us. This is the instruction of the Scripture.

Worldliness, of course, has many forms and there are specific dangers. The Apostle warns Timothy in the First Epistle, chapter 6, verse 9: 'They that will be rich fall into temptation and a snare, and into many foolish and hurtful lusts, which drown men in destruction and perdition. For the love of money is the root of all evil: which while some coveted after, they have erred from the faith, and pierced themselves through with many sorrows. But thou, O man of God, flee these things.' Here Paul is condemning the love of money. Money as such is not evil if a man uses it properly as a steward of the Lord Jesus Christ. But the moment a man begins to love money sin enters. I am old enough to be able to say that I have seen many a good man go wrong at this point. Once that happens there is always a lowering of the spiritual temperature, and a speedy loss of spiritual vigour. I have known cases of men who were converted from a very evil life, and who, because of their conversion, began to pay attention to their work and to get on and succeed; and I have had the miserable experience of watching some of them fall into this trap. Before, they threw their money away; now they begin to love it. Both extremes are wrong.

Another cause of loss of spiritual vigour and energy, and of failing to be 'strong in the Lord, and in the power of his might', is the enervating atmosphere of respectability. This is a very common danger in the Church. I sometimes wonder whether this is not the greatest curse of all at the present time. The statistics, at any rate, prove quite clearly that, for one reason or another, Christianity today is not touching the working classes of this country. Is it, I sometimes wonder, because we are giving the impression that Christianity is only for the respectable middle classes? Let us examine ourselves about this. Are we afraid of the manifestation of the Spirit? Are we guilty of quenching the Spirit? Are we afraid of life and vigour and power? How often have I seen men who started with fire become just respectable, nice Christians – useless, without any energy and vigour and power!

Let me illustrate this again from the realm of the ministry. I have known men who went into the ministry undoubtedly called of God, with a passion for souls, and with preaching power. I have seen them end up as just good pastors, good visitors. Visiting is a part of a pastor's ministry; but if a man becomes just a pleasing man, a good pastor, a nice man to have in the home, one who will drink a cup of tea with you, it is tragic. What a tragedy that a prophet should end up as just a nice man and a good pastor! Once more we see that we are always seeking to avoid extremes. But there is nothing that can be so enervating as this kind of nice respectable atmosphere in which we are afraid of almost anything, and above all, afraid of the manifestation of the power of the Holy Spirit; and so we begin to 'quench the Spirit'!

It is clear that there are endless applications of this theme. It is the real background and rationale of the teaching in 2 Corinthians 6 about 'not being unequally yoked together with unbelievers'. That applies, primarily, to marriage. The reason why a Christian should not marry an unbeliever is that by so doing he is putting himself into a wrong atmosphere which is bound to sap his spiritual energy and vitality. It is inevitable from the very fact that he is thus associated with and bound to someone who has no spiritual life and understanding. He, not the other partner, is the one who is bound to suffer. So we are told not to be unequally yoked together with unbelievers.

In the third place, avoid diseases and infections. Here we advance
to a more positive danger. We are not now talking merely about
an enervating atmosphere, bad though that is. There is something
worse, namely, a diseased atmosphere, a place in which there is
active infection. If you know that there is infection in a house
or in a room, the obvious thing to do is to avoid going there,
unless you have to go there for some good and valid reason. You
should not 'walk' into infection. Again, of course, you have to be
careful, for there are extremes here also. You may be so afraid of
infections that you never go out-of-doors at all, and you will end,
perhaps, by living in some sort of glass-house where you will die
of inanition! We have to maintain this spiritual balance and common sense at every point in our lives.

I am referring, of course, to the avoidance of bad company.
I have already indicated the danger of more or less innocent
company which is not spiritual. How much more are the warnings
required about bad company! The first Psalm deals with this
matter: 'Blessed is the man that walketh not in the counsel of the
ungodly, nor standeth in the way of sinners, nor sitteth in the seat
of the scornful.' He is a 'blessed' man, a right man, a happy man;
he is a man who will know the blessing of the Lord because he
avoids polluted atmosphere. If you 'walk in the counsel of the
ungodly', have intimate friendship with people who are literally
ungodly, and evil and bad, they are bound to affect you. If you
'stand in the way of sinners' and put yourself where you know
they are, it will not be surprising if you fall; and if you 'sit in the
seat of the scornful' you will soon lose the edge off your spiritual
life. This has happened frequently. There is only one thing to do:
avoid bad company; 'avoid it as the plague', as the expression
puts it. For it is the plague, the plague of hell, the plague of the
devil and all that is foul. Keep clear of it.

I like the Apostle's term – 'Flee'! Run away from it, get as far
away from it as you can. This is the only thing to do with 'bad'
company. You will find very instructive teaching about this in
1 Corinthians, chapter 5. At the end of that chapter the Apostle
shows us the perfect balance that always characterizes scriptural
teaching. In verses 9–11 he says, 'I wrote unto you in an epistle
not to company with fornicators'. The balancing statement
follows – 'Yet not altogether with the fornicators of this world,

or with the covetous, or extortioners, or with idolaters; for then must ye needs go out of the world. But now I have written unto you not to keep company, if any man that is called a brother be a fornicator, or covetous, or an idolater, or a railer, or a drunkard, or an extortioner; with such an one no not to eat'. You must not keep company with a brother who is guilty of these sins, you must have nothing to do with him. But note the balance in the way in which Paul puts it.

We have similar teaching in the fifth chapter of this Epistle to the Ephesians where he says at the beginning at verse 8: 'For ye were sometimes darkness, but now are ye light in the Lord: walk as children of light.' Verse 10: 'Proving what is acceptable unto the Lord. And have no fellowship with the unfruitful works of darkness, but rather reprove them. For it is a shame even to speak of those things which are done of them in secret.' We must have nothing to do with them, and not even speak about them. Then there is that terrible warning in the Epistle of Jude, verse 23. Jude has been telling Christians how to help people: 'Of some,' he says, 'have compassion. . . And others save with fear, pulling them out of the fire; hating even the garment spotted by the flesh.' You have to help these people but to be very careful as you are doing so, that they do not drag you down and pollute you. People say glibly: 'But our Lord was a friend of publicans and sinners.' True, but never forget that He was the Lord! Many a man acting on that maxim foolishly and thoughtlessly has ended by being dragged down to the level of the publican and sinner! But if you do so, 'hating even the garment spotted by the flesh', there will be no danger.

Furthermore, avoid bad reading – I mean general reading, polluting reading. There is much nonsense being talked about this at the present time. We are being told that Christians must read this kind of filth in order to be able to help people. You need not wallow in the filth in order to be able to understand something about it and to deal with it. You need not read that type of 'literature'. It is bad, it is polluting; avoid it, whether it is in books or in newspapers. Have you not found in your own experience that to read certain things does you harm? Then do not read them. If you find that as the result of reading a certain type of newspaper report about divorce, or something similar, you become subject to temptation in a more acute form, do not read that kind of thing. Avoid it, set it aside; if necessary, buy a different type of newspaper that does not glory in moral pollution, but very rightly only gives a few lines to it and says that such and such a verdict was passed. You need not know the details, you do not gain anything by knowing them. In fact you will nearly always suffer harm as the result of reading them. The Apostle states it thus in Romans 13:14: '. . . make no provision for the flesh to fulfil the lusts thereof'. If you feed the flesh do not be surprised if you fall to its temptations and its lusts; make no provision for it. Let us watch our general reading.

And again, under this heading, keep a watch on your thoughts and imaginations. 'Flee also youthful lusts!' That is the point at which to watch. The first thought, the first imagination, 'Flee', get away from it, cut it out, stop it. Thoughts and imaginations can be evil, and we are to mortify them speedily.

Furthermore, we are to avoid people who do not believe in the Bible as the Word of God, for they will do you harm; they will take from your spiritual energy and you will eventually become diseased. How often has this happened! How often have we known young men, truly converted, full of passion for souls, and zeal and enthusiasm, who after they have been to a theological college come out quite useless! What has happened is that their faith in the Word of God has been undermined. What harm it does, what ruination it has so often produced! I am referring to a certain attitude to the Scriptures, to the teaching that man with his reason is able to determine what is right and what is wrong. The critic believes this about the Lord, he does not believe that; he does not believe in His Virgin Birth, he does not believe in the miracles, he does not believe in the atoning death and resurrection. The Bible is no longer the Word of God, there is no real Gospel, there is no message. Have no fellowship with people who do not believe the Bible to be the Word of God. I am talking about people who call themselves Christians. Of course you have got to deal with others; but if a man says he is a Christian and claims to be such, and yet undermines the very basis and foundation of the faith, have no fellowship with him.

I am not asserting this on my own authority; there is scriptural warrant for what I say. The Apostle John in his Second Epistle says: 'If there come any unto you, and bring not this doctrine, receive him not into your house, neither bid him God speed.' We must act on this principle. It is my duty never to allow a man to occupy the pulpit of the church where I am the pastor who has a wrong view of the inspiration of Scripture, or who has a wrong view of any one of these cardinal doctrines. He is not only not a true preacher, he is an enemy and a menace. He is not only of no value, he is a danger. If I can help him, all well and good, but I must not welcome him into my house, I must not regard him as a brother, I must not be friendly with such a man. I must show that there is an essential difference between us.

There is nothing that is so fatal to spiritual vigour and power as a wrong attitude to the Word of God and to the cardinal Christian doctrines. That is why the Apostle wrote the First Epistle to the Corinthians, chapter 15. Certain people were denying the Resurrection. Why is Paul concerned about this? 'Because evil communications corrupt good manners.' The life will go wrong if the doctrine is wrong. And I have no hesitation in asserting again that one of the main causes of the condition of the Christian Church today is the departure during the past century from a belief in the divine and plenary inspiration of the Holy Scripture, and its final authority in all matters of faith and conduct. There is no question about this. The Christian Church herself by casting doubt upon the veracity of the word and the authority of the Scripture has literally sown the seeds of unbelief in the minds of the masses of the people, with the result that they are now outside the Church. And they will remain there until the Church returns to a belief in the authority of the Word of God.

In his First Epistle to Timothy the Apostle says that certain men have 'swerved away' from the truth, with the result that, in respect of the faith, they 'have made shipwreck'. He says virtually the same thing again and more extensively in his Second Epistle to Timothy, chapter 2. Take verse 18 for instance: 'Who concerning the truth have erred, saying that the resurrection is past already; and overthrow the faith of some.' They have erred themselves and they are doing harm to others; and accordingly, spiritual life and energy and vigour have been lost to the Church. Avoid all such heresies as the very plague; develop a sense of discrimination. Do not say, 'So-and-so is a very nice and lovable man, he talks about Christ, and about the death of Christ'. The vital question is. what is he saying about that death? What is his teaching concerning it? Let us develop a spirit of understanding and discrimination lest we become victims of the noxious, insidious infections which will rob us of our spiritual life and vitality. I dislike having to say such things, but it is one's duty to warn people against infections. The preacher is a man who is called upon to placard notices warning people of dangerous, infectious, spiritual diseases. The Church should put false teachers into quarantine and isolation hospitals, but until she does so I say, Avoid such men and their teachings, and have no fellowship with them.

One further emphasis is found in our text at the end. The Apostle says in verse 13: 'Wherefore take unto you the whole armour of God, that ye may be able to withstand in the evil day, and having done all, to stand.' 'Having done all!' What does he mean? 'Having done all' means 'having fought'. The Christian has put on the whole armour of God, he is filled with the strength and the power, and he has fought the battle in the evil day. Then having done all, he is tempted to take off his armour. 'I have gained the victory,' he says, 'all is well.' Then, taking off his armour, he lies down on his bed. 'No,' says the Apostle, 'having done all – stand!' Go on standing. Do not relax. 'Maintain the field', as Martin Luther puts it at this point. 'Maintain the field!' You are always on duty in the Christian life, you can never relax. There is no such thing as a holiday in the spiritual realm. Beware of overconfidence, because you have had a great victory. Paul says in 1 Corinthians 10:12: 'Let him that thinketh he standeth take heed lest he fall.' Never relax, never give way; having done all things, go on standing, that is to say, maintaining the position. To relax is a very real danger. I hear many foolish, evangelical people saying: 'We are winning all along the line, things are going well.' Are they? Does the state of the world prove the claim? Or the state of the Church? Many a man has been defeated immediately after his greatest victory. He foolishly put off the armour and settled down to have a rest and a quiet time. 'Having done all things, go on standing', ever; always be on the alert and ever ready for this most subtle foe.

May God give us grace to apply these things to ourselves. I have been indicating some of the things to avoid; for if you fail to do so you will soon lose your strength, you will become limp and weak. It was because he failed to do so that Samson fell into some of the pitfalls and traps against which I have been warning you. He lost his strength because he was not sufficiently careful as to the company he kept. May God preserve us; may God give us grace and wisdom to apply these things!

11

'Stand therefore'

'Finally, my brethren, be strong in the Lord, and in the power of his might.'

Ephesians 6:10

We are now in a position to sum up our consideration of the first particular exhortation in this statement. For this purpose I call attention to a word that is used in these very verses themselves, namely, the word *stand* in the eleventh verse. Having been told to 'be strong in the Lord, and in the power of his might', we are told to 'put on the whole armour of God' in order that we may be able to 'stand against the wiles of the devil'. Then again in verse thirteen: 'Wherefore take unto you the whole armour of God, that ye may be able to *withstand*.' It conveys the same idea with something added to it. 'Stand against', 'withstand', all the things that are likely to meet you, particularly in the 'evil day', 'and having done all, to *stand*'. Then the Apostle goes on: '*Stand*. therefore!' In other words we have this particular exhortation in this immediate context four times; and at the beginning of verse fourteen he is really summing it all up, as if to say: Now the summary of all I have been saying is this, 'Stand therefore!'

It puts emphasis particularly upon the first exhortation, to 'be strong in the Lord, and in the power of his might'. We shall need the armour also, but the great thing is that we have to stand thus fully equipped against the devil and against his nefarious forces. This is the great call that comes to all of us who are Christians. We are called to be victors in the fight, indeed to be 'more than conquerors' over everything that is set against us. This one word sums up the exhortations of the New Testament, stated though they may be, in a variety of forms. It is all designed to this end, that we should be enabled to 'Stand'.

The 'order for the day' for all Christian people is 'Stand!' 'Stand therefore!' – We have seen already the frequency of the use of military terms in the New Testament Epistles. We are not regarded there as sick people, we are always addressed as people who should be healthy, and who are to stand. The image that you should keep in your mind is that of a barracks, a training ground. We must think of ourselves as troops, as soldiers, as people in the army of the living God. What a difference it would make to the Christian Church if she viewed herself in this manner! The world outside is not interested in Christianity, for it thinks that it is something sentimental, sloppy, and spineless. Do our lives suggest that there is some truth in the criticism? Are we guilty of a kind of softness which is an utter misrepresentation of Christian truth? That should not be the case, for all the exhortations here, as I am showing, partake of the military character. We are to rouse ourselves, we are to 'stand'.

Let us look, therefore, and see something of the content and force of this word. Its first suggestion is that we must not feel disappointed and unhappy because there is a conflict, because there is a battle. Many Christian people seem to be disappointed when they find that the Christian life is a fight. They seem to have got the idea that from the moment you become a Christian you will never encounter any problems or difficulties; there will be no fight, there will be no struggle; effort will not be required. So when they find that, on the contrary, they have grave difficulties and a mighty battle they are utterly discouraged. And, of course, the moment that discouragement enters, they are already made weak, and in danger of becoming slack and lethargic. Soon they tend to mope and to be sorry for themselves, and to ask why this should happen to them. The very tone of voice in which they raise the query indicates that they are already defeated.

The Apostle's word comes to such people and calls on them to 'stand', to pull themselves together, to brace themselves for conflict. The Apostle Peter deals with the same position in his First Epistle, where he says: 'Beloved, think it not strange concerning the fiery trial which is to try you, as though some strange thing happened unto you' (1 Peter 4:12). Indeed it is quite

obvious as one reads these New Testament Epistles that such
words had to be spoken constantly to the first generation of
Christians. This is quite clear in the case of The Epistle to the
Hebrews. Those Hebrew believers were asking, Why is this
happening to us? We are being persecuted by our fellow-
countrymen, the Jews; everything is against us; we have been
robbed. We thought when we came into this Christian life that
there would be no more trouble, no problems, nothing to
disturb our happiness. The result was that they were beginning
to find their faith shaken and to look back to their old Jewish
religion. Similarly there is no real key to the understanding of the
Book of Revelation except this selfsame idea. The Book of
Revelation is a prophecy of the kind of life that Christian people
will always have in this world of time until the very end, because
of the devil and his powers, and because of the ravages of sin in
human nature. In various ways and by a diversity of symbols the
forces set against us are portrayed and we are shown exactly
what we must expect. In the same way the Apostle Peter writes,
'Beloved, think it not strange concerning the fiery trial which is
to try you' (1 Peter 4:12) – do not be surprised; because if you are
you will already be defeated.

Nothing is more important than that we should recognize the
inevitability of trials and troubles and conflicts in this world
because of the devil and because of sin. Therefore, whenever we
find ourselves tending to be discouraged, and to feel that we have
a sense of complaint and of grudge that the Lord does not seem
to be fulfilling His promises to us, that very moment we must
heed this exhortation to 'Stand!' 'Pull yourself together', 'brace
yourself up'. We must not give way to the self-pitying thoughts
that come crowding into our mind and heart. As Christians we
should never feel sorry for ourselves. It matters not what our
position may be, or what may be happening to us, we must
never feel sorry for ourselves. The moment we do so, we lose our
energy, we lose the will to fight, and the will to live, and are
paralysed. However strong you may be, once you give way to
such a feeling, you are already losing something of your vital
energy.

So this word comes as a strong exhortation to us to get rid of
all lassitude. 'Away dull sloth and melancholy.' We all need this

word. We recognize that certain practical things are sinful, and we would not dream of doing them. But let us remember that one of the greatest sins is the sin of self-pity, being sorry for oneself and allowing thoughts to enter into the mind which cast doubt upon God's love and goodness and care for us. Never think it strange or surprising that the life into which you have come is a life in which you have these difficulties. This same Apostle Paul, in writing to Timothy makes this quite explicit. He says: 'Yea, and all that will live godly in Christ Jesus shall suffer persecution' (2 Timothy 3:12). Indeed in the Epistle to the Philippians it is put as clearly as this: 'Unto you it is given in the behalf of Christ, not only to believe on him, but also to suffer for his sake' (Philippians 1:29). The same Apostle, we are told at the end of chapter 14 of the Book of the Acts of the Apostles, when making a round of the churches, reminded them of this, 'that we must through much tribulation enter the kingdom of God'.

There then is our first deduction from this great and rousing word 'Stand!' Indeed I can go further and almost say this – that because we are Christians we are to expect more difficulties, in some senses, than other people. The man of the world, the man who is without new life in Christ, is not attacked by the devil and his hosts as we are. Because we are Christians the devil is unusually active with respect to us; and therefore of all people we should be the least surprised when these things happen to us.

A second deduction is that not only must we not be surprised, we must not be frightened. 'Stand' says the Apostle. The man who is frightened is not seen standing; he is half running away already, he is terrified, he is alarmed. 'Stand', says the Apostle. It does not mean that you underestimate the devil and his power. Paul goes out of his way to tell us not to do so. That is why he enters into detail about the character and the nature of these powers. He is not advocating foolhardiness. We must realize to the full the nature of the power which opposes us. But – and this is the wonder of the Christian message – though we realize that the power is so great and so terrible and so mighty, second only to the power of God Himself, we still are exhorted not to be frightened.

This is so because of the reality of the power that is in us, and

[158]

that undergirds us. We are enabled to resist the devil. This is stated clearly in the First Epistle of Peter: 'Be sober, be vigilant; because your adversary the devil as a roaring lion, walketh about seeking whom he may devour' (1 Peter 5:8–9). But the exhortation is, 'Whom resist, steadfast in the faith'. James gives a similar exhortation: 'Resist the devil, and he will flee from you' – though he is indeed a roaring lion! How important it is that we should realize this! Important psychologically! Whenever you are frightened you are already defeated. The moment you begin to quake and to shake and to indulge thoughts of possible defeat, your energy is simply pouring out of you, it is being wasted and dissipated. So we need this exhortation to 'stand'. 'In nothing terrified by your adversaries!' (Philippians 1:28). You just do not allow this as a Christian. In other words realize that you are 'strong in the Lord, and in the power of his might', that you are a part of this Body which is controlled and governed and fed by the Head out of which all power comes. You are 'in Christ' and His power is in you through the Spirit. Realize that, and then you are strong. The Apostle expresses it in this striking way – 'Stand!' Before we have time to work out the argument we must simply 'Stand'. It has a kind of electric effect upon us immediately. There we are, tending to quiver and to tremble and to quake; and in that condition the enemy can do what he likes with us. But suddenly we are told to 'Stand'; and immediately we brace ourselves for the battle once more. As Christians, we must never be frightened.

This is what we may call the paradox of the Christian position. The Christian at one and the same time realizes how terribly weak he is, and yet how tremendously strong he is. In and of himself, helpless; but in the power of the Lord and His might, invincible, 'more than conqueror'. Therefore when depressing thoughts come, and when the devil tries to terrorize us like a lion, and roars at us, let us remember the exhortation to 'Stand'. We must not allow him to frighten us. 'The whole world', says the Apostle John in his First Epistle, 'lieth in the evil one' – in his embrace. 'But he cannot touch us' (1 John 5:18–19). We have to remind ourselves of this; he cannot touch us. We have been translated out of his kingdom into 'the kingdom of God's dear Son'. He can roar, but he cannot touch us. Therefore let him roar. Stand! 'Resist him in the faith.' Though he is the devil, and though you are very weak, you are made strong. He can do nothing when you remind him of the blood of Christ which is upon you, and of the power which is in you as the result of your relationship to Him. Stand! Oh that we might all hear this word as the devil comes and tries to tempt us or entice us! Whatever may be tempting you, or trying you, you need not fail, or falter, or fall into temptation. Stand! – Don't be frightened!

But this word 'stand!' also suggests that we must not be half-hearted and uncertain. Do not slouch, do not droop; stand at your post. We must never be half-hearted or uncertain in the fight. If you are doubtful about the warfare in which you are engaged you will fight very badly. That has often happened; it has happened in nations, and also in the case of individuals. Any doubt or uncertainty or hesitation with regard to what we are engaged in, will deprive us of our energy and more or less paralyse us. So the call to stand is another way of bringing us to realize clearly what the position is. In other words, it is another way of telling us, once more, that we must remember what it means to be a Christian. We must have a clear understanding of the Christian life. The Church of God is very largely as she is today because there are so many people in her who do not quite know why they belong to her ranks. Many are there simply because of their upbringing. They do not understand it, and it is against the grain; half the time they wish that they were not Christians and that they had never heard of the faith. They see other people, whom they know, who do certain things and enjoy them because they were never brought up in a Christian atmosphere; and they are almost sorry that they themselves are Christians because that is what they would really like to do. Surely all in that condition are already defeated because they are half-hearted.

If Christianity is a task, if to worship God in His house is something that we have to force ourselves to do, we are already defeated. We are not 'standing'. We are staggering, and slouching; we are having to be held up by other people, we are being carried along by some momentum other than our own. That is the position with many; they are not clear in their minds about these things.

Anyone who claims to be a Christian, who feels that the New Testament teaching is narrow, is proclaiming that he or she does not really know anything about it. If you are kicking against the teaching of the New Testament, and trying to do the minimum, it is a confession that you are not 'standing', that you have a divided mind, that you are half-hearted, that you are uncertain in your whole attitude.

The Bible condemns that condition wherever found. The Psalmist says: 'Ye that love the Lord hate evil.' Hate it! Not only don't do it, but hate it! And if we know anything in reality about the Lord we must hate evil. God hates it. The difference between God and evil, God and the devil, is the difference between light and darkness. 'Thou art of purer eyes than to behold evil, and canst not look on iniquity' (Habakkuk 1:13). 'God is light, and in him is no darkness at all.' And you and I say that we are children of God!

We must look at these things and remind ourselves of them. Stand up, realize that you are a child of God, and that the world and the flesh and the devil are set against you. Get it clear in your mind and then you will brace yourself to the task and to the duty. In the Epistle of James we read: 'Know ye not that the friendship of the world is enmity against God?' And it is true of necessity. The world is against God. 'The world' means, life, outlook, everything that is organized by the devil and his powers. It is altogether against God. And James tells you that if you are a friend of the world, to that extent you are an enemy of God. You are trying to have a foot in both camps at one and the same time. You are in the Church, and you are in the world; you are for God, you are for the devil. You are like a man of double mind and you are useless. You are like a wave of the sea tossed to and fro. But, 'you cannot serve God and mammon', you cannot be in light and in darkness at the same time. The Apostle John speaks even more strongly about this: 'He that saith, I know him [the Lord], and keepeth not his commandments, is a liar' (1 John 2:4). Now that is plain speaking, but it is the New Testament way of teaching holiness. Scripture does not just comfort and pat you on the back and say that you are doing very well, and urge you to try to do a little better. Not at all; but 'you are a liar'. Does that shock you? We must not have this divided, double mind. 'The friendship of the world is enmity against God.' So John goes on, 'Love not the world, nor the things that are in the world – the lust of the flesh, and the lust of the eyes, and the pride of life' (1 John 2:15ff). These, he says, are not of the Father, they have got nothing to do with God at all, they are the exact antithesis of godliness. Therefore have nothing to do with them.

Are we quite happy about these precepts? are we wholeheartedly in this matter? Are we proud of ourselves because we come to church on Sunday morning? Do we take pride in ourselves, instead of being proud of the fact that we have the privilege of worship because we are God's people? Is worship in spirit and truth against the grain? Do you have to force yourself to it? If not, then you are in line with Scripture, you are standing. But if you do, then the exhortation is spoken to you – Stand!' Do not be half-hearted, do not be half in and half out. Be 'all out', be thorough! It is a totalitarian demand that comes to us; so let us give a total full response to it. Our Lord calls for complete allegiance: 'Thou shalt love the Lord thy God with all thy heart and with all thy soul and with all thy mind and with all thy strength' (Mark 12:30). Do not keep anything back from Him. He wants it all; give Him all. Stand, brace yourself, take up your position. It is all here in this one word.

Then let me suggest a fourth meaning of the word 'stand'. It follows, of course, from all I have been saying. Having got rid of the things that prevent your standing properly, never give even a thought to possible retreat. A General who is planning a campaign and looking back over his shoulder to possible retreat will probably have to retreat. He is already defeated before the battle is joined. We must never be guilty of such conduct. There are no backdoors in the spiritual life, and you must never turn your back to the enemy. 'Stand!' The world is full of backdoors at the present time. It seems at times that the majority of people who are getting married today are already thinking of divorce even as they are getting married. That is why there is such a breakdown of morality today. Certain doors should be bolted and barred, never to be opened again. You must not look back at all, look forward. You are facing the enemy; do not think of retreat. Never toy with even the possible thought of failure; it is utterly opposed to this teaching.

Do not talk or think too much about your weakness or your defeats, or the weaknesses and failures of others. It is depressing to do so, and it is bad propaganda. The enemy's agents like us to do so, and he has them amongst us everywhere. He has his spies, and they insinuate thoughts and make suggestions, and try to depress us by telling us of the greatness of the enemy and our weakness, and so on. We certainly have to take note of these things: but do not talk too much about them. Let us not spend too much time in holding one another's hands. Does this sound harsh? But this is New Testament teaching. If the Church gives the impression to the world that she is but a collection of people who are holding one another's hands and saying nice, comforting, sentimental things, she is finished and useless in a world such as this is today. The devil and his forces are active, and we need to fight! The Church is not a place in which people do little but sympathize with one another; that is a totally wrong conception of the Christian Church.

> *Onward, Christians, onward go,*
> *Join the war, and face the foe.*

Notice how the hymn puts the matter, and how rightly it puts it! And again:

> *Shrink not, Christians! Will ye yield?*
> *Will ye quit the painful field?*
> *Will ye flee in danger's hour?*
> *Know ye not your Captain's power?*

We must not even think of fleeing in danger's hour. Many have done so of course. That is why the Church in this country is as weak as she is today. The 'passengers' tend to drop off, the people who do not know why they are in the Church always go at such a time as this. In the end that is good, of course, and the Bible shows that it is a part of God's method. Remember what He did with the army of Gideon, how drastically He reduced it until it had almost come to nothing; and then God used it. That is His way! There must never even be a suspicion of a

[163]

thought of a possible retreat. It should be unthinkable in the case of the Christian Church, and in the case of Christian individuals.

In the light of all this, my fifth point is: Take up your position and always be alert at it. 'Stand!' There are many thoughts here. The Apostle Peter's exposition of this word is, 'Be sober . . .' That is not a reference to the matter of not being drunk with wine or with alcohol. That is included, but that was not uppermost in the mind of the Apostle. He means, 'Be free from every form of mental and spiritual drunkenness'. Not physical only, but mental and spiritual drunkenness! Do we not know something about this? Mental drunkenness means that you are harbouring so many defeatist thoughts and so many discouraging ideas that you become incapable of doing anything. You are paralysed, you are like a man who is 'paralytic drunk'. There are people who say, 'I don't know where I am, I do not know what to do'. They are like drunken people. They have not taken any alcoholic drink, but they are suffering from mental drunkenness, confused by many thoughts and possibilities and ideas. They are so muddled that they cannot take action. Mental drunkenness!

The same thing happens in the spiritual realm. To be sober means that you are well-balanced, that you are not staggering mentally or spiritually, not being 'carried about by every wind of doctrine', not being upset when you hear something that you have never heard before. It means self-control, to be self-possessed under all circumstances. The characteristic of drunkenness, whether it is physical, or spiritual, or mental is that the person cannot control himself. He says things, and does things that he should not. He does not think things out, he has no balance, he lacks complete understanding, he acts on the first impulse that comes. That is to be drunk; so the command to the Christian soldier is, 'Be sober'. A man who is standing on duty, a sentinel, must of necessity be sober. He has to be in full control of himself. His mind, his thought, his energy, must be concentrated upon his task.

So Peter adds another word, 'Be vigilant'. That means 'keep wide awake'. A sentry who is half asleep at his post is not only a danger to himself but to the whole of the army and everything that is being protected. He may have to be on duty for a long time, and he may be feeling very tired and weary, so it may be that he leans against the door at his post. But the enemy suddenly comes, catches him dozing, and so gains an entry. Be on the alert, be watchful! The New Testament constantly emphasizes this – 'Watch!' 'Watch ye!' 'Be vigilant!' Be on the alert, be wide awake, stand! You cannot afford to relax, because if you do you will probably sleep. The only way to keep yourself awake is to stand. Brace yourself up and make sure that you are standing, and in perfect control, and that you are always watching. You have a very subtle foe. He may come at you from any direction – keep awake, watch and pray! Do not relax the tension for a moment, but always be vigilant.

These are the New Testament terms. How different they are from what we have often thought! But let us listen to the Scriptures; these are the divine exhortations that come to us as they came to the first Christians. Be vigilant, be sober, because of the character and the nature of your enemy. In other words watch for his very first approach; attack him and resist him at once without any hesitation. If you once begin to listen to the devil he has captured you. Do not listen to him, do not take a single sentence from him; at the first approach reply immediately, as our Lord in the Temptation, and you will beat him. But if you once begin to accept any of his suggestions, if you once begin to reason or to argue, he has already defeated you. Fire at him immediately whatever he says. He will say that he is coming as a friend, he wants to make overtures, he has a suggestion . . . Do not listen to him. Fire! He is always the enemy, he is always a liar, he is always 'the father of lies', he is 'a liar from the beginning'. Have nothing to do with him in any respect. Be vigilant, be sober, always ready, always alive, alert, fully awake, and watching in all directions. Do not become weary, do not think the battle long, do not begin to say: 'Is there no end to this?' The answer is, Stand, go on! 'Onward, Christians, onward go.'

Finally, realize the privilege of being in such a fight. Not only stand, but stand proudly. Indeed, you cannot stand without standing proudly. It is in the word itself – 'Stand!' because it is such a tremendous privilege. The cause of God is something worth standing for. The Apostle Paul himself calls it 'the good

[165]

fight' of faith (2 Timothy 4:7). 'Fight the good fight of faith!' And if that does not make us 'stand', what will? Think of the kingdom to which you belong, think of your whole position. If we but realized this we would never be half-hearted, we would never slouch. We should be so filled with pride, and a sense of glory at the great privilege that is given to us, that there would be no need to exhort us to stand; we would be standing already. I have at an earlier point mentioned the order for the day issued by Nelson on the morning of Trafalgar: 'England expects that every man this day will do his duty.' Remember what you are fighting for, remember the Cause. The fact is, it is God's battle. We are not fighting a personal fight; this is not some personal skirmish. We are fighting the battle of the Lord. 'The battle is not yours, but God's.' Christianity is not our affair, it is God's; and the Christian Church as an army, is the army of the living God. Israel in her great days always fought in that way – she fought as the army of the living God.

Recall the story of David and Goliath, and how David said to Goliath: 'Thou comest to me with a sword, and with a spear, and with a shield: but I come to thee in the name of the Lord of hosts, the God of the armies of Israel, whom thou hast defied'. Remember too the cause of Gideon and the battle-cry – 'The sword of the Lord, and of Gideon'. It is God's battle; and what we are fighting for is the name and the glory of God. That type of 'Holiness teaching' which comes to us first of all as something for ourselves is wrong at the outset. You should be concerned primarily not about having help for yourself, but about the battle of the Lord, God's battle. That is the way to start. 'Stand', realizing that it is God's battle. We must not be too subjective, as we tend to be. In the first instance we start with God, and then we shall very soon understand and solve our own problem. We are fighting in the name of God for the glory of God. The devil is not primarily our enemy, he is the enemy of God. It was against God he lifted up himself, it was against God that he rebelled; and it is against God that he wages the conflict. He uses us in our ignorance and folly to attack God. It is God who made us, and God who redeemed us at tremendous cost; and if the devil can defeat us he defeats God. The battle is not ours, and you and I have the privilege of fighting this battle – 'the battle of the Lord'.

And so we are bidden to 'stand'. You and I, such as we are, are being given the privilege of fighting one of the battles of the Lord God Almighty! The devil is plainly trying to drag the whole world down at the present time. Cannot you see him apparently succeeding, and the Name of God being blasphemed or else utterly ignored? Why do we attend church? Is it merely to get benefits? That should not be our first motive; our primary aim should be to fight against the enemy of God, this devil, this Satan, this hell that is let loose in the universe. It is through us that God is waging this warfare. 'Stand therefore.' But remember, too, that the devil is also *our* greatest personal enemy and adversary. He is our accuser, 'the accuser of the brethren'.

Take a second thought. Who is your Captain? your Leader? The Captain of our salvation is none other than the Son of God, the Lord Jesus Christ Himself. What a difference the general and the leader make! We all knew something of that during the last world war; a change in leadership often makes a vital difference. Men have confidence in the new leader, and the same men who were defeatist and on the run, as it were, before, receive new strength and power from the new arrival. The Imperial French Army, it seems, could always tell by instinct when Napoleon was present. The mere presence of the 'Little Corporal' always galvanized the energy of the troops. Multiply that by millions and by infinities, and you begin to realize that we are being led by the Lord Jesus Christ.

> *O loving wisdom of our God,*
> *When all was sin and shame,*
> *A Second Adam to the fight*
> *And to the rescue came.*

Here is 'The Captain of our salvation'. He came down to earth in order to lead us in this battle. And we are standing behind Him, we are with Him, He is our leader.

Or think of it in this way. We are engaged in the same fight as He was engaged in Himself when He was in this world, 'tempted in all points like as we are, yet without sin'. If ever anyone was confronted by disappointments and the misunderstanding of friends; if ever anyone was maligned and persecuted, His own friends running away from Him because they did not understand

His teaching, it was the Son of God Himself! We are following such a Captain, we are in the same kind of conflict. As a hymn reminds us:

> *It is the way the Master went,*
> *Should not the servant tread it still?*

We can sum it all up by saying that we are fighting for the honour of the faith. Paul writes: 'Even as it is meet for me to think this of you all, because I have you in my heart; inasmuch as both in my bonds, and in the defence and confirmation of the gospel, ye all are partakers of my grace' (Philippians 1:7). Verse 27 also: 'Only let your conversation be as it becometh the gospel of Christ.' What a phrase! Live in such a way, the Apostle says, as is becoming to, fits in with, the gospel of Christ, 'that whether I come and see you, or else be absent, I may hear of your affairs, that ye stand fast in one spirit' – holding the line, everyone standing alert, nobody slouching, nobody retreating – 'with one mind striving together for the faith of the gospel'. The gospel of Jesus Christ, its honour, its reputation, its glory, is in your hands and mine. You read in the newspapers frequently that there is a division in the councils of the West at the present time; and the newspaper writers say, 'There is laughter in Moscow' concerning us. Of course there is! They are very happy when they see division in the West. And when you and I fall there is rejoicing in hell. 'There is rejoicing in heaven over one sinner that repenteth.' Yes, and there is rejoicing in hell when any child of God falls or quits or fails to stand. The honour of the faith, the glory of the faith, is in our hands. 'Stand therefore.' Do not think so much about yourself; remember what and whom you represent.

My last word is this: Think of the crown of glory that is awaiting you. Do you feel the battle is long? Are you weary, are you tired, and, at times, struggling in the heat and burden of the day, do you feel that you are forsaken? If so, listen to the Apostle as he writes in the last chapter of the last Epistle he ever wrote – the Second Epistle to Timothy: 'I am now ready to be offered, and the time of my departure is at hand. I have fought a good fight, I have finished my course, I have kept the faith.' He had not slept; he stood – 'Henceforth there is laid up for me a crown of righteousness, which the Lord, the righteous judge, shall give me at that day'. But, you may say, this is only for the Pauls of the Church, there are not many such, indeed there is only one. He may have a crown of righteousness, but who am I? Listen: 'And not to me only, but unto all them also that love his appearing.' There is a day coming when you and I shall be given a crown of glory from the hand of the blessed Lord Himself, and we shall hear the words: 'Well done, thou good and faithful servant; enter into the joy of thy Lord.' You will kneel before Him, and He will put the garland upon your head, the garland and the crown given to every victor in the fight, to all men and women who, realizing that they had the privilege of fighting His battle, maintaining His Cause, in His glorious army, have stood, and gone on standing. 'Stand therefore', knowing that 'The crowning day is coming, bye and bye'.

12

The Whole Armour of God

'Put on the whole armour of God, that ye may be able to stand against the wiles of the devil.'

Ephesians 6:11

Having dealt with the first exhortation – 'Be strong in the Lord, and in the power of his might' – we now come to the second which emphasizes the importance of 'taking' to us and 'putting on' 'the whole armour of God'. Note that the Apostle first of all puts this exhortation in general, and then, from verse fourteen onwards, he proceeds to deal with it in detail, giving us instructions about particular portions of this armour. This is very characteristic of him; he puts the whole first and then he takes the individual parts.

My first comment must inevitably be that the very fact that this armour is needed at all, and that we are told to avail ourselves of it, is surely a very striking confirmation of all that we have seen and learned in dealing with the first exhortation. There, we were at pains to emphasize that we are in a fight, a conflict, and that we have to do the fighting. 'We wrestle.' If this were something that is done for us, then we should not need the armour, we would just look on, as it were, and reap the fruits and benefits of the victory. The very fact that we are told to clothe ourselves in the armour, that we have to put on each piece, and are more or less told how to use each piece, brings home again that part of the teaching which emphasizes that every one of us is engaged in this battle, and that the first thing we have to learn as Christians is how to 'fight the good fight of the faith'. We are in it, we can never contract out of it, and therefore it behoves us to make certain that we know exactly what to do.

My second comment – I have already hinted at it several times – can be stated in the form of a question. Why does the Apostle put these two things in this particular order – 'Be strong in the Lord, and in the power of his might' first, and then the armour in the second place? That, to me, is not only an interesting but a very important and vital question. The answer must be that the first thing we have to do is to deal with the whole situation. We start with the whole before we come to the individual parts. In the first exhortation Paul has been dealing with our general resistance to the enemy. Having dealt with this, he is then in a position to deal with the particulars.

The analogy of a war or a great campaign will help us to understand this point, for the relationship between the first and the second exhortation is precisely that between strategy and tactics in the art or science of war. You should always start with strategy and not with tactics. In other words, you must have an over-all picture, you must consider the enemy in his totality, and your general strategy must cover the whole field. It is only after you have started with strategy that you can rightly proceed to the realm of tactics which is more concerned with particular fronts, particular sectors, particular movements, particular methods and ways of attack. This is a most fascinating subject. You will find in the history of war that there has been many a general who has been very good as tactician but who might be a positive menace and danger if he were made supreme commander and put in charge of the strategy. The latter calls for a different type of mind, and demands a different outlook. A man who may be very good at local dispositions may fail in his grasp and understanding of the whole theatre of war. That seems to me to be the distinction which we have here between these two things. First and foremost the Apostle is saying to us, 'Well, now, there is your enemy, and you have to be in every way fit to fight in the war. Before you begin to fight you must be possessed of the strength which can only come from the Lord and "the power of his might".' This is the general requirement. Then you come down to the level of the particulars.

But there is another reason for the Apostle's method; it is the difference between the positive and the negative. In talking about being 'strong in the Lord, and in the power of his might' the

Apostle, as we have seen, is dealing with the question of building us up, and making us strong and capable and ready to do everything we have to do in this great fight. That is positive. But in this matter of the armour the outlook is somewhat more negative. You are waiting for something to happen to you. Or, to use other terms, it is the difference between the offensive and the defensive. The strength, and the power of his might, is an 'offensive' characteristic, but the armour is in the main, and almost exclusively, concerned with our protection, and the defensive side of our skirmishing and struggling and wrestling with the devil and the principalities and powers.

So, I repeat, it is not surprising that the Apostle uses this order. The positive should always come, in this particular matter, before the negative. We are not here concerned with analysis of truth, but with the fight and the call to battle, and are bound to start with the positive and follow it with the negative. In other words, if you enter into this spiritual conflict on the defensive only, and have entirely forgotten the offensive and the positive, you are already defeated. We have seen that in working out the first principle. The exhortation is to 'stand', to 'resist'; not to be afraid of this enemy though he is as a 'roaring lion'. We are to 'resist him steadfast in the faith'. If we fail to put the positive before the negative, the offensive spirit before the defensive, we have become defeatist; and that, of course, is always fatal. Therefore we cannot but admire the excellence of the strategy which is put before us here by the Apostle.

But there is a third reason why it is quite inevitable that the first exhortation should come before the second. It is, simply, that none of us could possibly use this armour if we had not first been given the strength. You need to be strong in order to use the armour. If you clothe the weakling in this kind of armour it will make him quite helpless and useless. He will have to use so much of his energy in trying to handle and to move inside the armour, that he will not have energy left to deal with the enemy. In other words, this armour is of such a character that you have to be capable of using it. So you start with the exhortation to 'be strong in the Lord, and in the power of his might'.

This is a most important principle in respect to Christian life and Christian living. If we neglect this matter of our personal strength and deal immediately with these various exhortations about the armour, we shall find that we are utterly defeated. The principle works out in the following way. We shall see that this armour consists partly in the understanding of doctrine and the right use of it. Many people are very capable in the matter of handling doctrine, nevertheless they are defeated in their Christian lives, simply because they have forgotten something that is more important still, namely, their spirits. You can put yourself right in this and in other respects intellectually but if, as a whole, you are not right, if you are not filled with this glorious power we have been considering, your expert handling of particular portions of the armour will finally avail you nothing. So the Apostle for these three reasons mentions our being 'strong in the Lord, and in the power of his might' before he bids us 'Take the whole armour of God'.

But why is this armour necessary at all? Why is it not sufficient to tell us to 'be strong in the Lord, and in the power of his might'? There are many who teach just that. They stop at Paul's first exhortation and never proceed to the second. Their idea is that if you are strong in the Lord, and in the power of His might, no more is necessary. They preach nothing but the need of power and are really not concerned about exposition of the Scriptures in detail. To them that does not seem to be necessary. They have a magic formula, and once you have accepted it you have every-thing. So they do not really know their Scriptures, they fail to expound them, they do not see the importance of every single item. They say, 'Once you get this power all is well, nothing can stand against it'. But the Apostle, having told us to 'be strong in the Lord, and in the power of his might' goes on to say twice for emphasis, 'Take unto you [put on] the whole armour of God!' And the reason for his exhortation is that we need protection. The strength alone is not sufficient, wonderful though it is; we still need the protection which is provided by this armour. In other words we have to realize that, as long as we are in this world, defence against the subtle attacks of the enemy is a constant necessity never to be neglected.

The Bible is full of this particular type of teaching. Take, for instance, what this same Apostle says in his First Epistle to the Corinthians: 'Therefore let him that thinketh he standeth take heed lest he fall' (10:12). He pictures a very strong man who thinks he stands. 'I have power', he says, 'what more do I need? I have had a great spiritual experience'. He feels he is filled with power. That is a common temptation. After some particularly high and exalted experience there often comes a period of very great danger. You will find this in the history of David, king of Israel, after he had conquered all his enemies and was somewhat elated with pride as the result of such mighty conquests. It was just then that the devil came and tempted him to count the children of Israel; and that led to great trouble and great suffering among his people. The principle which this incident illustrates is taught everywhere in the Bible. When you think that you are strong, and probably invincible, when you have had some great victory, the danger is to feel that nothing more is necessary, that you have become such a strong Christian that you imagine you can easily stand. You forget the exhortation which says, 'Let him that thinketh he standeth take heed lest he fall'.

The downfall of Samson, of some of the greatest saints that figure in the Scriptures, came in this way. It happened to the Apostle Paul himself after the great experience he described in 2 Corinthians 12 about being 'lifted up to the third heaven'. It was then that 'the messenger of Satan' was sent to buffet him, to keep him humble and to safeguard him against trusting to himself and his experiences.

That then is the principle that is brought out here. Though we may be very strong, though we may have grown in grace marvellously, and have had great victories, we must never rely upon that strength and growth, we must never rest upon it, we must never assume we are beyond reach of the enemy. The enemy that is for ever confronting us never admits defeat, and is always watching and waiting for our unguarded moments. He never relaxes, and he commands great powers. It is not the devil only, but also these 'principalities and powers, the rulers of the darkness of this world, the spiritual wickedness even in the heavenly places'. The devil himself is ubiquitous, and his emissaries are everywhere and always watching for a moment of slackness when one is off guard. 'Wherefore', says the Apostle, 'take

unto you the whole armour of God'. Put it on, and keep it on.
Our enemy is not only powerful but is also subtle; and, as we
have seen, his methods and the variety of his weapons are such
that we cannot afford to take anything for granted. We must
never relax. Wherever we are, whatever our circumstances,
whatever we have done, whatever we have to do, there is never
a holiday in the spiritual realm. Though we may feel ourselves to
be thrilling with power, let us be careful! He always knows the
Achilles' heel, the point of weakness. Therefore, though we may
have great strength and power, the Apostle reminds us that
this defensive armour is always an absolute necessity.

To those who are interested in the strategy of war, I would say
that I have often felt that such matters are a great aid to our
understanding of some of these illustrations in the Bible. That
does not mean that you need to be a war-like person, it does not
mean that you are a bloodthirsty person. But the whole art of
warfare is a fascinating subject, and though you may know nothing
in practice about fighting you can understand these matters with
your intelligence. If you have ever read books on that subject
you will have found that in his over-all strategy a general must
never neglect defence. History provides eloquent testimony on
this subject. There have been generals who have been excellent
always when on the offensive; but sometimes their very genius
and brilliance has made them become somewhat neglectful of
their defence; with the result that while they are attacking here
they have ignored the defence there, and the enemy comes in and
causes havoc. Some indirect strategy and approach was employed
by the enemy, and despite his brilliance the general was finally
defeated. We must never neglect defence; and that is why this
'whole armour of God' is so essential.

That brings us to the fourth point, which is to emphasize that it
is called 'the armour of God'. Note how careful Paul is to repeat
the words, 'the whole armour of God'. He does so because this
is the key to the whole situation. Nothing but 'the armour of
God' will ever suffice us in this terrible conflict in which we are
engaged. There is no protection, there is nothing we can do, that
will ultimately protect us against this wily, subtle, powerful enemy

but the armour of God Himself. Essentially, of course, it is the armour that is provided by God. That is the real meaning of the phrase. In other words, you are not left to your own resources and devices. You do not have to think of something new; everything that you need is provided by God.

This is a most comforting and encouraging thought. Whatever may come to meet us in this Christian life, God in His infinite wisdom and kindness has already provided for it. The Apostle Peter says in his Second Epistle in the first chapter that 'all things that pertain unto life and godliness' are already provided for us. Hence we are all without excuse when we fail. There is not a single contingency that can ever be conceived of that has not been dealt with beforehand by the Lord.

But as we look at matters in detail, let us look at them in the first instance negatively. If we try to fight the devil and these powers solely in terms of our own wisdom and understanding we shall inevitably be defeated. Sometimes we are tempted to think that, having read the Scriptures, and having lived the Christian life for a certain length of time, we are now able to deal with the enemy by ourselves. We think we can do so by means of reason, and by argument and common sense, or in terms of psychology or will-power. Let me give one illustration. Take the tendency to worry, to become anxious, and to spend time in worrying about what you may have done in the past or of what may happen to you in the future. The enemy often attacks Christian people in this way. If he can get us to be absorbed in ourselves and our problems – things that once happened, things that may happen – he is quite happy. The moment he gets us to turn in on ourselves, he has plunged us into a vortex in which we go round and round, and become defeated and utterly useless as Christians.

There are those who teach that the way to deal with such an experience is as follows: They say to us, 'Why do you not stop and think? What is the use of crying over spilt milk? The thing is done, you cannot undo it; what is the point, therefore, of thinking about it?' That is obvious common sense, simple, reasonable. But have you ever tried to deal with your problem in that way alone? The whole difficulty facing the person who is attacked by the devil at this point is that that is the very thing he cannot do. He wishes he could do so, but he cannot. He is prepared to admit – 'Yes, I quite agree, as you put it to me I can see that my reaction is utterly ridiculous, it is a waste of energy and I am really very foolish'. And yet he goes on doing it. He just cannot stop doing it because the enemy will not leave him alone. He wears the sufferer down, until he is so tired that he can scarcely think. The fact is that any one of us who imagines that he can argue with the devil is simply showing that he is the merest tyro in the spiritual realm. The moment you start engaging the enemy in argument with your own reason and understanding you are already defeated. He will beat you every time.

It is for that reason that you need 'the armour of God'. All other methods are right up to a point, but the tragedy is that when you need them most of all they do not seem to help you. If you are handling someone else's case all seems simple; but when the trouble comes to you, you somehow cannot see the remedy and you are defeated. There is only one way to fight this battle, and that is with 'the whole armour of God'. The enemy can defeat your mind, your reason, your arguments, your common sense, your psychology, your will-power, everything – and he does so. The only way to obtain real victory is to make use of this 'whole armour of God', which is specially designed to protect us. It does protect us, and nothing else, finally, will protect us. We are dealing with a foe that is inferior in power only to the blessed Holy Trinity, a foe who is altogether above man in brilliance, and mind, and power. Therefore, nothing less than this protection that God provides is adequate to our need.

The second idea conveyed by this term 'the whole armour of God' is that this is a very special type of armour, as the very terms used indicate – 'truth', 'righteousness', 'faith', 'salvation'. Clearly there is only one kind of person who can ever put on and use this armour, and that is the Christian. This is the case not only because he is the only kind of person who is 'strong in the Lord, and in the power of his might', but also because the very nature of the armour makes this quite inevitable. You may know someone who is not a Christian, maybe a relative, or friend or somebody who is brought to you. You can see at once exactly how and why this person is in trouble but you cannot help him. And for this reason, that he is not a Christian. The only method that you know of for dealing with this position, and for meeting with success, is by means of 'the whole armour of God'. But this person cannot use that armour. What is the use of saying to a man who is not a Christian, 'Are your loins girt about with truth?' What is the use of saying to him, 'What you need, of course, is "the breastplate of righteousness".' He does not know what that means, he does not believe in it. So, obviously, he cannot use this armour. It is called 'the whole armour of God' because it is an armour provided by God. It can only be used by the Christian, by the one who is, as it were, initiated into the truth, the one who, having believed, is now in a position to take hold of, to wear, and to use the armour which God provides.

In other words we are led to this point, that this armour consists of an understanding and an application of the truth of the Gospel. We must not think of it, in and of itself, in material terms. The Apostle is using an illustration from the physical realm in order to bring out his point. Notice the terms: the Christian's loins are girt about with truth, he puts on the breastplate of righteousness; his feet are shod with the preparation of the gospel of peace; he carries the shield of faith, he dons the helmet of salvation, he wields the sword of the Spirit, which is the Word of God. Now as every part and portion of this armour is obviously spiritual in its nature it means that it can only be used by a spiritual kind of person.

Here again is something that is constantly verified in practice. You will find as you talk to another, and try to help him, that the first thing you have to do is to get this person to become a Christian. You cannot help him until that happens. In other words all you can do until he becomes a Christian is to use arguments from common sense, and from reason, and from psychology. There is nothing else you can do for him at that point. If he is not a Christian you cannot give him spiritual help. The reason is that he has not the basis of understanding, he has nothing that enables him to put on the armour. It is 'the armour of God'.

All this can be stated as a question. As we examine ourselves and our experience, what do we find we are actually using in this battle? How do we meet our problems and our trials? Are we meeting them as does the natural man, or are we meeting them as does the spiritual man, the man clothed with the whole armour of

God? The world has its own methods for dealing with its problems. That is what makes society possible, and why everything does not collapse. But as the world becomes more and more dark and difficult, and the strain becomes greater, the neuroses also become greater, and the work of the psychiatrist is in greater demand. That is a proof of the inadequacy of the worldly methods. But, up to a point, the world can help. It has its adages and proverbs and maxims – 'It's no use crying over spilt milk'; 'Put on a bright face'; 'I can take it', and so on. All these things are right, up to a point.

But the question is, 'How do you fight?' As a Christian you should always be clad with 'the armour of God'. We should not be fighting this battle in a worldly way or in a merely rational way. Our fighting should always be waged in a spiritual manner. The whole armour of God is provided for us. So let us make sure that we are clad with this whole armour of God, which, ultimately, is an understanding and an application of the truth of the Gospel.

Notice, further, the double emphasis upon the 'whole' armour. 'Put on the *whole* armour of God.' 'Wherefore take unto you the *whole* armour of God.' This again is something of crucial importance. It means that we do not pick and choose in this matter. If you are to be a soldier in this army, if you are to fight victoriously in this crusade, you have to put on the entire equipment given to you. That is a rule in any army. You cannot select which parts of your uniform you are going to put on. If you say, 'I do not think this is going to suit me, I do not quite like that', you know exactly what will happen to you. And that is infinitely more true in this spiritual realm and warfare with which we are concerned. The moment you begin to say, 'I need this helmet, but I do not need the breastplate', you are already defeated. You need it all – 'the *whole* armour of God' – because your understanding is inadequate. It is God alone who knows your enemy, and He knows exactly the provision that is essential to you if you are to continue standing. Every single part and portion of this armour is absolutely essential; and the first thing you have to learn is that you are not in a position to pick and choose.

This means that we take the whole body of Christian doctrine; we do not concentrate on particular parts of it. It is not surprising that the Christian Church is as she is, forming movements to emphasize one doctrine only. That is a crucial part of our whole trouble today. We must take the complete doctrine. The Apostle Paul refers to this in his last words to the elders of this Church at Ephesus as recorded in Acts, chapter 20. He was on his journey to Jerusalem and the elders of Ephesus came down to meet him at Miletus. The Apostle is glad and proud of the fact that he can say that he had declared unto them 'the *whole* counsel of God'. There was nothing he had left unsaid. Similarly, there is no part of Christian doctrine that you and I can afford to ignore. We must study every part of Scripture: and it is good to read the whole Bible every year. Leave nothing out, read the history, read everything. Take every part and portion of the doctrine. Do not stop at evangelism, do not stop at justification, do not stop at sanctification; take in glorification, study prophecy, take the whole doctrine. Nothing causes such weakness and failure in the Christian Church as a failure on our part to put on 'the *whole* armour of God'.

It is also necessary to emphasize that every part of you has to be taken up in this Christian life. For instance, your mind needs the protection of the 'helmet of salvation'. Never neglect the mind in connection with these matters. The notion that Christianity is but a form of emotionalism or some sob-stuff – as the world is so constantly suggesting – is altogether wrong; and if we are giving the world occasion to think and to speak thus, we are very poor soldiers in the Christian army.

But do not stop at the mind. The heart needs protection in the same way. Certain people are very careful to protect the mind; they are experts on theology and on errors and heresy; but they pay no attention to the heart, and the result is that they are often wounded and defeated. They fall by the wayside through neglect of this vital organ.

Similarly with respect to the will. The Apostle Paul, in writing to Timothy, speaks of 'holding faith, and a good conscience; which some having put away concerning faith have made shipwreck' (1 Timothy 1:19). They were paying attention to the intellectual aspect of faith but they were not 'maintaining a good conscience'; they were neglecting the will, and the practical aspect. The result is, Paul says, that they have 'made shipwreck' of their faith and their lives.

'Take unto you the whole armour of God', every part and portion of it, in order that every part of your personality may be covered and protected. There is nothing that should so cause us to rejoice in the Christian life as the fact that it affects the whole man. Nothing else does so. You can find intellectual societies in the world; but they are cold and heartless. There are emotional, sentimental interests in the world; but they have nothing for your mind. Others concentrate on ethics, but they have no spiritual understanding, and they have no comfort and consolation to give us. But the biblical teaching takes up the whole man and governs the entire personality. 'The whole armour of God'!

But having emphasized that, observe how the Apostle is very careful at the same time to enter into details about the various pieces. The 'whole' includes every single piece. Never neglect the details. Leave no unguarded place in the soul – 'Each piece put on with prayer'.

> *Put on the Gospel armour,*
> *Each piece put on with prayer.*

What perfect balance there is here, as there is always in the Scriptures, in the teaching of the Word of God.

That is the balance we are to display as we go on in this spiritual fight and this Christian warfare. As the enemy is still waiting, and watching in all his subtlety, ingenuity and power, there is only one way to stand. 'Be strong in the Lord, and in the power of his might.' Take unto you the whole armour which God has provided for you. Put it on, piece by piece. Leave no unguarded place in your soul, but avail yourself of the full equipment which God in His infinite grace has provided for you in the Lord Jesus Christ and in His great and glorious salvation.

13
'Loins girt about with Truth'

'Stand therefore, having your loins girt about with truth.'

Ephesians 6:14

We come now to the beginning of our detailed study of the 'whole armour of God' which the Apostle has exhorted these Ephesian Christians, and all other Christians, to 'put on'. In withstanding the wiles of the devil, and in wrestling against the principalities and powers and the rulers of the darkness of this world and spiritual wickedness in high places, it is essential, he says, that we should first 'be strong in the Lord, and in the power of his might'. Then, after that, we must 'take unto ourselves, and put on, the whole armour of God'.

Having introduced the subject in general, let me remind you, once more, that what we have here is a picture, an external picture of something which is itself internal and essentially spiritual. The danger with a picture such as this is to materialize it overmuch. Many have fallen into this trap. It is, perhaps, the one real defect in William Gurnall's great book, *The Christian in Complete Armour*. His tendency is to over-elaborate the details. It was, perhaps, the common temptation that confronted the Puritans – the tendency to allegorize overmuch, or to turn a parable into an allegory. We must bear this in mind as we proceed to the interpretation of the significance of these different parts in this whole armour of God. The Apostle as a prisoner was familiar with Roman soldiers and always having to look at them. Chained sometimes to a soldier on the right hand and on the left, it came very naturally to him to use such a comparison and to say, in effect, 'This is a picture of what we have to do in a spiritual sense.'

These pictures, however, have to be handled always in a fairly general manner.

There are six main pieces to this armour altogether. Paul says that we are to have our 'loins girt about with truth', we are to put on 'the breastplate of righteousness', and our feet are to be 'shod with the preparation of the gospel of peace'. Then we are to take up 'the shield of faith', to put on 'the helmet of salvation', and to use 'the sword of the Spirit'. Those are the six pieces mentioned. The Apostle surely never meant this to be exhaustive. There are other aspects to the warfare and to the defence. What he does is to pick out the most important pieces, those that are absolutely essential as we look at this spiritual warfare in general.

As we come to classify these six pieces I tend to agree with the majority of commentators who say that they can be divided into two groups of three. The basis of the division is roughly that the first three are parts that are actually fixed on to the body. The girdle about the loins, for instance, is actually fixed in position on the body. So is the breastplate. They do not hang loosely, or as some loose attachment to the body; they have to be tied, or braced on. The sandals likewise have to be fixed firmly upon the feet. Those three parts of the armour have that feature in common. But when you come to the shield you are obviously dealing with something that is not fixed to the body. The same is true of the helmet. We must not think of the helmet in terms of what is more familiar to us, the kind of helmet that was worn in the Middle Ages. The helmet that was worn at the time of the Apostle consisted of a leather cap with pieces of metal on it which a man placed on his head. It was not fixed; the attachment was not as firm as was the case with the first three pieces. And, obviously, the sword is not fixed and attached to the body. We shall see the significance of that distinction as we proceed with our interpretation of the meaning of the pieces individually.

The only other general comment I make before we come to the detailed consideration of the first piece is that the order in which the pieces are mentioned is of very great importance and significance. The Apostle did not set down these different items at random in a haphazard manner as they might occur to him, or as he looked at a soldier. He builds up a case; and it is essential that we should adopt his method and look at these separate pieces of the armour in the order in which he introduces them to us.

So we start with '. . . having your loins girt about with truth'. The Authorized Version translation in this instance is not as good as it might be; it is misleading in the sense that it puts it in a passive way instead of an active manner. Instead of reading 'Stand therefore, having your loins girt about with truth', as if someone else did it for you, a better translation is, 'Stand therefore, having girded your loins about with truth'. In other words it is we who have to do this. The girdle is not put on us, we have to put it on; and we have to put it firmly in position.

This belt or girdle is to be fixed upon that part of the body known as the loins. It is obvious that it is not to be put on merely for the sake of decoration; it is not an adornment. Belts are often worn purely for adornment, and for the sake of appearance: but that was not at all in the mind of the Apostle. He assures us that this girdle is an absolutely essential part of the equipment; and it is therefore the first thing we have to put on.

The girdle is vital because of its function. Here we have to remember that the Apostle was writing for his own day and generation when it was the custom for people, men included, to wear long and loose garments, something like a Geneva gown, perhaps even longer. Now the purpose of the girdle was to gather up and to bind together these loose garments. That was its essential function. When a man was sitting down and relaxed he took off his girdle; but the moment he wanted to become active he gathered his garments together and fixed them in position by a girdle. He did so because otherwise these flowing garments would have been a hindrance to him. He would constantly be stepping on them; he would be stumbling when trying to handle the sword, or when he held up his shield. So the first thing the soldier always did when he was getting ready to meet the enemy, was to gather all his clothing together and fix it firmly in position by means of this tight band or belt which then held all his clothing in position. And the very putting on of the girdle in and of itself braces one up and prepares one for action.

But still more important is the fact that putting on the girdle frees the soldier for action. He is now unencumbered in all his actions and movements, and is able to hold up his shield with one hand and handle the sword with the other. He need not be afraid that he will trip or fall or become entangled in any part of the garments. It was essential for him to have free and unencumbered action.

In the third place, the girdle gave the soldier a sense of security. He was ready, he was keyed up, he was alert, he was tense, he was toned up for action and felt that everything was in order and in position; he had no mere collection of loose parts militating against what he was proposing to do. That immediately gave him confidence and a sense of security.

You will find that this picture is one which is used frequently in the Scriptures. We find our Lord Himself using it in the twelfth chapter of the Gospel according to St Luke where He is warning His disciples to be ever watchful and wary and careful. It is the same point exactly as the Apostle makes here. Our Lord states it in this way, 'Let your loins be girded about, and your lights burning'. Be ready for action. That is the first step always. Never be caught, He says, in a condition in which you are not ready for action. That is another way of saying, 'Stand therefore, having your loins girt about with truth'. The first thing we have to make sure of is that we are ready for action and prepared for any eventuality that may come.

There is no doubt that the order in which the Apostle puts these things before us is adopted deliberately. It would be idle and useless to proceed to the other parts of the armour unless we are clear about this. There are those who say that the girdle should be interpreted in a still more fundamental sense, that it is a kind of foundation garment; that you start with it and then put other things on top of it. I am prepared to accept that. But what is clear in both cases is that it is foundational, that the soldier cannot hope to do anything without it, that there would indeed be nothing but confusion if he did not start with it and make sure of it – the girdle!

Now we come to the way in which Paul uses this picture of the girdle in a spiritual manner. 'Having girded your loins', he says, 'with truth'. As it is foundational, it is vital to know exactly what he means by 'truth' here. There has been much discussion about the matter. Indeed it is interesting, not to say almost amusing at times, to observe the way in which the expositors deal with it. The trouble, I feel, is that many of them tend to become too rigid about it. This applies, alas, even to Charles Hodge.

In working out the analogy they ask, 'What is meant here by truth?' They reply by saying that your first instinct, of course, is to say that it is the Word of God, the truth of the Scriptures. 'Ah but', they say, 'it cannot be that', and for this reason, that later on Paul says, 'Take the helmet of salvation and the sword of the Spirit, which is the Word of God'. So they argue that the girdle cannot possibly stand for objective truth.

The expositors then go on to say that as the girdle cannot stand for objective truth it must mean something more subjective in us. Here, some of them go so far as to say that it means nothing more than a spirit of sincerity and truthfulness in us. Not so much truth itself as truthfulness in us. As David says in Psalm 51, 'Thou desirest truth in the inward parts – Sincerity! Candour! Truthfulness! Openness! This, they say, is the basis of everything; we have to be honest. The Christian puts on the girdle of truthfulness, of sincerity, of candour, and of openness, because without this he is helpless and hopeless.

But this seems to me to be a very grievous and almost a dangerous misinterpretation. I answer it by saying that the expositors' objection to objective truth here is not valid for this reason – that there are two ways in which we can look upon truth. There is a purely objective way and there is a purely subjective way. But you must not confine it to that. We have to accept the statement, of course, that 'the sword of the Spirit is the Word of God', but I am equally anxious to say that the girdle is also the Word of God looked at in a different manner.

There is a great difference between truth as a whole and truth in its separate portions. Let me illustrate what I mean. Take the phrase 'The sword of the Spirit, which is the Word of God'. There is a perfect illustration of what is meant by the expression in what we see in the temptation of our Lord and Saviour Jesus Christ in the wilderness by the devil. The devil came tempting Him, and our Lord answered him by saying, 'It is written'. There He is using 'the sword of the Spirit, which is the Word of God', but what He actually does is to quote particular scriptures. That is very different from talking about the whole truth of the Bible, the whole truth concerning the doctrine of salvation. I therefore suggest that the girdle represents whole truth, the truth in and of itself. Paul is speaking of truth in an objective manner; but it also comes to us subjectively.

Furthermore, the girdle cannot possibly stand for truthfulness and sincerity and candour for this good and sufficient reason – that if we are going to rely upon our sincerity and truthfulness as the fundamental piece of the armour in the fight with the devil, then we are already defeated and the campaign is lost. The truth about us all, alas, is that expressed in the lines of a hymn, 'I dare not trust the sweetest frame'. Are you prepared to trust yourself? No, we are all in the position of having to say, 'I am what I am by the grace of God'. The foundation piece in my armour is not my own sincerity and truthfulness. It cannot be that, because the Apostle is emphasizing here that it is a piece of armour provided for us by God. It is therefore primarily not a part of ourselves, but something that we are able to put on, something that is given to us.

To interpret the word 'truth' as it is used by the Apostle, let us adopt the method of approach which we should always adopt whenever we find ourselves face to face with a difficulty of this nature. There is a difficulty on the surface; let us grant that. 'The sword of the Spirit, which is the Word of God.' That seems to settle the matter. But it does not! Let us see then whether we can arrive at the meaning of this word 'truth' by searching the Scriptures and comparing scripture with scripture. That is surely the royal method of exposition at all times.

A scripture which comes to mind at once is found in the eighth chapter of the Gospel according to St John. There we read, in verses 30 and following that, 'As he spake these words, many believed on him. Then said Jesus to those Jews which believed on him, If ye continue in my word, then are ye my disciples indeed; and ye shall know the truth, and the truth shall make you free'. Notice the terms our Lord uses. He talks about 'knowing the truth'; in other words, He is speaking about it as a whole – the whole Christian doctrine in its entirety, the full summation of truth. 'And that truth shall make you free', free from the devil. Notice particularly the emphasis. He says: 'You seem to have believed; very well, if you continue in my word, in my instruction concerning the truth, then you will be my disciples indeed, and then the truth, which will thus be imparted to you and which you will be continuing in, will make you free'. In order to be free from the devil and his wiles you must put on the girdle of truth – 'My word'.

But consider also our Lord's phrase in the 'high priestly' prayer recorded in the seventeenth chapter of the Gospel of John and in the seventeenth verse: 'Sanctify them', He says, 'by thy truth: thy word is truth'. Sanctification is by the truth, but it works by means of 'thy word' – this Word of God. What we are dealing with here in Ephesians 6 is sanctification; therefore I maintain that the meaning is exactly the same here as it is in John 8 and in John 17.

Then take another example. The Apostle Paul, in the First Epistle to the Corinthians, chapter 16, verse 13, says, 'Watch ye, stand fast in *the faith*,' the faith! 'The truth' and 'the faith' are virtually synonyms. 'Stand fast in the faith.' Here in Ephesians the exhortation is the same, but it so happens that the alternative term is used – 'Stand therefore, having your loins girt about with truth'. The Apostle is speaking of truth as a whole, for the truth like the faith, is one.

Notice also that the Apostle Peter says a similar thing in his First Epistle to people who were in trouble and in difficulties, and having a great battle against the world, and the flesh, and the devil. Having outlined the whole position he takes up the real argument in the thirteenth verse of the first chapter and he says: 'Wherefore gird up the loins of your mind'. Now the mind deals with 'truth', with 'the faith'. It is illuminating to note how Peter in this same connection uses the expression 'the loins' of the mind exactly as Paul does in our text. Undoubtedly Paul is thinking about the mind rather than the body. Do not materialize the illustration. He is thinking spiritually, so it is the 'loins' of the mind, because the greatest thing in man is his mind, and his mind must receive enlightenment if he is to fight successfully.

Peter repeats his teaching in the fifth chapter of that First Epistle and in verse 9, where he writes about 'your adversary the devil, [who] as a roaring lion, roameth about seeking whom he may devour'. He says, 'Whom resist, steadfast in the faith'. In other words, the first thing to realize is that you can only resist by being 'steadfast in the faith'. And to become steadfast in the faith, you must 'girdle' it upon you, you must bind up yourself and your clothing with 'the faith'. Those examples surely help to throw great light upon the problem facing us. I therefore interpret the word 'truth' in this context to mean a belief in, and a knowledge of, the 'truth as it is in Christ Jesus'. It is the objective truth, which I possess in a subjective manner. It means a mastery of the truth, but it also means being mastered by the truth. I am held by the truth. This is the thing that binds me and holds me together and puts me on my feet and gives me vigour and strength and power. Or, to express it more particularly, it means that I do not merely look at the Bible intellectually and study it as if it were, say, the Works of Shakespeare, but rather that its truth gets hold of me and governs my whole attitude to the world, the flesh, and the devil, and to everything that happens. I have girded myself with it. 'Gird up the loins of your mind, be sober, and hope to the end for the grace which shall be brought unto you', as Peter says.

Truth is the first thing we put on. Without it we are completely lost. It means that we have a settled conviction with regard to the truth; it means that there are no uncertainties, no doubts. It means also that there must be no lack of clarity. There is no hope, Paul says, unless you put this on first. And that means nothing less than that we should know whom we have believed, and we should know what we believe. The girdle is truth – looked on, understood, appropriated, and in such a manner that it governs the whole of my outlook in every respect. Only in this way, says the Apostle, can you possibly fight a successful warfare against the enemy.

This follows of necessity from what we have already considered in our earlier studies. The devil tries to confuse us, to lead us astray with regard to what we believe. He is a 'liar', he is a 'murderer', he is 'the accuser of the brethren', he is 'the adversary'; and, as we have seen, he exercises these nefarious powers with particular subtlety and eagerness in his attempts to create confusion and uncertainty. How does one repel him? 'Gird your loins about with truth!' If you fail to do so, you are defeated almost before you have started to fight.

This principle is illustrated abundantly in Church history. Is it not clear that the need for putting on the girdle of truth had already arisen even in New Testament times? In the early Church the devil early tried to sow the seeds of confusion and of uncertainty. He did it first, of course, with regard to the question of the admission of the Gentiles into the Church. He tried to make the Jewish Christians hold on to circumcision as being absolutely essential, and also other observances of the Law. You can read about that in the Book of the Acts of the Apostles chapter 15, and likewise in the Epistle to the Galatians. The devil came in at the very beginning and tried to sow this seed of doubt. 'Ah', he said, 'it is right to believe in Christ, but if you are not circumcised you are not a true Christian; every one has to become a Jew before he can become a real Christian'. And so confusion tended to come in, and the Apostles had to deal with the problem.

In the twentieth chapter of the Book of the Acts of the Apostles we have an account of the Apostle Paul bidding farewell to the elders of the church at Ephesus. He warns them of what will happen after his departure from them. 'Take heed therefore', he says, 'unto youselves, and to all the flock, over which the Holy Ghost hath made you overseers, to feed the church of God, which he hath purchased with his own blood. For I know this, that after my departing shall grievous wolves enter in among you, not sparing the flock. Also of your own selves shall men arise, speaking perverse things, to draw away disciples after them. Therefore watch, and remember, that by the space of three years I ceased not to warn every one night and day with tears'. Paul had spent much time, teaching and preaching, enlightening them, giving them understanding, because he knew that these evils were certain to arise. The girdle of 'truth' is absolutely essential; you are defeated if you do not have this knowledge.

Then when you come to a somewhat later period in the history of the early Church you find the same thing again. How easy it is at a funeral service to listen thoughtlessly to the reading of that magnificent fifteenth chapter of Paul's First Epistle to the Corinthians! The language is wonderful, and the balance of the sentences, the cadences, and the glory and the beauty of the words fascinate us, and we say 'Marvellous!' But we often fail to realize what the Apostle is saying! He wrote that chapter because there were people who were teaching that there was to be no final resurrection of the body. It is a purely polemical piece of writing. He was writing to counter the attack of the devil upon the doctrine of the resurrection. It was essential that he should do so. He says: 'If in this life only we have hope in Christ, we are of all men most miserable'. He has to write it to counter the subtle attempt of the devil to subtract from the truth.

Paul does the same thing in the second chapter of the Second Epistle to Timothy. He says: 'Certain people in the church are saying that the resurrection is past already; and undermine the faith of some'. What is the remedy? 'The foundation of God standeth sure.' What is that foundation? It is the truth of the Gospel, which he also describes as 'my gospel' (verse 8). It is the only way in which you can answer that particular attack. The New Testament Epistles are in a sense the very girdle that you and I are to put on – 'the girdle of truth'. We have to be equipped with this if we are going to meet this enemy. We need to have the whole truth in our minds. All our thinking must be governed by it, so that when an attack comes we have the answer, and are ready – 'girded about with truth'.

But this problem did not end with the early Church; it continued into later centuries. Read the story of the Christian Church and you will find that certain great Councils were held. Christian leaders came together from different countries in order to define the truth. They did so because heretics had arisen, false teachings were being propagated, and the whole Church was in a state of confusion. No one knew exactly what to believe; one said this, another said that – teachings diametrically opposed – yet they all called themselves Christians. And the early Christians, led by the Holy Spirit, met together in solemn Councils where they defined the truth. They said, this is right, that is wrong. They defined heresy, and condemned it, and excommunicated men who taught it. If they had not done so there would have been no Church today. Greek philosophy came in, and men were trying to understand and to explain what cannot be understood, and explained, and so the heresies arose; and the leaders of the Churches had to meet in Councils.

The result was that we have the so-called great creeds of the Church – for instance, The Apostles' Creed. The Apostles' Creed would never have been written were it not for this very thing we are discussing. The devil in his wiliness had tried to cause confusion in the Church, so they met together and they said, 'These are the essentials of the faith'. Recite it, get it into your mind, put it on, gird yourself with it. But not only the Apostles' Creed, the Nicene Creed also, and the Athanasian Creed. All these Creeds came into being in exactly the same way. That is one way of girding the loins with truth. The Church made sure of the teaching and then tried to ensure that it was preached and taught everywhere.

But such action is not confined to the early Church. The same always happens whenever there is a period of reformation and revival. I suppose that in many ways the greatest characteristic of the Protestant Reformation was the way in which the early Protestant Churches proceeded to draw up their Confessions – the Augsburg Confession, the Belgic Confession, the Second Helvetic Confession, the Heidelberg Catechism, and others. They are all documents which contain definitions of the truth in order that people might know what was right and what was wrong. In England in that same sixteenth century, the Church of England drew up the Thirty-nine Articles. In the seventeenth century the Westminster Assembly drew up its famous Confession of Faith. The Church in every period of revival and awakening, when she is really alive, and realizes the character of the spiritual conflict, has always done this very thing. The drawing up of a Confession is nothing less than a way of 'girding up the loins of your mind', or 'putting on the girdle of truth'.

Such action is essential for a reason which the Apostle himself gives us: 'Evil communications corrupt good manners' (1 Corinthians 15:33). Truth does matter! If you begin to go wrong in your 'communications', in what you say to one another and in your thoughts, it will lead to bad practice, bad manners, and bad behaviour. And eventually you will make shipwreck of the faith. Error in doctrine is always fatal, both in the life of the individual and in the life of the Church. Paul has clearly said in this Epistle to the Ephesians that Christ has given to the Church apostles, prophets, evangelists, pastors and teachers, 'for the perfecting of the saints, for the work of the ministry, for the edifying of the body of Christ, till we all come in the unity of the faith, and of the knowledge of the Son of God, unto a perfect man, unto the measure of the stature of the fulness of Christ'. There the fact is stated positively. But the Apostle immediately adds the negative: 'That we henceforth be no more children, tossed to and fro, and carried about with every wind of doctrine, by the sleight of men, and cunning craftiness, whereby they lie in wait to deceive'. The characteristic of children is that they tend to believe any and every story. A plausible 'nice' man comes selling books at the door and they say, 'It sounds very good, he talks about the Bible, it must be right!' So they buy the books without further investigation. 'Tossed about by every wind of doctrine', because they do not know their own doctrine, because they have not girded their loins about with truth, because they do not know where they stand and on what they are standing.

This, then, is the first particular exhortation with respect to our armour. There is really no hope for us in this fight with the devil, and all his wiles, unless we possess, and are possessed by, the truth. Without a knowledge of what we believe, and of Him in whom we believe, we are already undone, we are already defeated. 'Stand therefore, having girded your loins about with truth.' 'Gird up the loins of your mind.' The girdle is the first in the list of 'the weapons of our warfare'. Let us be resolute to obey the Apostle's exhortation, 'and having done all things, to stand'.

14

The only Authority

'Stand therefore, having your loins girt about with
truth.' (A.V.)
'Stand therefore, having girded your loins with
truth.' (R.V.)

Ephesians 6:14

We have seen that the fundamental reason for starting with the
girdle of truth is what the Apostle says in 1 Corinthians 15:33,
'Evil communications corrupt good manners.' This has been
forgotten in the present century. The whole tendency of this
century has been to say that you can preserve 'good manners'
without truth. But it is impossible! There is no greater fallacy
than to think that you can hold on to the morals and ethics of the
Bible and shed the truth it teaches. The whole Bible testifies
against such an idea. Morals and truth are indissolubly linked
together. There is, therefore, no hope apart from a firm
grasping of biblical truth and living our lives according to its
teaching.

Someone may say: 'You as a preacher tell us to "Stand therefore, having your loins girt about with truth", but what does that
mean in practice?' Another may say, 'I admit, I confess, that my
life is a life of defeat; the devil masters me constantly; and you
say that the remedy is that, having made sure that I am "strong
in the Lord, and in the power of his might", I should "put on the
whole armour of God", and that I start by girding my loins
about with truth. But what is this truth?'

This is the question to which we must now turn. Unfortunately
it is a question about which there is the greatest confusion in
the Christian Church at this present time. I speak in a spirit of
sadness, almost of depair. Would to God that it were not necessary
to say such a thing, or, indeed, to say what I shall have to say. But
it is essential that we should do so because of the state of the

Christian Church in this country. The statistics speak eloquently. Compare the Church today with the Church depicted in the New Testament, or the Church you can read of at certain periods and eras in her long history. The Church is in a pathetic, indeed in a perilous condition. There is one main reason for this, namely, that she does not accept the Apostle's teaching at this point. The Apostle's exhortation is thoroughly unpopular today, and being argued against in almost every quarter.

The modern attitude in the Church herself is almost the exact opposite of this exhortation. The Apostle says that if the Church is to function as a body, and if you are to function successfully as an individual Christian, the first thing you have to do is to put this 'truth' about your loins so that it may bind and band you together and set you on your feet and energize you. But the modern attitude in the Church with its international congresses, its 'weeks of prayer for Christian unity', or its 'octaves' of prayer is far astray from the apostolic plan. It places its whole emphasis upon some general spirit rather than upon particular principles – a general spirit or attitude of friendship and of love and of worshipping together. That of course, in and of itself, is an excellent thing. We should love one another; there should be a 'unity of the Spirit in the bond of peace'. But the whole question is how to arrive at it. You cannot 'put on' a vague spirit. But according to the Apostle there is a piece of armour which you can take hold of, can take up and can put on. Yet at the present time we are told that the hope for the Church and the hope for the individual lies in some vague general spirit of fellowship.

Another way in which the matter is stated is that the life is more important than the belief. The whole tendency today is to say that, no matter what a man may say in words about what he believes, and what he does not believe, if he lives a good life, he is a Christian. For instance, an article recently written about a great man who had done much good said: 'Though he, of course, would have said that he was not a Christian, his life proves that he was a Christian'. That was said in the name of the Christian Church. So it is not surprising that the average Christian says, 'I am told to "gird my loins with truth", but what is truth? What am I to gird myself with? Is belief of any value at all? If we are going to "meet atheists in heaven", does what I believe matter to the slightest extent? What is truth? Does truth count at all? Is it possible to know what it is?'

Believing that I shall have to stand before the judgment throne of Christ and give an account of the deeds done in the body, I cannot be silent in the midst of all this terrible confusion. The things which are being said are not only confusing people, they are undoubtedly driving people to hell! For to tell people that what a man believes does not matter as long as he lives a good life and does good, is not only a denial of the Gospel, it is bound to discourage people from believing the only truth which can save them.

Not only so, I am concerned as a pastor. If I accept this modern attitude, what am I to say to people who come to me asking for advice and help, as they do, because life is difficult and trying? Am I to say to them, 'Try to think thoughts of love, just try to go on doing as much good as you can, and let us all be friendly together'? That, patently, does not help them. And the more this kind of vague, nebulous teaching is given, the greater the number of people who turn their backs upon the Church. And I do not blame them, for frequently there is more teaching given in the cults than there is in the Christian Church herself. No, our loins are to be girded about with truth.

But to come to grips with this yet more closely, what is being actively, seriously taught, is that truth cannot be defined. That is the essence of this modern attitude, the basis of its appeal. People say: 'The Church is divided and separated because people have been insisting on particular doctrines. Such a policy always divides. We must all agree that truth is so great and so glorious that it cannot be defined.' In other words we are being told that truth is something which is 'caught not taught'. You cannot put it into definitions, you cannot state it as a series of propositions, they say; it is just something you become aware of in yourself.

Let me give one illustration of this taken from a book which actually had the title, *Ultimate Questions*. The author was concerned to deal with fundamentals. He says that the trouble in the past has been that people have been trying to define what is right and what is wrong; but that, he says, cannot be done. What then is Christianity, what it truth? As his reply he gives a picture of a man who hears that if he climbs to the top of a certain mountain he will see a wonderful view, a great panorama. So one day he sets out to climb to the top of the mountain. After much effort and striving, and sweating, and cutting his knees and his hands on rocks and crags, he' reaches the summit, and there he sees the great panorama. 'What does he do', asks this author, 'does he go home and write all that he has seen in propositions and definitions – one, two, three?' Of course he doesn't! You cannot describe such a glorious view in such terms. No, there is only one thing to do; he just stands there in utter amazement. He is speechless. The writer says: 'I can imagine him dancing, I can imagine him singing, but what I cannot imagine the man doing is writing down what he has seen in propositions, and dissecting it, analysing it, defining it, and contrasting it with something else'. He says that that would be to ruin it. You cannot analyse a flower, you cannot analyse an aroma. You can sense it, you can feel it, you can be thrilled by it; but you cannot analyse it. The moment you bring these rough hands of yours and try to analyse you have lost the thing. That is truth!

That is typical of the modern attitude. In the light of that, of course, to express criticism is terribly wrong. If you venture to criticize or to say that a certain teaching is wrong you are dismissed as a contentious person. It is said that your spirit is not Christian any longer, you have become narrow; you are claiming that you alone are right. You must not do that. Who can define truth? One person sees it in this way but another sees it in that! No matter! We are all concerned about the same thing! So you must not criticize, and you must not say about any teaching that it is wrong. If a man really is doing his best, and trying to uplift himself and humanity, what right have you to say that he is wrong? Truth eludes definition. So your critical faculty must be stifled; and you must allow anyone to believe what he likes, as long as he aims at doing good.

In other words, unity is put before doctrine. There is only one thing, it seems to me, which is believed by the majority, and that is 'unity'. 'Unity' is the sole article of belief. We must all come together at all costs, believing what we like. It has indeed come to this; and this is increasingly the prevailing view. Rome and ourselves must be one. The Reformers were wrong. Who is to say that they are wrong and that we are right? What right have they to say that we are wrong and that they are right? You cannot define truth. Anyone who says he is a Christian is my brother. We are all one! And so the leaders of the Movement for Unity – the ecumenical movement – are concerned about 'bringing together again' Roman Catholicism and Protestantism into one great 'World Church'.

Let us be clear about this. A world-wide unity is the logical end of the argument. You have no right to stop short at the unification of the different sections of Protestantism; you must follow the argument right through. If the argument is that you cannot define truth, and that if a man claims to be a Christian, then you must be one with him whatever he says or believes, the end of that attitude is that we must all go back to Rome. You cannot stop short of that; you must be consistent. It therefore means that the Reformation was a disaster. Many say so quite openly. It is the logical end of this argument which says that you cannot define truth, that you must not criticize, and that you must not ask questions. It is the logical end of the position that says that you must take every man at his face value, and that in a spirit of charity and friendship you must be ready to work with him.

At the back of all this is the belief that the ultimate standard and test of everything is modern knowledge. I read in a religious journal recently the specific statement that the Bible is of great value but, of course, it would be foolish to expect it really to help us at the present time. The Bible was written in days when society was primitive and simple. It deals with the problems of those times, and deals with them very adequately. Not only so, the article went on to say that the Bible has insights – that is the word, 'insights' – which are of great help to us today, but obviously in the complexity of modern civilization and modern society, it would be ridiculous to expect the Bible to be adequate. We have advanced beyond it. So we rest upon modern knowledge, modern understanding and modern learning.

The question I ask, in the light of all this, is – How am I to put on the girdle of truth? The Apostle tells me that it is absolutely essential, that it is the first thing I have to do, that if I do not do it, I cannot put on the whole armour of God, and that without the whole armour of God I am already defeated. The Apostle says that truth is something that I can take up, and can put on; but today we are told that you cannot define it.

There is but one answer to this modern attitude. In the Bible, truth is defined and error is condemned. There is a perfect illustration of this in the second chapter of the Second Epistle to Timothy where the Apostle throughout the chapter virtually says just one thing, namely, that we must hold on to the truth. There were some who were denying it, 'saying that the resurrection is past already'. The Apostle calls that type of teaching 'a canker'! But if I call it a canker today I should be vilified as an arrogant person, a contentious person whose spirit is wrong.

The Apostle Paul defines doctrine. Look at verse 8 of that chapter, 'Remember that Jesus Christ of the seed of David was raised from the dead according to my gospel'. 'My gospel!' Sheer arrogance! Today the Apostle would be dismissed as a contentious, arrogant fellow. That is certainly what they are saying about all who maintain the apostolic teaching today. There are many who do not hesitate to say the same about the Apostle himself. They do not like the Apostle Paul; they prefer what they call 'the simple gospel of Jesus', the 'gospel of love'. They regret that Paul 'with his legalistic mind foisted his Jewish pharisaical ideas on the simple gospel of love'. It is not surprising, therefore, that the Christian Church is as she is.

Paul talks about 'my gospel'! But note that he also says, 'Thou therefore, my son, be strong in the grace that is in Christ Jesus. And the things that thou hast heard of me . . . the same commit thou to faithful men who shall be able to teach others also' (vv. 1-2). The Apostle Paul, as we see quite clearly from the Book of Acts and the Epistles, did not content himself with saying 'Let us all be friends together, the love of God will cover everything. Let us believe anything we like as long as we are all nice and kind and friendly, and are all presenting a common front'.

'The things that thou hast heard of me among many witnesses, the same commit thou to faithful men, who shall be able to teach others also.' These things are not mere generalities, but particulars; and in the chapter of which I am speaking, Paul takes up one particular matter – the resurrection. Today we are told that it is quite immaterial whether a man believes in the literal physical resurrection or not. That does not matter, we are told, as long as he belongs to a church. As long as he claims to be a Christian let him deny the resurrection or anything else. 'No!' says the Apostle, 'the foundation of God standeth sure'. Notice, too, what he says at the end: 'The servant of the Lord must not strive; but be gentle unto all men, apt to teach, patient, In meekness instructing those that oppose themselves' (vv. 24–25). You have to instruct them, and you cannot instruct them unless you believe that they are wrong and you are right. And you instruct them, 'If God peradventure will give them repentance to the acknowledging of the truth'. Those men had gone wrong at particular points in their doctrine; and Timothy is to be patient with them, to see that they are in error, and to instruct them. We must likewise put the truth to such in order that they may come back to the truth, and 'recover themselves out of the snare of the devil, who are taken captive by him at his will' (v. 26).

The Apostle is saying in effect that these men are to be pitied and we must feel sorry for them because they have fallen into the 'snare of the devil'. The devil, like a trapper of animals, is setting his snares everywhere to catch ignorant people, people who do not believe in teaching, and who say that it does not matter what you believe as long as you are living a good life, and are a good and nice man, and so on. The devil has set snares for them, and they drop into the snare. The snare suddenly closes upon them and they cannot get free. You and I are to set them free.

If that is true, then it follows that you will never know true peace, you will never know the joy of the Lord, you will never know true Christian living, until you believe the Christian doctrine. You can persuade yourself that all is well, but remember that the devil is able to put upon us what are called 'strong delusions'. A poor man who is mad may feel that everything in the world is perfect, or a man under the influence of alcohol may say that everything is going well. In the same way the devil can make people think that all is right by means of his 'delusions'. 'Believe not every spirit', says the New Testament, 'but test the spirits whether they are of God' (1 John 4:1).

The New Testament itself is quite clear about all these things. The truth can be defined, it can be stated in propositions. That is what we find in these Epistles. It teaches clearly that you must therefore say that any other teaching is wrong and you must condemn it. The New Testament argues; the New Testament is polemical. The Apostle Paul uses very strong language. He says that some people 'believe a lie', that there are 'false teachers', and he warns people to flee from them. He says, 'Though we or an angel from heaven preach any other gospel unto you than that which we have preached, let him be accursed' (Galatians 1:8). He did not write that to people in the world outside the Church, he was referring to false teachers in the Church. Yet if you say such things today, if you even repeat them, you are 'contentious', you are 'narrow', you are 'negative', you think that you alone are right, you are opinionated, and intolerant.

Is it surprising that the Christian Church is as she is at the present time? All this modern teaching is not only a denial of the New Testament, it is a denial of what the Church herself has taught throughout the centuries. If truth cannot be defined, if you cannot state it in propositions, then scrap the Apostles' Creed, and the Athanasian Creed, and the Nicene Creed. Stop repeating them. Burn up all the great Confessions of the faith. They were wrong in principle, let alone in details. The modern teaching is a denial of, it is going back upon what the people of God have done under the guidance and the power and the leading of the Holy Spirit in all the greatest and the most glorious periods in the history of the Christian Church.

However, I am concerned about all this, not so much in that general aspect, as in the personal. How am I to put on the girdle of truth? What is 'truth'?

How am I to know what is truth? What is my authority in this respect? The great question of today is the question of authority. What am I to say amidst this babel of voices? The first answer is that my authority must not be human reason. That is the supreme authority today – human reason based upon modern knowledge. We are told that because we are living in a scientific age the entire situation is different. But that is clearly and patently quite inadequate, because there is so much that I do not know, there is so much that I do not understand. My mind is too finite, it is too small.

Then I am told that our position is today dependent upon modern knowledge, and that I must not rely upon knowledge from the past. But that leaves me in this position: If I say today in the light of my knowledge that the bulk of past 'knowledge' was wrong, I know perfectly well that people in fifty and a hundred years time will be saying exactly the same about what I know now; therefore what I know now will probably be wrong. I have got nothing; I am on shifting sand, and confronted by a sliding scale of truth.

But apart from that, what is human reason – or the reason of any man – when faced by the reason and the knowledge and the cleverness and the subtlety of the devil? 'We wrestle not against flesh and blood'. We are not merely arguing with men, we are arguing with the greatest mind in the whole universe apart from the mind of the Triune God. That is, you must remember, the Apostle's constant emphasis – the wiles and the subtlety of the devil. And the history given us in the Bible is an illustration of that subtlety. It shows how the best, the greatest, the most saintly minds have been trapped by the devil; the best of men have gone astray. If I am to rely upon human reason I am already defeated. You cannot rely upon your reason; it is too small, it is too inadequate. Yet that is what men are doing today. They are relying upon their reason and criticizing the Bible; they are even criticizing the Lord Jesus Christ Himself! 'He was a child of His age', they say, 'He could not possibly know what we know'. That is human reason, human knowledge, set in the supreme position; and you are left without any higher authority. Our final authority cannot be reason.

What about my feelings? Feelings are placed in the position of authority by many today, because the more honest minds have to admit that reason ultimately fails. The two world wars have shattered the faith in human reason that characterized the first part of the present century. Humanism was largely discredited and ridiculed by the two world wars. Many are therefore turning from it today and are making this leap into the realm of 'feeling'. 'Ah', they say, 'don't try to understand too much, don't try to reason. It is what you feel, it is what you experience that matters – this indefinable something that "gets" you!'

But feelings cannot be our ultimate authority because, as we all know, they are so changeable, and unreliable. They come and they go, and you never know what they may be. 'I dare not trust the sweetest frame', says a hymn-writer, because it may have gone by tomorrow. If I am to be governed by my feelings I shall find myself constantly changing – sometimes happy, sometimes miserable, sometimes feeling that all is well, sometimes that everything is going wrong, sometimes thrilled by reading the Bible, at other times having to force myself to get something out of it, feeling dry, arid, dull, stupid! Is not that your experience? If so, how can you rely on feelings as your authority?

Then remember, too, that feelings can be so easily counterfeited. If what is nice is of necessity good, if what gives me a pleasant, comfortable feeling must be right, then I have no answer whatsoever to the cults. I would just have to say: 'Well, go to them. Anything that makes you feel better, anything that gives you a kind of release and relief is good; follow it. Anything that makes you a better man must be right, go after it.' If we rely merely upon the pragmatic test of what makes me feel better we have no standard at all. I cannot criticize any teaching. It is so entirely subjective that I have no standard whatsoever.

But let us go further. If the authority is not reason, not feeling, is it possible that it is the Church? There stands ever, of course, the Roman Catholic Church claiming that her authority is final. 'Oh yes', she says, 'the Bible is very good, but it is not enough. We have added to it, we have had further revelation. You must believe in the Church as well as the Bible.' There is this 'drift', so rapidly becoming a flood, back in the direction of Rome. It is inevitable in the light of what we have been considering. If we have no valid tests to apply, there is only one conclusion – Go back to Rome.

There are many reasons why I say we cannot accept Rome as our authority. The way in which she has so obviously departed from the doctrine and practice of the early Church is sufficient in and of itself. I once asked a Roman Catholic priest who came to speak to me at the close of a meeting this one question: 'Can you see your Church as she is today in the New Testament?' He said: 'I had never thought of that.' 'Well,' I said, 'think of it now.' And he did so and said: 'I have got to admit that I cannot see it there.' Of course he could not! It is the creation of men. They have borrowed ideas from pagan religions and from the political system of the Roman Empire. You cannot see that Church in the New Testament. It is totally unlike the early Church. And that, I say, is sufficient in and of itself to disprove its claim to authority.

[203]

'But', asks someone, 'what has all this to do with me?' It has this to do with you, that if you are in trouble, one day you will perhaps become desperate, and by chance you will be confronted, perhaps in a bus, or working next to you in your office, by a Roman Catholic who will say to you, You cannot deal with these things. You have been fool enough to think you can do so all these years. There is only one thing for you to do, come back to Mother Church; she will take the problem from you, the priest will take it from you. You do not have to carry your burden; come and hand it over, hand yourself over.' That is what takes people to Rome, sometimes very intellectual people, like the late G. K. Chesterton and hundreds of others. Intellectual people in the U.S.A. at the present time are apparently crowding back to Rome, the reason being that they are bewildered!

But I repeat that Rome is no authority because of these additions by men for which there is no authority at all. Furthermore their additions contradict basic Christian teaching. The Church of Rome has not abandoned belief in the deity of Christ, in the facts concerning Him, in His atoning death, in His literal physical resurrection. She has held on to those, but she has added other things which deny the original teaching concerning Him and His work for our salvation. She is a mass of contradictions. Take but one illustration – the growing cult of Mariolatry, the worshipping of the Virgin Mary, in the Roman Catholic church. 'Roman Catholics are Christians', we are told, 'so let us pray with them, let us be one with them'. But before you do so consider this quotation from an article by a monseigneur, a high official in the Roman Church. He says: 'Each time we repeat the prayer, "Save us, O Queen", we spontaneously admit the Queenship of Mary. Mary is Queen of heaven and earth because she is the Mother of Jesus, the King of the universe, thus becoming the co-Redemptrix of the human race' – he means the co-Redeemer with our Lord. He goes on: 'It is because Mary gave life to a Son Who is King and Lord of everything that she is somehow mysteriously the Mother of the Trinity'. The Mother of the Trinity! the Father and the Holy Ghost as well as the Son! 'Mary is still our Queen and co-Redemptrix of our salvation. It was she, one who was free from guilt and sin' – Where do they find that in the Scriptures? Nowhere! None of this is to be found in the

Scriptures. 'It was she, who was free from all guilt and sin that offered her Son on Calvary's Cross, sacrificing her maternal love and rights for our eternal salvation. Mary, Queen of goodness and mercy, full of love and grace, guides all humanity towards Paradise. Sitting beside Christ, Who is the Ruler of the world, is Mary, whom our Redeemer has entrusted as the official dispenser of grace. The authority that Mary has is based on the power of intercession and mediatorship because she has access to the heart of Christ the King. She has the key to His heart and distributes all the grace and treasures that are enclosed therein.'

Let that suffice. I cannot regard the Roman Church as the final authority because her teaching denies the plain teaching of the Scripture, denies what was taught by the early Church, and the Church for a number of centuries afterwards, and is a contradiction of her own teaching at other points.

Another reason why I cannot accept Rome is because of the whole system which characterizes that Church, a system which asks me to believe in miracles wrought by the relics of saints, to believe in miracles which are not miracles, and are not authenticated. My object in saying all this is not just to denounce the Roman Catholic Church. I am saying these things because I believe I am called of God to preach the Gospel of truth to modern men and women, to bring them to a knowledge of salvation through the 'truth as it is in Jesus'. I speak thus because I know that I shall have to give an account of my stewardship. Hence I warn against these things. We have been told that we cannot be happy until we are one again with that Church that teaches what I have quoted. That, to me, is nothing but an attempt to entice and to incite people to walk deliberately into error, to believe as truth that which is a lie, and which derogates from the unique glory of the Son of God, our only Saviour and Redeemer. The Apostle assures us that 'There is one God and one' [and only one] 'Mediator' – no co-Mediator, no co-redemptrix – 'between God and men, the man Christ Jesus'. To add anything to Him is to take from Him; and that is the final blasphemy. I say these things in the name of truth, for the sake of, and for the honour of, my blessed Lord who died for me. I say them because I feel a responsibility not only for my own soul but for the souls of others.

You must gird yourselves and your loins with truth. If you do not, you are defeated. And I am asserting and maintaining that truth can be known, that there is an authority. It is not reason, it is not feelings, it is not the Church, any church, It is the Book called the Bible.

15
The Scripture of Truth

'Stand therefore, having your loins girt about with
truth.'

Ephesians 6:14

We have reached the stage where we see the absolute necessity for
some external, objective authority; not my reason, my feelings,
or the traditions of men, which ultimately are but the outcome of
reason and feelings. The Roman Catholic Church and all the
churches which follow her speak much about tradition, but for
the most part it is of human, not divine origin. Our Lord Himself
speaks about 'the traditions of the elders' whereby the commandments of God were violated. It is essential for us to have an
external, objective authority by which we can test our reason,
our feelings and all else. I assert once more that this is a question
of superlative importance. What do you see when you look into
the future? How do you explain the tendencies that are so obvious?
Is it a matter of indifference to you if the whole Church should
go back to Rome? Did the Reformers die in vain, or was the
Reformation, as so many are saying today in Protestant circles,
the greatest disaster in the history of the Church? These matters
are absolutely vital to us. The day has come when we have to
face them with all seriousness and take our decision and our
choice with respect to them.

In my attempt to make this clear, let me relate an experience
that came to me very recently. It brings out the importance of
this whole matter of authority. I was seated in a train travelling in
the direction of Southend. I was reading a book, but suddenly I
became aware of a commotion in the compartment. It was one of
those open compartments subdivided into sections. I looked up,
and I saw people standing round a man who was obviously in

[207]

some kind of trouble. So I approached, and there I saw a fellow-traveller having an epileptic fit. He was struggling, bluish red in colour, frothing at the mouth and so on. I soon realized that these good people who were standing round him, and who had been paying attention to him while I was still reading, had arrived at a decision. They said that there was only one thing to do. They must stop the train at the next station. One of them knew that there was a hospital up the road not far from the station, and urged that the thing to do was to get an ambulance and take him there. Their idea was that the man had had a stroke, or that he was suffering from a very serious heart attack, and he was on the verge of death. Because they took this view they very rightly and naturally were proposing to make these arrangements. Having listened to them I had to arrive at my decision. What should I do? It was quite clear to me that this man was not in any danger at all as regards his life. He was suffering from an epileptic fit, as he had probably done many times before. I knew that the man, when he came round, would be very much annoyed if he found himself in a hospital. So I decided that in the interest of the man I would intervene. But then I had to take a second decision. Should I tell them that, as it happened, I did know something about such matters, or should I not tell them? Well, not desiring to be involved in a delay which would make me late for my preaching engagement that afternoon, I decided that I would not give them any indication as to who or what I was, so I simply said to them quite firmly, 'No, you must not do this; it is quite unnecessary. This man is suffering from an epileptic fit, and will be all right in a short time, and he will be very annoyed if you put him into hospital'. I added, 'There is no danger whatsoever'. They looked at me with considerable doubt and hesitation, but I could see that I was making an impression. So I persisted, and after a while I was able to persuade them. Obviously some of them were still doubtful, and really did not quite believe what I said, but I was able to persuade them not to do anything. I assured them that the man would soon regain consciousness; which, of course, he did. Eventually he left the train with me at Southend, as I had anticipated he would do, and went home unaided.

My only reason for relating that incident is to show how the question of authority came in there. Here were a number of people – we were all strangers to one another – deciding to do something. I alone, for they were all agreed about what they vere going to do, was able to persuade them not to act. I succeeded because they detected the note of authority in what I was saying. They did not know the cause of the man's trouble. Was it haemorrhage in the brain, was it a heart attack, what was it? They were all agreed that he was dying, that the case was desperate, but they did not know what it was. But suddenly someone speaks with authority, and says, 'All is well; you need not do that; you need not stop the train, you need not send for an ambulance, you need not take him to hospital; he will soon recover'. And they listened to me, they accepted my opinion and they acted upon it. The significant point is that they did not know the basis of my authority. I had not told them the grounds on which I was able to speak in this dogmatic and certain and authoritative manner. But in spite of their lack of knowledge they listened to me, they changed their opinion, and they acted upon my advice.

That, it seems to me, is a parable. It illustrates the case of many in the Church, and as a consequence, the case of many outside the Church. People are bewildered as they face an alarming situation. What is about to happen? What ought to be done? And they do not know. They consider and discuss many ideas and proposals. Then suddenly they hear someone speaking dogmatically and with authority, and they are ready to listen.

The material point that emerges is that, without knowing the basis of the authority, they are ready to listen to an authoritative statement. Is not that the very thing that has happened? It explains why the cults are succeeding today, why certain freak religious movements are succeeding today, and why the Roman Church has succeeded. They speak with authority, they speak with certainty. The Protestant churches, on the other hand, are fumbling and hesitant and doubtful. They say that they do not know what the truth is, some even saying that you cannot tell what it is, that it is something that is 'caught, not taught', and so on. The people in their bewilderment, when they hear a word of authority, something spoken definitely, believe it. They accept it, and act upon it; but they do not know the basis of the authority.

I was able to speak as I did to my fellow-travellers because I had authority. It was not merely an opinion, it was not only a feeling that I had; I was speaking on the basis of knowledge and of facts. I was not making what the doctors sometimes call 'a spot diagnosis'; it was perfectly simple; it was a 'textbook case' of an epileptic fit; there was no question at all about it. Knowledge! information! truth! So I was able to speak as I did. And what I said was verified, because it was based upon and established upon facts and upon a knowledge of medicine.

What is needed today is not merely a note of authority, but the authority which leads to the authoritative statement. There are many people in the world who are ready to make dogmatic pronouncements, and speak with great certainty and an assurance born of nothing but their own self-confidence, and sometimes their delusions! That is where the danger arises. People are ready to listen, as these people listened to me in the train, without knowing the basis of the authority. I was glad they did, and yet, at the same time, there was to me something pathetic about it, because it showed this terrible danger. However, what the incident illustrates is that it is essential that we should have some authority which is based upon knowledge.

So we return to consider the only authority that can answer these desiderata. It is found in the Bible. There can be no doubt whatsoever that all the troubles in the Church today, and most of the troubles in the world, are due to a departure from the authority of the Bible. And, alas, it was the Church herself that led in the so-called Higher Criticism that came from Germany just over a hundred years ago. Human philosophy took the place of revelation, man's opinions were exalted and Church leaders talked about 'the advance of knowledge and science,' and 'the assured results, of such knowledge. The Bible then became a book just like any other book, out of date in certain respects, wrong in other respects, and so on. It was no longer a book on which you could rely implicitly. There is no question at all that the falling away, even in Church attendance, in this country is the direct consequence of the Higher Criticism. The man in the street says, 'What do these Christians know? It is only their opinion, they are just perpetrating something that the real thinkers and scientists have long since seen through and have stopped considering'. Such is the attitude of the man in the street! He does not listen any longer, he has lost all interest. The whole situation is one of drift; and very largely, I say, it is the direct and immediate outcome of the doubt that has been cast by the Church herself upon her only real authority. Men's opinions have taken the place of God's truth, and the people in their need are turning to the cults, and are listening to any false authority that offers itself to them.

We all therefore have to face this ultimate and final question: Do we accept the Bible as the Word of God, as the sole authority in all matters of faith and practice, or do we not? Is the whole of my thinking governed by Scripture, or do I come with my reason and pick and choose out of Scripture and sit in judgment upon it, putting myself and modern knowledge forward as the ultimate standard and authority? The issue is crystal clear. Do I accept Scripture as a revelation from God, or do I trust to speculation, human knowledge, human learning, human understanding and human reason? Or, putting it still more simply, Do I pin my faith to, and subject all my thinking to, what I read in the Bible? Or do I defer to modern knowledge, to modern learning, to what people think today, to what we know at this present time which was not known in the past? It is inevitable that we occupy one or the other of those two positions.

The Protestant position, as was the position of the early Church in the first centuries, is that the Bible is the Word of God. Not that it 'contains' it, but that it is the Word of God, uniquely inspired and inerrant. The Protestant Reformers believed not only that the Bible contained the revelation of God's truth to men, but that God safeguarded the truth by controlling the men who wrote it by the Holy Spirit, and that He kept them from error and from blemishes and from anything that was wrong. That is the traditional Protestant position, and the moment we abandon it we have already started on the road that leads back to one of the false authorities, and probably ultimately to Rome itself. In the last analysis it is the only alternative.

People will have authority; and they are right in so thinking. They need authority because they are bewildered; and if they do not find it in the right way they will take it in the wrong way. They can be persuaded even though they do not know the source of the authority; in their utter bewilderment they are ready to be persuaded by any authoritative statement. So that it comes to this, that we are back exactly where Christians were 400 years ago. The world talks about its advance in knowledge, its science, and so on, but actually we are going round in cycles, and we are back exactly where Christians were 400 years ago. We are having to fight once more the whole battle of the Protestant Reformation. It is either this Book, or else it is ultimately the authority of the church of Rome and her 'tradition'! That was the great issue at the Protestant Reformation. It was because of what they found in the Bible that those men stood up against, and queried and questioned and finally condemned the church of Rome. It was that alone that enabled Luther to stand, just one man, defying all those twelve centuries of tradition. 'I can do no other' he says, because of what he had found in the Bible. He could see that Rome was wrong. It did not matter that he was alone, and that all the big battalions were against him. He had the authority of the Word of God, and he judged the Church and her tradition and all else by this external authority.

We are back again in that exact position, and I am concerned about the matter, not only from the standpoint of the Church in general, but also from the standpoint of our own individual experiences. How can we fight the devil? How can we know how we are to live? How can we answer the things we hear, the things we read, and all the subtle suggestions of the devil? Where can I find this truth that I must gird on, as I put on all this armour of God? Where can I find it if I cannot find it in the Bible? Either my foundation is one of sand that gives way beneath my feet, and I do not know where I am, or else I stand on what W. E. Gladstone called 'The Impregnable Rock of Holy Scripture'.

Why should we return to the Bible, why should we believe it? Because we should not be as children, 'carried about by every wind of doctrine, by the sleight of men, and cunning craftiness, whereby they lie in wait to deceive'. The only way to avoid such a catastrophe is to have a compass, to have a chart, to have an authority, to have something solid on which we can base our whole life, and if necessary sacrifice our lives for it.

But – to speak more in detail – the first answer is that the Bible itself claims that it is this authority. Sometimes it does so explicitly,

and at all points it does so implicitly. No man in and of himself
can ever arrive at a knowledge of God. That is the whole basis
of the New Testament teaching, as it was the whole basis of
the apostolic teaching. I cannot understand how anyone can hold
any other view who has read the first two chapters of Paul's
First Epistle to the Corinthians. The Apostle lays down the following as his fundamental position: 'For the preaching of the cross is
to them that perish foolishness; but unto us which are saved it is
the power of God'. Then he goes on: 'For it is written' – he is
quoting from the Old Testament – 'I will destroy the wisdom of
the wise, and will bring to nothing the understanding of the
prudent'. 'Where is the wise? where is the scribe? where is the
disputer of this world?' That is to say, where is the man who
relies on modern knowledge and science and learning, and on his
own ability and on what the philosophers are saying? Then Paul
continues: 'Hath not God made foolish the wisdom of this world?'
How? Paul answers, 'For after that in the wisdom of God the
world by wisdom' – by philosophy, by learning, by knowledge and
understanding and human reason – 'the world by wisdom knew
not God'. It had failed to find Him; but when the world had failed,
it then 'pleased God by the foolishness of preaching' – by what
the world regarded as the 'foolishness' of the thing preached, the
'foolishness' of the Gospel and the message of the Gospel – 'to
save them that believe.' The Apostle states there the whole
position; and there is no answer to it. This is where we see the
wisdom of God. People often ask the question: 'If God had proposed to send the Messiah, the deliverer, His own Son, into this
world, as He had foretold throughout the centuries, why did He
wait so long to do so? Why did He not do so much earlier?' The
answer is that God sent His Son into the world with His message
after He had given the world a full opportunity to deliver itself,
and particularly through Greek philosophy. All the great Greek
philosophers – Plato, Socrates, Aristotle, and the rest – had lived
and died before the Lord Jesus Christ came. They represented man
at his very acme. There is no question but that the flowering
period of the human intellect in so many senses was reached in
that great era of Greek philosophy which preceded the coming of
the Lord Jesus Christ. There you have man's ability and thinking
at its very best and highest; but it proved quite unable to rise to

a knowledge of God. 'The world by wisdom knew not God', and it never has known Him ever since, and it never will.

Yet, today, men continue to put their trust in human philosophy. The Church is doing so; she is quoting the philosophers, finding 'insights' in a variety of religions and in the philosophers' teachings whether they are Christians or not. If they are able men, men of learning and deep thinkers, it is argued that they must have something to tell us! But that is a complete denial of the whole basis of apostolic preaching.

'The world by wisdom knew not God': and the reason for that is obvious. It is obvious because of the character of God. In 1 Corinthians, chapter 2, Paul says that 'the princes of this world did not know' and did not recognize our Lord. 'We speak wisdom', says Paul, 'among them that are perfect: yet not the wisdom of this world, nor of the princes of this world, that come to nought' (v. 6). Human wisdom, even in its princes, its greatest men, is inadequate; it will never bring us to the truth. It is because God is what He is! God is infinite and absolute and eternal in every respect. God is! And the moment you realize that truth, you see how man can never possibly arrive at a knowledge of Him. How can the finite encompass the Infinite? How can mortal man arrive at a real knowledge of the immortal God, the God who says, 'I am that I am', the God who is from eternity to eternity, absolute in every respect, the God who is 'light and in him is no darkness at all'?

Even if man were perfect he could not arrive at a knowledge of God the infinite, for in comparison with God he is nothing. If you can encompass any knowledge with your brain it means that your brain is greater than the thing that you encompass. So when man tries to understand God, and to find Him by his own searching and power and intellect and understanding, he is postulating that he is greater than God, and that God is someone open to examination. The very idea is monstrously ridiculous.

But when we realize that man is not only finite but also sinful, and fallen, and unclean, and twisted, and perverted, the position becomes still more ridiculously impossible. Take the Apostle's argument: 'What man knoweth the things of a man, save the spirit of man which is in him?' (1 Corinthians 2:11). There must be a correspondence. If you want to appreciate music you must have some musical sense. There are people who have no appreciation of music at all. They may have great intellects, but they are tone deaf, they have no appreciation. There must be some correspondence before there can be understanding. And the same applies to the spiritual realm. God is not only infinite and absolute and eternal; 'God is light, and in him is no darkness at all'. There is no communion between light and darkness, there is no correspondence between black and white. God is everlastingly holy, and every one of us is sinful and unworthy and vile. And the result is, as the Apostle says, that to every such 'natural' person the things of God's Spirit are 'foolishness' (1 Corinthians 2:14). Man by nature not only cannot arrive at the knowledge; when he is given the knowledge he rejects it with scorn. It is nonsense to him, it is foolishness. 'The Greeks seek after wisdom', but the Gospel is 'foolishness' to them. It is so utterly different from what they believe, and what they are, and what they have. And it will be so throughout eternity. The passing of the ages makes no difference. God does not change, man does not change, sin does not change, and therefore, whatever we today may know scientifically which our forefathers did not know, makes not the slightest difference. So we are back again in the old position, 'The world by wisdom knew not God'. It could not know. 'The natural man receiveth not the things of the Spirit of God . . . neither can he.' Man cannot, because of the greatness of God and his own weakness and inability and sinfulness.

We are all therefore in this position, that by all our efforts we can never arrive at this knowledge of God. Well, then, is knowledge possible? If I am to gird my loins about with truth, how can I find it? There is but one answer: if we are to have any knowledge of truth at all, then God must give it us. It has to be revealed to us. 'It is high, I cannot attain unto it,' says the Psalmist (Psalm 139:6). But God, if He so chooses, can give us the knowledge which we desire. And the whole message of the Bible from beginning to end is just this, that He has done so. 'In the wisdom of God, when the world by wisdom knew not God, it pleased God, by the foolishness of preaching' – by the message which He sent out through His servants – 'to save them that believe'. That is another way of stating the fact of revelation. Consider for a moment the way in which the Apostle Paul stated the matter when he was preaching at Athens, and addressing Stoics and Epicureans. It is, to me, not only the tragedy of tragedies, but almost inexplicable that the Christian Church in the last century deliberately brought philosophy back into the Church and put it in a central position. It is a fundamental denial of the whole of the Gospel. And she is still doing so. We are to stand before the world and say what Paul said at Athens: 'Whom ye ignorantly worship . . .' (Acts 17:22ff). They were trying to find Him; they had not only erected temples to all their various gods, but there was this strange altar bearing the inscription, 'To the unknown God'. They had a feeling that He was there somewhere. The most primitive races have a belief in some supreme God. They do not know Him, they are trying to find Him – and so were the Greeks! 'The unknown God!' And Paul looks at them and says, 'whom ye ignorantly worship' – or try to worship – 'him *declare* I unto you'.. He is making a declaration. Here are people fumbling and groping in the dark, and then a man with authority comes and says, 'him declare I unto you'. Here is knowledge, here is the information. That is revelation! That is the whole biblical position. In our inability, in our finite condition, in our sinfulness, we cannot, and we never shall be able to arrive at a knowledge of God. And we are shut up to this position, that if God is not pleased to give us the knowledge, to give us revelation, we have nothing, we are undone, we are hopeless, 'we are without God, in the world'. But, says the Bible, God has done this very thing! That is the whole glory of the message, that is the good news of the Gospel of salvation; God has been pleased to give us this revelation. That is the message of the whole Bible; that is what it is proclaiming from beginning to end. 'In the beginning God . . .' It is an authoritative statement. How does Moses make the authoritative statement? It was given to him. So you find the author of the Epistle to the Hebrews saying that it is 'through faith we understand that the worlds were framed by the Word of God'. We know it 'by faith'; it was given; it is a revelation.

Such is the claim of the Old Testament; and the Old Testament in this matter is as important as the New Testament. The two go together, the one leads to the other. Moses wrote his five books, not by his own wisdom, not by his own philosophy. He does not give us his own ideas and understanding. The truth was revealed to him and he was enabled by the Spirit to write it. When you come to the prophets, you find exactly the same thing. Not a single prophet ever stood up and said, 'I am saying this because I have thought very much about this subject; I have meditated and read much about it, and I have come to this conclusion'. That is not what they say. Instead, they speak about 'the burden of the Lord'; 'the message of the Lord came unto me', or 'the Spirit of God came upon me'. Some of them did not want to give the message. Jeremiah says, 'I wish I had not got to speak, I only get into trouble when I do speak'. He decided more than once that he would never speak again, but he said 'The Word of God was like a fire burning within me and I could not refrain'. That is their position. The Psalmist says much the same thing.

The Bible is the result of God disturbing men by the Spirit, giving them the message, and then enabling them to deliver it in speech or in writing. And the Apostles, writing in the New Testament, about these very things, fully confirm what the Old Testament claims. Take the famous statement of the Apostle Paul to Timothy in 2 Timothy 3:16: 'All Scripture is given by inspiration of God'. It is 'God-breathed'. It has come from God. He has 'breathed' it into men. It is not of men, it is not human literature, its source is divine. 'And it is profitable for doctrine, for reproof, for correction, for instruction in righteousness, that the man of God may be perfect, thoroughly furnished unto all good works'. The truth is the girdle which you have to put on around your loins. Peter confirms that in his own language in an important statement in his Second Epistle, chapter one, verse nineteen to the end: 'We have also a more sure word of prophecy; whereunto ye do well that ye take heed, as unto a light that shineth in a dark place, until the day dawn, and the day-star arise in your hearts: knowing this first, that no prophecy of the scripture is of any private interpretation'. Peter does not mean that you and I cannot interpret it as we read it, but that 'no prophecy of scripture' is the result of any private human ex-cogitation; it is not the result of human reason and thinking and understanding. The prophetic writings do not give us a man's own private interpretation of contemporary events and his attempt to forecast the future – it is not that! Peter goes on to say,

'Prophecy came not in old time by the will of man, but holy men of God spake as they were moved by the Holy Ghost'; they were 'carried along by', 'borne along by' the power of the Spirit. The claim is made first in the Old Testament; and we find it stated explicitly in the New Testament.

But over and above the testimony of the Apostles Paul and Peter to the Old Testament writings, we have our Lord's own attestation of them. Read the Four Gospels and note how He quotes Scripture, and always as the final authority. Notice that He says on one occasion, 'The Scripture cannot be broken' (John 10:35). He quotes from Genesis as well as the other books. He talks about man at the beginning, obviously accepting the teaching about Adam and Eve and the first marriage and so on. There is never any question about the authority of the Old Testament anywhere in the whole of His teaching. He accepts the entire Book. And note how after His resurrection when He talks to the two on the road to Emmaus whose faith had been shaken, and who were dejected and disappointed, 'O fools,' He says, 'and slow of heart to believe all that the prophets have spoken'. And so He began to take them through the Scriptures – Moses and the prophets. He showed them in the Scriptures 'the things concerning himself'. He had already said to the Jews, 'The Scriptures testify of me' (John 5:39). And then, later, when these two from Emmaus had arrived back in Jerusalem, where the entire company had assembled, and some were still somewhat bewildered and unhappy and not able to understand exactly what was taking place, we read in Luke 24:44: 'And he said unto them, These are the words which I spake unto you, while I was yet with you, that all things must be fulfilled, which were written in the law of Moses, and in the prophets, and in the psalms concerning me'. He teaches plainly the authority of the Old Testament; He refers to prophecy as foretelling – and foretelling accurately! The knowledge could only have come from God; and it had been recorded by God's servants. 'Then opened he their understanding, that they might understand the scriptures.'

The Old Testament Scriptures are authoritative because they are the Words of God. When you come to the New Testament the same holds good. There is the towering figure of our Lord Himself, with all that He says about Himself, and what He claims for His teaching. He does not hesitate to speak with authority; and the people recognized it. They said that 'he taught them as one having authority, and not as the scribes' (Matthew 7:29). 'I say unto you' – this carpenter, this man who had come out of Nazareth of all places, this man who had never been trained in the schools of the Pharisees, stands and speaks with authority. He claims to be the Son of God, not a human teacher; He has come from God. He is the Son of Man who comes down from heaven and who is still 'in heaven'. 'Before Abraham was, I am', He says. That is His claim everywhere. He commands them to listen because of the unique authority that belongs to His Person, and therefore to His teaching. That anyone could read the Scriptures without noting these claims would indeed be inexplicable were it not that we know how sin blinds, and how sin fills us with such prejudice that we cannot see. The crime today is that people are sitting in judgment, not only on the Scriptures, but also on the Lord of the Scriptures! They say that He was wrong in His belief in the Old Testament and that 'He was a child of His age'. They do not hesitate to say that he was wrong in certain claims which He made for Himself. People who speak thus abandon all authoritative utterance, for there is no alternative. The supreme and only authority is the One who is the Son of God and who has come out of the eternal bosom. He was 'with' God. He has looked into the face of God. And He has come on earth and He has revealed God. 'No man hath seen God at any time; the only begotten Son, who is in the bosom of the Father, he hath declared him' (John 1:18). And what do we know apart from this revelation?

This is the beginning of the matter, the foundation, the bare minimum, the absolute. We either take everything from this, or we have no authority at all. You either submit completely to it, or else one man's opinion is as good as another's – and that means that you have no authority at all. Before you can ever succeed in girding your loins about with truth you have to come to God's Word as a little child, or, to use the stronger word that Paul uses, you have got to come to it as a 'fool'. 'If any man seemeth to be wise in this world', he says, 'let him become a fool that he may be wise' (1 Corinthians 3:18); which means, 'Let him say he knows nothing, let him say that his philosophy is of

[219]

no value to him, let him agree that "the world by wisdom knew not God" and cannot know God, and that therefore he knows nothing, and is prepared to bend his knees and to look up and receive the divine revelation'.

In other words, if we are to gird our loins about with truth, we have not only to admit that we know nothing, but that before the Holy Spirit works upon us and gives us enlightenment we cannot even receive God's revelation. The natural man cannot do so; 'but God hath revealed them unto us by his Spirit; for the Spirit searcheth all things, yea, the deep things of God' (1 Corinthians 2:10). If you want to be girt about with truth you have to come as a little child, acknowledging not only your weakness and insufficiency and inability and complete impotence; you have got to realize that the Spirit of God must work upon you and enlighten you and cleanse your understanding and give you an anointing before you can receive the revelation that God has graciously been pleased to give us. Here is the authority – God's revelation, which we can receive and understand as the result of the working of the Holy Spirit of God within us and upon us.

Do you know where you stand? What are you fighting with? How do you face the future? How do you deal with temptation and the devil and all the uncertainty of life today? Here is the only answer. May God give us grace and strength to have our loins girt about with truth!

16
The Breastplate of Righteousness

'. . . and having on the breastplate of righteousness.'

Ephesians 6:14

Thus far we have dealt with 'having your loins girt about with truth'. That is the foundation of everything, and we have interpreted the word 'truth' as standing for the whole truth concerning salvation, the great message of salvation, which is, of course, the peculiar message of this book which we call the Bible. But next we must proceed to put on the various parts of the armour, and here we come to the piece which the Apostle describes as the 'breastplate of righteousness'.

Let me first remind you of what I mean by 'putting on the whole' and then 'putting on the parts', and to illustrate it by the story of what happened when Great Britain conquered Canada from the French. The conquest was accomplished, in one sense, at the Battle of Quebec in 1759 when General Wolfe beat General Montcalm; and yet we know from history that it took many decades to possess that portion of North America. There was one decisive battle, the Battle of Quebec, and from that moment Canada became British; but there were still pockets of resistance which had to be dealt with, and it took until the 'thirties' of the nineteenth century before it could be said that the British Crown really had taken and possessed that great piece of territory. It is much the same here. We start by putting on the 'whole truth' – our acceptance and our understanding of the whole way of salvation. But having put that on, we are taught by Paul that it is equally important for us to be clear about the particular aspects and applications. When we are dealing with an illustration such as this which the Apostle is using, just as when we are dealing with a picture, an image, we must be careful always to remind ourselves that it is but a picture. The Apostle is dealing with something purely spiritual, and yet he is talking about parts of the human body and what we put on – material things that we put on different parts. It is a very good picture, but we must remember that he is interested in the spiritual aspect. For instance, we have been talking about the 'loins'. The Apostle is not interested in our actual physical loins, he means the loins of our mind. 'Gird up the loins of your *mind*' as the Apostle Peter says (1 Peter 1:13). That was the idea when we dealt with the loins, and it is the same now that we come to the breastplate. We must not press the details too much. Much confusion has been caused by expositors through a failure to understand this principle, with the result that they become quite mechanical.

I say this for the reason that, as we come to deal with putting on the 'breastplate of righteousness', we remember that in I Thessalonians 5:8 the Apostle says, 'But let us, who are of the day, be sober, putting on the breastplate of *faith and love*'. Here, it is 'the breastplate of righteousness'. We learn, therefore, that we must not be too mechanical about interpretations, or begin to feel that the Apostle is contradicting himself. The Apostle is concerned that we should realize the importance of these different aspects of our spiritual warfare, and realize that God has made a special provision for each particular portion as well as for the whole.

Let us keep that principle in mind. At the same time, however, it cannot be doubted that there is a very real significance in the order in which the Apostle places these pieces of armour. He started with the girdle for the loins, as I reminded you, because the body's loins determine the body's strength. They form the pivot on which the whole body turns, and therefore you must start with them. Not only so, the girdle pins together and holds and fastens together everything else.

Now we must move on to consider the breastplate. The breastplate Paul has in mind is that which in those ancient times was worn by the Roman soldier. He may have been chained to soldiers on the right hand and on the left when he dictated his Epistle; in any case it was a very familiar picture in the Roman world at that time. This 'breastplate' generally extended from the base of the neck to the upper part of the thighs, so it covered what we would now call the thorax and abdomen. That is actually the term that is used here in the Greek – the 'thorax'. But it also covered the abdomen, the abdominal cavity. So here Paul is talking about the portion of the armour that is to be put over the whole of what you may call in general 'the trunk'. This is, clearly, an important part of this armour because of the parts of the body which it covers.

First and foremost, of course, there is the heart. Then after that the lungs. Both are essential and vital to existence, not to say to true living. Then come all the various organs in the abdominal cavity. We today do not attach the same significance to those as did the ancient people. The biblical writers very often refer to the various organs of the abdominal cavity. We read of the 'reins' in the Book of Psalms. The kidneys are meant. In the same way, 'My bowels, my bowels!' says Jeremiah. And we find a similar usage in the New Testament in the writings of the Apostle Paul. In the Epistle to the Philippians he says: 'If there be therefore any consolation in Christ, if any comfort of love, if any fellowship of the Spirit, if any bowels and mercies' (2:1). The ancients believed that these various organs were the seat of the 'affections', and they attached significance to practically all of them. This idea has in a sense persisted. A man speaks of being 'liverish' and so on; he is referring to a mood which arises from the condition of the liver. We also talk of men 'venting their spleen'. The ancients were aware, when they had various feelings and sensations, that there was some kind of local reference, so they deduced that the cause of a particular trouble was in a particular local organ. It does not matter whether they were right or wrong, the important thing is to know that that was how they viewed it. So the Apostle, here, when he tells us to put on the breastplate of righteousness, is concerned that in this conflict, this wrestling that we are engaged in with the world, and the flesh, and the devil, there should be no part we should be more careful about in regard to protection than that where the feelings and the affections are controlled. And not only the feelings and the affections, but the conscience also, and the desires and the will.

This is, for those who like such terms, what I would call biblical psychology, and it is very profound. The biblical writers were given the enlightenment of the Spirit to understand man and the personality of man. The Apostle Paul knew that the feelings and affections play a prominent part in our life. The devil also know that, and is ready to play on them and to use them to serve his own pernicious ends and purposes. So they need to be protected very carefully.

Likewise, of course, the conscience. What a powerful instrument is the conscience! One of the greatest difficulties in life for all of us is to live with our conscience. We cannot get rid of it; it is there and always speaking. And again, of course, the devil knows this, and he is very ready, as we shall see, to come and to attack us in the realm of the conscience. There are many who are held captive by the devil at this point. They 'live laborious days', as Milton put it, very largely because the devil confuses their consciences, and they do not know how to deal with him. Somehow they have not put on the breastplate of righteousness as they should have done.

Then there are the desires and the will. Here, again, is a most involved and complicated matter. There is nothing wrong with the desires as such. It is God who has given us our desires. The desires are good in and of themselves; they are a part of life, a part of our human nature and constitution. But what the devil does is to come and to create 'inordinate desires'; he inflames the desires. Through these desires the will is affected. Thus it is of high importance for us to see that that part of our life, that part of our personality where these vital forces and factors are centred, should be adequately protected.

I am to protect these parts which I have been describing with the breastplate of righteousness. Here, again, there has been much confusion. There are some who claim that what is meant here by 'righteousness' is 'moral rectitude'. You will find that the *New English Bible*, so-called, translates it as 'integrity' – we are to be sure of our own personal 'integrity', we must be men of 'moral rectitude', we must be just and righteous and good people.

Such teachers tell us that we stand no hope or chance in fighting the devil and all his emissaries unless we are honest persons, unless we have an inherent integrity of personality. It is essential, they say, that we be not guilty of hypocrisy, that we are not two persons at one and the same time, and that there is no lie at the centre of our life.

We cannot possibly accept 'integrity' as the right and the adequate interpretation here. Obviously we do not reject it because we are opposed to integrity. Integrity is essential everywhere. You cannot hope to do anything without it; but it is of very little value when you are face to face with the devil. Man's integrity at its best is but as wax before the devil. If you imagine that by relying upon your own inherent goodness and rightness and moral rectitude, you can withstand the wiles of the devil, you are the merest tyro in these matters. Read the biographies of some of the greatest saints the Church has ever known and you will find that, the more saintly they are, the less confident they are about their own integrity, their own goodness, their own moral rectitude. Some of the greatest servants of God have felt themselves most acutely at the end of their lives to have been 'unprofitable servants' and to have done nothing. Read the autobiography of such a man as Andrew Bonar and you will see how useless personal integrity and goodness and personal righteousness are when you are confronted by the wiles and the attacks and the insinuations of the devil.

Integrity is not a 'breastplate' that is adequate to meet the 'fiery darts' and all the other instruments and implements the devil uses against us. Integrity is good, but natural integrity and goodness is as nothing when confronted by the guile and the wiles and the subtlety of the enemy who is standing opposed to us. He can bring us into utter condemnation if we rely upon our own goodness.

I could very easily become the devil's advocate in this respect. If you are tending to be proud of yourself as a Christian, read some Christian biographies, and you will soon begin to realize what you are and where you are. Read about Whitefield and the Wesleys, read about Hudson Taylor and such people, and you will sometimes begin to doubt whether you have ever been a Christian at all. Personal integrity is insufficient at this point. It is not armour provided by God; and we are concerned about 'the whole armour of God'.

Let me put before you what seems to me to be the only adequate answer. We obviously need a righteousness which is provided by God Himself. That is what is described, for instance, in the third chapter of the Epistle to the Philippians. There the Apostle states the matter very clearly. He begins by a reference to his own natural righteousness, and he says: 'If any man thinketh that he hath whereof he might trust in the flesh, I more'. If there is to be a competition in personal integrity and natural righteousness, he says, I am ready to enter the competition. And he has very good standing ground – 'Circumcised the eighth day, of the stock of Israel, of the tribe of Benjamin, an Hebrew of the Hebrews; . . . touching the righteousness which is in the law, blameless'. He was a paragon of all the virtues! He could stand up and challenge all aspirants; he was undoubtedly at the head of the list. But listen: 'What things were gain to me, those I counted loss for Christ. Yea doubtless, and I count all things but loss for the excellency of the knowledge of Christ Jesus my Lord: for whom I have suffered the loss of all things, and do count them but dung [refuse], that I may win Christ, and be found in him, not having mine own righteousness, which is of the law, but that which is through the faith of Christ, the righteousness which is of God by faith'. 'The breastplate of righteousness' refers to 'the righteousness which is of God'. It is from God, made and prepared by God, given to us. I want that, says the Apostle. That is the thing I am concerned about, everything else is 'dung' and loss, useless, not worth talking about. I used to think my own righteousness was very wonderful, he says, but I have had my eyes opened and I have come to see that it is of no value at all. Thus, you see, how at first the devil had completely defeated Paul, as he did all the Pharisees. That was the very essence of their tragedy. The Pharisees were very good men. It is a mistake to think they were bad men. They fasted twice in the week, they gave a tenth of their goods to the poor; they were very godly and very religious. As Saul of Tarsus the Apostle Paul was a Pharisee and proud of it. But he came to see that that was nothing but the devil blinding him. Putting on the breastplate of his own integrity and righteousness he was hopelessly defeated. Consequently he is no longer interested in his own righteousness and integrity; but he is interested in this other righteousness. This alone can defend him; here is the thing that can keep him safe – 'the righteousness of God which is by faith'.

In defining exactly what this means we cannot do better than accept the definition of this 'righteousness of God which is by faith' which was always taught by those who are certainly the master-teachers in this particular subject, the Protestant Reformers and their noble successors the Puritan divines. It is as the Church has forgotten them, and their teaching, that she has become vague and indefinite about this glorious matter, and has suffered such defeats at the hand of the devil and the powers he commands. They draw a careful distinction between 'imputed' righteousness and 'imparted' righteousness. We are living in an age when people say that they do not understand these terms. Several have even done away with the word 'righteousness' in their translations and substituted 'integrity' and 'goodness'! But the correct term is 'righteousness', and we must strive to learn the meaning of it. 'But we do not understand what "imputed" means,' says the modern Christian. Of course we do not. It is the business of preaching and the Church to make these things plain and clear. We should not expect people to know these things when they read the Bible, not even the instructed Christian. Hence they should come to Church and be taught, instead of expressing their foolish opinions with regard to these matters. Whoever expected any natural man to understand these profundities and immensities? All of us at our best and highest are but beginners, but learners.

'Imputed righteousness' is the whole foundation of our standing as Christians. An alternative term is 'Justification by faith'! Modern man does not know what that means either. Of course he doesn't! But that is what he needs to know. He is what he is because he does not know anything about 'Justification by faith'. Men may go on producing fresh translations of the Bible until they are tired of doing so, but the natural man will still not understand it. He has to be taught the meaning, and taught it not merely in words but by 'the demonstration of the Spirit'. It is something that calls for heavenly enlightenment.

Justification by faith means 'imputed righteousness' as described by Paul in Philippians 3. This is the righteousness to put on, says Paul. However good the life you live, whatever you are, whatever you have done, when you come to stand in the presence of God you will find that you are a hopeless sinner, utterly condemned. 'Ah', you say, 'but I intend to live a better life, I intend to turn over a new leaf, I intend to start reading my Bible, and praying, and doing good – I intend to make myself a righteous man in the presence of God'. You might as well stop at once, says the Bible, because you cannot do it. If you give the whole of your life to that work you would be as bad at the end as you are at the beginning. If you forsook the world, and became a monk or a hermit, it would not help you. Why not? Because God 'seeth the heart' and because God's standard is an absolute one. God does not demand only a little goodness. God's demand is stated in the words: 'Thou shalt love the Lord thy God with all thy heart, and all thy soul, and all thy mind. This is the first and great commandment. And the second is like unto it, Thou shalt love thy neighbour as thyself' (Matthew 22:37–39). That is God's standard. You may be highly moral but that is not what God wants of you. What can a man do? The answer is, he can do nothing. And that is the first thing he has to learn. And that is the only way in which he will ever be able to fight the insinuations of the devil. The devil can examine your righteousness; he has tests and standards, and he can ridicule it, he can show how useless it is. When you are preening yourself on your good life he will take up a book and show you a man who has sacrificed everything. You will feel that you have done nothing, that you have only given your spare money as it were, only given that which you could easily afford to give. Here is a man who has given everything, and so the thing you have boasted of, and prided yourself on, becomes refuse in your hands.

Because we can never attain to God's standard of righteousness, God sent His only Son into this world, in order that He might be able to give us *His* righteousness. He came, the spotless, sinless Son of God, and He rendered a perfect obedience to God's law, obeyed Him in every jot and tittle of the law. He lived a perfectly righteous life. But more than that; He made Himself responsible for our sins, He bore them in His own body and was crucified for them. 'God laid on him the iniquity of us all.' And at the Cross

God smote His dear Son as our sinbearer. And in raising Christ again on the resurrection day God has proclaimed to us that Christ's death was more than sufficient to satisfy His righteous demands.

Imputed righteousness is defined in 2 Corinthians 5:21: 'God hath made him to be sin for us, who knew no sin'. In other words, God took our sins and 'imputed' them to His Son, put them on Him, put them to His account. That is the meaning of 'imputation' – that you take something that belongs to one person and you put it to the account of another. A man owes a debt; you take it out of his page in your ledger and you put it into the page of another man in the ledger. You have 'imputed' the debt to another. That is what God has done with our sins. He has imputed our sins to His Son, and He has punished them in Him.

But that has not exhausted the meaning of the term. That leaves me, as it were, with my sins taken away; but that is not enough. Before I can stand in the presence of God I must be positively holy, I must be positively righteous. God is righteous, and just and holy. 'God is light, and in him is no darkness at all'. To stand in His presence I need to be positively righteous. And this is how it happens. As I believe on God's Son and His work for me, He 'imputes' His righteousness, His perfect observance of the law, to me. I have not kept the law; Christ has kept it perfectly and He is righteous before the law. God puts to my account, imputes to me, the righteousness of His own Son. He clothes me with it. So, as I stand in the presence of God, God does not see me, He sees the righteousness of His Son covering me, clothing me completely. That is what I now rejoice in, says the Apostle. 'I count all things but loss for the excellency of the knowledge of Christ Jesus my Lord: for whom I have suffered the loss of all things, and do count them but dung, that I may win Christ, And be found in him, not having mine own righteousness, which is of the law, but that which is through the faith of Christ, the righteousness which is of God by faith' (Philippians 3:8, 9).

Salvation by 'imputed righteousness', means that Christ's perfect righteousness is put to my account, imputed to me, put upon me by God. And, looking at me, clothed in the righteousness of Christ, God pronounces me to be a just man, a righteous man; and the law cannot touch me. 'There is therefore now no condemnation to them which are in Christ Jesus' (Romans, 8:1). The law has nothing to say against me because I am covered by this perfect, spotless righteousness of the Son of God Himself, and have on 'the breastplate of righteousness'.

That is part of righteousness, but it is not the whole. There is also what the Puritans called 'imparted' righteousness, and it is equally important for us to lay hold on that also. The difference between 'imputed' and 'imparted' righteousness is, that if we stop at imputed righteousness, I am left where I was before. I have no righteousness inherent in me at all, although I am clothed and covered by the righteousness of the Lord Jesus Christ. That is the beginning; that is what makes me a Christian; that is the foundation. But God does not stop at that, He now begins to work in me the righteousness of His own Son. He 'imparts' it to me, He makes it a part of me, He puts it into me. This happens of necessity as the result of the rebirth, regeneration, the new life. There is a new seed of life 'implanted' in me.

The seed has been put into me, and that seed grows and develops. This is what is meant by the idea of 'imparting' righteousness. Another term that has sometimes been used states that the righteousness is now 'infused' into me. It is not only put upon me as a cloak and a covering, but also 'infused' into me. It is comparable to a blood transfusion where the blood from one person is put into the circulation and the blood of another. It can be 'transfused' or 'infused', 'injected', 'imparted' – these are all terms which stand for the same operation.

This is how the Apostle expresses the truth to the Philippians: 'Wherefore, my beloved, as ye have always obeyed, not as in my presence only, but now much more in my absence, work out your own salvation with fear and trembling. For it is God which worketh in you both to will and to do of his good pleasure' (2:12, 13). We are to 'grow in grace', and in the knowledge of the Lord. These are different ways of expressing 'imparted righteousness'. It is important for us to remember this, and particularly in the context of the matter with which we are dealing. For the devil attacks us in many ways. He not merely attacks us concerning our justification, he also attacks us in the realm of desire and of will, in the realm of feelings. And the only way to deal with him at these points is to 'put on the breastplate of righteousness'. This is the righteousness that will protect us at these very sensitive points – the heart, the conscience, the desire, the will – where this conflict is going on ceaselessly and the devil is trying to defeat us.

The breastplate of righteousness helps us in the first place by giving us a general sense of confidence, and this is always essential to our warfare. If you enter into this fight with the devil uncertainly or hesitantly you are already defeated. We need confidence. Here I stand, as it were, as a soldier, and I know something about the enemy. I have examined his dispositions, I have discovered something about the powers that he commands, and the armaments that he is able to use, and I know that they are characterized by subtlety and by power and by strength. I am also aware of these sensitive organs within me which are exposed to his attack. Until I have a feeling of confidence that they are covered I cannot possibly stand and be ready for some particular onslaught that is coming. But the moment I have this breastplate I know that all is well.

In a sense this means, therefore, assurance of salvation; a realization of our whole standing and position. Ezra has a very profound remark to make about this matter. He was leading God's people at a very difficult time after everything had gone wrong, and they were beginning to put things right again. But there were enemies, and Ezra (with Nehemiah), addressing the people on one occasion says, 'The joy of the Lord is your strength' (Nehemiah 8:10). Without the joy of the Lord we are very weak. 'The joy of the Lord is your strength' – and this is the strength we need. You can only get the joy of the Lord as you appropriate this truth concerning 'the righteousness of God which is by faith' (that is to say, it comes to us through the instrumentality of faith). It is God's righteousness which is given to us in this extraordinary manner. In other words it means the confidence which arises from the knowledge that we are the children of God.

There is nothing else that will enable us to stand against the devil. The writer of a certain hymn expresses it perfectly. He had had wonderful experiences, he knew what it was to bask in the sunshine of God's face and smile, he knew what it was to have his heart drawn out in praise and in thanksgiving, but when he comes to write his hymn this is what he says:

> *I dare not trust the sweetest frame,*
> *But wholly lean on Jesus' name;*
> *On Christ the solid rock I stand,*
> *All other ground is sinking sand.*

That is true of all Christians. If we stand on anything but Christ Himself and His righteousness, we shall find that it is 'sinking sand'. If you have been relying upon your feelings or upon your moods and your 'frames' you will find that you have nothing. We are told in the Book of Revelation that 'they overcame him by the blood of the Lamb, and by the word of their testimony' (12:11). There is no other way whereby finally you can overcome. John refers to the matter in his First Epistle, chapter 5: 18–19: 'He that is begotten of God sinneth not' – does not go on sinning, does not sin habitually, does not fall and remain fallen in sin – 'but he that is begotten of God keepeth himself'. That may be better translated by 'he that is begotten of God keepeth him' – ultimately it comes to very much the same thing – 'and that wicked one toucheth him not'. Because you are in this position, 'that wicked one cannot touch you'. 'And we know that we are of God, and the whole world lieth in the wicked one.' The whole world is 'lying in the wicked one', helpless in his clutches. But we are not! We know that we are of God! We have been taken out, 'translated' from the devil's kingdom and we are clothed with the righteousness of Jesus Christ. We are not in the clutches of the devil, he cannot touch us, because we are protected by 'the righteousness of our Lord and Saviour Jesus Christ'.

Are you relying on your own righteousness? Or on 'the righteousness of God which is by faith in Jesus Christ'? Do you know the grounds of your standing at this moment? Have you got this solid rock beneath you? Are you relying utterly upon the Son of God and His perfect work on your behalf? If not, you have not got the breastplate of righteousness, and that means that you are already defeated by the devil. This is the only righteousness that avails, not only when we go to God in prayer, but when we are confronted by the wiles of the devil, and as we wrestle against the principalities and powers, the rulers of the darkness of this world, the spiritual wickedness in high places.

Do you know this longing of the Apostle for a yet more perfect understanding and receiving of the righteousness of God which is by faith? He, above all, was clear about justification, but this is what he says: 'Not as though I had already attained, either were already perfect'. His desire is 'That I may know him, and the power of his resurrection, and the fellowship of his sufferings, being made conformable unto his death; if by any means I might attain unto the resurrection from among the dead'. This righteousness of Christ which is being 'imparted' to us will finally bring us to perfection, 'without spot, or wrinkle, or any such thing'. We shall be holy and blameless, perfect and entire, in the presence of God. Are you relying upon this righteousness which is given by God? Do you know that it has been imputed to you? Is that your sheet anchor – justification by faith only; being clothed with the righteousness of Christ, and being more and more conformed unto His blessed image?

Jesus, Thy blood and righteousness
My beauty are, my glorious dress;
'Midst flaming worlds, in these arrayed,
With joy shall I lift up my head.

Bold shall I stand in Thy great day;
For who aught to my charge shall lay?
Fully through Thee absolved I am,
From sin and fear, from guilt and shame.

O let the dead now hear Thy voice;
Now bid Thy banished ones rejoice;
Their beauty this, their glorious dress,
Jesus, Thy blood and righteousness.

17

'The Righteousness which is of God by Faith'

'. . . and having on the breastplate of righteousness.'
Ephesians 6:14

We now go on to consider further ways in which this 'breastplate of righteousness' helps us in our conflict with the wiles of the devil, and in our wrestling with the principalities and powers. Consider first the way in which it protects us in the realm of our feelings and sensibilities. There are many Christians who, because they have not put on the breastplate of righteousness, are very unhappy; the devil has 'got' them, and has defeated them simply because they have never known exactly what it means to put on this breastplate.

I am referring, primarily, to moods and variations in our feelings and sensibilities. We must all have discovered long since that feelings come and go; and the devil, of course, is well aware of that. So his special strategy at this point is to try to make us rely unduly upon our feelings and sensations and sensibilities. He persuades many people to base the whole of their Christian position upon them. They had some wonderful feelings on a certain occasion and they have based everything upon that experience. Or they may have had wonderful feelings in the presence of God in prayer, or in a service, or elsewhere; and they have been relying upon them. Then, for some reason or another, their feelings seem to desert them. They are aware of a dryness and a coldness; they do not feel any longer what they used to feel; and their whole position is shaken. The devil suggests to them that they are not Christians at all, that they have never been Christians. The one thing which had proved to them that they were Christians has gone, and so they are left with nothing.

The danger arises because feelings are a part, indeed a vital and essential part, of the true Christian experience. Let us be clear about that. If we have never felt anything in connection with our faith, then we do not have a true faith. You cannot really believe in this great salvation without feeling something. A man who has a real knowledge of the truth we have been describing is a man who is deeply moved by it. It must be so. You cannot truly realize the presence of God and remain unmoved.

But, unfortunately, the devil comes and tries to cause a division of the human personality; and he does so in many different ways. A particularly common way which he uses is the following. The Gospel having brought us to see that the affections, the emotions, must be involved and must be 'moved', he then deliberately exaggerates that element. He presses it, and would have us believe that this, and this alone, is the one thing that matters. And so he gets us to rely exclusively upon our feelings. Then, of course, when for some reason or another they suddenly change – and there are many reasons why it may be so – we are left without anything at all.

Now it is just here that the breastplate of righteousness is all-important; indeed at this point it is the only adequate protection. The saintly man who wrote in his hymn 'I dare not trust the sweetest frame', did so because he knew how fallible these 'frames' are, as they used to be called. It is quite a good term. We talk about 'a frame of mind'. Well, you can have a 'frame' of feeling and of emotion, of the affections, in exactly the same way. I am not thinking at the moment particularly of people who are emotionalists. Emotionalism is always wrong, and they of all people are the ones who are most deluded by the devil. I mean the people who work themselves up into some sort of ecstasy of emotion, a mere riot of emotions. That can be done through singing. If you keep on singing, and work it up, and shout, and get into a certain rhythm, you can easily get into a highly emotional state. I am not now thinking of that. It needs no attention; it stand self-condemned. Once a man has lost control of himself in that way he is clearly a victim for any evil spirit that may be at hand and watching for his opportunity. I am thinking, rather, of people who stop short of that, but who nevertheless tend to be of the intro-spective type. Such people are very much concerned about their feelings; and their danger is to put their feelings in the foremost place and to rely upon them. And so they often find themselves like poor William Cowper crying out in agony, 'Where is the blessedness I knew, when first I saw the Lord?' It has gone.

This is a very common condition. Every pastor, every physician of souls, will have met this with greater frequency than perhaps anything else. People complain 'I cannot feel anything any longer; I used to, but I cannot now'. They are dejected and downcast, and querying whether they are Christians at all. The answer to all that is, 'Put on the breastplate of righteousness'. It is the only answer. So let me complete the quotation from the hymn:

> *I dare not trust the sweetest frame,*
> *But wholly lean on Jesus' name;*
> *On Christ the solid rock I stand,*
> *All other ground is sinking sand.*

Your highest frames, your best feelings, can be most treacherous, and may desert you at any moment; and then, the thing on which you were leaning entirely having vanished, you wonder whether you are a Christian at all. The only remedy is 'the breastplate of righteousness'. While we are to enjoy feelings, they are to be subservient to, and the outcome of, our standing on the basis of justification by faith only. It is 'the righteousness of Jesus Christ by faith' that saves me, not any feelings we may have with respect to it.

There is an inevitable order in these matters. The subjective must always follow the objective. The tragedy is that people often put the subjective before the objective. Others, of course, do the exact opposite, and the devil will come to them and say, 'Quite right, it is the only thing that matters'. They are so objective that they have never felt anything at all! And they are not Christians! The true Christian is the man defined in Romans 6:17: 'But God be thanked, that ye were the servants of sin, but ye have obeyed [by the will] from the heart [affections, emotions] that form of doctrine which was delivered you' [to your mind]. There you have the intellect, the heart, and the will; and they must all be engaged, and in that order.

Let us then beware of the subtle temptation of putting the feelings and the emotions in the first place, and relying upon what we feel for our ultimate assurance of salvation. Feelings must never be isolated as if they could stand alone. The way to avoid doing so is to put on 'the breastplate' which is 'the righteousness of God in Jesus Christ'. That, and that alone, can save us from this subtle temptation.

Then, in a similar, and closely related manner, we have the whole question of 'experiences'. There is a difference between 'feelings and emotions' and 'experiences'. Sometimes as Christian people we are given remarkable and unusual experiences. God in His grace sends them to us. This is described frequently in the Scriptures. God, for His own inscrutable reasons, grants His people some manifestations of Himself, something which is quite out of the ordinary, something unusual and exceptional. Here again is something for which we should thank God. But here again we have to be careful to put on the breastplate of righteousness, because the devil will come and try to make us rely upon those very experiences.

This danger is described in the book of Job. One of the friends of Job was most eloquent on the experiences which come to a man in the night. There have always been such people in the Church, people who may have come into the Christian life in some dramatic manner. They talk about seeing a ball of light, or of a whole room being lit up. Such things may be a part of a true spiritual experience; but they may not, and may be sheer counterfeit. The danger is that, if they have been vouchsafed to us, we will tend to base our whole belief, and our whole position, upon them. Then, of course, the day comes when suddenly, for some reason or another, we begin to query and to question it all. It has often happened. People have had such experiences and have relied upon them. Then they may read a book in which they learn that certain other people who obviously have never become Christians at all have had similar experiences, and so they begin to doubt everything. There are people who talk about 'having visions of our Lord'. You should always be a little suspicious at that point because that is not the normal way. And if it is not God's normal way of bringing the soul to salvation, always be careful, because the devil can give counterfeit experiences.

The general principle is that we must be careful not to rely upon experiences. Do not base your everything upon them. The history of the Church bears eloquent testimony to the folly of such a course. There are people who seem to come into the Christian life through some amazing experience which makes the rest of us wonder whether we have ever been Christians at all. You will find, however, that after a short time, far too often they have gone back; they do not know where they stand; and they have to be brought again into the Christian life in a more ordinary and usual manner. They have never understood the doctrine of justification by faith, but have relied entirely upon the amazing experience which they had. Thank God for experiences, but do not rely on them. You do not put on 'the breastplate of experiences', you put on the breastplate of 'righteousness'. You must realize the only true ground of your standing in the presence of God, so that in the absence of anything unusual or dramatic or extraordinary you nevertheless know where you are, and how you stand, and how to answer all that the devil may suggest to you.

Consider again, under this heading, the whole matter of discouragement. Discouragement is very frequently used by the devil. The devil well knows that man's final trouble always is his pride. It is pride that keeps a man from believing in the Lord Jesus Christ. Most of those who are not Christians, particularly the intellectuals, are unbelievers because of their pride. They refuse to say, 'Vile, and full of sin I am'. Of course they are not! They will not say that they are 'helpless' and that they can do nothing. They are convinced that they can do a great deal, and they are trying to do so. They have confidence in their own morality, confidence in their own understanding, in their views, and in many other things. Their reliance upon these things prevents them from becoming Christians.

Pride is fundamental in fallen human nature, and the result is that, even when we come into the Christian life, and have seen initially how utterly wrong we have been, and how our own 'goodness' avails nothing, and how we have to rely in utter simplicity and helplessness upon Christ and His perfect work for us – I say, even when we have entered the Christian life the devil may still trap us. He tries to bring us back into a subtle reliance once more upon works, and upon ourselves, and upon our own activities. We are living the Christian life, we are active, and working hard, and making a great contribution; and in a subtle way we begin to be proud of it, and to rely upon it, and feel that after all we are as we are because of all the good we have done since we became Christians. We begin to imagine ourselves to be perfect Christians! Without knowing it we have come to rely upon our own activities and actions.

This is one of the greatest temptations that meets a preacher, a minister of the Gospel, a pastor of a church. But it applies to all Christians. And it especially applies to certain types who are active by nature. The devil knows us so well. He brings us into this position in which we are relying upon our own activities and actions. Then a time comes when for some reason or another things begin to go wrong, troubles and problems arise, even in connection with Christian work perhaps. Or, after a period of success and blessing, there seems to be a kind of stalemate, with nothing happening at all; and the devil comes in and begins to seek to depress us. He begins to make us feel that we have never done anything, that everything we have done is merely something temporary and of no real value; and, so, all the works that we have been relying upon suddenly seem to be nothing at all. The result is that we are cast into depths of gloom and despair, and even wonder whether we have ever been Christians at all. This is an extraordinary condition. It is quite common among the best workers, the most active people in the Christian life. Everything seems to come to a standstill; nothing goes well; and the poor man who had unconsciously been relying upon his own activity and works finds himself lost and shaken and wondering what is happening.

The first thing we have to learn is that all the good we may do, and all the activity in which we may be engaged, will not help us at the day of judgment. Our Lord Himself taught this. The disciples could not follow this, so He tells them in the parable recorded in the seventeenth chapter of Luke's Gospel, that when you have done everything you can do, you must still say 'I am an unprofitable servant' (Luke 17: 7–10). That is the only healthy position for a Christian. Any man who realizes exactly what he is, and who contrasts himself with some of the great saints who have gone before him, soon begins to see his nothingness.

But he must not be downcast on that account. His position amounts to what the Apostle teaches the Corinthians in the First Epistle, chapter 3: 'For other foundation can no man lay than that is laid, which is Jesus Christ. Now if any man build upon this foundation gold, silver, precious stones, wood, hay, stubble; every man's work shall be made manifest: for the day shall declare it, because it shall be revealed by fire; and the fire shall try every man's work of what sort it is. If any man's work abide which he hath built thereupon, he shall receive a reward. If any man's work shall be burned, he shall suffer loss: but he himself shall be saved; yet so as by fire'. Here we have the governing principle in connection with this – 'the day shall declare it'. But, as I am suggesting, sometimes the devil gives us a preview of that day, and he makes us look at our own work and see what we have done, and he convinces us very quickly that we have done nothing at all. So, if you have been relying upon your own works, your whole position has collapsed. The only answer is this – at that great day, whatever may happen to me, and though all my work may be burned, thank God I am still saved, 'yet so as by fire'. What saves me is the 'one foundation', than which none other can be laid, 'Jesus Christ'. It is the breastplate of righteousness that saves me! So as I think of myself and my work, and eternity and judgment, the only thing I can be sure of is the righteousness of Jesus Christ which I have received by faith. We must always keep on this breastplate of righteousness, so that when the devil tries to discourage us we do not listen to him, and can repel him.

It is clear that there are many forms of discouragement. There are people who say, 'I have been in the Christian life so long; what have I got to show for it, what have I done?' And the devil casts them down, and they begin to doubt whether they are Christians. I am not excusing slackness in the Christian life. God forbid that the devil should use even what I am trying to say in order to lead someone astray! I know he is very ready to do so. I am not encouraging indolence. It is inexcusable. But what I am emphasizing is that we should not go to the other extreme and rely upon our activity and keep ourself happy in terms of what we are doing. One of the saddest spectacles to me in Christian life today, and particularly perhaps among evangelical people, is to see the number of people who are living on their own activities. Some are even breaking down in health. It is the devil who drives them to live on their works! It is a real danger. Finally, it will always let you down. There is only one breastplate – the righteousness of Jesus Christ.

But let us look at this matter in terms of a general kind of spiritual depression. What I have been referring to are, of course, particular manifestations of spiritual depression. Let us take a look at general spiritual depression. We need not spend much time in describing it. It is a state in which the whole tone of one's spiritual life has become lowered. It is like the weather that we have to endure at certain times – cold, everything at a standstill, with no evidence of spring and of life. A similar condition seems to descend sometimes upon the soul. It is sometimes very difficult to diagnose exactly how it has happened. But one just finds oneself in a period of aridity and dryness, lethargy and lifelessness. Many saints have testified to this.

If you know nothing about this I suggest that you had better examine your foundations. There is this kind of variation in spiritual experience as there is in natural physical life. You do not always feel the same physically; and it is the same in the spiritual realm. I find that the people who never have any variations are the people who follow the cults; because it is a part of that teaching that there should be no variations. But in the spiritual life variations are seen and known. This is 'life' and wherever you have life you tend to get variations. And, of course, we are in the body, and sometimes the cause of this depression may be purely physical. Physical depression can lead to spiritual depression and can mislead people. It is not easy for us to remember that the body and soul and spirit are very intimately related. Because you are feeling slack and enervated and lethargic in a physical sense, and for a good physical reason, the devil may say that it is all due to your spiritual state. So you begin to doubt whether you have ever been a Christian at all.

Other causes of depression are trials and tribulations. We have to meet them in this world. Our Lord had to endure 'the contradiction of sinners against himself', and there are people who hate Him and who hate every Christian, and do everything they can to entangle us and discourage us. You have but to read the fourth chapter of the Second Epistle to the Corinthians in order to remind yourself of this. The Apostle was being beset on all hands. There were people inside the Church and outside the Church trying to harm him, and to bring him down, and to frustrate all his work. And there was the physical aspect as well. He says: 'We have this treasure in earthen vessels, that the excellency of the power may be of God, and not of us. We are troubled on every side' – from all quarters he was being attacked, it could not be worse – 'yet not distressed, we are perplexed' – he could not understand it, wondering why it was happening – 'but not in despair; persecuted, but not forsaken; cast down' – the great Apostle! – 'but not destroyed; always bearing about in the body the dying of the Lord Jesus, that the life also of Jesus might be made manifest in our body. For we which live are alway delivered unto death for Jesus' sake, that the life also of Jesus might be made manifest in our mortal flesh'.

The Apostle Peter describes the same thing. He was writing to certain Christian people 'scattered abroad' in various parts of the world, and this is what he says to them: 'Wherein' (talking about the great salvation) 'you greatly rejoice, though now for a season, if need be, you are in heaviness through manifold temptations [trials]' (1 Peter 1:6). He says, I have heard about you; that is why I am writing to you. You are rejoicing in the great salvation and in Christ Jesus, though for a moment, 'for a season' for some strange reason, you are in heaviness through manifold trials, troubles and tribulations. Such are the conditions to which Christian people are often subjected.

These things may come with such power, such overwhelming force at times, that the poor Christian scarcely knows where he is or what is happening. And the devil tempts him and says, 'Do you still believe? do you still say you are a Christian? do you still say that your God is a God of love?' He may appear 'as an angel of light' and say, 'Of course, God is love, but it is obvious that He does not love you, for if He loved you He would not be allowing this to happen to you, you would not be going through this experience'. And so you are cast down into the very depths. You cannot help yourself, you find yourself in this state of 'heaviness', of spiritual depression. You do not see, you do not understand, you do not know, you cannot explain; and the devil is pressing you hard to give up, to abandon it all because 'there is nothing in it'.

There is only one protection against such assaults, it is 'the breastplate of righteousness'. Nothing else can avail you at this point. If you have not put on this breastplate the devil will cause you to doubt, or to grumble, or to complain and to say hard things against God. You will be like the man in Psalm 73 who said 'My feet had wellnigh slipped'. He almost said, 'I have cleansed my heart in vain'. What saved him was that he went into the house of God. That is just another way of 'putting on the breastplate of righteousness'. The only hope is to say, 'Well, I do not understand; but there are certain things I am sure of whatever happens'. That is to put on the breastplate of righteousness.

To put it in the words of the Old Testament: 'Rest in the Lord, and wait patiently for him'. When you do not understand; when you really are perplexed, as the Apostle was; when everything is going against you 'to drive you to despair', 'Rest in the Lord, and wait patiently for him'. It is the only thing you can do, but it is a wonderful thing to do. Thereby you put on the breastplate of righteousness, and the moment it is in position you are protected and are quite safe, even though you do not understand what is happening. Or look at the matter in terms of the Apostle's statement to the Romans: 'We know that all things work together for good to them that love God'. He does not say, 'We understand it'. He says we do not understand always how it is working, but 'We know that all things work together for good to them that love God, to them who are the called according to his purpose'. That leads you directly to justification by faith, the righteousness of Jesus Christ. You rest on that, it is the only thing to do. Toplady expresses it thus:

> *The work which His goodness began,*
> *The arm of His strength will complete;*
> *His promise is Yea and Amen,*
> *And never was forfeited yet.*

You cannot understand the particular happenings, you cannot give any explanation. All you know is that you are banking utterly upon this glorious purpose of God in Christ. That is simply another way of obeying the injunction, 'Put on the breastplate of righteousness'. You say to yourself, 'I have this on; and therefore I know that God is concerned about me; He would never have given me this, He would never have clothed me with this if He had not set His love upon me and saved me. I must take courage. I do not know what is happening to me now, I cannot fathom it; but I know this, If He has started His work in me He will go on to complete it'. So we can go on to say:

> *Things future, nor things that are now,*
> *Not all things below or above*
> *Can make Him His purpose forego*
> *Or sever my soul from His love*

The devil may be trying to convince you that you have been severed from God – if ever you were attached – and that these things are proving that your union with God is impossible. But you possess the breastplate of righteousness and nothing can penetrate it. Put it on! Remember the words you sometimes sing:

> *In every high and stormy gale*
> *My anchor holds within the veil*

Have you not known that? Thank God for it. These are different metaphors which say the same thing. I am like a little ship, a little boat out in mid-Atlantic, and a terrible storm arises; the billows are rolling and the gale is howling at me, and my frail bark is tossed hither and thither and I feel that at any moment I may sink. No, never! 'In every high and stormy gale, my anchor holds within the veil.' It is the anchor of Christ. He is 'the forerunner that has for us entered'. His righteousness is upon us and nothing will ever be able to touch us. Put on the breastplate of righteousness, no matter what may be happening to you, even the worst storm conceivable. This will protect you; it is the only thing that will do so.

Let me, then, summarize this whole section, which is concerned with the feelings and the sensibilities, by quoting a hymn which

'The Righteousness which is of God by Faith'
unfortunately is not in many modern hymnbooks although it is in
many of the old hymnbooks:

'Twixt gleams of joy and clouds of doubt
Our feelings come and go;
Our best estate is tossed about
In ceaseless ebb and flow:
No mood of feeling, form of thought,
Is constant for a day;
But Thou, O Lord, Thou changest not;
The same Thou art alway.

I grasp Thy strength, make it mine own,
My heart with peace is blest:
I lose my hold, and then comes down
Darkness, and cold unrest.
Let me no more my comfort draw
From my frail hold of Thee;
In this alone rejoice with awe –
Thy mighty grasp of me.

Out of that weak, unquiet drift
That comes but to depart,
To that pure heaven my spirit lift
Where Thou unchanging art;
Lay hold of me with Thy strong grasp,
Let Thy almighty arm
In its embrace my weakness clasp,
And I shall fear no harm.

Thy purpose of eternal good
Let me but surely know;
On this I'll lean – let changing mood
And feeling come or go –
Glad when Thy sunshine fills my soul
Not lorn when clouds o'ercast,
Since Thou within Thy sure control
Of love dost hold me fast.
(John Campbell Shairp)

That hymn is a glorious expression of what it means to put on the breastplate of righteousness. And if we do not know how to put it on we shall inevitably be defeated by the devil at one or other of these points which I have been mentioning. And there are many others. The ways and methods by which the devil comes are almost endless, And there is only one answer – Christ! Christ in me! Christ's righteousness upon me! My whole relationship to Him!

Not hell, nor anything else can penetrate the righteousness of Jesus Christ. Put it on! 'Having on the breastplate of righteousness.' So whatever the assault may be, and whatever form it may chance to take, we know that we are quite secure and that finally 'nothing can separate us from the love of God which is in Christ Jesus our Lord'. God has put upon us 'the righteousness of Jesus Christ'. And you put 'the breastplate of righteousness' on yourself by reminding yourself of this truth, and by relying utterly and solely upon it.

18

Putting on the Breastplate

'. . . and having on the breastplate of righteousness.'

Ephesians 6:14

In our previous study of 'the breastplate of righteousness' we have seen that the wearing of the breastplate gives us a general sense of confidence and of reassurance. That is one of the great advantages of putting on this armour – you feel better the moment you put it on. You feel you are not as exposed as you were; you are ready, you can rely upon its protection. That is very wonderful – assurance of salvation in general! Then we were considering how we need to be protected in the realm of our moods and feelings which are so variable and come and go. There is only one protection, namely, 'the righteousness of Christ'. Not our integrity, but 'the righteousness of God which is by faith through Jesus Christ'. 'Imputed!' 'Imparted!' Justification by Faith! Yes, and the working out of it – Sanctification! And it is the only protection against our varying moods and states and feelings; against discouragement, depression, and all that the devil tries to insinuate into us in order to mar our experience and to ruin our work. We have been considering all that.

Similarly, the breastplate of righteousness is absolutely essential as a protection against the accusations of the devil, whom Scripture describes as 'the accuser of the brethren'. At the same time he is also 'the adversary'. He not only accuses us to God, but he accuses us to ourselves, and it is essential that we should know how to protect ourselves against his attacks.

The Bible has much instruction with respect to this. Satan attacked all the patriarchs and the Old Testament saints; David, perhaps, in particular; and he likewise attacked the saints of the New Testament. The history of the Church, the biographies of the saints, tell us a great deal about how they endured and suffered the accusations of the devil. The Christian life is 'the fight of faith'! We are not promised a life of ease and of rest. We are not carried passively, as it were, to heaven. That is the false teaching of the cults. We experience 'the fight of faith!' We face the adversary! The accuser! He is ever threatening us; and he brings his terrible accusations against us.

Let us note some of the ways in which he does so. He does so above all when we try to pray to God. We turn to God in prayer, perhaps because of some need, or perhaps because we have felt the desire to do so; and the moment we get on our knees the devil begins to act. What he does is to suggest that we are in no condition to pray to God. He reminds us of our unworthiness, of our sinfulness, rakes up perhaps from a dim and distant past something we did, and holds it before us. Then turning himself into an angel of light he tells us about the greatness and the glory, the majesty and the holiness of God, and he says: 'How can such a person as you pray to God? What access, what entry, has such a miserable, sinful worm into that glory everlasting? God is light, and in Him is no darkness at all; He is of such a pure countenance that He cannot even look upon sin, and here are you proposing to enter into the presence of God!' The devil ridicules the whole thing and shows how utterly and completely impossible it is.

You will never be able to argue with the devil out of that position. He will defeat you every time. He knows us well; he has a record of our past; he knows our present; he knows all about us – and, as I say, he can tell us about God. There is only one way of withstanding his attacks, and that is, to 'put on the breastplate of righteousness'.

What that means at this point is the application of something we have already been considering; it means utter, absolute dependence upon the Lord Jesus Christ and His righteousness. It means an application to our case and condition of the glorious doctrine of justification by faith only. There is no hope apart from that. Anyone who is not clear about this doctrine is already defeated by the devil.

Let me give some illustrations of how it works. The only way to answer the devil when he comes in that way is to say: 'Therefore, being justified by faith, we have peace with God through our Lord Jesus Christ: by whom also we have access by faith into this grace wherein we stand' (Romans 5:1, 2). That is a final, conclusive, complete answer, because it takes the ground from under the devil's feet. He has reminded us of our sinfulness and our unworthiness. But then, when you quote these two verses, instead of being frightened by these accusations of the devil, you say to him: 'You do not frighten me by saying that, I know all about it as much as you do'. And speaking in this way you have already defeated him. If you do not understand justification by faith, of course, he has defeated you. But if you do understand it, then you say to him, 'I never proposed to go into the presence of God in my own righteousness; I do not plead before Him my good life or my personal excellence. You are quite right, there is no dispute at that point. If you say even more against me, if you try to damn me to the vilest hell, I will agree with it all. My integrity was not the basis of my approach to God. My access to Him is based upon the Lord Jesus Christ, 'by whom also we have access by faith into this grace wherein we stand'. It is all in this blessed Person. That is one of the meanings of 'putting on the breastplate of righteousness'! When the devil comes with his accusations, let us rout him in that way.

But do not be content with one quotation only when you are dealing with the devil. Rout him completely, hurl many texts at him. Take him to Hebrews 4 and read, or recite, to him verses 14 to 16: 'Seeing then that we have a great high priest, that is passed through the heavens, Jesus the Son of God, let us hold fast our profession; for we have not an high priest which cannot be touched with the feeling of our infirmities, but was in all points tempted like as we are, yet without sin. Let us therefore come boldly unto the throne of grace, that we may find mercy and find grace to help in time of need.' Tell the devil that you are dependent upon Christ, our great high priest, Jesus the Son of God. He is our representative! He is our high priest, He has died for our sins! Yes, we need mercy! And we know that we shall have it because He is on the throne of grace.

But the devil says, 'Ah yes, but hear me further. God is on the throne, and God is the Judge, and there is the law of God. Have you considered His righteousness and all His holy demands?' We reply, 'we agree that God is almighty and eternal and that He is upon the throne. But we know that for us that throne has become a throne of grace'. 'How do you know it is a throne of grace?' asks the devil. Our answer is, 'There is One seated at the right hand of the Judge, and He is our great high priest. He has satisfied every demand of the law, and God has acknowledged this by raising Him from the dead – Jesus the Son of God! He has passed through the heavens, and He is seated there'. So we can go to God with boldness and confidence in spite of our being what we are. Our Lord even knows what it is to be tempted. He has been here in the flesh, He understands it all; and He is there on our behalf. So that we are able to go 'boldly unto the throne of grace, to obtain mercy and find grace to help in time of need'. It is the same answer again. We wear this 'breastplate of righteousness'! Jesus Christ Himself! It is His righteousness that is put upon me, and that righteousness is sufficient for all my needs.

But let us give the devil another answer. Go to the tenth chapter of Hebrews and begin at verse 19: 'Having therefore, brethren, boldness to enter into the holiest by the blood of Jesus, by a new and living way, which he hath consecrated for us, through the veil, that is to say, his flesh; and having an high priest over the house of God, let us draw near with a true heart in full assurance of faith, having our hearts sprinkled from an evil conscience'. The devil has been reviving this 'evil conscience' – making it condemn us – in the way I have indicated; and we cannot answer it. We know that what it testifies against us is true. But the conscience can be cleansed and has been cleansed! It is sprinkled by the blood of Jesus Christ Himself, and 'our bodies washed with pure water'. This is just a very graphic and dramatic way of re-stating this glorious doctrine of justification by faith only.

For one further quotation turn to 1 John 3:21: 'Beloved, if our heart condemn us not, then have we confidence toward God'. There is only one way in which that can happen. It is the way in which you should ever approach the throne of God. It is by putting on this breastplate of righteousness. Let Toplady sum it up for us:

A debtor to mercy alone
Of covenant mercy I sing;
Nor fear with Thy righteousness on
My person and offering to bring.
The terrors of law and of God
With me can have nothing to do;
My Saviour's obedience and blood
Hide all my transgressions from view.

I am nothing, I am nobody; and my little offering, what is it? But all is well – 'Nor fear with Thy righteousness on, my person and offering to bring'. So when the devil comes and tries to discourage me and tells me I am not fit to pray, I repulse him in this manner.

The practical question for us is: Are we using this breastplate of righteousness in this respect as we ought? There are still too many Christian people who never take part in public prayer because they say that they are unworthy and unfit to do so. That is a very good reason, and a very wrong reason. Are you clear about justification by faith? Why are you talking so much about your own unfitness? It is the breastplate of righteousness you need! We are none of us fit. Who am I to stand in a pulpit to expound this holy Word and to lead in public prayer? 'Who is sufficient for these things?' We are to put on this blessed breastplate, the righteousness of Jesus Christ. Of yourself you will never be fit enough to enter into the presence of God. Though you may become a monk or a hermit or an anchorite and segregate yourself from the world, and fast, and sweat, and pray, you will have no entry to that presence except by the blood of Jesus. There is no other entry. But in Him you have access, you can 'stand' in this grace, you can go with boldness and confidence and assurance. It is by His blood! 'A new and living way'!

Never was it more necessary that we should know something about this boldness! Never has there been such need of prayer. Look at the world! Look at the Church! Are you interceding for them? Are you concerned about the desperate condition of the souls of men and women? Why do we not pray more? I sometimes think it is because the devil defeats us at this point, and we have never known what it is to 'put on' in this manner this breastplate of righteousness which God has provided for us.

We go on now to a second method of attack – the accusations of the devil when we fall into sin. It is a part of our doctrine that a Christian may fall into sin! There is no perfectionism in the New Testament. We are saved, but we are still fallible. The 'old nature' is still here – not the 'old man', but the 'old nature'. And while that old nature is in us we are ever liable to sin, and do fall into sin. Then the devil comes to us and tries to bring us into a sense of utter condemnation and of complete hopelessness and despair. He says, 'You have believed the Gospel. Good! But then you were ignorant, you did not know! Now you do know, and therefore you have now sinned against the light. Before, there was that excellent, adequate, and sufficient excuse of ignorance. But you cannot plead that any longer. Because as a child of God you have fallen into sin there is no hope for you now'. And so he hurls this accusation at us, and tells us that we have forfeited the love of God. He does this not only in the matter of open, public sinning; it may be that God was manifesting Himself to us and leading us, but we disobeyed, we put our own desires and our own ease first. And the devil then comes and torments us by telling us that there can be no forgiveness for such conduct, for we have sinned against the light.

There is again much that one could quote with regard to this aspect of the matter also; but the ultimate answer to this, as to the first accusation is still the breastplate of righteousness. This is always sufficient and will never fail us. The First Epistle of John seems specially written for this very condition. In the first chapter, beginning at verse 6, we read, 'If we say that we have fellowship with him' (who is light, and in whom there is no darkness at all) 'and walk in darkness, we lie and do not tell the truth. But if we walk in the light, as he is in the light, we have fellowship one with another, and the blood of Jesus Christ goes on cleansing us from all sin'. It is the continuous tense. 'Cleanseth' says the Authorized Version. It means that the blood of Christ keeps on cleansing us. Then 'if we say that we have no sin, we deceive ourselves, and the truth is not in us. If we confess our sins, he is faithful and just to forgive us our sins, and to cleanse us from all unrighteousness'. Then again in the first two verses of the second chapter: 'My little children, these things write I unto you, that ye sin not. But if any man sin, we have an advocate with the Father, Jesus Christ the righteous: and he is the propitiation for our sins: and not for ours only, but also for the sins of the whole world'. That is as clear and as explicit as anything could be; and yet I am quite sure that I have had to quote these verses in my vestry more frequently, possibly, than any other verses in the whole of the Bible. That shows that the devil succeeds in persuading many at this point that they have no hope. He tells them: 'There is no point in praying; you have no right to approach God. Surely you are a cad to go back to God to ask forgiveness after that sin, or after that failure, or after that disobedience. You have no standing at all, you have sinned against the light and there is no hope for you'. So they are held in the bondage and the despair and the utter hopelessness and sense of desertion which are the inevitable concomitants of listening to the devil at this point. It is obvious that they have not realized the significance of these verses in John's First Epistle because there they have the complete answer to their fears. 'If any man sin . . . If we confess our sins He is faithful and just to forgive them.'

The Apostle John expresses the matter in this way because he would have us understand that our relationship to God is a legal one. God always acts according to His own law. That is why foolish people who regard the notions of the wrath of God and the love of God, or the justice and the mercy of God, as being incompatible are denying the Scriptures. God's love is not a sentimental love. It is a just love, it is a holy love, it is a legal love. 'He is faithful and just!' God Himself has made a way whereby He can with justice forgive this sin into which the believer has fallen. I dare to go further and say that I believe that it means that when I go to Him in penitence and contrition, and with a broken heart because of what I have done, if He does not forgive me He is not being just, He is not being faithful to His own word. He has set His own Son forth as the 'propitiation' and I come to Him pleading that fact. God – I say it with reverence – cannot refuse you if you come to Him confessing your sin, truly penitent and casting yourself utterly upon your beloved Lord who has died for you and risen again for your justification. Such is John's argument.

You find the same argument, equally clearly, in Romans 8:1, which contains one of the most majestic statements concerning this matter in the entire Bible. The Apostle has been working out this great doctrine of justification by faith, particularly in the first four chapters; and then he has shown in the summary in chapter 5 some of the inevitable consequences. Then in chapters 6 and 7 he has dealt with two obvious objections to what he has just been saying; and, having finished that, he says: 'There is therefore now no condemnation to them which are in Christ Jesus'. There is no condemnation now; there never will be, and never can be, condemnation in the future. Remember that the Christian, as the Apostle has been demonstrating so abundantly, is out of the whole realm of the law. He is 'dead to the law', 'dead to sin'. How then can there be condemnation? Nothing can condemn the believer. He is in Christ Jesus! The Christian has to realize that he is in this entirely new relationship to God, he has been entirely removed out of the whole realm of law and of condemnation – the 'law of sin and of death'. 'The law of the Spirit of life in Christ Jesus hath made me free from the law of sin and death' (verse 2). The law that leads to death and condemnation has been fully answered and satisfied, and removed as far as the Christian is concerned.

We must learn to realize and to understand what the righteousness of Jesus Christ does to us. It covers us. It is God who has put it on us, and it is there for ever. 'But surely' says someone, 'this is the preaching of sheer Antinomianism. You are virtually saying, "Go out and sin as much as you like; all will be well with you".' That was the very charge brought against the Apostle Paul. His critics said: 'What shall we say then? Shall we continue in sin, that grace may abound?' (Romans 6:1). 'God forbid', says Paul. 'If you say that, it means you have not understood my teaching.' 'How shall we that are dead to sin, live any longer therein?'

In other words, what we have to realize at all points, and always, is that our standing is never based upon our actions or goodness. It is because we tend to think that it is so based that, when we fall into sin, we say, 'It is all over', and so we listen to the devil when he brings his accusations against us. Obviously we have been relying upon *our* goodness, *our* righteousness. The wearing of the breastplate of righteousness is our one security. Keep it on! And when the devil comes and says, 'You have no standing, you are condemned, you are finished', you must say, 'No! my position did not depend upon what I was doing, or not doing; it is always dependent upon the righteousness of the Lord Jesus Christ'. Turn to the devil and tell him, 'My relationship to God is not a variable one. The case is not that I am a child of God one day, and not a child of God the next day; then a child of God, and then again not a child of God. That is not the basis of my standing; that is not the position. When God had mercy upon me, He made me His child, and I remain His child. A very sinful, and a very unworthy one, perhaps, but still His child! And now, when I fall into sin, I have not sinned against the law, I have sinned against love. Like the prodigal, I will go back to my Father and I will tell Him, "Father, I am not worthy to be called thy son"! But He will embrace me, and He will say, "Do not talk nonsense, you are My child", and He will shower His love upon me'. That is the meaning of putting on the breastplate of righteousness! Never allow the devil to get you into a state of condemnation. Never allow a particular sin to raise again the whole question of your standing before God.

A simple illustration will help here. When your little child disobeys you, and is very naughty, and does something which is very wrong, you are displeased with the child, and you are certain to reprimand and punish him; but has that affected the relationship between you? Of course not! Transgressions do not affect relationship: so do not listen to the devil when he tells you that they do. Say to him: 'I know I am wrong, I am unworthy, I deserve to suffer for what I have done, but, thank God, I am still His child, and I know He forgives me.' And have you not felt that it is this certain knowledge that you are still the child of God, that He still loves you, and that He is going to forgive you – that it is this that breaks your heart most of all at that point? But it should not bring you into condemnation. The breastplate of righteousness is more than sufficient.

This does not mean the excusing of sin in a believer. Indeed, if we understand this doctrine truly, it is more calculated than anything else to keep us from sin. It is when we know the love of God to us, and when we love Him as we ought, that sin becomes most hateful. Nothing so keeps us from sin as the fear of hurting or offending or grieving the One who has loved us with such a love.

I must mention one further manifestation of the accusations of the devil, namely, his accusations when we come to die. Some of the greatest saints have had a terrible conflict with the devil on their deathbed. 'Let him that thinketh he standeth, take heed lest he fall!' You may be well now and brim-full of health, and you may tend to say, 'He would never shake me!' But let me remind you that you are facing the wiles of the devil. He has tried to shake some of the greatest of the saints on their deathbeds, reminding them of their past sins, reminding them of all they had not done, the poverty of their work and their service – showing it to be nothing! In the time of their physical weakness, and with death staring them in the face, the devil tries to shake them. The only answer to give him is still the same; it is 'the breastplate of righteousness'. You can apply it at this point by using the words of our Lord Himself in John 5:24: 'Verily, verily, I say unto you, He that heareth my word, and believeth on him that sent me, *hath*' – he has already got it – 'everlasting life, and shall not come into condemnation; but is passed from death unto life'. You feel that you have nothing to recommend you, but you can say, 'I rest upon His word. I have already passed from death unto life, I shall not come into condemnation, because of Him!' And to that you can add Paul's telling argumentation in Romans 8:31–37: 'What shall we then say to these things? If God be for us, who can be against us? He that spared not his own Son, but delivered him up for us all, how shall he not with him also freely give us all things? Who shall lay any thing to the charge of God's elect? It is God that justifieth. Who is he that condemneth?' Does Christ condemn us? No! 'It is Christ that died, yea, rather, that is risen again, who is even at the right hand of God, who also maketh intercession for us. Who shall separate us from the love of Christ?' Nobody! Nothing! But let Paul give his own conclusion in verses 38 and 39: 'For I am persuaded that neither death, nor life, nor angels, nor principalities, nor powers, nor things present, nor things to come, nor height, nor depth, nor any other creature, shall be able to separate us from the love of God which is in Christ Jesus our Lord'.

Ever wear the breastplate of righteousness. Never depart from it. Keep it on always. Let me put the truth to you in the well-known words of Count Zinzendorf, translated by John Wesley, part of which I quoted in an earlier study:

> *Jesus, Thy blood and righteousness*
> *My beauty are, my glorious dress;*
> *'Midst flaming worlds, in these arrayed,*
> *With joy shall I lift up my head.*

> *Bold shall I stand in Thy great day;*
> *For who aught to my charge shall lay?*
> *Fully through Thee absolved I am*
> *From sin and fear, from guilt and shame.*

> *Jesus, be endless praise to Thee,*
> *Whose boundless mercy hath for me,*
> *For me a full atonement made,*
> *An everlasting ransom paid.*

'Put on the breastplate of righteousness!'

19

Marching Orders

'Stand therefore, having your loins girt about with
truth, and having on the breastplate of righteousness.'

Ephesians 6:14

As we continue in this struggle against the devil and his forces we
must also realize that to have and to continue in a right view of
our life as Christian people in this present world is one of the
ways in which we put on the breastplate of righteousness. This
thought runs through the Old Testament and the New Testament
alike. Do we modern Christians remember this as we should?
Surely one of our greatest dangers is the worldliness that has crept
into the Church, and we have lost sight of this notion of the
Christian man's attitude towards life in this world. The whole of
the biblical teaching is to the effect that we are God's people and
therefore a separated people. In the Old Testament, the children
of Israel were marked off from everyone else by a great number of
rules and regulations and commandments. That was done simply
to differentiate them from others, and to show that they were
God's people. That is the meaning not only of the Ten Commandments but also of all the ceremonial law which taught that
they should not eat certain animals. And how constantly God
reminds them of that! 'You only have I known of all the people
[the nations] of the earth', He says through Amos (Amos 3:3).
They were a 'separate' people because they were His people. The
overruling commandment was 'Be ye holy'! Why? 'For I am holy.'

God separated Israel with the object of revealing Himself and
to bring in the great salvation. It was the Church in the Old
Testament. But the principle is found quite as plainly in the New
Testament as in the Old Testament. The Christian by definition
is to have an entirely different view of this present world from all

others, one reason being that he has a new view of himself. We are in this world, sharing its life, its affairs, with all other people; and yet though we are in it, we are not of it. And our biggest problem is the fighting of the devil as he confronts us in and through 'the world'. We must realize that if we are going to 'withstand' the devil we must see 'the world' as it is. As the Apostle John says '. . . this is the victory which overcometh the world, even our faith' (1 John 5:4).

'The world' in Scripture means, not the physical universe of course; it does not even mean the people in the world as such. It means the world of men as organized by the devil against God. It means the world as ruled by the devil. The Apostle Paul in the Second Epistle to the Corinthians, chapter 4, refers to him as 'the god of this world'! In the Epistle to the Ephesians chapter 2, verse 2, he calls him 'the prince of the power of the air, the spirit that now worketh in the children of disobedience'. He controls the mind and the outlook of the godless world. We must realize this.

Our position is based, ultimately, upon what our Lord Himself taught immediately before His death on the Cross when He offered up His last intercessory prayer on behalf of His people. It is recorded in the seventeenth chapter of John: 'I pray for them: I pray not for the world, but for them which thou hast given me; for they are thine'. He draws a fundamental distinction. He does not pray for the world, He prays only for the people whom God has called out of the world to be His own, to be His servants, His representatives, those through whom He is going to do His work after His departure. But then He goes on: 'I have given them thy word; and the world hath hated them, because they are not of the world, even as I am not of the world. I pray not that thou shouldest take them out of the world, but that thou shouldest keep them from the evil. They are not of the world, even as I am not of the world. Sanctify them through thy truth: thy word is truth'. He is going to leave these disciples, these poor followers of His. He knows their ignorance; knows that they do not understand what is coming, do not know the devil as He knew him, and do not know the world as He knew it. Though He had come into the world He never belonged to it, He was not of it. He was a stranger here. But as He passed through it He realized the power of the world; so He prays the Father that He will keep them. He says, I have kept them while I have been here, I am now going back to Thee; keep them, 'sanctify them through thy truth; thy word is truth'. The disciples would be engaged in this mighty fight against 'the world'.

This same teaching is found in all the Epistles. We find it in chapter 5 of the Epistle to the Ephesians in verse 8. Paul says, 'Ye were sometimes darkness, but now are ye light in the Lord'. You are no longer what you were, says the Apostle, you are no longer darkness, you are light, you are no longer in the world, you are in the Church. This great change has taken place. Observe the way in which He states it in writing to the Philippians: 'Our conversation [our citizenship] is in heaven'. Though we live in this world, and are still in a sense citizens of this world, our real citizenship is in heaven. That is where we belong. Someone has translated it, 'We are a colony of heaven'. In other words, we do not belong to this world, heaven is our home, heaven is our city. Our ultimate citizenship is there; heaven is the place to which we owe our first allegiance.

It is said about God's people in the eleventh chapter of the Epistle to the Hebrews: '. . . they confessed that they were strangers and pilgrims on the earth' (v. 13). That is said about the great heroes of the faith in various generations. It was the great characteristic of such people as Abel, Noah, Abraham, Isaac, Jacob, Moses, and David. That is how they viewed life in this world. They were in it, they played their part in it; but they never belonged to it; they were separate. They knew that they were strangers and pilgrims, mere sojourners and travellers. They did not settle down in this world, they did not live for this world; their activities were not for this world primarily. They played their part, they did not segregate themselves, they did not go out of the world; but they did not live for it, their horizon was not limited by it. They looked beyond it, 'they looked for a city which hath foundations, whose builder and maker is God'. Similarly you find the Apostle Peter, in appealing to Christian people, writing, 'Dearly beloved, I beseech you as strangers and pilgrims, abstain from fleshly lusts, which war against the soul; having your conversation honest among the Gentiles: that whereas they speak against you as evildoers, they may by your good works, which they shall behold, glorify God in the day of visitation' (1 Peter 2:11, 12).

I am emphasizing that an essential part of putting on the breastplate of righteousness is to start with that realization. If you say, 'Isn't life wonderful, isn't the world wonderful?', if you are fascinated by this world and controlled by it, you are doomed to failure. The Apostle John says, 'The world passeth away and the lust thereof; but he that doeth the will of God abideth for ever'. So we have to start with this realization, that the whole organization of the life of this world is against us as Christians. The newspapers are a perfect representation of the mind of the world. Look at what they say, what they teach, what they insinuate. Look at their representation of life, and look at what they are advocating. The same is true of the other instruments – television, wireless, and the rest – all belong to the world. The power controlling them is what the Bible calls 'The world'. They do not urge us to think about the soul and our relationship to God and eternity. They are all earth-bound, all within the temporal, the material, the physical. And the world hates the Bible; it is anti-God. You need not go to Russia to get evidence of it; you can find it in your newspapers – the blatant, open, criticizing and ridiculing of the Bible and its teaching. The world is doing that constantly. Most of the great men of the world today are doing this very thing. Such is 'the world'!

If we fail to realize these things, we are already defeated. The Christian has to realize that the world is against him, that the devil is using the visible, the seen, to defeat God's people, to bring them into confusion, to entangle them, to ensnare them, and thus to stand between them and the blessings that God is ready to give them. How slow we are to realize this! Our Lord says, 'If the world hate you, ye know that it hated me before it hated you'. Do not be surprised, He says. It hated the Lord, and He says, 'The servant is not greater than his Lord. If they have hated me they will hate you'. And God's people have always been hated. One main point of the eleventh chapter of Hebrews is to show how the world treated them. The world was 'not worthy of them'; it persecuted them, it maligned them, it hated them. And 'the world' let us remember, can come into the Church; which explains why Christian people often receive persecution from merely nominal Christians. They have always had it, they are still getting it. The mind of the world says, 'Religion is all right, but you must not go too far, you must not take it too seriously'. There is always a hatred on the part of the world for true Christianity.

Obviously, therefore, an essential part of putting on the breastplate of righteousness is to realize that you can afford to take nothing for granted, that you have to be on the watch always, that you must walk circumspectly, for the times are evil. We are surrounded by that which is utterly opposed to us and trying to get us down. I am not thinking of open sin only. Worldliness is not confined to flagrant sinning. There are many highly respectable people who are utterly worldly. To be worldly means that God is shut out, Christ is shut out, the holy life is shut off. Very respectable perhaps, but not Christian; that is the essence of worldliness.

We have to realize that this world in which we are living is not really our world. As Christians we live in it, and we must take our part in it. But we must not get excited about it; our biggest ambition must not be World Reform. What must matter most to us is that 'our citizenship is in heaven'. If we are true Christians we know that this world will never be truly reformed. It cannot be reformed, because it is under the power and dominion of the devil. It is also under 'the wrath of God', under judgment, and will finally be destroyed. Therefore a man whose whole idea is to make the world a better place and who thinks that such a programme makes him a Christian is denying the essential teaching of the Scripture. 'Our citizenship is in heaven.' The world is under 'the god of this world', the devil; and it is facing nothing but final disaster and final judgment. 'Put on the breastplate of righteousness.' Realize the state of the world in which you are living; do not look to it for your pleasure, your happiness, your joy. Use it, but do not abuse it. Keep your eye upon your heavenly home, the place to which you belong -- 'set your affection on things above'.

We must take this matter a step further and say, that we must have a more practical realization of the character of the place to which we are going. We are travellers, 'strangers and pilgrims'. The world, as the poet Dryden put it, is an inn. In it you spend the night, pay your bill in the morning, and go on. We are but travelling through this world. But we must obviously know where we are going, and something of the nature of our destination. We shall have to consider that in detail when we come to look at 'the helmet of salvation'. I mention it at this point, because it is an essential part of the breastplate of righteousness. We must realize the obvious need of preparation.

This again is a theme which is found throughout Scripture. A journeyman, a stranger, a pilgrim, obviously keeps in the forefront of his thinking the place to which he is going. He can do certain things *en route*, but if you set out upon a journey, surely your object is to arrive at your destination. You are not interested in travelling as such. Travelling is but a means of bringing you to the goal at which you wish to arrive. It is a perfect picture of the life of the Christian in this world; he is a traveller. It means, therefore, that he does not settle down in this world, and feel anxious to do so, and regret the fact that he has to go out of it. He should be anxious to arrive, and so he constantly reminds himself of the place at which he is going to arrive. He would never have set out for it if he did not desire to get there.

It is a part of putting on the breastplate of righteousness, that I remind myself daily of where I am, and where I am going. Paul states this in his letter to the Romans in chapter 13 beginning at verse 11: 'And that, knowing the time, that now it is high time to awake out of sleep: for now is our salvation nearer than when we believed'. He means that you are nearer to the goal than when you started; you have travelled a certain number of miles; '. . . our salvation is nearer than when we believed'. Then Paul adds, 'The night is far spent, the day is at hand . . .' This world is a place of darkness and of night, and we are making for the dawn, for the day, the everlasting day of God. Then follows the Apostle's exhortation: 'Let us therefore cast off the works of darkness, and let us put on the armour of light. Let us walk honestly, as in the day; not in rioting and drunkenness, not in chambering and wantonness, not in strife and envying. But put ye on the Lord Jesus Christ, and make not provision for the flesh, to fulfil the lusts thereof'. In other words you say to yourself, 'I do not belong here, I am passing through this country, this is the night, this is the darkness. I am making for heaven, for light, for God, for glory. Time is passing and I must be prepared for the great moment which is coming!' When you say this you are putting on the breastplate of righteousness.

But we have still more specific instruction in the Book of Revelation, in chapter 21, verse 27: 'And there shall in no wise enter into it [the city] anything that defileth, neither whatsoever worketh abomination, or maketh a lie: but they' – and they only – 'which are written in the Lamb's book of life'. And in the last chapter in the Bible, verses 14 and 15: 'Blessed are they that do his commandments, that they may have right to the tree of life, and may enter in through the gates into the city'. Here 'the holy city' is in view and we are told that certain people have no right of entrance. Indeed it is only those that 'do his command-ments' who have a right to the tree of life and may enter in through the gates into the city. Outside are spiritual dogs, the scavengers, that nose about picking up this and that for their delectation and enjoyment – 'sorcerers, whoremongers, murderers, idolaters, and whosoever loveth and maketh a lie'. They will not enter into that city. We may fool man; but we cannot fool God. There is an examination as you enter through the gates of that city.

A Christian is a man who realizes that he is making for a city. The chief ambition of a Christian is to enter through those gates and to partake of that 'tree of life' for ever and for ever. If he really believes the words I have just been quoting, it will be the first thing in his life, and he will be preparing for that. 'Our salvation is nearer than when we believed. The night is far spent, the day is at hand.' We are drawing nearer. There is no time to waste.

It is a contradiction in terms for Christian people to be giving so much of their energy to this world. Church conferences and assemblies spend most of their time in considering 'this world', passing resolutions about this world. But our first business is to prepare for that other world! This world is doomed. It is under the condemnation of God; it will never be made a better place. Recall how men have tried in the last hundred years to reform it, and how ministers of religion and leaders in churches have given themselves to politics. But look at the state of the Church and the world! The men who have been the greatest benefactors to this world have been such people as those in Hebrews 11 who realized that they were 'strangers and pilgrims' and kept their eye 'upon the recompense of the reward' – such men as Moses, who did not glory in being called the son of Pharaoh's daughter, but was prepared to suffer affliction with the people of God rather than 'to enjoy the pleasures of sin for a season'. Worldliness has often ruined the testimony of the Church; and we must return to this biblical view of the Christian. To do so is 'putting on the breastplate of righteousness'. Surely we must give our energy to this very practical matter. We must apply this truth which we claim to believe, and as we do so we are putting on the breastplate.

In many other respects also we are to wear the breastplate. John in his First Epistle, in the first chapter and the fifth verse, states clearly: 'God is light, and in him is no darkness at all'. So it follows that 'If we say that we have fellowship with him, and walk in darkness, we lie and do not the truth'. The Apostle means that if we claim that we are Christians and not like others in the world, if we claim that we are church members having fellowship with God, yet walk in darkness at the same time, then we are liars in whom the truth has no place. John returns to the theme in his second chapter: 'He that saith, I know him, and keepeth not his commandments, is a liar, and the truth is not in him'. To put on the breastplate of righteousness is to realize the force of such words and to prove that you realize it by ceasing to walk in darkness.

Let me draw certain practical deductions from these aspects of Christian doctrine which we have been mentioning. We do so, as do the Epistles themselves, by bringing in the word 'Therefore'. Paul has already done that in this Epistle to the Ephesians. Having stated his doctrine in the first three chapters he begins chapter four by saying: 'I *therefore*, the prisoner of the Lord, beseech you that ye walk worthy of the vocation wherewith ye are called'. He has reminded them of the doctrine; 'therefore', he says, put it into practice. He does the same thing in the twelfth chapter of the Epistle to the Romans: 'I beseech you, *therefore*, brethren, by the mercies of God' – the mercies about which he has been telling them in the eleventh chapter. If I were asked to state in a word what it means to put on the breastplate of righteousness, I would say that it means to understand the meaning of the word *therefore* in the New Testament Epistles.

But, of course, we cannot leave it at that; the Apostles themselves do not do so, for they proceed to work out the 'therefore' for us. We must content ourselves with a number of headings. Shout these at yourself, and as you do so you are putting on the breastplate of righteousness. Christ says, 'If you know these things, happy are ye if ye do them'! You can listen to this glorious doctrine of the blessed God, but if you do not apply it, it will be of no value to you. Many Christians are in that miserable condition because of this wretched failure. They do not come to the 'Therefore'! They stop at the doctrine. They think they know it, but they fail to apply it.

We can divide these headings or slogans into negative and positive. The negatives are found in the Epistle to the Ephesians from chapter 4, verse 17 onwards: 'This I say therefore, and testify in the Lord, that ye henceforth walk not as other Gentiles walk, in the vanity of their mind, having the understanding darkened, being alienated from the life of God through the ignorance that is in them, because of the blindness of their heart: who being past feeling have given themselves over unto lasciviousness, to work all uncleanness with greediness'. The Christian must not walk in that way any longer. And then Paul continues: '*Wherefore* putting away lying, speak every man truth with his neighbour . . . Be ye angry, and sin not: let not the sun go down upon your wrath: neither give place to the devil. Let him that stole steal no more'. These are the negatives – slogans. He sums it all up, as it were, in chapter 5: verse 11: 'Have no fellowship with the unfruitful works of darkness, but rather reprove them'. That is a command to us today as much as it was to these Ephesian Christians in the first century.

This does not mean, I repeat, that you are to go out of the world. You still have to meet people, and have acquaintances, and do business; but you have no 'fellowship' and 'friendship' with them, you do not become one of them. In the Epistle to the Romans in chapter 6, verse 12, Paul having said, 'Reckon ye also yourselves to be dead indeed unto sin, but alive unto God', continues, 'Let not sin *therefore* reign in your mortal body, that ye should obey it in the lusts thereof. Neither yield ye your members as instruments of unrighteousness unto sin'. If you do these things you are contradicting yourself, you are denying what you say you believe. Again in chapter 8, in verse 12, he says, '*Therefore*, brethren, we are debtors, not to the flesh, to live after the flesh. For if ye live after the flesh ye shall die'. And then at the beginning of chapter 12: 'I beseech you *therefore*, brethren, by the mercies of God, that ye present your bodies a living sacrifice, holy, acceptable unto God, which is your reasonable service. And be not conformed to this world . . .' But so many are still conformed to this world, even after coming into the realm of the Church. You see worldly distinctions, class distinctions, the mere sophistication of men, the appearance of gentility in the Church! These things are of 'the world', and we must not be conformed to this world because we do not belong to it. What should be obvious about the Christian in the first instance is not that he belongs to a certain stratum of society, or that he has been educated in a certain manner, but that he belongs to Christ, that his citizenship is in heaven.

And then we have the statement in chapter thirteen already quoted. 'The night is far spent, the day is at hand: let us *therefore* cast off the works of darkness, and let us put on the armour of light. Let us walk honestly, as in the day.' And next, those words that had such a profound effect on Augustine, 'Not in rioting and drunkenness, not in chambering and wantonness, not in strife and envying . . .' 'Not', 'not'. These are the negatives. 'We are not of the night, nor of darkness'. Once more, in 1 Thessalonians 5:22: 'Abstain from all appearance of evil', which means, 'abstain from every form of evil'. It does not matter what it is, abstain from it. Jude says, 'hating even the garment spotted by the flesh' (v. 23). The very garment is spotted by sin. Do not touch it, have nothing to do with it. This is typical of the negative exhortations of the New Testament. The apostle John writes: 'Love not the world, neither the things that are in the world . . . the lust of the flesh, and the lust of the eyes, and the pride of life'. They are the very antithesis of that which delights the heart of God.

Turning to the positives we find that they are addressed to

'the new man' whom the believer has 'put on', as for example in Romans 6:13: 'Yield yourselves unto God, as those that are alive from the dead, and your members [your faculties] as instruments of righteousness unto God'. In Romans 8:13 we read: 'If ye through the Spirit do mortify the deeds of the body, ye shall live'. Similar exhortations appear in Colossians, chapter 3: 'Mortify therefore your members which are upon the earth; fornication, uncleanness, inordinate affection, evil concupiscence, and covetousness, which is idolatry: for which things' sake the wrath of God cometh on the children of disobedience: in the which ye also walked some time, when ye lived in them. But now ye also put off all these; anger, wrath, malice, blasphemy, filthy communication out of your mouth. Lie not one to another, seeing that ye have put off the old man with his deeds; And have put on the new man, which is renewed in knowledge after the image of him that created him' (vv. 5-10).

Going back again to Romans 12, we find the negative followed by, 'Be ye transformed by the renewing of your mind, that ye may prove what is that good, and acceptable, and perfect will of God' (v. 2). Walk circumspectly, redeem the time, do not waste a moment. You are children of the light, you are children of the day. Then in Colossians 3 again: 'Set your affection on things that are above, not on things that are on the earth'. Set them! You have to set them as if you are setting a compass, plotting a course. And you have to do this deliberately. The world will not help you, but rather hinder you. If you start the day with your newspaper and the wireless you will be setting your affections elsewhere. 'Grow in grace, and in the knowledge of the Lord Jesus Christ'. 'Every man that hath this hope in him purifieth himself, even as he is pure.'

'The crowning day is coming, by and by.' The night is far spent, the day is at hand.' The investiture is coming. People who go to be invested and receive medals and honours in Buckingham Palace spend much time in preparing for the occasion. They prepare their clothing, their bodies, their manners – everything. Christian! the day of your investiture is coming, the day when you will stand before the King 'immortal, invisible, the only wise God', and be invested with your crown of glory, and enter into the enjoyment of that glory for all eternity. It is coming!

'Our salvation is nearer than when we believed!' We have not a moment to waste. Realize all these things, and as you do so you will be able to 'withstand' all the wiles of the devil, even in the evil day, and having done all things you will be able still to 'stand'. 'Put on the breastplate of righteousness!'

20

Stand Fast

'And your feet shod with the preparation of the gospel of peace.'

Ephesians 6:15

In these words we come to examine yet another piece in this 'whole armour of God' which is provided for us as God's people in our fight in this world against the devil, and the principalities and powers, the rulers of the darkness of this world, and spiritual wickedness in high places. I would remind you as we come to this next piece that the Apostle is using a figure; and we must be careful not to over-literalize it or press it too far.

This third piece, which has reference to the feet, reminds us again that the entire personality is engaged in this Christian warfare; and that therefore nothing must ever be neglected. Nothing is more important in the Christian life than balance. Many of our troubles are due to lack of balance, a fact of which the enemy is well aware. The very figure the Apostle uses reminds us of the wholeness, and that every part of us as Christians is engaged in this conflict. We are not Christians in sections and portions. Our faith takes up the whole life, and the whole man; so we have to protect ourselves at every single point.

It is interesting, nevertheless, to notice that the different parts have their relative importance. One might be tempted to feel at first that the feet are comparatively unimportant. When you compare the heart and the feet from the standpoint of mechanism and subtlety there is, of course, an obvious difference. The foot seems coarse and comparatively unimportant. There is the danger, therefore, in the Christian life of regarding certain aspects as relatively unimportant. But we are told here that we must protect our feet, and for the obvious reason that they play a vital part in life. However powerful your chest may be, and however wonderful your loins, if you get wounded in your feet, or if you slip and fall in the battle, you will be easy prey for your antagonist. So the feet, while having their own importance, contribute to the welfare of the whole body.

The word the Apostle emphasizes shows the importance of the feet. It is the word, 'stand', 'withstand'. After all, you stand upon your feet! You do not stand on your chest! So in a sense everything depends upon the security and the safety and the good functioning of the feet.

This selfsame Apostle has dealt with this matter very clearly in what he says about the body in the twelfth chapter of the First Epistle to the Corinthians. There he uses this analogy of the body in a different way. The Church at Corinth was divided into groups and sects, and his way of dealing with that evil is: to say, Do you not remember that you are the body of Christ and that you cannot divide the body? The eye may sometimes say to the hand, I have no need of you; what is a hand in comparison with an eye? There are comely parts, and less comely parts, and we tend to treat with disdain the less comely parts. But says Paul, that is foolish; every part of the body is essential to the true functioning of the whole body. Because of the nature of the body, when there is anything wrong in your little finger the whole body will suffer. We are reminded, therefore, that the feet are absolutely essential to the body's welfare because of the unity of the body. The Christian man is one personality; every part of him counts; so we must not treat any part with disrespect or with any kind of negligence.

So we come to consider what must be done about the feet. Our feet with which we walk along the roads in the dust and the mud and the mire are very important. Let us be careful that we know exactly what to do with them. What we are told is: 'Have your feet shod with the preparation of the gospel of peace'. The best way to understand the meaning of these words is to start with the actual analogy the Apostle uses. He was thinking, undoubtedly, of a Roman soldier. The provision made for the Roman soldier's feet was a certain type of sandal. Not a boot, but a sandal, which consisted essentially of a sole with straps which held firmly on to the foot. But still more important this sandal had hobnails or studs underneath.

The sandal provided the Roman soldier with firmness of hold, to prevent his sliding and slipping and falling; hence the studs. But there was another reason for providing him with sandals made of stout material. A very familiar device in warfare in those days was to place certain traps or gins in the ground. They would take a piece of wood, or a stick, and chisel it into a narrow point, then they would fix this into the ground with the sharp point sticking up slightly above the surface, almost invisible. When an enemy came running along, if he had no sandals on, these spikes would suddenly penetrate the sole of his foot. This would not only cause severe pain, it would also cause bleeding, and it might also become infected and put the soldier entirely out of action. It was most important, therefore, that the feet should be protected against these traps that were camouflaged and hidden in order to cause this trouble.

The third obvious reason for providing these sandals was mobility. Nothing is more important in an army than mobility. The Romans were very interested in this aspect of warfare. The man who first saw the importance of mobility in a military sense was Alexander the Great, one of the greatest captains of armies and of war that the world has ever known. He lived in the fourth century before Christ and had had his greatest successes by moving his armies quickly and unexpectedly, while his foes were stationary, or moving in a ponderous and slow manner. So he provided his soldiers with the right kind of footwear, and the Romans and others had by this time copied Alexander. In this way the Apostle was provided with a valuable and instructive lesson for Christians who were fighting and standing against 'the wiles of the devil'. He says to them, 'Have your feet shod with the preparation of the gospel of peace'.

We are interested in the spiritual application of this analogy. The term 'preparation' is the key to that. 'The gospel of peace' is not difficult to understand, but what is the meaning of the word 'preparation', as it is translated, in the Authorized Version? There are two main interpretations, and both can claim, up to a point, that they are based upon the original basic meaning of the word used by the Apostle. The first is, that it simply conveys the notion of 'firmness', that the 'preparation' of the Gospel of peace means the firmness which is given to us by the Gospel of peace. The so-called *New English Bible* adopts that meaning in its translation, 'to give you firm footing'. But the common idea which is adopted very generally, with few exceptions, is something much nearer to what we have in the Authorized Version, and, indeed, is but a variant of it – 'Your feet shod with the "preparedness" [or the "readiness"] . . .' John Wycliffe was the first to see that that is the real meaning. He translated it 'in making ready', which means 'readiness', or 'being prepared'. The Revised Standard Version of America supplies a good translation, namely 'equipment'; 'having your feet shod with the equipment of the gospel of peace'. The translation given by the *New English Bible* is not even considered by Arndt and Gingrich in their lexicon. They concentrate entirely on the 'preparedness', 'readiness', and especially on the idea of 'equipment'. There is no doubt, it seems to me, that this is right.

The same word is used in the Epistle to Titus in the third chapter and the first verse, where the Apostle says: 'Put them in mind to be subject to principalities and powers, to obey magistrates to be *ready* to every good work'. I propose therefore to accept as the best translation the word 'equipment', because it seems to me that the word 'equipment' includes both the idea of preparedness and also the element of stability and steadfastness.

Why does the Apostle tell us that we must have our feet shod with the preparedness, the readiness, the equipment of the Gospel of peace? There are some who say that what is meant is our readiness to take the good news of the Gospel of peace and of salvation to others; that it means that as Christians we should be ready to evangelize, always ready to obey the command to go and 'preach the Gospel'. In Dr John Henry Jowett's book on *The Armour of God*, in the chapter devoted to this matter of the feet, there is a characteristic sermon emphasizing our being ready to obey the call of God and to engage in missionary activity; that we are always to be on the *qui vive* as it were, so that when the command comes to us we shall be ready to go. 'For My sake and the Gospel's, go, and tell redemption's story.' I imagine that this interpretation was suggested by those Bibles which have marginal references which direct to two portions of Scripture. The first is Romans 10:15: 'How shall they preach, except they be sent? as it is written, How beautiful are the feet of them that preach the gospel of peace and bring glad tidings of good things!' – a quotation from Isaiah 52:7. So in the marginal reference you will find opposite 'feet' in Romans 10:15, Isaiah 52:7. And so the notion comes in of being ready to run with the Gospel, the good news of peace with God through the blood of Christ.

It seems to me that this interpretation must be rejected completely, and for one all-sufficient reason. The Apostle is dealing here with one thing only, namely our fight and conflict with the devil. 'We wrestle not against flesh and blood, but against the principalities and powers.' His whole object is to enable us to 'stand' against the wiles of the devil. He is not thinking of evangelizing, he is picturing a Christian who is being attacked night and day by the devil and all his powers, and warning him that if he is not filled with the power of God, and if he does not put on this whole armour of God, he will be defeated. It is a defensive warfare. How can the question of evangelism possibly come into this matter of defensive warfare?

But someone may ask, 'Well, how did anyone ever come to interpret it in that way?' Here we have a most interesting point in connection with our reading and interpretation of the Scriptures. It is good to use a Concordance, but it can be a very dangerous instrument! You can read this verse, 'And your feet shod . . .' and then turn to your Concordance and you are referred to Romans 10:15, Isaiah 52:7 etc.; and this determines your interpretation. Now that is a bad use of a Concordance. There are many who always interpret Scripture in such a manner. They take a word, turn up the references, and the sermon is based upon the uses of the word. And an interpretation is produced which has little relationship to the context. Here, then, is a most important lesson. We must never interpret a word or a phrase without being sure that the interpretation fits the context. Do not isolate it and think of possible meanings or uses; everything must be taken in its context. The moment you adopt this method here, you see that that particular interpretation of 'preparedness' and 'readiness' and 'eagerness' is altogether wrong. Indeed, it is quite misleading at this point, it makes you forget all about the devil and the principalities and powers. In the sermon by Dr Jowett to which I have referred they are not even mentioned at all. He speaks of nothing but preaching the Gospel, and taking it to the distant parts of the world, and being ready to obey the call. It is important, I say, always to take a word, or a phrase, in its context. If people paid attention to the context most of our problems of interpretation would be solved. Most heresies have arisen because men have lifted a word or a phrase entirely out of its context and elaborated a false theory or a point of view out of it.

Since, then, the Apostle is speaking about our fight against the devil, our interpretation of his words must include the following principles. The first is firmness, confidence, a sense of assurance. If you are engaged in a mortal conflict with a powerful, wily, nimble adversary, you must guard against falling and slipping and sliding, by making sure that you are well shod. That is important in all kinds of physical conflict; and it is even more important in the spiritual realm. You have to be quite sure that you know what you are doing, and where you are standing. You must not suddenly find everything slipping from under your feet because your feet have not got a firm grip.

This means that you must be resolute; that you have to resolve to be 'a good soldier of Jesus Christ', come what may. You have to resolve to adhere to this Gospel, no matter what hosts of foes may be arrayed against you. You have to take a firm grip of yourself. You must not come into the Christian life and continue in it half-heartedly, half in and half out, desiring benefits but objecting to duties, wanting privileges but rejecting responsibilities. You have to start by being firm and solid and resolute and assured. Paul's mention of the sandals carries that notion. If you want to 'stand', make sure that you can stand and that you want to stand. Do not rush out as it were in your bare feet, but put on the sandals with the studs. Pay great attention to this requirement.

The Apostle teaches the same truth in 1 Corinthians 16 in the command, 'Stand fast in the faith!' (v. 13). As I look at the Church today I see large numbers of people whose feet are not shod with the preparation of the Gospel of peace. I see them slipping and sliding – Evangelicals as well as others! Men are no longer standing, they are no longer resolute, they no longer know what to believe, and they do not hold to it, come what may. Compromise is all too common. Be pleasant, be nice, be affable, are today's slogans. Many Protestants seem to be ready to return to Rome at any moment! It is because they have not got their feet shod with the equipment of the Gospel of peace. They are slipping and sliding, shifting and moving, not knowing where they are, and the devil is rejoicing in the meantime. This is applicable to Churches as well as to individuals.

Do you know what to believe? Is there anything for which you are prepared to 'stand'? I do not apologize for putting such questions. It seems to me that people are ready today to compromise on everything. Do you really believe that the Bible is the Word of God, divinely and uniquely inspired, and inerrant? Are you ready to stand on that truth? That is what is meant by putting on the sandals. Are you ready to stand for the deity of Christ? for his Virgin Birth? for the miracles? Are you ready to stand for the substitutionary, sacrificial, atoning death of our Lord? Are you ready to stand for the resurrection of Christ as a literal physical fact? Are you ready to stand for the Person of the Holy Spirit? Do you know where you want to stand, do you know your position? How can you fight the enemy if you do not know your own position? I sometimes feel that the art of warfare should be made compulsory reading, that we should read about the great commanders of armies such as Alexander, Cromwell, Napoleon and others. They chose their place and position always; they knew where they were going to stand. And we must not allow the enemy to decide. Take up your position and say, 'I stand here!' 'Stand' with Martin Luther who was not troubled by the fact that he had twelve centuries of Roman Catholicism and tradition against him. 'Here I stand; I can do no other', he said; and we too have to learn to 'stand'. We have to know what we believe; and be resolute and determined to stand for it, come what may.

Have you a definite position? Are you prepared to stand in it, and say, 'I will never yield, I will never move from this?' The moment you begin to compromise on this Word of God you will soon be slipping and sliding both in doctrine and in practice.

Some people are constantly contradicting themselves; they praise the Protestant and the Nonconformist Fathers in the first half of their address or article; then criticize them in the second half. That is not 'standing'; that is sliding. They do not know where they are, and no-one else knows.

As the Apostle Paul says in 2 Corinthians 1:19, the Gospel of Christ is not yea and nay at one and the same time. That is true of politics, of ecclesiasticism, of 'the world'; but it is not true of Christ. The Gospel of the Son of God, Jesus Christ, is never 'yea and nay'. Paul's teaching does not tally with the popular creed of today – 'dialecticism', they call it – which teaches 'Yes and No' in the same breath. But, says Paul, the Gospel is not 'yea and nay', but 'in him [Christ] was yea. For all the promises of God in him are yea, and in him Amen, unto the glory of God by us'. And that means, according to some interpreters, that you and I must add our Amen to his Amen, to his great 'Yea'. Stand on it, at all costs.

But our standing applies not only to doctrine; it applies to the whole life. Once you have come into this life you have to take your stand unflinchingly on the Lord's side. When you meet your old friends from the world, and they propose that you go on doing what you used to do with them, you know that you cannot, and you refuse to do so. You stand resolutely. You do not slide towards them. No! Have your feet shod with the preparedness of the Gospel of peace. Once you come into this life and realize that it is entirely different from your former life, you must say, 'I stand here!' You may be tempted by someone you like very much, but you must say 'I cannot betray my Lord; I am pledged to obey His commandments. My feet are shod, I am not moving.' We are not meant to behave ridiculously, of course; but to stand on principles, and to apply those principles. This applies intellectually, doctrinally, and in conduct and behaviour. It applies in every department of life.

Are your feet shod? That is the great need of this hour; it is the call of God, I believe, to the Church and to every Christian at this present time. God is looking for people who will 'stand'! I believe He is doing in these days what He did in the days of Gideon. The 'hosts of Midian' had come up, and a large army of about 32,000 was gathered together by Israel. But God reduced that army to a mere handful. Of the 32,000 there were only 300 whom God could trust. He knew these would stand, that they would never quit, that they would never compromise. So He dismissed the rest, and with the little 300, the remnant, He discomfited and routed the hosts of Midian. God has always done His greatest work through a remnant. Get rid of the notion of numbers. What God wants is a man or a woman who is prepared to 'stand', whose feet are 'shod with the equipment of the gospel of peace'. He knows that He can rely upon such; that they will stand no matter what is happening round and about them.

Are you standing? Do you propose to stand? Are you ready to stand? Have you truly come into the Christian life, or is one foot in the world, one foot in the Church? Which is it? You 'cannot serve God and Mammon'. You may think you can; you will soon find that you cannot. You will be defeated, and you will be miserable, and when you face God in the Judgment you will be ashamed of yourself. Have your feet shod with the preparedness, the firmness, the equipment of the gospel of peace. 'Stand!' 'Ye that are men, now serve Him.'

The second great principle in addition to firmness and confidence and dependability, is watchfulness, that is, alertness. In the words of a well-known hymn, 'Where duty calls, or danger, Be never wanting there'. We must realize, in other words, the character of the foe we are confronting. We have already looked into the matter in great detail in previous studies, but we are concerned now about the practical application of what we have learned. Watchfulness! Alertness!

'Watch ye, stand fast in the faith, quit you like men, be strong,' says Paul in the last chapter of his First Epistle to the Corinthians. His first word is 'watch'. Our Lord says, 'Watch and pray'. Why? 'Lest ye enter into temptation.' Watch! Pray! This precept runs through the whole of the New Testament. Paul exhorts the Colossians to 'walk circumspectly'. His words warn us to watch where we put our feet. This is because of the gins, the traps, and the spikes set by the enemy whom we are confronting. This is emphasized for many reasons; the first is that we are confronted by an enemy who is restless, and ceaseless in his activities. The Apostle Peter describes him as 'a roaring lion', continually walking about. Have you ever been in a place like the Kruger National Park in South Africa? Have you ever seen films of these creatures in the wide open spaces where Nature is still to be seen 'red in tooth and claw'? Have you seen a lion prowling about, dragging himself along the ground, concealing himself and ready at any moment to pounce? That is a picture of 'the devil as a roaring lion, roaming about, seeking whom he may devour'. 'Gird your heavenly armour on', says the hymn very rightly, We 'wear it ever, night and day', because of the character of the evil one who is opposing us. He never wearies, he never tires, and he commands principalities and powers, and all evil influences, forces and factors. The result is that we have always to be ready – 'night and day', as it were.

Another element is the unexpectedness of his attack. You never know when it is coming, where it is coming from, or how it is coming. If only we knew, of course, the whole position would be different. When we have had a time of great spiritual uplift in a service or in our homes, we tend to think that we are now going to be immune. Yet it may be the most dangerous moment for you. 'Let him that thinketh he standeth take heed lest he fall.' You never know when the enemy is coming. You cannot rely upon the fact that you have recently been blessed by God in an unusual manner; the enemy may take advantage of that to trip you up. It was after our Lord's baptism, when the Holy Ghost had descended upon Him, that He was driven into the wilderness to be tempted of the devil. You never know when temptation is coming. Beware of the unexpected!

Another most important consideration is the subtlety, the 'wiles' of the devil. 'Ambushed lies the evil one' says the hymn. The Apostle reminds us of this in the fourth chapter of his Ephesian Epistle where he says, 'Henceforth be no more children, tossed to and fro, and carried about with every wind of doctrine, by the sleight of men, and cunning craftiness, whereby they lie in wait to deceive' (v. 14). It is the devil who uses men to produce 'cunning craftiness'! By 'the sleight of men' he means the cleverness by which the quickness of the hand deceives the eye. That is what is happening doctrinally, theologically, says the Apostle. False teachers abound. You must not believe everything at its face value; you must not assume that if a man does not say something outrageously wrong he is a fine evangelical. But that is what is happening today; there is no discrimination. It is because Christians are not 'ready', they are not 'watching', they are not prepared for the wiliness and the subtlety of the devil's tactics.

In the Second Epistle to the Corinthians Paul uses the expression, 'We are not ignorant of his [Satan's] devices' (2:11). He was writing to them about forgiving a man who had wronged them, and he says that he was doing so not only for the man's sake, but because he knew the devil is ever ready to come in and take advantage of the situation. And those devices are many. Do we know Satan's subtlety? Do we know about his wiles? Do we recognize the camouflage that he is so expert in using? Do we know the different forms and guises in which he appears? If you wish to defend yourself, get your feet shod with this preparedness. You must always be on the alert, and always watching, always aware of what the enemy is doing.

But we must not only be aware of Satan's subtlety, but also of his changing tactics. Ignorance of this point causes many to be defeated. Sometimes he changes his own appearance. Not always is he comparable to a roaring lion. In the Second Epistle to the Corinthians again, in chapter 11, Paul says that the evil one can appear 'transformed into an angel of light' (v. 14). The devil does not always appear ugly and foul and harsh and cruel. He can be most pleasant, affable, and ingratiating. Many are deceived by these changes. Affability is what most people mean by saintliness today. 'So nice', they say, 'so pleasant'. 'I talked to the man and he was so kind.' But the question is, What does he believe? The important question in this realm is not whether a man is nice or not; the question is, What is he saying? what does he say about the Bible? what does he say about the truth? 'Ah, but he is so nice', people say, 'he never says an unkind word about anyone'. 'Therefore he must be a wonderful Christian', says the believer who has not got his feet shod with the preparation of the Gospel of peace.

But the devil often changes his methods also. Sometimes he comes to you, opposing you violently and condemning you. The next moment he will come flattering you. Sometimes he will inflame your passions to drive you into sin; the next time he comes, in a most subtle and enticing manner he will achieve the same end before you know that anything has happened. Sometimes he will come and bludgeon you on the head, as it were, and club you in order to make you do what he wants you to do; the next time he will employ a most sweet reasonableness. The devil contradicts himself; he does not mind doing so. His one object is to get us down. He will contradict himself utterly and shamelessly; what does it matter? As long as we believe him on both occasions, he is perfectly content. Sometimes he attacks the Scripture; the next moment he will be quoting it, as he quoted it to our Lord. One moment he comes to us, and tells us that we are not good enough to be Christians, another time he tells us we are so good that we do not need the death of Christ in order to save us; our lives are so good that God will accept us on our merits. One moment he comes to us and tells us that we have to justify ourselves by our good works, that nothing counts with God but good works, and that if we do not live this good life and do good works we are not justified; the next moment he will come and tell us that works do not matter at all; as long as we say that we believe in Christ and His blood we can go where, and do what, we like. Antinomianism! One moment he comes to the Christian and says, 'Do not overdo yourself; look after your health, look after your interests; read more, do nothing'. The next moment he comes and fills us with a carnal zeal, and makes us so busy that we ruin our health, perhaps, or do not have time to read at all; and so we lose our grip of the truth, and do not know where we are. One moment the brake is on, the next moment it is wild fanaticism. The same devil tempts to both extremes.

Nothing matters to the Devil as long as he can get us into trouble. One moment he comes and fills us with doubts about truth and about the faith; the next moment he comes and fills us with credulity which makes us ready to regard anything as a miracle, and to expect 'signs and wonders' constantly. He drives us to extremes, and is perfectly happy as long as we are obeying what he tells us. One moment he persuades us to be lax, the next moment he will drive us to a morbid scrupulosity, or make such legalists of us that we become afraid to move because we are hide-bound by law.

These, then, are some of the reasons why we must all 'be shod with the preparation of the gospel of peace'. We are fighting 'the wiles of the devil' and the 'principalities and powers' and the devilish ingenuity of it all – the camouflage, the paint, the powder, the appearances, the guises, the quick changes. There is only one safe defence; always be ready, always be on the alert. 'Watch and pray, lest ye enter into temptation'. That is, at least, the beginning of what is meant by 'having your feet shod with the equipment [the preparedness, the readiness] of the gospel of peace'. May God make us wise in this vital matter!

2I

Mobility

'And your feet shod with the preparation of the
gospel of peace.'

In our previous study we noted that 'having your feet shod'
means that we must have firmness and confidence, and that we
should be watchful. The Christian life is not a sinecure. Christians
do not rest on a bed of roses in expectation of being carried
passively in some celestial railway to heaven. They are called to
'fight the good fight of faith', to 'Watch', to 'Be strong', to
'Stand', to quit themselves as men. And we are examining the
interesting and pictorial way in which the Apostle conveys such
instruction.

Our next application of this 'picture' of having our feet shod
with the preparation of the Gospel of peace has reference to the
whole question of 'mobility', which is another big element in the
interpretation of 'preparedness', 'preparation', 'equipment'. We
have seen that this whole notion of mobility in warfare came in
really with Alexander the Great. It was then practised by the
Roman generals at the time when the Apostle lived. Indeed most
of the really great captains in war have attached great significance
to this matter of mobility. It was a part of the genius of Oliver
Cromwell, the thing that made him such an outstanding general.
He would suddenly move a section of his troops, particularly the
cavalry, halfway through a battle, see an opportunity, and take
advantage of it. It was also a chief part of the genius of one of his
contemporaries, Montrose, who so frequently achieved his
amazing victories by extraordinary marches which he planned

and executed and thereby discomfited the enemy. The study of military strategy, if properly used, has much to teach the Christian. We are justified in saying so by the Apostle's own use of this image here. Many a battle and a campaign has been lost through failure to implement this principle. Think of the Cromwells and the Montroses rather than the Douglas Haigs if you want to work out this principle as it should be worked out, and grasp the spiritual message that is imparted here. This is of unusual and exceptional importance today, not only for the individual Christian, but particularly, perhaps, for the Church as a whole, which is at this present time in terrible trouble. If we fail to recognize the appalling state of the Church today, then we are utterly defeated.

The Church does not count in Britain. We are but a little remnant, only some ten per cent of the population. Why is the Church failing? That is the question. And in so many other lands the same is true. Even in lands where there appears to be religious prosperity the truth is that there is real failure. Evil and sin are rampant even in such countries. There can be an appearance of success which is not success. It is of vital importance, therefore, that we should face this whole matter. We not only have to watch the enemy, we have to be ready to counter his every move, and to meet him where he is, not where we think he should be. This whole notion of readiness, quickness, watchfulness, mobility is inherent in the image and picture which is employed here by the Apostle. In other words, I am emphasizing the importance of tactics. I am not so much dealing with strategy as with tactics. It is just in this realm that this whole matter of mobility is of first importance.

What then is the spiritual application? The first point, clearly, is that we must not be slow, we must not be heavy-footed, there must be no dragging of the feet. There is nothing which is so fatal to successful progress as a sluggish, lifeless Christian. Ask the average man in the street why he does not come to a place of worship, why he is not a Christian, and you will find that the answer he is most likely to give you is that it is all so dull, and so dead. He says there is nothing in it, no life. And of course there is much to justify what he says. You have but to compare and contrast a typical sample of worldly people with a typical sample of

Christian people to see the basis on which he makes his statement. Look at the enthusiasm and the excitement of people who watch the football on Saturday afternoon in the winter, or the people who go to the races. Listen to the shouting and the excitement! Look at those people who go after their sports or whatever they are interested in! They want to be there in time, they want the best seats, and they want the sport to go on and on, and are disappointed when it finishes. Contrast that with Christian people who seem to think they are doing something wonderful by going to a place of worship on a Sunday morning. They are not quite sure whether they will go or not when they wake up in the morning, but at last, as a matter of duty, they decide they will go – hoping the service will not be too long. Is not that the position?

Do we give the impression when we come to our places of worship that we are doing the most wonderful and thrilling thing in the world? Are we alive, are we rejoicing? How do we compare with these other people? A staid, lifeless Christian is a denial, in many respects, of the Gospel at its most glorious point. To be heavy-footed, slow-moving, lethargic, having to be whipped up and roused constantly, and urged to do this and that instead of running to it, and rejoicing in it, is a sad misrepresentation of Christianity. 'Let every man examine himself.'

Or look at the matter in the following way. Many of us simply follow a routine in a thoughtless, unintelligent manner. It sounds a strange thing to say at a time like this in the history of the Christian Church, but there are many people in the Church who have no idea why they are there except for the fact that they were brought up to attend services. They would not be there otherwise. They have never even thought about these matters sufficiently to break the habit; they are following a routine. There are thoughtless, unintelligent Christians who have no idea of the spiritual conflict, no idea of the crucial importance of the Christian Church at an hour such as this. They take the same journey and do the same thing Sunday after Sunday simply as a part of the routine of life. But they are without understanding. That is the kind of thing the Apostle has in mind. Such a Christian, of course, is already defeated, and useless in the battle. He does not count at all in the army. Active Christians have to carry them for they cannot move; they are not ready for any sudden change of tactics. They are passengers, and they are always a great hindrance to an army. They have been a great problem throughout the history of warfare.

On the other hand there are also many people who live on their own activities, and who are not aware at all of a spiritual conflict. Christianity to them is what they do. It is a part of the danger of conforming to type. It is sad to observe people who have recently come into the Christian life and to find them in a very short period of time repeating phrases and clichés. They have no idea what they mean; they are merely imitating someone else; they are picking up the language and the expressions and activities. And on and on it goes. One feels that they are not alive to the true situation.

Let me be honest and admit that these strictures apply throughout the Church, to preachers as well as to congregations. There is nothing that I know of that is so utterly opposed to what the Apostle is teaching here as the professional preacher, the man who adopts a manner and a voice, the so-called parsonic voice, and all the other characteristics of 'the cloth'. The professional in a pulpit is a great curse. He is a man who is really fighting for the enemy. He is a quisling in the army of the living God!

Let us have our feet shod with the preparation of the Gospel of peace. Let us know what we are doing. This professionalism is found among liberals, and also among evangelicals. Some affect an artificial brightness and cheerfulness, a kind of 'muscular Christianity'. Those who do so are conforming to a pattern. They are not being intelligent, and show a failure to understand the profound character of the Christian life. And there are others, sometimes young men, who try to look as if they were Puritans living three hundred years ago, and who talk in Puritan language. That is equally bad. Any putting on of a mask or a cloak, or professionalism, is the exact opposite of what the Apostle exhorts to do.

All such things are but manifestations of being 'at ease in Zion' while a mighty battle is going on. Respectable or formal Christianity at such a time is useless. That is why the Church is declining, and exhibiting nothing more than respectable Christianity, 'Morality touched with emotion', as Matthew Arnold described it, of no value. I am not surprised that the state of the Church is what it is. There is a lack of spiritual understanding, or, to use the Apostle's figure, the feet are too heavily shod by mere traditions and formal worship. There is none of the mobility and quickness that is essential at such a time as this.

The Church today too much resembles David in Saul's armour. Goliath challenges Israel with his armour and his spear and sword; and Israel quakes and trembles, and does not know what to do. All are frightened of this man, who has killed so many. Then David, the stripling, a mere shepherd, arrives in the Israelite camp, and, moved by the Spirit of God, shows himself to respond to Goliath's challenge. Saul and his company, not having their feet 'shod with the preparation of the gospel of peace', and thinking in the old terminology instead of spiritually, say, 'He seems convinced that he can do it; let us fetch Saul's armour and put it on him'. They believed that the only way in which anyone could fight Goliath was in Saul's armour. So they put it on him. But David realized at once that if he went in that armour he would be killed. He could scarcely move, the armour was too heavy for him, and too big for him. So he got rid of it. He said, 'I cannot fight in Saul's armour; I must use my own method of fighting, and in the name of the living God I am going to do so'. David as it were realized the importance of being 'shod with the preparation of the gospel of peace'. He wanted to be mobile, and to be able to move quickly and respond and react to every move of Goliath.

My meaning is that Christian people often get into trouble because they try to fight this battle in a manner of which they are incapable. For instance, I have often found Christian people in trouble and saying, 'I put up a very bad show the other day in a discussion with some people about religion; I really feel I did more harm than good'. 'Well', I said, 'what were you discussing?' They tell me they were discussing Evolution or some other scientific question. 'Tell me', I say, 'are you scientifically trained?' 'Oh no', they answer. 'Well', I ask, 'why did you ever enter into such an argument?' You should not do so. David refused to fight in Saul's armour. If you do not know the case say nothing; or say, 'I do not know'. Keep the battle to what you do know. Insist always upon controlling the place where the battle is fought.

[287]

Do not let your friends put Saul's armour on you. Your business is to do what you are capable of. Get out your sling and your stones, and use them. Do not try to do something that is beyond you.

We are not called upon to defend the whole of the Christian faith. No one man can do it at all points. Keep to familiar ground. Make sure that your feet are shod with 'the preparation of the gospel of peace'. You must be mobile, you must be free in every way and without encumbrances. You must not be shod with heavy boots in which you can scarcely move about, and which compel you to spend all your time watching your feet and considering how you are going to move. That is the fatal truth about professionalism. The whole tragedy today is that the Christian Church is moving ponderously, slowly, heavily, while the world is in the grip of the devil. She is setting up committees to investigate the problems, and commissions to examine various situations, and calling for reports, interim and final, to be produced in a year, or perhaps several years, which will then be considered. And she is doing this while the world is on fire, and people are going to hell, and the devil is rampant everywhere!

Is it surprising that the world is as it is? Our feet are not shod with the preparation of the Gospel of peace. You can never fight the devil in that way. We must fight in the way God has indicated, however ridiculous it may appear to be to modern man. Remember how ridiculous David appeared to be to Goliath and to many in Israel also. A mere stripling! Goliath, you remember, roared at him, and thought he was virtually going to blow him out of existence with the breath of his nostrils. Nevertheless it was Goliath who was killed. So the Christian Church needs to consider this particular text very urgently. When will the Church of God awake and realize that her strength lies not in her numbers but in her relationship to God, and her ability to respond to His every suggestion, His every stimulus, His every move. We must not be slow and heavy-footed.

But let us look at this more positively. I am urging the vital principle of adaptability, and elasticity in tactics. This, I know, can be misinterpreted, and is being misinterpreted at the present time by numbers of people, so we must be careful. Fundamentally the battle is always the same. In every age and generation, first century as twentieth century, the battle is against the devil and the principalities and powers. Fundamentally, there is no change. Therefore we need the same essential strategy at all times and in all places. We need two things at one and the same time. We must have the firmness and the mobility. The trouble is that we are either too firm – so firm and solid that we are useless – or else we get so excited that we break rank, and there is no cohesion, and no discipline. In both cases the enemy is triumphant. I could illustrate that even in terms of singing, congregational singing. Some are always ahead of the congregation, others drag and hold out at the end of each line. Both are wrong. The army must move as one unit. You must have firmness, and yet quickness, mobility and adaptability.

While I thus emphasize that you need adaptability, it is most important that the adaptability should always be within the limits of truth. We must never move away from truth. 'Everything', says the Scripture, 'must be done decently and in order'. Our methods must correspond to our message and we must not take the opinion of some atheistical journalist with respect to them; but act on the wisdom of the New Testament and the saints of the centuries. We are not interested in art for art's sake, and modernity and novelty, but in adaptability which is nevertheless always true to the fundamental teaching. Like Wordsworth's skylark we are to be –

Type of the wise who soar, but never roam;
True to the kindred points of heaven and home!

You can 'soar' but you must 'never roam'. In other words, this Christian man has his feet firmly on the ground, and yet he is mobile. He does not become a fool, he does not 'lose his head', he does not forsake his principles in his excitement to be doing something, and in an attempt to convert people.

Adaptability means we must beware of a slavish adherence to old forms. That is always a temptation. One of Britain's troubles in the First World War was that her generals and leaders were old cavalry men who could not get rid of the notion that a war must of necessity be fought by cavalry. Some of them did not learn the lesson even by the end of the war – hence the terrible slaughter which took place. With minds rigidly attached to their old school they thought they were fighting another Boer War. They had not realized that it was a new type of warfare altogether. So you get your Passchendaeles. And this tendency still continues. One of the main troubles in the last world war was the mentality of France. It was Maginot Line thinking. There was to be no movement. The impregnable Maginot Line was going to block all enemy advance, nothing could pass through it, everything was going to be static – that was the way to fight the Second World War. It was that mentality and thinking that produced the collapse and the fall of France, and very nearly the collapse and the fall of the whole free world. The French Government and its generals would not listen to General de Gaulle, who had written a book pointing out that the next war was going to be a war of movement, that the Maginot mentality was fatal, that it was going to be a war of tanks and of movement – armoured vehicles in abundance – and that unless they realized this they were lost. He had written his book several years before the war; but he was ridiculed.

We could carry our illustrations further. By now we are faced with nuclear warfare; and we must not think any longer in terms of masses of men and personal valour. The next war will be nuclear, and we have to understand this and adapt our methods. We must not expect to fight the next war with the methods of the First World War. Fundamental strategy must not be changed, the basic principles adhering to tactics must not be forsaken, but you have to be adaptable.

Is the Christian Church adaptable? As I see it, the tragedy is that we still seem to be clinging to the forms and the methods of the Victorians. Nothing is more extraordinary than to see men who have forsaken the Gospel long ago still clinging to the methods and the forms and ceremonial of the Victorians. It is not surprising that people no longer attend churches. The people who have forgotten the Gospel cling to the old forms and methods; and the world scoffs. The whole thing is ridiculed. And, indeed, we have no right to complain of the ridicule.

I do not want to be unfair, so let me balance my statement. We are not going to fight this modern battle successfully by repeating the sermons of the Puritans verbatim, or adopting their classifications and sub-divisions, and their manner of preaching.

That would be futile. We must learn to hold on to the old principles but we must apply them, and use them, in a manner that is up-to-date. Forgive a personal reference. I am going to do what the Apostle did in the eleventh chapter of his Second Epistle to the Corinthians. I am going to be a fool, and to say something about myself. I remember how, in the very first year when I began to preach, I was preaching in a service with an old preacher who was over eighty years of age. Having listened to my feeble effort, and having heard me for the first time, the old man made this comment which encouraged me very greatly. He said, 'Though you are a young man you are preaching the old truths I have been trying to preach all my life'. He went on, 'You are preaching the old truths, but you have put a very modern suit on them'. That is what I am trying to say. We need the old truths in a modern suit. You must not clothe them in the old staid terminology or manner or method that was appropriate in the past. The moment we become slaves to any system – I do not care how good it was in its age and generation – we are already defeated, because we have missed this whole principle of adaptability. So we do not need gramophone records, not even of the Puritans! We need the truth that was preached by the Puritans, but preached in a manner that will show its relevance, its adaptability to the most urgent modern situation. God forbid that our methods should deny the very message we are trying to preach, either by imitating the latest methods of worldly entertainment or by methods that are so archaic as to make our message irrelevant.

To state the matter in different terms, it is the danger of concentrating on old problems instead of present problems. The Christian Church is still fighting rearguard actions. The impression of Christianity given by the newspapers is that it is nothing but a protest against the opening of public houses, or of Sabbath desecration, or this or that – always protesting, always negative. You cannot expect people to come and listen to the Gospel if they think that Christianity is nothing but a negation or negative protest. But that is the impression that is given. A hundred years ago when the Church was in a very powerful position and could influence governments, her protests really did have an effect. But who listens to the resolutions of church assemblies today? Do you imagine that any government pays the slightest attention? Of course not! And the people in general are uninterested. Neither must we deal with the wrong problems. Far too often the man in the pulpit is preaching about his own problems, not the problems of the people. He has certain philosophical problems as the result of his reading philosophy, and he brings his great philosophical problems to the pulpit. But they are not the problems of the people listening to him; and the business of a preacher is to preach to the needs of the people who are listening to him.

There are those who seem to think that the one problem in the Church today is the problem of unity. So they give all their time and attention to this. That people are going to hell does not seem to matter to them, they are always preaching about unity, and writing books about it. 'The Unity of the Church' is their Gospel. But that has never saved anyone. If all the Churches in the world, including the Roman Catholic Church, became amalgamated and you could say that now we had one great world Church, I venture to prophesy that it would not make the slightest difference to the man in the street. He is not outside the Churches because the Churches are disunited, he is outside because he likes his sin, because he is a sinner, because he is ignorant of spiritual realities. He is no more interested in this problem of unity than is the man in the moon! And yet the Church is talking about the problem of unity as if it were the central problem. And while we are talking about unity the devil is getting his great victories, is conquering individual people, and the whole position of the Church is shaking. Unity is not the first or the greatest problem.

In much the same way many evangelicals are fighting what we may call 'the old modernism'. We are fighting a new modernism today. The problem today is not so much that people are saying things which are not true. It is a fact that they are doing so, but the main problem is that they are saying now that what you say does not matter at all. Fifty years ago there was the problem of R. J. Campbell's so-called New Theology. What he was saying about the Person of Christ was the urgent problem. And it was rightly faced and denounced by the stalwarts at that time. But there has been a great change. By now the attitude of many in the Church is that what you believe does not matter as long as you call yourself a Christian. That a man does not see the truth about the deity of Christ does not matter as long as he is trying to do good, and to bring in the Christian emphasis on art, education, politics, industry, and so on. By now we are faced with this position, that what you believe is not important. Believe what you like; as long as you claim to be a Christian, all is well. Are we facing the wrong problem?

In other words the enemy today is complacency. The enemy at the moment is a sentimental, nondescript idealism which is passing for Christianity. Vital principles are regarded as unnecessary. Affability passes for saintliness. The man who is idealized today is a man who is an aggregate of negatives. The absence of qualities constitutes greatness today. People do not believe in true greatness any longer. They do not believe in goodness, in manliness, in truth itself. It is the smooth, nice, affable man who is popular.

There is, however, a ruggedness about truth. Look at the Apostle Paul, this man who stands, and who speaks boldly, and who denounces heretics as the enemies of truth. 'These men', he says 'are enemies of the cross of Christ, whose god is their belly, who glory in their shame'. 'How terrible', says the modern man, 'to speak like that!' But such is the Apostle Paul. The trouble is, that the devil has persuaded us that niceness is saintliness. Remember how the serpent 'beguiled Eve', says the Apostle.

But the Apostle not only says that we must be ready and prepared; he further says that the preparedness is produced by 'the gospel of peace', because without this peace we can do nothing. Any uncertainty in the Christian tends to failure and disaster. Ezra and Nehemiah say rightly, 'The joy of the Lord is your strength'. The Psalmist also says, 'I will run the way of thy commandments when thou shalt enlarge my heart' (119:32). So Paul says that we shall have this mobility and adaptability and watchfulness as the result of the Gospel of peace. The Gospel of peace means, firstly, peace with God. This always makes one ready. If I am in any doubt about my salvation I shall not be able to fight the enemy. I shall have to spend the whole of my time struggling with myself. The soldier has to be clear about certain things; and the Christian must be clear about his relationship to God. 'Therefore being justified by faith, we have peace with God through our Lord Jesus Christ; by whom also we have access by faith into this grace wherein we stand' (Romans 5: 1, 2). It is only as we are clear about the fundamental fact that our sins are forgiven and that we are reconciled to God, that God can do His gracious work of sanctification in us. Paul in 1 Thessalonians 5:23 says: 'And the very God of peace sanctify you wholly; and I pray God your whole spirit and soul and body be preserved blameless unto the coming of our Lord Jesus Christ'. As God does that to us we are able to fight the enemy; and it is as the 'God of peace' that He accomplishes the work.

The Epistle to the Hebrews says the same thing in chapter 13, verses 20, 21: 'Now the God of peace, that brought again from the dead our Lord Jesus, that great shepherd of the sheep, through the blood of the everlasting covenant, make you perfect in every good work to do his will, working in you that which is well-pleasing in his sight, through Jesus Christ; to whom be glory for ever and ever. Amen'. Peace with God! If you have not got that you are a poor soldier in the army of the living God. You are probably a casualty. You had better be sent back behind the lines to some casualty clearing station, or even to some hospital.

But you must also have peace within. I must know that 'all things work together for good to them that love God, to them who are the called according to his purpose' (Romans 8:28). Similarly I must believe what Paul says to the Philippians in chapter 4; verse 6: 'Be careful for nothing'; that is to say, have no anxieties. If you are anxious as a soldier in God's army, worried perhaps about what is happening at home, you are a poor soldier. You have to concentrate entirely on the fight with the enemy. 'Be careful for nothing; but in every thing by prayer and supplication with thanksgiving let your requests be made known unto God. And the peace of God, which passeth all understanding, shall keep your hearts and minds through Christ Jesus.' We must have peace within. But we must also be peaceable people, we must be gentle, longsuffering and patient. We must not be worried, anxious Christians, troubled and frantic. So much of the time in the Christian army is taken up in keeping the troops healthy and happy. 'I am worried about this', says one; 'I am troubled, and everything is a burden and a problem', says another. How can you fight the devil if he has already defeated you in that way? Peace within as well as peace with God is an essential.

And lastly, peace with others: 'As much as lieth in you', says Paul to the Romans in chapter 12, verse 18, 'Be at peace with all men'. 'As far as you can and as far as it is possible' is what he urges upon them. 'Recompense to no man evil for evil. Provide things honest in the sight of all men . . . Dearly beloved, avenge not yourselves, but rather give place unto wrath: for it is written, Vengeance is mine; I will repay, saith the Lord. Therefore if thine enemy hunger, feed him; if he thirst, give him drink: for in so doing thou shalt heap coals of fire on his head. Be not overcome of evil, but overcome evil with good'. If the members of the army of the living God are fighting one another, what hope have they of fighting the enemy? It is quite impossible. The Apostle teaches this yet again in the Epistle to the Philippians, chapter 2, 'Fulfil ye my joy, that ye be likeminded, having the same love, being of one accord, of one mind. Let nothing be done through strife or vainglory; but in lowliness of mind let each esteem other better than themselves. Look not every man on his own things, but every man also on the things of others' (vv. 2–4). That is the way to fight the enemy. If we are jealous and envious and selfish, concerned about ourselves only, and heedless of the welfare of others, the position is hopeless. There is no discipline, there is no cohesion. We are to be the exact opposite of the Church at Corinth which was divided up into factions and groups. We must obey Paul's exhortation to the Colossians, chapter 3, verse 13: 'Forbearing one another, and forgiving one another, if any man have a quarrel against any: even as Christ forgave you, so also do ye. And above all these things put on charity' – be clothed with charity – 'which is the bond of perfectness. And let the peace of God rule' – or act as umpire – 'in your hearts, to the which also ye are called in one body; and be ye thankful'.

That is the 'preparation of the gospel of peace'! Be shod in that way! Be certain you have peace with God, peace in your own heart, peace with one another. Let the peace of God arbitrate, act as umpire, between you as members of this great army; so that together, and for His glorious name's sake, you may be able to face the enemy and conquer him, and win resounding victories for your blessed Lord and Saviour, the Captain of our salvation.

22

The Shield of Faith

'Above all, taking the shield of faith, wherewith ye
shall be able to quench all the fiery darts of the
wicked.'

Ephesians 6:16

We now proceed to consider yet another piece of this 'whole
armour of God' which the Apostle reminds the Ephesians is so
essential to a successful warfare against the devil, and against
'the principalities and powers, against the rulers of the darkness of
this world, against spiritual wickedness in high places'.

We note first that when the Apostle introduces this fourth
piece of armour there is a kind of break. Obviously we have come
to a point of transition. 'Above all', he says, 'taking the shield of
faith'. The pieces of this armour, as we indicated in introducing
the whole subject, can be divided into two main groups; and we
have already dealt with the first group. Now as we come to the
second group, we shall see that the parts differ in certain respects
from those of the first group. The Apostle calls attention to this
fact by saying, 'Above all'.

Concerning the interpretation of that expression, the tendency
is to take it, as translated in the Authorized Version, as meaning
'above everything else in importance'. But it really means 'in
addition to all', that is to say, in addition to the three parts of the
armour that I have already mentioned. Furthermore 'Above all'
introduces everything that is to follow – not only 'the shield of
faith', but also 'the helmet of salvation', and 'the sword of the
Spirit' as well. It is a general introduction to these additional
portions which Paul is about to put before us.

We must notice also another way in which he calls our
attention to the difference. So far he has been using the word
'having'. 'Stand therefore', he says, 'having your loins girt about

[296]

with truth, and having on the breastplate of righteousness, and your feet shod with the preparation of the gospel of peace'. But now he changes his word. 'Above all', he says – 'not "having" the shield of faith, but *taking* the shield of faith, wherewith ye shall be able to quench all the fiery darts of the wicked.' 'And *take* the helmet of salvation', 'and *take* the sword of the Spirit which is the word of God'. The difference between the three portions that are to come and the three portions already mentioned is the difference between 'having' and 'taking'.

Two main things are thereby suggested. The first three portions of the armour are parts that are fixed to the body by special fastening. We noticed that that was so in the case of the girdle; it is something that you fix on; you clamp it on as it were, and put it firmly in position. The same is also true of the breastplate of righteousness – you fix it on to yourself. And the same obviously must be true about the sandals.

The first three parts of the armour are firmly fixed to the body by this special fastening so that they are immovable. But with the next three there is an obvious difference. You do not fix a shield on to your body; it is something separate from you. You take it up and use it but it is not attached to your body. The same applies to the helmet, which was more like a cap that was put on the head and taken off quite easily. And the sword is clearly not a part of us but a thing that we take up and use as the need arises. That shows why the Apostle drops his term 'having' and says 'taking'. You 'have' those other pieces on always; but you 'take up' the shield and the sword and the helmet and put them on.

A further difference, and one which is really an outcome of the first, is that the first three portions are more or less passive and preparatory; the soldier puts them on and keeps them on. But when you come to the second group there is a suggestion immediately of activity. The soldier may be sitting down in his room in the barracks and taking a period of rest, but he still keeps on his girdle of truth, his breastplate and his sandals. Then suddenly an alarm is given that the enemy is already attacking, and he immediately takes hold of his shield and his sword and puts on his helmet and rushes out. There is the suggestion of activity, of an actual fight and battle. You do not have the shield in your hand when you are resting; you put it down, and likewise your sword. But the moment the enemy becomes active again and there is an engagement, you have to take up these things in order that you may be ready for the conflict.

We must say something about shields as such, because the Apostle is conveying spiritual truth by means of these pictures and analogies, and he means us to examine them in detail. The shield which was used by the Roman soldier, whom Paul is taking as his example, was a very large shield. We have become accustomed to thinking of shields as being something smaller; but the shields that were used then were often about four feet in length and two-and-a-half feet wide. The original idea was of a door which you held in front of you, and behind which you could hide. Later it was altered into an oblong shape; but it was still meant to cover most of the body. But still more important is the fact that this shield had a fire-proof metal lining placed upon it, the significance of which, of course, is immediately obvious. The shield was made of wood, but it had this fire-proof metal lining on its surface so that as you held it up to face the enemy who was throwing his fiery darts at you, the darts would fall upon this fire-proof metal lining.

Clearly the idea is, that in addition to the breastplate which you already have on, and the girdle of truth about your loins, and your feet shod, you must protect yourself in a still more general manner. You need your shield to protect you against the things that may be hurled at you as a preliminary before the enemy comes in person, sword in hand, and attacks you still more directly. That is clearly the picture which is meant to be conveyed.

The Apostle says that the shield is necessary in order to 'quench all the fiery darts of the wicked'. The 'fiery darts' really explain themselves. They were made either of wood or of metal, but their special feature was that they had a sharp point. They were like arrows or darts. They were made of material which was soaked in some inflammable substance. Then this material, impregnated with this inflammable substance, was wound round the point of the dart very tightly until it was firmly in position. Then, when they were ready to attack the enemy, they would ignite this inflammable material so that it would burst into flame, and they would then hurl the darts in the direction of the enemy. If one of these darts should happen to penetrate, it would burst into flame yet more, and burn some portion of the enemy's body and so render him inactive. In this manner they prepared the way for the mass attack of the troops upon the enemy opposed to them.

Soldiers used to throw these darts at the enemy in great profusion from all conceivable directions so as to cause confusion. And having prepared the way in that manner the troops would then advance. This was the ancient way of doing what in modern warfare is known as the preliminary barrage of the guns to prepare for the advance of the infantry. Or you can think of the preliminary bombing that was used in the Second World War.

According to the Authorized Version, these darts are thrown at us by 'the wicked'; but that is an unfortunate translation. The word used in the original means 'the wicked one', or 'the evil one'. The exact translation is particularly important here because the Apostle has reminded us that we do not fight 'evil', regarding it as something abstract or impersonal. He has already assured us that we are confronted by 'the wiles of the devil', and not only by the devil, but also by 'principalities and powers, the rulers of the darkness of this world, and spiritual wickedness in high places'. His whole purpose is to say that we are fighting spiritual persons, forces, beings. And if ever it was necessary to emphasize that, it is at the present time. As we have already pointed out, the world no longer believes in the devil, still less in spiritual beings and entities. The world does not believe in angels or in devils. That is one of the main causes of its troubles.

The 'wicked one' is the devil, and he commands and controls a diversity of powers and agents. Never was it more important that we should realize that we are involved in a tremendous spiritual warfare. We believe in the Triune God, Father, Son, and Holy Spirit, Three Persons in one godhead. God is Personal. God is not a force or a power. But neither are the forces against us only a force or a power, but personal agencies, personal intelligences. As I have often pointed out, we do not begin to understand the problem of life in this world at the present time unless we understand this teaching. We do not understand our own personal experience, still less do we understand the whole state and condition of the world, apart from this. We do not wrestle only against 'flesh and blood'. Our striving, our problem, is not merely man and his sin and his evil. Behind man there are these infernal powers, these devilish agencies, these spiritual entities. There is no more important theological, and indeed practical question than that of 'The Origin of Evil'. You must not think of evil and wickedness as something abstract. The whole teaching of the Bible is that evil is manipulated and propagated by these beings, these entities, these persons. Our Lord had to meet the devil, a person, in the temptation in the wilderness. So it is of great importance that we should translate the Apostle's words as 'able to quench all the fiery darts of the wicked one'.

There is a similar statement in the nineteenth verse of the fifth chapter of the First Epistle of John. Again there is a poor translation in the Authorized Version, which reads, 'And we know that we are of God, and the whole world lieth in wickedness'. That, of course, is true; but what the Apostle really wrote was, 'the whole world lieth in the wicked one', in the embrace of Satan, the one whom the Lord Jesus Christ described as 'the strong man armed'. We must get rid of the notion of abstract evil: there is no such thing. Evil is a personal being. There would be no evil in the world if there were no evil persons; there would be no evil human beings unless there were evil spiritual beings who entered into God's creation and tempted man and seduced him in the calamity of the Fall. The evil state of the world today stems from that calamity.

But now let us turn to the spiritual application of our theme. The Apostle is telling us that we must be prepared for what we may describe as Satanic attacks and assaults which at times can be unusually fierce and fiery. In addition to all his other activities, and all the implements or the instruments he employs, the devil employs these fiery darts. And they are fiery; they burst into flame and are very destructive.

An understanding of this is of vital importance to us in our spiritual warfare. Many masters of the spiritual life have described these attacks in detail. The best known examples are Martin Luther and John Bunyan. No two writers have ever dealt more specifically or clearly with this particular aspect of the Christian's warfare than those two men. Most Christians have heard the famous story of Luther and his inkpot, and of his throwing it at the devil. He was deeply conscious of the devil's presence in his room, and he could not get away from him. Whatever he tried to do, the devil was there hurling his darts at him. John Bunyan testifies in his own way to a similar experience.

But what of our experiences? Do we not all know something of this? Do we not know something of what it is, perhaps, to wake up in the morning and to find that before we have had time to do any thinking, thoughts come to us, evil thoughts, perhaps even blasphemous thoughts? You were not thinking, you were doing nothing, you had just awakened; but suddenly the darts reach you. That is what the Apostle means by 'the fiery darts of the wicked one'.

It is important for us to realize this because it is a part of the enemy's strategy to prevent our understanding that he is the cause of this. He would have us believe that all these things originate in ourselves, and then he persuades us that, in consequence, we must be very evil persons who have no right to be called Christians at all. And so he drives us down into the depths of despair and utter hopelessness about ourselves. So nothing is so vital for us as to realize that it is the devil whose fiery darts are responsible for our condition. But let us consider some examples of this. Have you not found that, when you have been engaged in prayer or are trying to pray, these darts come from all directions at you? When your one desire is to be concentrating on God, and on worship and prayer and adoration, you seem filled with all these distracting, and perhaps evil thoughts and notions and ideas. Where do they come from?

Have you not experienced this also when you are reading the Bible? You can read a newspaper and concentrate on it, but when you start reading the Bible, thoughts and ideas come from all directions and you find it almost impossible to concentrate. Where do they come from? These are 'the fiery darts of the wicked one'. The point we must grasp is that they obviously come from outside ourselves. They are not generated by us; they come to us. They strike us. We give evidence of some awareness of this in such expressions as, 'it suddenly struck me', or 'the thought came to me', and so on.

But we can add this further point, that there is a curious

periodicity about these experiences. They are not with us permanently but can happen at any moment. But there are times and seasons when the enemy is unusually active in this respect. The analogy of warfare is very helpful here. In the First World War, in particular, when trench warfare was practised, there were days when there was a kind of lull. The enemy was still there, and you could not afford to take any risks. If you exposed yourself you would be shot at, but on the whole there was a lull with nothing much happening. Then suddenly a barrage would come from the enemy's lines. Something comparable to that happens in the spiritual realm. You never know what a day is going to bring forth. The fact that you may have had a wonderful day of blessing does not guarantee that all will be well tomorrow. That may be the very occasion when the enemy will suddenly hurl his darts upon you, of all types and kinds and shapes, and from all conceivable directions. He may continue to do so for a number of days. Such happenings can be definitely categorized as Satanic attacks. There are times when the enemy concentrates on individual Christians, on Christian churches, or sections of the Christian Church, almost upon countries at times, and in this malign manner he does his utmost to destroy the work of God by hurling these 'fiery darts' at us. These darts can take almost any form. The commonest of all is with regard to thoughts. The devil hurls doubts at us. Some of the greatest saints have been plagued from time to time by horrible doubts. They were hurled at them, thoughts came into their minds; suggestions, queries, questions arose. They did not want them, they did their utmost to drive them out; but still they came and kept crowding in upon them. Many of the greatest saints have testified to such trials.

But there is something even worse! The devil has often plagued some of the noblest saints with blasphemous thoughts—blasphemous thoughts about God, blasphemous thoughts about the Lord Jesus Christ. Horrible, horrifying! And as I was explaining earlier, what the devil hopes and trusts will happen, is that the saint under attack will assume that they are his own thoughts and begin to doubt whether he is a Christian at all. Or the devil may hurl words and phrases, oaths, horrible language, at the Christian. His mind may appear to be filled with these. But none of them arise from the believer himself. They come from the devil who is trying to shake him, trying to confuse him, trying to persuade him that he is not a Christian, and that he has never been a Christian.

These are some of the ways in which the fiery darts come, and chiefly, as I say, in the realm of the thoughts. It is indeed instructive to read of this in the lives of saints. Thank God that they have ever been recorded; because it is a great help to a Christian under assault, who may imagine that such trials never happened to anyone else, to remember not only what the Apostle says here, but also to see its confirmation in the life and in the experience of some of the greatest and most wonderful saints that have ever adorned the life of the Christian Church.

But sometimes the darts take the form of imaginations. There is nothing the devil cannot do in that respect. We are confronted by the 'wiles' of the devil, and his ingenuity is almost endless. He can conjure up scenes, he can depict events, he can paint things very vividly, he can make them real. Thus he hurls his fiery darts at us in the realm of the imagination. He does the same in the realm of the desires and the passions and the lusts – inflaming, inciting, rousing them with tremendous heat. Do you not realize how true it all is? If not, then you are so much in the grip and in the arms of the devil that you are not even aware of the fact that it is happening. Temptation is the lot of every Christian; it happens to all at some time or another, in some shape or form. We must be ready for it. We must always have our shield of faith in a convenient position so that we can take it up at any moment. It is our only hope.

I would add one further item to this list of the ways in which the devil may hurl his darts at us. A well-known hymn says, 'If through fiery trials your pathway should lie'. The history of the Church has much to say about 'fiery trials'! Indeed there are many Christian people today who are passing through fiery trials; they are in a furnace, as the young men were in Daniel's time. The Apostle Peter in the fourth chapter of his First Epistle uses that very expression in the twelfth verse: 'Beloved', he says, 'think it not strange concerning the fiery trial which is to try you, as though some strange thing happened to you'. It is not strange, it is the lot of God's people. It always has been, it always will be. 'Yea, and all that will live godly in Christ Jesus', says Paul to

Timothy, 'shall suffer persecution' (2 Timothy 3:12). The wicked one can bring all these things suddenly to bear upon us.

By these means Satan tries to alarm us, tries to fill us with fears. Do our enemies intend to kill us? Do they propose to take everything from us? Am I going to lose my position because I am a Christian? Or you will be troubled about your wife and family, you will be troubled about your church, about the whole cause of Christ. Terrible periods of persecution come to the Christian Church. Again there may be long intervals when there is no persecution except in some minor manner, just an occasional shot here and there. But sometimes the devil, as it were, has been preparing a great mass of fiery darts, and he hurls them all together at the same time; and the onslaught may continue for a period.

Many good Christian people endured grievous trials during the Hitler regime in Germany: and there are Christian people enduring this kind of fiery trial at the present time. Persecution may come even through those who are dear to us, but who are not Christians. They may leave us alone for a long time, then, suddenly, as if the devil were let loose in them, they suddenly attack us and continue to do so for a period. Then they desist, then return to the attack, and so on.

The Apostle's teaching is that there is only one way to deal with these attacks. We must take and use the shield of faith. It is the only thing that can quench all the fiery darts of the wicked one. As these things are hurled at you, you do not hold forward your breast and allow them to strike the breastplate of righteousness. What you must do is to take your shield and hold it up, so that they may hit against that portion of the shield which is specifically meant to deal with them as they burst against it, and so do you no harm. You must be ready to meet them from all directions. Remember your feet must be shod with the preparation of the Gospel of peace. You must be mobile and agile, and hold your shield in all necessary directions. You quench one dart here, one there, another in yet a third direction, and so you save yourself much trouble. Caught in this way by your shield, you will not need to extricate them from the joints of the armour; and so you save yourself much trouble.

The Apostle Peter expresses the same idea in the words, 'Be

sober, be vigilant; because your adversary the devil, as a roaring lion, walketh about, seeking whom he may devour: whom resist stedfast in the faith' (1 Peter 5: 8 and 9). Faith alone enables you to meet these particular attacks. John says exactly the same thing: 'This is the victory that overcometh the world; even our faith' (1 John 5:4). Faith is always the shield that you have to hold up to quench these fiery darts of the wicked one.

Faith here means the ability to apply quickly what we believe so as to repel everything the devil does or attempts to do to us. Faith is not merely an intellectual belief or theory. Of course, faith includes what you believe, but faith never stops at mere intellectual assent and belief. Faith is always practical. Faith always applies the truth. 'Faith without works is dead.' There is always this element of activity in faith. 'Faith is the substance of things hoped for, the evidence of things not seen' (Hebrews 11:1). So I define faith in 'the shield of faith' as meaning the quick application of what we believe as an answer to everything that the devil hurls at us.

But how does faith act as our shield? The answer is that faith never points to itself, it always points to its object. That is absolutely crucial. The cults produce people who have faith in faith. But if you put your faith in faith you are eventually undone. There are people who try to work up faith, the quality of faith, in themselves; but they will never succeed. That is Couéism, a thing purely psychological. We are not told to work up faith or to put our faith in faith. No, faith never points to itself. Faith never protects a man in and of itself.

Faith always points to its object, and in that way it makes us strong. Paul deals with this matter in chapter 4 of his Epistle to the Romans, beginning at verse 18. He is writing about Abraham, 'who against hope believed in hope, that he might become the father of many nations; according to that which was spoken, So shall thy seed be. And being not weak in faith, he considered not his own body now dead, when he was about an hundred years old, neither yet the deadness of Sara's womb: he staggered not at the promise of God through unbelief; but was strong in faith, giving glory to God; and being fully persuaded that, what he had promised, he was able also to perform. And therefore it was imputed to him for righteousness'.

Faith saved Abraham by 'giving glory to God', by pointing to God. And that is what faith always does! It never points to itself; faith points to God. The secret of Abraham was that his faith led him to God, and God's character and promises; and he relied upon them, and all was well. We are told about the great heroes of the faith in Hebrews 11, that 'out of weakness they were made strong'. Always by faith! Not faith in faith, but faith in God! They were men who believed God, they accounted Him able to do that which He had promised. That was their secret.

Faith never turns in upon itself. So you should not be looking at yourself and trying to cultivate faith in yourself. Faith always points to God, to the character of God. He is One on whom we can rely. Faith points to His promises – and the Bible is full of them. Get to know them, and then you will be able to hold up the shield of faith. The moment the enemy comes, and the darts are flying round you, you will be able to hold up a statement of the Scripture, a promise of God, knowing that He is always true and faithful to His promises. He is unchangeable. He is 'the Father of lights, with whom is no variableness, neither shadow of turning'. So when the devil comes to you and says, 'I grant you that God did bless you once, and seemed to be your Father; but He is no longer interested in you', lift up the shield of faith and say, 'But that is impossible, God is "the Father of lights, with whom is no variableness, neither shadow of turning". He cannot change. What God promised He will perform. His promises are ever sure. He has taken an oath and He will never break it'. That is how you must hold up the shield of faith.

Then, too, you must remember the power of God. When the enemy sends over his barrage of fiery darts and you feel very weak and frail, and tempted to believe that they are bound to hit you and you will certainly be defeated, take up the shield of faith, hold it up. It points you straight to God and to the power of God. Remember an incident in Abraham's life, how he was tired and exhausted after a great stand, and the enemy began to attack him and to say to him, 'What is the point of God blessing you in this way? He has not given you an heir, you have no-one to carry on the line; what is the use of all these great promises of God if you have not a son?' And Abraham was on the point of shaking when God reminded him of the shield of faith by saying to him, 'Fear

[306]

not, Abram: I am thy shield, and thy exceeding great reward' (Genesis 15:1). 'I am thy shield!' God is our shield, and His power is endless and eternal. 'God is our refuge and strength, a very present help in time of trouble', says Psalm 46. And the book of Proverbs adds, 'The name of the Lord is a strong tower: the righteous runneth into it, and is safe'. That is the shield – the Name of the Lord, the power of God! David delights to tell us in Psalm 84, 'The Lord God is a sun and shield'. The shield of faith points you to the power of God, and the moment you are hidden behind it, all the fiery darts of the wicked one are quenched and come to nothing; they cannot touch you. And remember, His power is eternal, illimitable, everlasting; He is the omnipotent God. Let the forces of hell come together, they cannot touch you: 'Whom resist steadfast in the faith'.

But not only is God the Father on our side, our blessed Lord and Saviour brings it to us still more definitely. His love for us in the past proves His interest in us. 'Who can condemn?' asks Paul. 'It is Christ that died [for us], yea rather, that is risen again, who is even at the right hand of God, who also maketh intercession for us' (Romans 8:33, 34). So when the devil hurls these darts and doubts at you, hold up the shield of faith by saying, 'Christ has proved His love to me by dying for me and rising again'. Then take this thought. He has been in the world Himself as a man; 'The Word was made flesh'. He came 'in the likeness of sinful flesh'. He was tempted by the devil. The devil hurled all his fiery darts and brought out all his reserves against Him. But He defeated him completely and routed him finally. Remember, too, that He is now seated at the right hand of God, with all power in His hands, and that He is there as our representative, that He is there to help us to fight all our battles, and 'waiting until his enemies are made his footstool'.

When you are in the heat of the battle, and when the fiery darts are coming from every direction, remind yourself then that because He came into this world, because the Incarnation is true, because He suffered, fighting against sin even unto blood, because He has been tempted like as we are, He is fully able to sympathize with us when we are tempted. 'We have not an high priest that cannot be touched with the feeling of our infirmities, but was in all points tempted like as we are, yet without sin.' You are not left to yourself; He is with you and He 'is able to succour you'. You are 'in Him', and He is watching over you and caring for you! He has given proof of His love by what He has done, He is continuing that proof by what He is still doing.

The holding up of the shield of faith reminds you that you are looking to God the Father, God the Son, and God the Holy Spirit. It means that you are depending upon God and His grace in Christ. It means that you link yourself in your mind and thought to Him who has all power, and who will enable us to be 'more than conquerors'. There are times when we are so hard-pressed that we can do nothing but call on the name of the Lord. We feel almost incapable of holding up the shield of faith, but we still do so by saying,

> *I need Thee every hour, stay Thou near by;*
> *Temptations lose their power when Thou art nigh.*

That is all you can say! You just desperately cry to Him, 'Stay near; stand by' – and He will!

> *I need Thy presence every passing hour,*
> *What but Thy grace can foil the tempter's power?*

But grace can do so. 'My grace is sufficient for thee'. So we can say:

> *I fear no foe, with Thee at hand to bless;*
> *Ills have no weight, and tears no bitterness.*
> *Where is death's sting? where, grave, thy victory?*
> *I triumph still, if Thou abide with me.*

That is what it means 'to take up the shield of faith, wherewith you are able to quench all the fiery darts of the wicked one'. It is not trying to work up some kind of feeling called faith. Faith leads straight to the Almighty God who is our Saviour, and who is a 'very present help in trouble'. 'Let us therefore come with boldness to the throne of grace, that we may obtain mercy, and find grace to help in time of need.' Do that, and then none of these darts will ever find a lodging place in you or burn you or damage you. Hold up the shield of faith. 'Whom resist stedfast in the faith.'

May God enable us to understand this teaching, and to implement it, whenever the enemy comes in his malignity and hurls his fiery darts at us.

23

The Helmet of Salvation

'And take the helmet of salvation.'

Ephesians 6:17

We come now to the second portion of the armour which is not fixed or attached to the body but which the soldier has to take up and put on – 'the helmet of salvation'. The Apostle was using the figure of a typical Roman soldier of his own day, and he knew that the soldier always required a helmet. Every part of the body has to be protected and has to be covered. And as this is true in ordinary warfare it is equally true in the spiritual application.

The helmet worn by the Roman soldier was a kind of cap which was made of leather; but this leather had been strengthened, and incidentally ornamented, with plates or 'bosses' of metal, to give it protection. Then surmounting all this there was a kind of crest or plume, again mainly for the purpose of ornamentation. When the Roman soldier knew the enemy was coming he took hold of his shield, then of this cap or helmet, put it on, then took hold of his sword and rushed into the battle.

The spiritual application of the helmet is obvious; the Apostle is drawing attention to the head, to the mind, the brain, the understanding, the thinking of the Christian. We have already dealt with the feelings and the sensibilities, the emotions, and the desires, and have seen how the enemy tends to attack us at those various points. But now we have to direct our attention to the particular aspect which involves the consideration of the mind and the understanding, the intellectual part of our whole position as Christians.

Again I would remind you that we must not make too much of these divisions and distinctions; yet they are present, and we

[309]

must pay attention to them. Of course, when we are dealing with the heart we also include the mind, for the devil can tempt us with doubts in that realm. Here, I suggest, the apostle is concerned not so much with our acceptance and understanding of the faith – that we have already dealt with, in the breastplate of righteousness – but with something that is even more general. Here, we are concerned not so much with our understanding of particular doctrines, such as justification by faith, as with our whole attitude towards the faith.

We have already dealt with the matter of particular doctrines; here we have something that is more general. In previous studies, I have indicated that warfare can be considered in terms of both strategy and tactics; that is to say, in terms of the campaign as a whole, or in terms of particular incidents and events in the campaign. The distinction is a vital one. Some great generals and captains of war have been experts on strategy – they could take a very good over-all view – but they were not always so well skilled in respect of local skirmishes, and tactics; and the reverse has also been true.

We have spent much time in looking at the tactics, now we become engaged in looking at the strategy, at the whole campaign. In this general sense our adversary the devil often attacks us through producing a sense of weariness or of tiredness; so much so that the Christian sometimes feels like giving up the entire battle. Notice the difference between this and what I have called the tactics. Christian people are sometimes in difficulties and trouble about particular doctrines, particular aspects of the faith. That does not raise the question of giving up the whole of Christian life. But here is something bigger and in a sense much more serious. It is that one tends to become weary and tired, and to feel hopeless about the whole campaign itself and its outcome.

This is the kind of problem that is dealt with in a well-known poem of Arthur Hugh Clough:

> *Say not the struggle naught availeth,*
> *The labour and the wounds are vain,*
> *The enemy faints not, nor faileth,*
> *And as things have been they remain.*

The poem deals with the condition in which a man begins to feel that the fight is in vain, 'naught availeth, the labour and the wounds are vain.' He says to himself, 'I have been in this campaign for a long time, I am wounded, I am striving, I am struggling; but what is the point of it all, I am the one who is tending to faint, "and as things have been they remain". Have I gained an inch of ground, have I done anything at all?'

The Apostle Paul deals with that same problem when he writes to the Galatians in these words: 'Let us not be weary in well doing' (6:9). The Christian becomes weary in well doing, simply through feeling the heat and 'the burden of the day'. The campaign is so long drawn out, the warfare is constant, and he is tempted to feel utterly hopeless.

This can afflict us in a personal sense, or in a more general sense. It often comes to a man individually in connection with his own personal problems and battles. He sometimes turns to himself and he says in the words of Rustum, in Matthew Arnold's *Sohrab and Rustum*:

> *For now in blood and battles was my youth,*
> *And full of blood and battles is my age;*
> *And I shall never end this life of blood.*

He says to himself, I have been fighting ever since I have become a Christian; and I am still fighting. Is there no end to it? That means that the devil is attacking and trying to get him to feel that the whole thing is vain and useless.

One can feel the same about the entire condition of the Church as one looks at it today. Here is an institution that has been in existence for nearly two thousand years: but what is her position in the world today? The Church in Britain is full of confusion and muddle and uncertainty. She counts for so little; and so the devil comes and suggests to us that she is useless. If otherwise, he suggests, things would not be thus after two thousand years. The enemy seems strong and powerful; while Christians seem weak and fainting. Is there any point in going on with the struggle? And there are undoubtedly many people who were once attached to the Christian Church but who have given up, feeling that the whole thing is vain. And this feeling can come to us in respect of our own individual and personal problems, or with regard to the whole state and condition of the Church.

The best way, perhaps, of looking at the matter is to see it in terms of the teaching of the Epistle to the Hebrews. Indeed the Epistle to the Hebrews is nothing, in a sense, but an extended commentary on this phrase that we are looking at – 'Take unto you the helmet of salvation'. The Hebrew Christians who are addressed, had been brought up in the Jews' religion; then they had heard the Christian message and had believed it, and had become members of the Christian Church. For a while their sun shone brightly, and they were happy in their new faith. But as the years passed they found that they were being persecuted by their own fellow-countrymen the Jews, who regarded them as traitors to their long history, and also by Gentiles. We read that they had been robbed of their goods. Moreover they had been told in the preaching and the teaching that the Lord would come back again and receive His own unto Himself and set up His kingdom. But there was no sign of His coming. The result was that these Hebrew Christians had become utterly discouraged, and some of them were beginning to look back to their old religion, and were wondering whether they had been a little too precipitate in leaving it and taking up the Christian faith. That is the background to the Epistle to the Hebrews – discouraged Christians! They were beginning to think, and to wonder, whether they were engaged in the true religion after all; they were beginning to look back to, and some were even tending to go back to, the temple worship and ritual.

In other words the problem facing those Hebrew Christians was not a question of tactics but one of giving up the whole campaign. They were weary, they were tired, they were persecuted, they were tempted; everything seemed to be against them, and they had got into a condition in which they were tempted by the devil to quit, to give it all up, to back out of the whole campaign, and to return to their former position.

There is a similar illustration in the third chapter of the Second Epistle of Peter. The Apostle is dealing there with the scoffers who came to the early Christians and said, 'Where is the promise of his coming?' They said in effect: You Christians have said that the Lord is coming back, and that He will conquer His enemies and set up His kingdom, but where is the promise of His coming? Everything remains as it has been since the foundation of the world. These enemies said to the Christians: You have made a mistake, you have believed a lie, your doctrine is not true. You might as well give it up because it has proved to be false.

We are facing the same problem in our twentieth century. The enemy comes and attacks our mind and our whole outlook in this way. He says, There is nothing in Christianity; it makes wonderful offers but what does it give you? He returns to the attack and says: That evangelist to whom you listened and who urged you to become a Christian, told you that all your troubles would end, that you would walk down the road with a light step, that you would be in a new world, and that all would go well with you. But has it turned out to be like that? Are you not encompassed by trials and troubles and problems? Are you not finding yourself in a very weary, tiring campaign? Indeed, do not things seem to be worse even than they were before you became a Christian; is not the fight hotter, and are you not being attacked as you have never been attacked before? So much for this Christianity of yours; it offered you so much, what is it really giving you in practice?

Such is the condition, with which we are dealing. It is a very old problem. God's people have always been tried in this way. The classical example of it in the Old Testament is Psalm 72, which shows the godly man full of troubles and trials; everything seemed to be against him. He looked at others, the irreligious, the godless, and he says, 'There are no bands in their death. Their eyes stand out with fatness, nothing goes wrong with them'. 'Verily', he is on the verge of saying, 'I have washed my hands in vain. I am trying to live a godly life and to please God, but everything goes wrong with me. Those other people defy God in rebellion; but they seem to be having a wonderful time.' The temptation that came to him was to renounce religion, and to say there was nothing in it. 'I have washed my hands in vain. I am trying to live the righteous life to no purpose, I might as well give up, I might as well give in.' That was the temptation, and that is the very temptation with which the Apostle is dealing as he tells us to put on this 'helmet of salvation'.

What it means is that the devil succeeds at times in persuading us to become so preoccupied with the details of the Christian life that we forget the grand truth covering the whole. We are so concerned about the trees that we miss the wood; we are so immersed in the local tactics that we forget the great campaign. 'The world is too much with us.' We are so keenly aware of the heat and the burden of the day that we forget who we are, we forget what we are destined for. The result of all this, of course, is that we begin to feel that we cannot go on, that it is too much for us. 'The struggle naught availeth.' Our wounds are all in vain, and all our labour is in vain. The devil, we feel, is too strong, too subtle for us; he is sure to defeat us.

Our Lord deals with that condition when He says that 'men ought always to pray, and not to faint' (Luke 18:1). The danger is to faint. The main problem in life is to keep standing, and not to be overwhelmed by all these things that come upon us from all directions, and make us feel, Oh, there is nothing in it, let yourself go; go back into the world, have your enjoyment, drown your sorrows. What is the point of struggling in this way, what are you getting out of it? Give up the whole thing! That is the temptation. This problem is in an entirely different category from the various detailed problems with which we have been dealing in our study of this section of Scripture up to this point. This therefore obviously merits careful treatment. The way to resist the enemy in this respect is dealt with extensively in many parts of the Scripture. Let us consider one other illustration of it in order that it may be quite clear to us. This was the peculiar trouble with the youthful Timothy. Timothy always had the feeling that everything was too much for him. How to go on was always the question and the problem. His old friend and teacher, the Apostle Paul, was in prison, and likely to be put to death at any moment, and the cares and burdens and problems in the churches fell to his lot. Oh, how can one go on with it all? The Apostle has to write to Timothy and say, 'God hath not given us the spirit of fear; but of power, and of love, and of a sound mind' (2 Timothy 1:7).

To deal with this, says the Apostle, there is only one course to follow: Take hold of the helmet of salvation and put it on your head! What does 'salvation' mean in this connection? At this point I venture to disagree with the great Charles Hodge who tells us that 'salvation' here means our awareness of the fact that we are saved, that we are Christians. He says it means the present enjoyment of our salvation. I agree that that is included, but I believe it misses the real thrust of this point, and is therefore inadequate.

I am satisfied that the Apostle Paul himself leads us to the right answer in what he says in the First Epistle to the Thessalonians in chapter 5, verse 8, where we read: 'But let us, who are of the day, be sober, putting on the breastplate of faith and love; and for an helmet the hope of salvation'. 'The hope of salvation!' So I interpret this as meaning, not so much the realization of our salvation at the present time but of the 'hope' of salvation.

The meaning of 'hope' in this connection is supplied by Scripture itself. The best way to interpret any passage of Scripture is to look at another similar Scripture. Scripture interprets Scripture. So we turn to what Paul says in his Epistle to the Romans, chapter 13: 'Love worketh no ill to his neighbour: therefore love is the fulfilling of the law. And that, knowing the time, that now it is high time to awake out of sleep: for now is our salvation nearer than when we believed'. 'Salvation' in this context is not so much something I am enjoying at the moment; it is something to which I am going, something which is coming to me; 'our salvation is nearer than when we believed'.

In other words I suggest that what the Apostle means by salvation here, is the Christian hope, or what he calls elsewhere 'the hope of glory'. The protection therefore which we put on our heads to counter the devil's particular assault and attack is 'the hope of glory'. Our Lord Himself in His teaching dealt with this at the very end of His life on earth. Take, for instance, chapters such as the twenty-fourth of Matthew or, the thirteenth of Mark and the twenty-first chapter of Luke. Our Lord is taking a preview of history, and He warns His followers that they are certain to have great trials, and will have to endure great tribulations. There are going to be 'wars and rumours of wars'. Get rid of the notion that Christianity is something magical, that you enter into a magic circle, and never have any more problems. It is not going to be like that, Christ says, but rather a life of trial and trouble and temptation. 'He that endureth to the end shall be saved.'

That is the picture! He does not say: My teaching is going to make the world better and better; My teaching is one of political reform which is going to banish war. There will be no troubles, the nations will all embrace one another, and you as Jews will be at the head of the nations. It is the exact opposite of that.

Nevertheless Christ gives His disciples real hope. He says, 'These things have got to be; these things must happen before the end comes'. But then He tells them about the end, and of how, when they think that everything is hopeless, and they are about to give way to despair, suddenly they shall see the Son of man coming, riding upon the clouds of heaven, King of kings, Lord of lords. That is what is meant here by 'the helmet of salvation'. When the enemy tells you to give up and to give in, that you are hopeless, that you are losing, your answer is – the hope! 'The hope of glory!' The hope of His coming! Everything that is contained in that teaching! The same is found in the teaching of the Apostle Paul, for instance, in the First Epistle to the Corinthians. 'But of him', he says, 'are ye in Christ Jesus, who of God is made unto us wisdom, and righteousness, and sanctification, and redemption' (1:30). In this context 'redemption' has the same meaning as 'salvation' in our present context. The Christian is already justified. Some think that the word 'redemption', as just quoted, is tautological; but it is not. Paul means by 'redemption' the ultimate, completed, final, full deliverance – complete salvation in glory! We have that already in Christ by faith.

But let us look at another example, namely, the central theme of 1 Corinthians 15. The Apostle's argument there is that the assurance that Christ has risen, and that we shall be raised also in incorruption, and so on, is the mainspring of all the Christian's activity. He says for instance, in verse 32, 'If after the manner of men I have fought with beasts at Ephesus, what advantageth it me, if the dead rise not? let us eat and drink; for tomorrow we die'. He says, in effect, I would not go on with this fight were it not that I know what is coming. What is the point of fighting with beasts at Ephesus? What keeps me going in the fight, he says, is that I know this redemption, this salvation, this ultimate victory is coming, is sure. If it were not so, he says, 'Let us eat and drink for tomorrow we die', – let us go back and give up!

Paul says a similar thing in the Second Epistle to the Corinthians, chapter 4, verse 6: 'God, who commanded the light to shine out of darkness, hath shined in our hearts, to give the light of the knowledge of the glory of God in the face of Jesus Christ'. One might suppose that a man who speaks in this way is surely a man who never has any troubles. But immediately he adds: 'But we have this treasure in earthen vessels, that the excellency of the power may be of God, and not of us'. Then there follows, 'We are troubled on every side, yet not distressed; we are perplexed, but not in despair; persecuted, but not forsaken; cast down, but not destroyed; always bearing about in the body the dying of the Lord Jesus, that the life also of Jesus might be made manifest in our mortal flesh. So then death worketh in us, but life in you. We having the same spirit of faith, according as it is written, I believed, and therefore have I spoken; we also believe, and therefore speak; knowing that he which raised up the Lord Jesus shall raise up us also by Jesus, and shall present us with you'. Were it not for this hope we would faint, the fight would get us down, we would give up, we would give in. So Paul continues: 'For which cause we faint not; but though our outward man perish, yet the inward man is renewed day by day'. And then comes the moving statement at the close: 'For our light affliction, which is but for a moment, worketh for us a far more exceeding and eternal weight of glory; while we look not at the things which are seen, but at the things which are not seen: for the things which are seen are temporal; but the things which are not seen are eternal'. Here Paul is 'putting on the helmet of salvation' and rejoicing in 'the blessed hope'. Keep your eye on that! 'Set your affection on things above.' All these are but variants of this command we are examining.

But this teaching is not confined to the Apostle Paul. As I have already hinted, it is the great theme of the Epistle to the Hebrews. In chapter 6, verses 11, 12 we read: 'We desire that every one of you do shew the same diligence to the full assurance of hope unto the end: that ye be not slothful, but followers of them who through faith and patience inherit the promises'. The author has already said to them, 'Beloved, we are persuaded better things of you, and things that accompany salvation, though we thus speak'. He has been talking about people who deny the faith and who had once said that they believed, and he has been saying terrible things concerning them. But he says, Beloved, I am persuaded that this is not true of you. 'For God is not unrighteous to forget your work and labour of love, which ye have shewed toward his name, in that ye have ministered to the saints, and do minister'. Then he appeals to them to put the same diligence as they had put into that work of ministering to the saints into making sure of the 'full assurance of hope unto the end'. In other words, use the same energy that you show in practical matters in this matter of fighting the enemy when he tries to discourage you. Then the writer goes on to speak about God having pledged Himself with an oath, 'that by two immutable things . . .we might have a strong consolation, who have fled for refuge to lay hold upon the hope set before us'. Thus, he says, we have an anchor 'within the veil', for Jesus, our forerunner, has gone there for us. Hold on to that truth, says the Epistle, make sure that you understand it and grasp it.

That is another way of putting on the helmet of salvation. Indeed it is the teaching right through the whole of the Hebrew Epistle. Its author has already said in chapter 2, verse 5: 'For unto the angels hath he not put in subjection the world to come, whereof we speak'. Who are the angels? 'Are they not all ministering spirits, sent forth to minister for them who shall be heirs of salvation?' (Hebrews 1:14). The 'world to come' is not being prepared for angels; it is being prepared for us, who believe in Christ. In chapter 4 he states the same truth by exhorting them not to be like the children of Israel who became discouraged in the wilderness, and listened to the devil who told them that they would never arrive in the land of Canaan, the land flowing with milk and honey, and urged them to turn against God. Hence they rebelled in the wilderness, and they never entered into the land of promise. Do not be like them, says the Epistle; hold on to the hope, hold on to the salvation that is coming.

The Apostle Peter gives the same teaching: 'But the God of all grace', he says, 'who hath called us unto his eternal glory by Christ Jesus, after that ye have suffered a while, make you perfect, stablish, strengthen, settle you' (1 Peter 5:10). The Apostle John writes in similar fashion. 'Beloved, now are we the sons of God . . . it doth not yet appear what we shall be: but we know that, when he shall appear, we shall be like him; for we shall see him as he is' (1 John 3:1-3). Then follows the words: 'Every man that hath this hope in him' – that is it! 'The hope of salvation! The helmet of salvation!'

The same message is found in the last book of the Bible, indeed it is the real message of the Book of Revelation. The vision was given to John, in order that he might prepare the Christians of that time, and the Christians of every subsequent age, for the kind of treatment they must expect in this world. 'Beasts' will arise – military power, political power, false power, against the Church. They will attack the saints, and the saints will almost be exterminated. But we need not fear or panic. He is coming – the Rider on the white horse with a sword in His mouth, conquering and to conquer. That is a part of the message of the Book. It is a Book that was designed to give God's people comfort, to enable them to repulse the enemy when he attacks them, in the realm of the mind, about the whole campaign. We are not dealing with particular doctrines here, it is the whole of Christianity that is involved. And the Book of Revelation shows us the only way in which we can succeed.

To conclude, we may say that nothing is more important for us than to learn what we may call 'the tenses of salvation'. An objector may say, 'Are you not trying to tell us, then, that a man can never know that he is saved? You are representing salvation as something entirely in the future'. The answer is that there are tenses in salvation, past, present, and future. The Christian is a man who *has been* saved. He is justified by faith. He is no longer 'under the law'. We saw that when dealing with the breastplate of righteousness. He will never come into condemnation. He is delivered also from the dominion of Satan. He is already free, and in that sense, he has been saved. But then the Christian is a man who *is being* saved. He is not perfect, there is a work going on in him. The present tense of salvation is the 'continuous present'. But then, also, salvation has a *future* tense. The Christian has yet to experience final salvation. There is a day coming when he will be absolutely perfect. Bearing that in mind, this word 'salvation' obviously means the hope of salvation. So you can describe the tenses thus: the past is justification, the present is sanctification, the future is glorification. 'Redemption!' 'Glorification!' The ultimate, the final, the absolute salvation!

So 'putting on the helmet of salvation' means that when you are attacked, besieged, tried, tempted, and the devil says, 'There is nothing in it, you might as well get out of it, Christianity makes false promises, it does not fulfil them – give up!', you answer by saying, 'No, I have not been led astray by this teaching. I have always known that there are steps and stages in salvation. I know that I am saved, I know that I am being saved, I know that ultimately I shall be completely saved'.

In other words, we have to realize what this 'hope' actually means; and there is no difficulty about our doing so. The Apostle has already told us in the fifth chapter of this Epistle to the Ephesians: 'Husbands, love your wives, even as Christ also loved the church, and gave himself for it; that he might sanctify and cleanse it with the washing of water by the word' – to this end – 'that he might present it to himself a glorious church, not having spot, or wrinkle, or any such thing; but that it should be holy and without blemish'. That is the ultimate in salvation. Believers are destined to be absolutely perfect, free from sin, free from all vestiges of evil, 'without spot, or wrinkle, or any such thing'. We shall be glorified, we shall be like Christ, we shall see Him as He is and be like Him; our bodies shall be changed, we shall be completely glorified – saved entirely, body, soul, and spirit; with nothing lacking. That is the hope! And putting on the helmet of salvation means realizing that that is coming.

Secondly, it means that we are certainly assured that we are predestined to glory. 'Moreover whom he did predestinate, them he also called: and whom he called, them he also justified: and whom he justified, them he also glorified' (Romans 8:30). It means knowing all these blessings are yours, knowing that you are no longer in the world, knowing that you have been redeemed by the precious blood of Christ, and that having been justified you can rejoice in hope of the glory of God.

Thirdly, it means that the Lord, having ever set His love and His affection upon us, and having called us, will never let us go; that whatever the strength and the power of the enemy, His power is greater. Our Lord tells us so in John 10, verses 28, 29: 'And I give unto them eternal life; and they shall never perish, neither shall any man pluck them out of my hand. My Father, which gave them me, is greater than all; and no man is able to pluck them out of my Father's hand'. That is the 'helmet of salvation'! No man shall ever be able to pluck us out of the hand of the Son, and the hand of the Father! They will keep us! Listen to Paul giving the same comfort to Christians in Romans 8: 'What shall we then say to these things? If God be for us, who can be against us?' When you see the enemy coming in droves, and in all his power and might, put on this helmet of salvation – 'If God be for us, who can be against us?' – and you will have already defeated him. For though we are led as sheep to the slaughter day after day, and everything is against us, 'I am persuaded, that neither death, nor life, nor angels, nor principalities, nor powers, nor things present, nor things to come, nor height, nor depth, nor any other creature, shall be able to separate us from the love of God, which is in Christ Jesus our Lord'. Let the enemy do his worst, he can never separate us! That is the helmet of salvation! The certain hope!

In other words it comes to this. Look at our blessed Lord Himself, the Son of God here incarnate in this sinful, evil world, with the devil attacking, and all the powers of hell let loose against Him. He went through with it. He knew what it would mean, He knew that the cross would mean separation from His Father; but He went on. What enabled Him to do so? The answer is given in Hebrews 12:2: 'Who for the joy that was set before him endured the cross, despising the shame'. That was the secret. He kept His eye on the joy set before Him, and therefore He was able to conquer His enemies. Let us then 'Look unto Jesus', let us follow His example. As the enemy comes and attacks the mind and the understanding, let us answer him by 'the blessed hope', the certainty of it, the glory of it! And let us realize that we are in His power, and that He will never leave us nor forsake us. The writers of our hymns have got hold of the idea and they have expressed it thus:

> *Mid toil, and tribulation,*
> *And tumult of her war,*
> *She waits the consummation*
> *Of peace for evermore;*
> *Till with the vision glorious*
> *Her longing eyes are blest,*

And the great Church victorious
Shall be the Church at rest.

Another hymn exhorts us:

Stand up, stand up for Jesus!
The strife will not be long:
This day the noise of battle,
The next the victor's song,
To him that overcometh
A crown of life shall be;
He with the King of Glory
Shall reign eternally.

Let us end with John Bunyan:

Hobgoblin nor foul fiend
Can daunt his spirit;
He knows he at the end
Shall life inherit;
Then fancies fly away!
He'll fear not what men say;
He'll labour night and day
To be a pilgrim.

Bunyan had seen it! He had the hope. He knew about this ultimate redemption, this final glorification, this completed salvation. He had put on the helmet of salvation.

That is the only way in which this battle can be fought. Has the devil tempted you to give up? Has he tempted you to give up the Church and your Christian profession and join the world and its supposed pleasures? Can you not see the subtlety of it all? Can you not see the folly of listening to him? We have never been offered an easy time in this world. Christianity is too honest to do that. It is the politicians and the philosophers who offer such things. Christ has warned us, 'He that shall endure to the end, the same shall be saved'. 'There shall be wars, and rumours of wars', everything will be against you, and you may well think that you are finally lost and defeated. 'Lift up your heads! The coming of the Son of Man draws nigh. Put on the helmet of salvation.'

24
The Sword of the Spirit

'And take . . . the sword of the Spirit, which is the Word of God.'

Ephesians 6:17

Here we are to look at the sixth piece of the whole armour of God which the Apostle exhorts the Ephesian Christians to take unto themselves and to put on. While it is the sixth of the entire series, it is the third in the second division into which we have seen that these pieces of armour can be divided.

The sword of the Spirit differs from all the others in three main respects. It is interesting in the natural realm, and therefore still more interesting when we come to the spiritual application. Every other part we have been looking at provides a protection for the body as a whole or particular parts of the body. But this is not true of the sword of the Spirit.

Another point of difference is that this weapon is defensive in a different way. It is defensive in the sense that it keeps back the enemy as a whole rather than some particular aspect of his attack or some particular method of attack. It is obvious that the breast-plate, as we have seen, protects the seat of affections. Similarly the helmet, and the sandals, protect different special parts. But when you come to the sword, it does not protect different parts of the body, or cover the whole body as the big shield does. It protects us in the sense that it helps us to hold back the enemy himself rather than some particular action on his part.

But the main, and the third point of difference and distinction is that this is also an 'offensive' weapon. This constitutes its uniqueness. There was no element of the offensive in any of the other five parts of the whole armour of God, but here there is. The sword serves a dual purpose, defensive and offensive. It is something whereby we can not only repel the enemy but also attack him.

It throws light on phrases in the Scripture such as, 'Resist the devil, and he will flee from you' (James 4:7). You will not merely hold him up, as it were, he will run away, he will 'flee'. We learn therefore that we have not merely to repel or to resist the enemy and his nefarious attacks in a negative sense, but that there is to be also a positive element in what we do with respect to him. He is to be discomfited, and to be caused to retreat; we are to drive him back.

One of our main troubles is that the devil tends to terrorize us and to frighten us, and to produce in us a craven spirit and a feeling of hopelessness. And if he succeeds in doing so we are already defeated. But the Apostle's statement about the sword is the final antidote to such feelings. It reminds us that if we view these things in a New Testament manner we must not shrink back from the devil in that craven sense of fear; we must be confident in our ability to resist him. We must have the assurance that though he is so great and powerful, and though all we have seen concerning him and his forces is true, it is not a hopeless battle. It is possible for the Christian so to resist the devil as to cause him to flee.

I must qualify my words, however, by saying that this is not an encouragement to foolhardiness, or to a spirit of jocularity with respect to the devil. The world regards the devil as a joke; and indeed there are many in the Christian Church who tend to do the same. But remember the warnings in the Second Epistle of Peter and in the Epistle of Jude. We are not 'to speak evil of dignities', we are not 'to bring a railing accusation against the devil'. The foolhardy Christian is nothing but a fool. We must never forget the might and the power and the strength of this great enemy that is set against us. But at the same time we are not to be terrified by him. We must 'stand' and 'withstand' and use this 'sword of the Spirit' in such a manner that we shall cause him to flee from us.

There is a balance with regard to this subject in the New Testament. We are not to indulge in a foolish over-confidence, making us feel that because we are Christians we can be care-free. Rather we are told, 'Let him that thinketh he standeth take heed lest he fall'. But at the same time we must avoid being terrorized by the devil, and being brought to a feeling of utter hopelessness because of his great power and strength.

But we must proceed to the detailed description given by the Apostle. We are 'to take the sword of the Spirit', which means that it is the sword which the Spirit gives or supplies. But then he adds to that the phrase, 'which is the word of God'. The so-called New English Bible translates it thus: 'For sword, take that which the Spirit gives you – the words that come from God'. I confess that I have no idea what they mean by that. I have consulted every other translation I know of, and without exception they all have 'the sword of the Spirit, which is the word of God'. But the N.E.B. says, 'the words that come from God', opening the door to mysticism, or to certain feelings or words that may come to us at a time of stress. That seems to me to be an entire contradiction of what the Apostle is teaching at this point. It is not, 'words that come from God', but 'The sword of the Spirit which is the word of God'.

Another false interpretation has sometimes been current, which states 'Take the sword of the Spirit, which is' – that is to say, the Spirit is – 'the word of God'. But this is obviously wrong because nowhere in the Scripture is the Holy Spirit described as the Word of God. That description is confined solely to our Lord Jesus Himself. The Spirit is not the sword.

What the Apostle is saying is this: Take up the sword which the Spirit Himself provides for you, that is to say, the Word of God; in other words the Scriptures, the Bible. I am anxious to prove this, and to show that it is not merely my idea but rather something which is inevitably true. In proof of my claim, I point you to what happened to our blessed Lord Himself when He was tempted by the devil in the wilderness for forty days and nights. First of all, He went to be baptised by John the Baptist in the Jordan, and as He was coming up out of the water the Spirit descended upon Him in the form of a dove. He was filled with the Spirit. Next notice the interesting thing that follows: 'Then was Jesus led up of the Spirit into the wilderness to be tempted of the devil' (Matthew 4:1). Then there follows the account of the

Temptation. But what interests us now is the way in which our Lord, filled with the Spirit, resisted the temptations of the devil. He did so by quoting the Scriptures. He did not merely speak words that were given to Him by God at the moment; He did not merely utter 'words that came to Him from God'. He quoted the Word of God, He quoted the Scriptures. And there can be no question but that the Apostle has all that in his mind as a background to what He is teaching at this particular point. The weapon used by our Lord was the Word of God, the Scriptures. And you and I are to fight the devil and all his powers with the same weapon, 'the sword of the Spirit, which is the word of God'.

This in turn leads us to ask this question, Why are the Scriptures described in this way and defined as the sword provided by the Spirit? There is nothing more important in this fight against the devil and all these powers than that we should be clear as to God's Word and its authority and its meaning. It is 'the sword of the Spirit', which means that it is He who gives it. It comes altogether from Him. It is the Spirit who inspired the men who wrote it; so it is 'the sword of the Spirit' in that sense. Let me remind you of certain most important statements concerning the Scriptures. 'All scripture is given by inspiration of God', or 'All scripture is God-breathed' (2 Timothy 3:16), a statement which assures us that the Scriptures are given to us by God the Holy Spirit. Then there is the equally important statement in 2 Peter 1:19-21: 'We have also a more sure word of prophecy; whereunto ye do well that ye take heed, as unto a light that shineth in a dark place, until the day dawn, and the day star arise in your hearts: knowing this first, that no prophecy of the scripture is of any private interpretation'. Peter means that the prophecies which we find in the Old Testament are not in any sense the private opinions of those prophets; they do not represent their own understanding and interpretation of the times and of the future. They are not ideas which the prophets excogitated, as it were, out of their own minds and put before us as their own thoughts and theories. Peter plainly says, 'the prophecy came not in old time by the will of man' – man is never able to produce this – 'but holy men of God spake as they were moved [or carried along, or borne along] by the Holy Spirit'. So there is every reason for describing the Word of God as 'the sword of the Spirit'. He

[326]

produced it. He gave chosen men the revelation; He guided them in the recording of the revelation. So the Bible is not a mere human document, a human word. It is indeed God's own out-breathed Word. It was breathed into these men and they wrote it.

It is a vital and fundamental matter for us that this particular weapon provided for us is indeed a part of the whole armour of God. We are not to fight the devil in our own strength or power, or with our own ideas; we are to fight him with this Word that the very Spirit of God Himself has produced. The Holy Spirit is the Author of the Scriptures. That does not mean that the men who wrote did so mechanically; but it does mean that the Holy Spirit is the Author who so took up these men, and guided them, and inspired them as to give them the revelation and the ability to write it without any error. When you consider the strength and the power of the enemy that is against us you will see the importance of realizing the strength and the power of this particular weapon.

But we must go further. The Holy Spirit alone enables us to understand this Word. One of the clear statements to this effect is found in 1 Corinthians 2:12: 'We have received, not the spirit of the world, but the spirit which is of God; that [in order that] we might know the things that are freely given to us of God'. We cannot know them in any other way. Paul's argument is that when the Son of God was present in this world in the flesh the princes of this world did not know Him, did not recognize Him. They dismissed Him and derided Him, 'for had they known him, they would not have crucified the Lord of glory'. How does anyone come to believe in Him? The Apostle gives the answer: 'Eye hath not seen, nor ear heard, neither have entered into the heart of man, the things which God hath prepared for them that love him. But God hath revealed them unto us by his Spirit: for the Spirit searcheth all things, yea, the deep things of God'. Again: 'The natural man receiveth not the things of the Spirit of God: for they are foolishness unto him: neither can he know them, because they are spiritually discerned . . . he that is spiritual judgeth all things, yet he himself is judged of no man'. It is the Spirit alone who enables us to understand and to receive this Word.

In the same way the Holy Spirit alone enables us to 'interpret' this Word. It is entirely the Spirit's work. Everything connected with this Word is always the result of an operation of the Spirit from beginning to end. However able a man may be in a natural sense, that ability does not help him to interpret Scripture. He may be a genius, or a great scholar, but it will not help him here. Truth is 'spiritually discerned'. It must be interpreted in a spiritual manner. And nothing and no one can enable us to do that apart from the Spirit of God Himself. So all along the line we see that our weapon is 'the sword of the Spirit'.

Lastly – and this is, perhaps, the consideration that was uppermost in the mind of the Apostle as he wrote the words – it is the Holy Spirit alone that enables us to use this Word properly. And as the Apostle is concerned about the very practical matter of fighting the enemy, and repelling him, and causing him to flee, clearly this is the thing that is uppermost in his mind. It is one thing to know the contents of this Book; it is a very different thing to know how to use it aright. The Holy Spirit alone can enable us to do so.

The relationship between the Spirit and the Word is an all-important one. Failure to realize this has accounted for many troubles in the long history of the Christian Church. People always tend to put the emphasis exclusively on one side or the other. The moment you separate the Spirit and the Word you are in trouble. There are some who say that having the illumination of the Spirit you do not need the Word at all. That was the tragedy of the Quakers. George Fox started with the right balance, but as he went on he increasingly tended to pay less and less attention to the Word and more and more to the 'inner light', the illumination of the Spirit, the message received immediately. That is why the so-called New English Bible translation is so dangerous. It substitutes 'words that come from God' for 'which is the word of God', the very thing the fanatics have always claimed. The 'enthusiasts', the fanatics, have always based their whole position on that.

But then there is the other tendency, at the other extreme, to discount the Spirit, and to say that as long as we have the open Bible and the Word before us, and as long as we know it in some mechanical sense, we need nothing further. So the Spirit is forgotten, and you may have a dead orthodoxy, or a mere intellectual academic knowledge of the Scriptures, which really does not enable one to fight the battle against the devil and the principalities and the powers. The Spirit and the Word must be kept together always. The Spirit has provided for us the instruction found in the Word, but we cannot use it without Him. It can be a dead letter to us: 'the letter killeth, but the Spirit giveth life'. What is needed is the Spirit opening the Word, and opening my mind and opening my heart. As long as you keep the two together as the Apostle does here, you cannot possibly go wrong; but if you separate them the devil has already 'divided in order that he may conquer', as it were. And as I say, he has done that very often in the long history of the Christian Church.

Error comes in many ways but we are concerned particularly now with the general attack upon the 'truth'. We have already considered specific attacks under the other headings. The enemy makes this general attack in many ways. He does so through philosophy which has been an enemy of the truth from the very beginning. One of the first battles the Christian Church had to fight was the fight against Greek philosophy. When the Gospel came to Europe it came first to Greece where there was a great philosophic tradition, the outlook which says that man by seeking can find out God, that man can arrive at truth as the result of meditation and the working out of his theories. There was a great fight in the early centuries between the Christian Church and the subtle attack that came from the direction of philosophy. It is still with us, of course, and perhaps more so than ever.

Coupled with philosophy is what is generally called 'knowledge' – any knowledge that man has. It is true of 'scientific' knowledge in particular. It is in terms of modern knowledge, the latest advances of knowledge, especially scientific knowledge, that most people reject Christianity. The only way in which we can repel this particular attack is to take up and wield 'the sword of the Spirit, which is the Word of God'. There is no other way of defence. This is what our Lord Himself did. We must ever follow in His steps in all matters; and in the pages of the Four Gospels you will find that our Lord did this repeatedly. Those clever men, the Pharisees, scribes, doctors of the law, came with their catch questions, saying to themselves, 'Who is this fellow? He has never been trained as a Pharisee, He is just a carpenter, He has never been to the Schools, what does He know?' So they brought their clever questions. They were experts in the details and the minutiae of the law. They were great scholars, so they came with all their scholarship and thought they could trap Him and bring an end to His ministry. He always met them in the manner we have already seen in the Temptation in the wilderness.

Take one instance out of St Luke's Gospel: 'And, behold, a certain lawyer stood up' – a clever man, a trained man, an expert in the Jewish law – 'and tempted him [the Lord], saying, Master, what shall I do to inherit internal life?' He hoped, of course, that our Lord would have delivered an opinion of His own which he, the lawyer, would then prove was not consistent with the teaching of the law. But our Lord met him by saying, 'What is written in the law? how readest thou?' (Luke 10:25, 26). In other words He took up 'the sword of the Spirit, which is the Word of God'. That is how our Lord dealt with the man. 'What is written in the law, what do you read, what do you find in the Scriptures?' There is a similar example in St John's Gospel: 'Then the Jews took up stones again to stone him. Jesus answered them, Many good works have I showed you from my Father; for which of those works do you stone me? The Jews answered him, saying, For a good work we stone thee not; but for blasphemy; and because that thou, being a man, makest thyself God.' A subtle attack indeed! Jesus answered them, 'Is it not written in your law, I said, Ye are gods? If he called them gods, unto whom the word of God came, and the scripture cannot be broken; say ye of him whom the Father hath sanctified, and sent into the world, Thou blasphemest; because I said, I am the Son of God?' (John 10:31–6). Note the weapon! He took 'the sword of the Spirit' and He smote them with it. He not only defended Himself, He discomfited them. And He did so constantly in that very way and manner.

In this way we too are to deal with these general attacks upon the whole truth. What these men were always trying to do was to discredit our Lord, to prove that He was not what He claimed to be, and to show that His teaching was wrong. And men are still doing the same thing. The so-called 'new approach' to 'truth', the philosophic questioning as to how these things can be true in the light of our knowledge with regard to miracles and such matters, is but an example of it. We are facing today an attempt to discredit the whole of revelation and the very essence of our Gospel. And the Apostle's teaching here is that the only way to withstand such attacks is to take up the 'sword of the Spirit, which is the word of God'.

Take another example of the use of this 'sword'. We read in Acts 17 of the Apostle Paul going to the synagogue at Thessalonica and facing gain-saying Jews. What we are told is that he 'reasoned with them out of the scriptures, proving and alleging that the Christ must needs suffer, and that this Jesus whom I preach unto you is the Christ'. He 'reasoned out of the Scriptures'. Invariably, that was his method. His Epistles are full of Scriptural quotations, necessarily from the Old Testament. The Gospels record the same procedure. 'So was fulfilled', they say, 'that which was said by the prophet'. And later, the Apostles, in writing to the churches in order to establish doctrine and to ground people in the truth, always bring out as their final argument a word of Scripture, the Word of God.

What was done by the Apostles was done also by the Church's martyrs and confessors. In particular we see that it was the very thing that was done by Martin Luther in the days of the Protestant Reformation. Luther was held in darkness by the devil, though he was a monk. He was trying to save himself by works. He was fasting, and sweating, and praying; and yet he was miserable and unhappy, and in bondage. Superstitious Roman Catholic teaching held him captive. But he was delivered by the word of Scripture – 'The just shall live by faith'. From that moment he began to understand this Word as he had never understood it before, and the better he understood it the more he saw the errors taught by Rome. He saw the error of her practice, and so became more intent on the reformation of the Church. He proceeded to do all in terms of expositions of the Scriptures. The great doctors in the Roman Church stood against him. He sometimes had to stand alone and meet them in close combat, and invariably he took his stand upon the Scriptures. He maintained that the Church is not above the Scriptures. The standard by which you judge even the Church is the Scriptures. And though he was but one man, at first standing alone, he was able to fight the papal system and twelve centuries of tradition. He did so by taking up 'the sword of the Spirit, which is the word of God'.

[331]

Our Protestant Fathers in this country did precisely the same thing. It was the one weapon which they used. The Puritans also did likewise. That is why the early Protestants were so concerned that there should be a dependable English translation of the Bible, which could be understood by all its readers. It was Tyndale's resolve that every ploughman, every boy at the plough, should be able to read and to understand it in order that they might be safeguarded against the false teaching of the Roman Catholic Church. The way to make people strong in that respect is to give them a knowledge of the Word of God. Hence the great anxiety for accurate and reliable translations of the Bible into the English tongue.

We can withstand the devil in this way whatever the argument that his agents may bring forward. We are not all experts in science, we are not all experts in philosophy. How then can we stand up against the people who bring unchristian arguments? There is only one thing to do. Take your stand. Take up the thing that you can use, the Word of God. Here is something that is available to every one of us. And if you know this word you will be able to answer philosophy, science or anything that may come against you. Keep to the Word, keep to its teaching, and you will invariably cause the enemy to flee.

There is one very interesting aspect of this matter. Ever since the Protestant Reformation in the sixteenth century true Protestantism has fought the battle against Rome in terms of the Bible because it was a way that had worked and been honoured by God. Throughout that period the Roman Catholic Church kept the Bible from the people, for clearly it was the knowledge of the Bible that delivered people from her false doctrines. She did not allow the people to have the Word in a language they could understand. She kept it from them; she discouraged them from reading it, saying they could not possibly understand it. She denounced the Protestant doctrine of the universal priesthood of all believers and the teaching that it is possible for one man with the Spirit upon him to understand. The Roman Church claimed that she alone can interpret Scripture.

By today, however, the Roman Catholic Church has changed her policy. She is now giving the Bible to her people, and encouraging them to read it. Why the change of policy? This, to me, is one of the most significant things in this century. Why does she now give the Scriptures to her people, and why is she no longer afraid to do so? The answer is significant. I quote the words of a dignitary in the Roman Catholic Church, not said publicly, but said privately to a Protestant who put the question to him. It is an honest explanation of the reversal of their policy. He said, 'I will tell you why we have changed our policy. There is no longer any need for us to be afraid of the Scriptures, for this reason, that you Protestants no longer believe the Scriptures. It is you Protestants', he said, 'with your destructive criticism of the Scriptures that have undermined the confidence of the people in the Scriptures. So we are able to say that it is we alone who are standing for the Scriptures'.

Such is the position we are confronting! The Roman Catholic Church says Scripture is the Word of God. It is true she adds her Tradition, but she does stand for the Word, and until recently she has been opposed to the higher criticism. But Protestantism, in its blindness and folly, and utterly defeated and duped by the devil, has undermined its own authority. It has nothing now wherewith it can fight the battle against Rome. It has nothing whereby it can fight philosophy. It has nothing whereby it can fight 'Science'. Its authority is no longer the revelation found in the Bible, and the fact that the Word is God-breathed and God-given and God-honoured. Modern Protestants claim to be fighting evil in terms of philosophy and science and modern knowledge, and that can lead to nothing but utter defeat. There is but one way to fight any enemy which attacks the whole Christian Gospel, whether it be an apostate church or whether it be infidels with their modern knowledge, and science, and philosophy. The only way to fight and to repel the enemy is to take up this 'sword of the Spirit, which is the word of God'. If you are not certain that it is the Word of God, if you do not rely utterly, absolutely upon it, if you do not believe it is inerrant, then you have a broken sword in your hand and you are already defeated by your enemy. Take up this sword and use it in the power of the Spirit, and I care not what universities or scholars or anything else may arise against you; like Martin Luther, with the Word you are divinely equipped and you will be able to repulse and drive back your enemies.

[333]

One further matter calls for consideration. When we were interpreting the first piece – 'having your loins girt about with truth' – I said I would have to show the difference between that truth which you gird about your loins, and the sword of the Spirit, which is the word of God. The difference is that when the Apostle says that we are to have our loins girt about with truth he is referring to the central truth of salvation, the great way and plan and scheme of salvation as a whole. But that is not the meaning here. When Paul says 'the sword of the Spirit, which is the word of God', he is referring to our detailed knowledge of that Word. He means our knowledge of particular Scriptures, and our ability to select and to use the appropriate word or passage at any given point. The picture is of the enemy advancing and of my taking up the sword. I repeat that it is illustrated perfectly in the account of our Lord's Temptation. The enemy comes with his three different suggestions. But our Lord knew exactly which part of Scripture to choose, which part to use, which word to apply in each particular case. By using the sword in this way, with the particular answer from the Scriptures, He repels the enemy and causes him to disappear, although only 'for a season'.

This, I believe, is the difference between these two pieces of armour. In other words, if we are to conquer as our Lord conquered, we must not only know the way of salvation, and know that we are saved, we must know our Scriptures, we must know them in a detailed manner. And not only so, we must learn how to use Scriptures, how to be able to quote the most telling word when someone tries to shake us. Any well-trained Christian must know this in his own experience both negatively and positively. I have known Christians who, when trying to help an unbeliever, have said, 'It says somewhere in the Bible . . .' But then the unbeliever says, 'Are you sure that that is in the Bible?' And the Christian says, 'Well, I know it is here somewhere'. But he does not know where it is. The unbeliever says, 'Well, you cannot prove to me that it is in the Scripture'. And he cannot of course, because he does not know where to find it. But on the other hand, if you can say, 'Here, look at this', the other is made to listen – and to look! It does not mean that of necessity you can persuade him to believe it, but at least he has been made to face the Scripture. And you will find that the unbeliever is generally very ignorant of the Scriptures, which explains in part, perhaps, why he is an unbeliever. He is reading philosophy, or science, he is reading the newspapers, he is reading the attacks upon the Scriptures; but he does not know the Scriptures. The best way of dealing with him is to teach him out of the Scriptures, to unfold their teaching, and to give him particular answers out of them. The term 'sword' I repeat, in this context, does not refer to the general knowledge of the way of salvation, but rather to the ability to use the Scriptures and to give the appropriate answer at any particular point, as our Lord did in His Temptation.

The sword is provided for us; we have an open Bible. But we must know it. We must know the whole of it. It is not sufficient merely to learn certain proof texts; you must know your whole Scripture. Observe how our Lord quoted the Book of Deuteronomy. He obviously knew the whole book. We must be soaked in Scripture, we must 'have it at our finger-tips' as it were, so that when we are tempted, the appropriate Word comes to us; the Spirit gives it to us; He leads us to the Word, Scripture. He enlightens us, He will lead us and guide us. We must not content ourselves with reading a few verses and imagining that when we have read our daily portion we have truly studied the Scriptures. We must give time to it, we must get down to the depths in it, we must read the whole of the Bible, and be really steeped in the knowledge of its every part. Then at any given moment we shall have the appropriate answer, and the enemy will not only be repelled, he will be discomfited, he will flee from us.

This knowledge is something which is possible to all of us. I have known many a workman without much education, but who knew his Bible, and who could make learned men look very foolish indeed. A clever man was trying to make fun of a poor road-man working on the highway. With his knowledge and his learning he was trying to shake the humble Christian. But he could not do so. The humble Christian knew his Scriptures, he knew the Word of God, and it was he who was enabled to make the learned man look foolish and walk away discomfited. This is not a matter of natural ability or learning or knowledge. God provides the Word, the Spirit offers it to us. And if He is upon you and in you as you read the Word, He will fix it in your mind and heart, and He will show you how to use it as the occasion demands.

We are living in desperate days when the enemy is trying to undermine our whole position. 'Take up the sword of the Spirit, which is the word of God'. Let us do so, and use it and wield it to His glory and to His praise.

25
Praying in the Spirit

'Praying always with all prayer and supplication in
the Spirit, and watching thereunto with all perseverance and supplication.'

Ephesians 6:18

The Apostle comes here to his last statement with respect to
what we as God's people have to do in this matter of our conflict
and struggle against the devil and the principalities and powers,
against the rulers of the darkness of this world, and against the
spiritual wickedness in high or in heavenly places.

Our blessed Lord when He was here in the flesh was engaged
in the same conflict. He was 'tempted in all points like as we are'.
The devil assailed Him, and all these powers were used against
Him. And the very fact that we are Christians means that we are
inevitably involved in this fight and conflict. Nothing is more
fatal than to start in the Christian life with the notion that now
we are Christian we have finished with all our difficulties and
problems. That is far from being the truth. Indeed it is almost the
antithesis of the truth. The New Testament rather gives the
impression that because we are Christians we must expect attacks
upon us in a way that we have never known or realized before.
But, thank God, we are not only told that we have to wrestle and
fight in this way, we are also told how we can be enabled to do
so successfully.

What is the meaning of this further and final exhortation?
What is the relationship of this 'praying always' to what the
Apostle has been dealing with hitherto? The answer is that this is
not an additional piece of armour. Some have taken it to mean
that Paul is still dealing with the whole armour of God and that
he is saying, 'Now the next piece, the final piece, is prayer'.
But that, surely, is entirely wrong were it merely for the reason

[337]

that in all the other cases, in dealing with the pieces of armour, the Apostle has followed his own analogy carefully and closely. He has in his mind a Roman soldier, and he takes the various pieces of armour that were worn by such a soldier, and he names them. He mentions, as we have seen, the girdle, the breastplate, the sandals, the shield, the helmet, and the sword. But there is no mention of any portion of armour here, and that, in and of itself, is sufficient to decide the matter. The Apostle has described six pieces of armour; and that is the total picture as regards the analogy concerning 'the whole armour of God'. Moreover there is no reference here to any particular part of the body, nor indeed to the body as a whole.

Neither are these words, as some have suggested, an elaboration of 'the sword of the Spirit, which is the word of God'. 'Praying always with all prayer and supplication in the Spirit' means, they suggest, that you use the sword of the Spirit by 'praying in the Spirit'. That seems to be an entirely artificial interpretation.

Well, then, what is the connection? Surely it is that this 'praying in the Spirit' is something we have to do, and to keep on doing, in connection with the use of the whole armour, and indeed with the whole of our position as Christians in conflict with the world and the flesh and the devil. Paul says, 'Take these various separate parts of the armour and put them on, and put them on carefully, and use them in the way described . . . but in addition to all that, always and at all times and in every circumstance keep on praying. There are two hymns which give what I regard as the correct interpretation of the connection between 'the prayer' and 'the whole armour of God'. One of the hymns puts it thus:

> *Put on the Gospel armour,*
> *Each piece put on with prayer.*

The other hymn expresses it thus:

> *To keep your armour bright*
> *Attend with constant care;*
> *Still walking in your Captain's sight,*
> *And watching unto prayer.*

Both those stanzas have clearly been inspired by the verse we are looking at, and I believe that their interpretation is sound and

right. 'Each piece put on with prayer.' In fact everything that we
have to do must be done in this spirit and attitude of constant
prayer.

This means, then, that the armour which is provided for us by
God cannot be used except in fellowship and communion with
God. The armour God provides for us must never be thought of
mechanically, still less magically. The danger, the temptation, is
to feel that as long as we put on this armour there is no more to
be done; all is well, the armour will in and of itself protect us,
and do so mechanically. So having put it on, we can relax, and
put watching aside. But that is the exact opposite of the true
position, says the Apostle; to think in that way means that you
are already defeated. The armour, and the spiritual application of
it must always be conceived of in a vital and in a living manner.
Every single piece, excellent though it is in itself, will not suffice
us, and will not avail us, unless always and at all times we are in
a living relationship to God and receiving strength and power
from Him. Look once more at the things we have been considering. 'Having your loins girt about with truth' – the great
and glorious truth about salvation as a whole and in general.
The 'breastplate of righteousness' – seeing clearly the doctrine of
justification by faith only, and proving that we see it, by living a
righteous life. 'Feet shod with the preparation of the gospel of
peace' – a zealous faith and all the wonderful things that it can do.
'Helmet of salvation' – that 'blessed hope'! And 'the sword of
the Spirit'. And yet according to the Apostle, having all these
things, we may still fail and be utterly defeated. In other words,
you cannot rely even upon these things in and of themselves,
and imagine that because you have them, you can never fall and
never fail.

To state it in a different form, what the Apostle is telling us is
that even orthodoxy is not enough. We must be orthodox, we
must have the whole armour of God; we are hopeless if we have
not got it. You cannot fight the devil with philosophy, you
cannot fight him with idealism, you cannot fight him with anything but with the truth of God which is provided for us. But the
point is that you cannot fight the devil even with orthodox
doctrine if you are attempting to do so in your own strength and
power. There is such a thing as a dead orthodoxy. It is possible

for a Christian to be perfectly orthodox and yet to be defeated, and to be living a defeated and a useless life. He understands the truth with his mind, he knows it, he can point out the errors in other people's teaching; and yet his life is of no value to anyone, because he is being defeated by the devil. He has perhaps become intellectually proud of his knowledge, of his understanding and apprehension of the Scripture. If so, he is already a defeated man. A mere intellectual acquaintance with the truth, though it is absolutely essential, cannot guard us against defeat.

The same applies, of course, to a church or to a group of churches or a denomination of churches. There have been, in the history of the Church, churches which have been thoroughly orthodox but which have been utterly ineffective and useless from the standpoint of evangelism and bringing men and women to a knowledge of the truth. They did not count in their own areas, or their various countries. This may arise because they have this false mechanical, almost magical, view of the whole armour of God. They have started with the girdle of truth, have donned all the other parts of the armour, and they are able to use, as they think, the sword of the Spirit. Yet they are paralysed by the devil. Somehow or other their possession of the truth does not seem to be of active value in their work as branches of the Church of God.

This state of things could be illustrated, as I say, from the long history of the Church; it can also be illustrated from the record of the Church at this present time. There is nothing so tragic as a dead orthodox church; and the explanation always is that they have forgotten this further exhortation. Having put on each single piece of the armour carefully and thoroughly they have not gone on to remember this injunction – 'Praying always'. This is an appalling fact and in some ways the most alarming position possible – alarming, perhaps, especially to those of us who are theologically-minded. It may happen that the people who are most orthodox are those who realize least the value of prayer. I have known Christians who have been well acquainted with the theology of the Bible, and known it in an extraordinary manner, but who did not believe in prayer-meetings, who did not seem to see the utter and absolute necessity of 'praying always' in the way that is indicated here by the Apostle.

It is possible, alas, for the devil to cause us to concentrate our attention so closely on one aspect of truth that we entirely forget other aspects. But we must not fall into this trap; we must follow the Apostle and go on as he leads us on. What he means is that everything must be done in a spiritual manner, brought to life and quickened by the Spirit. If this does not happen there will be little, if any, benefit. 'The letter killeth; the Spirit giveth life', and we can turn even this glorious doctrine of salvation into merely another kind of legalism or scholasticism. The moment we do so we are already defeated by the devil. So there must always be this 'living' quality, this 'power', this ability to use what God provides for us.

In other words the Apostle is really repeating in this verse what he has already said in verse 10: 'Finally, my brethren, be strong in the Lord, and in the power of his might'. He started with this precept, but he so well knows how we tend to concentrate on the last thing we have heard, that he goes on to tell us about the whole armour of God in detail. He also knows that many a man is likely to say, 'This armour is the one thing that matters', and then to forget that with which the Apostle started; so he brings it in again – 'Praying always'. It is in this way that we become 'strong in the Lord and in the power of his might'; 'praying always with all prayer and supplication in the Spirit'. We are utterly dependent upon God and upon the Lord Jesus Christ; and we must realize that if we do not remain in constant contact and communion with God, whatever we may have done by way of putting on the armour will avail us nothing. We must ever maintain this essential intimate relationship with God. Let us never forget that in the Christian life prayer is essential.

The place given to prayer in the New Testament is remarkable. See it in the life of our Lord Himself. As the Son of God He possessed marvellous knowledge, and displayed it at times to the amazement of the Pharisees and scribes and others; and yet note the frequency with which He turned aside to pray to God. He would spend a whole night in prayer, He would rise a great while before dawn in order to pray to God and maintain this communion. He found this to be essential to His ministry. And so it is not surprising that He should have taught His people that 'men ought always to pray, and not to faint' (Luke 18:1). It is the only alternative to fainting, it is the only way to avoid fainting. We must always pray, or else we faint.

So I ask a question at this point – What is the place of prayer in your life? What prominence does it have in our lives? It is a question that I address to all. It is as necessary that it should reach the man who is well versed in the Scriptures, and who has a knowledge of its doctrine and its theology, as that it should reach anyone else. What part does prayer play in our lives, and how essential is it to us? Do we realize that without it we faint? Do we practise it in the way the Apostle indicates here? There can be no question as to the answer given by the lives of the saints to this question.

Our ultimate position as Christians is tested by the character of our prayer life. It is more important than knowledge and understanding. Do not imagine that I am detracting from the importance of knowledge. I spend most of my life trying to show the importance of having a knowledge of truth and an understanding of it. That is vitally important. There is only one thing that is more important, and that is prayer. The ultimate test of my understanding of the scriptural teaching is the amount of time I spend in prayer. As theology is ultimately the knowledge of God, the more theology I know, the more it should drive me to seek to know God. Not to know 'about' Him but to know Him! The whole object of salvation is to bring me to a knowledge of God. I may talk learnedly about regeneration, but what is eternal life? It is 'that they might know thee, the only true God, and Jesus Christ whom thou hast sent' (John 17:3). If all my knowledge does not lead me to prayer there is something wrong somewhere. It is meant to do that. The value of the knowledge is that it gives me such an understanding of the value of prayer that I devote time to prayer, and delight in prayer. If it does not produce these results in my life, there is something wrong and spurious about it, or else I am handling it in a wrong manner. The trouble, I am convinced, is that we tend to stop at putting on the whole armour of God. 'Here we are', we say to ourselves, 'complete'. And so the devil puffs us up with our knowledge and thereby defeats us.

Let us then follow the Apostle as he gives us some detailed instruction with regard to this vital matter of prayer. Though he has all but finished his Epistle he still feels compelled to enter into details. What a wise man he was, what a profound teacher! He does not leave it at 'praying always'. That is what we tend to do. But he knows us, he knows our defects, our ignorance, he knows that we need to be taught in a detailed manner – 'praying always, with all prayer and supplication in the Spirit, and watching thereunto with all perseverance'.

Paul's teaching with regard to prayer, true prayer, can be divided, perhaps, into general and particular. The general instruction can be called the form of prayer as distinct from the spirit of prayer. 'Praying' is a general term and the Apostle subdivides it into two sections – firstly, 'all prayer', and secondly, 'supplications'. 'Praying with all prayer' means, partly, prayer in general, everything included under the heading of prayer. But there is a deeper meaning. The Apostle actually means that we should pray always with all forms or kinds of prayer. You should pray in private, you should pray in public. 'All prayer', every kind of prayer! There is secret prayer, there is closet prayer, there is lonely, isolated prayer, and we should always be engaged in it. But not only so, there is also public prayer, church prayer, common prayer, 'praying together', as you read of the early Christians doing in the Book of the Acts of the Apostles.

But there is another kind of division. Sometimes one prays in words – oral prayer! But you need not always use words in order to pray. You can pray without actually uttering words; it can be unexpressed as well as oral. Paul says, Indulge in all types. You need not of necessity get down on your knees when you pray. Sometimes as you are walking along the street, temptation may come, and you begin to pray in your mind and in your heart and in your spirit.

Again, prayer sometimes is formal in the sense that it is orderly. Take the order seen in the Lord's Prayer, for instance. There is an obvious order there and a design and an arrangement. And that is true of many of the great prayers we find in the Bible. We should pray in the same manner. Our prayers are to be intelligent. It is right that there should be a certain amount of order and formal arrangement in our prayers. But that is not the only form of prayer. There is another type of prayer that can be equally valuable, equally efficacious. Sometimes it is just an ejaculation, sometimes only a groan, a cry from the heart. 'The Spirit maketh

[343]

intercession for us', says Paul, 'with groanings which cannot be uttered'. They are our groanings. The Spirit does not need to groan, it is we who do the groaning. And sometimes that is all your prayer is; it is just a sigh, just a groan, an 'Oh'! Read the prayers of people like Isaiah: 'Oh that thou wouldest rend the heavens . . .' (64:1). That 'Oh'! What the Apostle Paul is saying is that we should pray in all ways and in all manners, using all forms and kinds of prayer. Be at it always and in endless ways.

But the apostle specifies a certain type of prayer in particular; and in his context this is obviously necessary – 'Supplication'! This refers to that very definite part of prayer which we call 'petition'; it means prayer with regard to special requests and desires. We are to engage in prayer in general, in every form and every type of it – adoration, worship, praise and thanksgiving. But then we move on to 'requests'. The Apostle always seems to adopt this same order. He does so in writing to the Philippians, where he puts it thus: 'Be careful for nothing; but in everything by prayer and supplication with thanksgiving let your requests be made known unto God' (4:6). In this kind of general prayer which we must always be offering, Paul says that in particular you must bring these 'supplications', these particular petitions, and keep on doing so as you see the various needs arising, and as you see the needs of others, and so on. In all these different ways be free, he says, and pray in general, pray in particular, bring your petitions, 'let your requests be made known unto God'.

Such, then, are the Apostle's general instructions with regard to prayer. But let us concentrate on the next section, which I venture to call the secret of true prayer. It is found in three words – 'in the Spirit'. 'Praying always with all prayer and supplication *in the Spirit*.' This is the real essence, the very life and spirit of prayer. It is found in this Epistle in the second chapter, verse 18: 'For through him', says the Apostle, referring to our Lord, 'we both have access by one Spirit unto the Father'. He has dealt with the same matter in the Epistle to the Romans, in chapter 8, verse 26. His theme there is the same – we are in a world of trials and of sufferings and of temptations. He reminds them – and is glad to do so – that 'the sufferings of this present time are not worthy to be compared with the glory that shall be revealed in us'. But life is very difficult all the same. 'Ourselves also which have the firstfruits of the Spirit, even we ourselves groan within ourselves, waiting for the adoption, to wit, the redemption of our body. For we are saved by hope: but hope that is seen is not hope' – we have not got it yet, we only see it as in a glass darkly, we see it distantly by faith – 'for what a man seeth, why doth he yet hope for? But if we hope for that we see not, then do we with patience wait for it' (Romans 8:23–25). Such is the position of the Christian in this world – persecuted and tried and tempted. But Paul continues: 'Likewise the Spirit also helpeth our infirmities: for we know not what we should pray for as we ought: but the Spirit himself maketh intercession for us with groanings which cannot be uttered. And he that searcheth the hearts knoweth what is the mind of the Spirit, because he maketh intercession for the saints according to the will of God' (vv. 26, 27).

The same idea is found in Philippians 3:3, where Paul, describing a Christian, says: 'We are the circumcision, which worship God in the spirit' – or, 'by the Spirit' – 'and rejoice in Christ Jesus, and have no confidence in the flesh'. The emphasis is upon 'We worship God'. Unlike the Jews and Judaisers we worship God 'in the spirit'. We find the same teaching in the Epistle of Jude, when he writes: 'But ye, beloved, building up yourselves on your most holy faith, praying in the Holy Ghost, keep yourselves in the love of God, looking for the mercy of our Lord Jesus Christ unto eternal life' (v. 20).

Why does not Paul content himself with saying, 'praying always with all prayer and supplication'? Why does he add, 'in the Spirit', as he does in other Epistles, and as Jude does? This to me is the vital point about prayer. The addition is as vital as this – that if we do not remember it, we do not really pray. Praying, Paul says, in various ways, whether audible or inaudible, or standing or kneeling or whatever, is not ultimately the vital element in prayer. Of course they have their place; but above all prayer must be 'in the Spirit'.

That means, negatively, that vain repetitions are not praying. 'Much speaking! The Pharisees thought they were heard on that account. They judged and evaluated a prayer by its length and its publicity. And surely the whole question of the use of liturgy is involved here. You can repeat prayers mechanically, reading the

[345]

same prayers or reciting them from memory Sunday after Sunday. That is not confined to the liturgical section of the Church; those who frown upon a liturgy can be guilty of the same thing; we can indulge in vain repetitions, merely uttering words. We can do so privately, we can do so publicly; we can pray out of mere habit and custom simply because we believe it is right to say our prayers morning and evening. But often that is not praying at all! We may be merely uttering words and not praying 'in the Spirit'. True prayer is prayer that is 'in the Spirit'. It is the opposite of relying upon forms and upon ritual.

Do not listen to those Judaisers, says Paul to the Philippians, they will tell you that you can only worship in a temple, or that you can only worship as long as you adopt certain forms and ceremonies and ritual. Then he speaks the positive word: 'We are the circumcision, that worship God in the Spirit', that is, in a spiritual manner. All other worship or prayer is mechanical, external, formal; it is not acceptable to God.

We see, therefore, the need of this exhortation, this addition 'in the Spirit'. There are people to whom certain types of building are essential before they can pray. I have heard such people say, 'Of course the Catholic section of the Church pays more attention to worship than does Nonconformity'. What they really mean by that is that they have certain types of building with stained glass windows, and that they use certain forms and ceremonies and ritual. They think that that is worship; and, of course, if you do not *kneel* in prayer in church, you are not praying. The mere posture is to them a great and vital matter. But to the Apostle what matters is whether your spirit is bowed before God. It is whether you are 'in the Spirit' that matters. That is the contrast.

We can further say that 'praying in the Spirit' is the opposite of cold, heartless, formal prayers. Nothing so appals me as to hear, sometimes in a religious service, on the wireless or television, people talking about 'saying a prayer'. I remember once hearing a man describe how he had been visiting a certain city. He told us that he suddenly saw a cathedral, 'and I went in' he said, 'and said a prayer'. Then he went on looking at the sights of the city. 'Saying a prayer'! That seems to me to be the exact opposite of 'praying in the Spirit'. Or still worse, you get the type of man whose religious deportment is perfect, who is trained perfectly in the niceties of how to conduct a religious service, and who, when he comes to a certain part of the service says, 'Now a prayer'. 'Now a prayer!' That is the antithesis of praying in the Spirit. 'Saying a prayer!' 'Now a prayer!' The glibness, the slickness, the ease of it all! I find it very difficult to refrain from saying that in my esteem such behaviour is little short of blasphemy; it is the antithesis of praying in the Spirit. It means that you are praying with your mind only. You can pray with your mind a very correct prayer, a very 'beautiful' prayer and yet never truly pray 'in the Spirit'. For this reason I never liked printed prayers. 'A beautiful prayer!' As if a man's diction and language when he is addressing the Almighty is the important thing! To be perfectly composed and doctrinally correct does not make it true prayer. You may also pray for the right things and still it is not true prayer.

Are you, says someone, suggesting that Paul means praying emotional prayer? I do not mean that, either, because the phrase does not refer to our spirit; it is the Holy Spirit – praying in the Holy Spirit! This means that the Holy Spirit directs the prayer, creates the prayer within us, and empowers us to offer it and to pray it. 'We know not what we should pray for as we ought, but the Spirit himself maketh intercession for us'. He does this in us, He gives us the petitions, He orders our mind, He gives the prayer, He directs it, He empowers it.

That always results in true worship, in adoration, in praise; and in us it is characterized by warmth of spirit and freedom. There is nothing on earth more wonderful than freedom in prayer. Are you not filled with delight and joy when you are suddenly given freedom. You may have been struggling in prayer, finding it difficult to concentrate, finding it difficult to gather your thoughts, finding it difficult to make contact – but suddenly freedom is given to you. Have you not noticed it also in public prayer? You may have been stumbling and halting, praying as you should with your mind, ordering your thoughts, gathering your petitions. It is right to do so. But that is only the framework, the scaffolding; and you are not to rest content at that point. Suddenly the Spirit comes and you are taken out of yourself, and the words pour out of you, and you know that you are speaking to God, and that an exchange is taking place. You are in the realm of the Spirit and enjoying something of the glorious liberty of the children of God.

'Praying in the Spirit!' Anyone who knows anything of this experience will know exactly what it is. How difficult to put it in words! I can look back, by the grace of God, and I thank Him for it, to two public prayer-meetings in which I was present when this was experienced in an unusual manner. I shall never forget them as long as I live. A prayer-meeting started one night at 7.15 in a church in South Wales. It was a hot summer's evening on a Monday night. Two men had taken part in prayer. Then a man stood up whom we all knew so well, an unimportant man, not a gifted man by any means, a man whose prayers could be stilted and formal and dry and discouraging. He began to pray, and suddenly something happened to him. The whole man was transformed. His voice deepened, and he began to pour out one of the most eloquent prayers I have ever heard in the whole of my life. And he lifted up the entire meeting, myself included. Every one of us was 'in the Spirit', in the realm of the Spirit. And on the meeting went, one after another praying. Men and women whom I had heard on other occasions, praying, were now praying as I had never heard them pray before – language, thought, everything was perfect, and the warmth and freedom and liberty were remarkable. And on and on it went until about ten minutes to ten. We had forgotten time. We were in the realm of the Spirit, we were in eternity. Time did not matter, nothing mattered. This is what you get in revivals: and we were being given a taste of it.

This is the thing to which the Apostle is exhorting us. Formal prayers are not sufficient, the world and the Church being as they are today. We need this 'praying in the Spirit'. We need to lay hold on God, to 'give him no rest' to use those expressive dramatic words of the Prophet Isaiah. And you will never lay hold of Him unless you are 'in the Spirit'. Formal prayers, read prayers – these are not the ways of 'laying hold upon God'. But if you are in the Spirit you can do so. That is what the Spirit enables us to do, and our hearts are warmed, and we know this glorious liberty and freedom that the Spirit alone can give. That is the most important part of prayer.

Is anything real prayer but that? Yes, I thank God it is. I believe He honours our intentions, poor and unworthy though they be. But let us not rest in intentions; let us try to learn how to pray 'in the Spirit'. Once you have known it you will be content with nothing less, you will feel that everything else is a failure and has fallen short. To be taken up by the Spirit, to know He is illuminating your mind and moving your heart, giving you freedom of utterance, liberty of expression, understanding of things in the spiritual realm, is what we need. And as we have it we will not only fight our spiritual foes, but we shall be 'more than conquerors'.

The Apostle ends by saying, Keep on at it; always, at every time, on every occasion, at all seasons. 'Pray without ceasing' he says to the Thessalonians. That is what, in a sense, he is saying to the Ephesians – and to us! 'Praying always'! Not now and again, not simply when we are in trouble, not only when things are going wrong. 'Always'! Always watching! Do not fall asleep, keep awake, be attentive, be vigilant, never be listless, rouse yourself, do not be slack. If you find you are neglecting prayer take yourself to task. Do this – 'watching thereunto, and with all perseverence'. Keep on at it, do not do it by 'fits and starts', do not have spasms of praying. Be unremitting, keep on and go on, never quit, never cease praying: 'Men ought always to pray, and not to faint'.

Surely this is the greatest of all needs at the present time. But let us keep to the apostle's order. You must have the 'whole armour of God'. Put on the whole armour piece by piece, but put on each piece with prayer.

> *To keep your armour bright*
> *Attend with constant care,*
> *Still walking in your Captain's sight,*
> *And watching unto prayer.*

Make prayer come alive! Let it burst into flame! Let your knowledge be illuminated, let the Spirit lead to a knowledge of God that is indescribable because of its glory. 'Praying always in the Spirit!'

26

Praying for all Saints

'Praying always with all prayer and supplication in
the Spirit, and watching thereunto with all perseverance and supplication for all saints; and for me,
that utterance may be given unto me, that I may open
my mouth boldly, to make known the mystery of
the gospel, for which I am an ambassador in bonds:
that therein I may speak boldly, as I ought to speak.'

Ephesians 6:18–20

We have arrived at the last, the final exhortation, which the
Apostle addresses to the members of the church at Ephesus.
Verses 21 to 24 form a personal postscript; the great teaching of
the Epistle ends at verse 20.

It is remarkable that Paul should end on this particular note of
prayer, because as we have remarked so often, this Epistle above
all others in the New Testament is an Epistle devoted to doctrine,
to teaching, and to the display of the great theological principles
which govern the life of the individual Christian and the life of
the whole Church. It is probably the acme even of this Apostle's
endeavours; and in it we have all the great doctrines. So it is
interesting to observe that as he comes to his last word it should
be concerned with prayer. I re-emphasize the fact, therefore, that
the ultimate test of the Christian life is the amount of time we
give to prayer. But my statement can be misleading because it
rather represents prayer as a duty. Prayer is a duty, but it is much
more than a duty. It should be a delight, it should be the ultimate
expression of the Christian life.

The end to which all knowledge and teaching in Scripture is
meant to bring us is to know God, to have fellowship with God,
to realize our utter dependence upon Him, and 'the power of his
might'. So the Apostle ends on this note. Knowledge is of little
value if we lack divine fellowship. What the Apostle says in
1 Corinthians 13 about love is equally true about prayer. Know-

ledge 'puffeth up' if it does not lead to love and to prayer and to communion with God.

We have already considered how to pray, and that what matters above everything is that we should be praying 'in the Spirit'.

But now we turn to consider what we are to pray for. Here, again, the Apostle leaves us in no doubt or uncertainty. First we should pray for ourselves. He is addressing people who are engaged in the Christian conflict and battle, and he tells us that, unless we are 'strong in the Lord, and in the power of his might', even the armour itself will be of no avail to us. So we must be constantly in touch with God and with the Lord Jesus Christ. 'Our fellowship is with the Father, and with his Son Jesus Christ.' So we must go regularly into the presence of God and thank Him that we are His people. Before we come to petitions there should be thanksgiving, praise, worship, adoration! We all know what it is to derive benefit from being in the presence of God. The more time we spend in the presence of God the stronger we shall be, and the more efficient and effective will be our service.

So the Apostle urges us to be 'watching thereunto with all perseverance', never allowing ourselves to become slack, but always to be waiting in the presence of God, speaking to God, making known our difficulties and our problems, and taking our requests and our petitions to Him. Such is Paul's exhortation to the Philippians. 'Be careful for nothing' – never be anxious, never get into that state in which you are filled with anxiety, and are 'on edge', and do not know what to do, and are almost beside yourself, says the Apostle. 'Be careful for nothing; but in everything by prayer and supplication with thanksgiving let your requests be made known unto God'. So if you find yourself passing through an unusually trying and difficult and strenuous period in your Christian life, pray all the more, remind yourself that you are not alone, that you are one of God's people, that you are a unit in the army of Christ, and that as you belong to Him you are entitled to look to Him for all your needs and necessities. He has endless, illimitable resources. Go as it were to the great armoury, go to the great headquarters, go there constantly. In other words, as day by day you continue your fight against the devil and the principalities and powers, make certain that you are renewed in strength. We can be renewed day by day! Whatever may have happened yesterday, 'day by day' we can be renewed in strength and power and everything we need. So the Apostle urges us to go to God constantly, and to pray in this manner for ourselves.

But that is not the main emphasis in what he tells us here. The main emphasis is on what is called 'intercessory prayer', that is to say, prayer for others. We start with prayer for ourselves but we do not stop with ourselves. The Apostle says, 'watching thereunto with all perseverance and supplication for all saints'. 'For all saints'! Why at the end of his letter does he urge these Ephesians not only to pray for themselves but to pray for one another? The answer is that we are all engaged in the same fight. We are partakers, as Jude says in his Epistle, of 'the common salvation' (v. 3). Salvation is not only private and personal, it is a 'common salvation', it is something we share with all Christian people. But it is equally true to say that we are facing a common foe, and that we are all subject to the same problems and difficulties.

Public worship is of great importance for this very reason. The devil would have us imagine and think that religion is entirely personal, and that we alone are involved in it. So, listening to him, we tend to sit in our corners, and to think that we are having an unusually hard time; we commiserate with ourselves, we feel very sorry for ourselves, and are utterly cast down. And so the devil is victorious. One of the best antidotes to that danger is to realize, as the Apostle says in 1 Corinthians 10:13, that 'There hath no temptation taken you but such as is common to man'. We are not alone in this: it is the lot of every Christian. That is what the Apostle emphasizes here – that we share the same salvation, and are confronted by precisely the same enemy. The same subtlety, the same arts, are deployed against every one of us.

This cannot be stressed too much. I speak out of some experience in a pastoral sense, and indeed even in a medical sense. I have found throughout the years that people are frequently amazed when I tell them that other people are having exactly the same difficulties as themselves. The devil, obviously, in his subtlety has got them to think, and has persuaded them, that they are alone. The moment they realize that others are involved, and are experiencing exactly the same trials, immediately they feel a sense of release; they also feel that they can stand up again and face the enemy. So the Apostle tells us to make supplication always for all the other saints because they are engaged in the same battle and conflict that we are in ourselves.

But, in the second place, we have to realize that the battle in which we are engaged not only involves us, and all the saints, but that ultimately it is not our battle but God's battle. We find this message emphasized in a clear and dramatic manner in the story of Jehoshaphat in the Old Testament. The enemy was confronting him, and Jehoshaphat and the children of Israel were in terrible trouble. They did not know what to do. But the command that came to them was this: Stand still and see the salvation of God, 'for the battle is not yours but God's' (2 Chronicles 20:15). Our trouble is that we always tend to view our problems in a personal and subjective manner only. I think about *my* problems, *my* difficulties, *my* fears and *my* hopes. The result is that I become entirely self-centred and introspective, and so I am defeated. What we have to realize is that what happens to us as individuals, what happens to us all together, is but an incident in a battle in a realm much bigger than ours. The ultimate truth is that it is God and the Lord Jesus Christ who are engaged in this battle. It is a cosmic battle. The more we think of it in these terms, and the less we think of it in terms of ourselves and our own personal position, the better it will be for us. This is the great battle of the ages – God and the devil, heaven and hell. That is the real conflict, and the Apostle is emphasizing that the extent to which we realize that we are involved in this great fight of God against the devil is the measure of the extent to which we shall be strong. We shall be delivered out of our morbid subjectivity and see exactly what is happening, and so we shall fight with a new spirit and outlook.

To use the obvious analogy, it is exactly the same as what happens when a country goes to war. It is not a private war. Of course, there are some men who seem to think that it is a private matter, but it is the concern of the country involved; individuals are in it because they are members of the country which is at war. The same holds good in the spiritual realm. So we must get rid of our subjectivity and think in terms of this mighty spiritual conflict, and realize that we are but units in it, and that we have been granted the great privilege of being allowed to take part in the battle of the Lord, the battle of God, the great Crusade of the Eternal God against the devil and all his forces and powers.

We must also think of other saints as being in exactly the same position. They, like yourselves, are but units in the great army of God, in the mighty spiritual Crusade that Heaven is waging against Hell. That is the way in which we are to think of it; so the Apostle obviously tells us to pray and make supplication for all saints because they are in it in the same way as we are ourselves.

Another point now emerges. Because 'we are members one of another', it follows that the failure of any one of us is bound to affect the entire campaign. Once more we make use of a military illustration. Think of a great line of battle – the forces of God. Facing it is the line of 'the principalities and powers, the rulers of the darkness of this world, the spiritual wickedness in high places'. The enemy begins to probe, at any point, trying to get an entry, trying to push back, to make a bulge, so that he may develop a kind of pincer movement. It follows, therefore, that failure at any one point is going to affect the whole line, the whole army. The Apostle therefore tells us to make supplication for all saints.

It is highly important, I repeat, for us always to think of ourselves in terms of the Church. We are not only individuals, we are members of the Church which is the Body of Christ. The Apostle has used that analogy two or three times in this Ephesian Epistle. And yet we constantly tend to be individualistic, and to regard our spiritual conflict as a personal battle and problem only. We think of no one else, and we do not pray for others – it is always *my* problem. I am always talking about it, thinking about it, praying about it, and I rarely pray for anyone else. That is thoroughly bad for me, as I am about to show. But it is also wrong, and especially from this standpoint: 'None of us liveth to himself, and no man dieth to himself' (Romans 14:7). We are mutually interdependent, whether we know it or not; and nothing can happen to any one Christian without all being involved. If any one Christian fails or falls, every one of us suffers inevitably, because we are all members of the one Body, we are all in this one army, we are all parts of this one line. Failure at any one point means that the whole line will be involved, and readjustments will have to take place.

We are all aware of this at times. We see how the devil and his forces rejoice when an individual Christian fails. We see the way in which it is placarded in the newspapers, and how they always rake up the man's past. If ever he was in a Sunday School, the headline reads, 'Sunday School teacher guilty of . . .' The man may not have been in a Sunday School for twenty or thirty years, but it is always dragged into public view. It is something for the devil to rejoice in; God has been defeated, as it were. And not only so, but how utterly discouraging and depressing to the rest of the Church! So the Apostle tells us to pray for one another and to make supplication for all the saints. Apart from anything else, it is foolish not to pray for all the saints. Nothing happens to them but it affects you; therefore, says Paul, remember the whole line of battle. Do not be for ever looking at yourself and concentrating on yourself; consider the whole position, and pray that every man may stand in his position. You must not only stand yourself, your neighbour must stand, and the next, and the next. Pray that they all may stand in order that this great Crusade of God may go forward. This is the way to avoid discouragement even for yourself. This is the way to have the assurance that you belong to a victorious army, and that nothing can possibly defeat the cause to which you belong.

Then the Apostle carries this still further in saying '. . . with all perseverance and supplication for all saints'. Some saints are in positions of peculiar difficulty and trial and stress and strain and trouble. How often do we think of them? How often do we think at the present time of Christian people in many another land? 'Oh,' you say, 'I am having a terribly hard time myself. I am having this problem and that difficulty, and the devil is attacking me'. I agree; but try for a moment to transport yourself into the position of some of these other people. They do not know what is going to happen at any moment, they do not know whether they are going to remain alive tonight or not, they do not know what the future holds for them. Their countries are passing through a period of transition, of uncertainty and of readjustment, and the whole position is as black and as terrible as it can be for many of them. How often do we think of them? They are brothers and sisters, they are units in the army of this living God; and many of them at this very moment may be in positions of such acute strain and stress that they can scarcely pray for themselves at all. But quite apart from other countries, there are many hard-pressed Christians in Britain itself who are carrying terrible loads, awful burdens, and who have crushing problems. How often do we remember them and pray for them? Do not always be thinking of yourself, says the Apostle, remember these others. Whatever may be happening to you, their position is very much worse. Remember those Christians who are almost at the point of collapse. Make supplication for them, pray for them.

Such is the background of this particular exhortation of the Apostle. He gives us remarkable teaching about prayer as one of the great mysteries of the Christian faith. Prayer does make a difference, prayer does help. People have sometimes asked foolishly, 'If God knows everything, what is the point of praying?' But it is God Himself who bids us pray. In 2 Corinthians, chapter 1, the Apostle is talking about a great trouble that had come to him, and he says: 'We would not, brethren, have you ignorant of our trouble which came to us in Asia, that we were pressed out of measure, above strength, insomuch that we despaired even of life: but we had the sentence of death in ourselves, that we should not trust in ourselves, but in God which raiseth the dead: who delivered us from so great a death, and doth deliver: in whom we trust that he will yet deliver us; you also helping together by prayer for us'.

Now that is remarkable; it is a problem, it is a mystery; do not try to understand it. All we know is that it is the New Testament which teaches us in this way to pray for one another. God could do all without us, but He has chosen to do it in us and through us. He blesses His people through the instrumentality of prayer. So we are exhorted to pray, we are urged to be persistent, and to persevere in supplication for all saints. Let us remember this at the present time as we contemplate the lot of our brothers and sisters in many a foreign land. Let us think of the hard-pressed, lonely, pioneer missionary whose supreme temptation, perhaps, is to discouragement and to a feeling of utter hopelessness and despair, struggling as he is against climate, and against physical illness and weakness, staggering on his feet, and facing the slowness of his people to learn, and their occasional lapses. To us is given the great privilege of making supplication for him and for all such people, of holding them up before God, of asking God to look upon them and to bless them, knowing that God is ready to hear us.

Prayer is the sovereign remedy for many of the ills and diseases of the soul that tend to defeat us all. It is the sovereign remedy for introspection, for morbidity and a morbid self-concern. Self is the last enemy. It is self that causes most of our troubles. We sit thinking of ourselves and what is going to happen to us, what the effect of something will be upon us. We turn in upon ourselves and pity ourselves and are sorry for ourselves, and spend our time commiserating with ourselves. One of the best ways of getting rid of such a condition is to pray for other people. Lift up your heads, look away from yourself, realize the whole position, and as you do so you will forget yourself.

This can be illustrated in a very interesting manner. There are statistics which prove beyond any doubt that during the Spanish Civil War, just before the Second World War, the very principle I am enunciating literally and actually worked in practice. In this instance it was not so much a matter of prayer as a purely psychological response. Before the outbreak of the Spanish Civil War, in Barcelona, Madrid and other places, there were psychological clinics with large numbers of neurotics undergoing drug treatment and others attending regularly for psychoanalysis and such like. They had their personal problems, their worries, their anxieties, their temptations, having to go back week after week, month after month, to the clinics in order to be kept going. Then came the Civil War; and one of the first and most striking effects of that War was that it virtually emptied the psychological and psychiatric clinics. These neurotic people were suddenly cured by a greater anxiety, the anxiety about their whole position, whether their homes would still be there, whether their husbands would still be alive, whether their children would be killed. The greater anxieties got rid of the lesser ones. In having to give attention to the bigger problem they forgot their own personal and somewhat petty problems. This was a literal fact.

In a measure that also happened in Britain during the Second World War. A greater fear drives out lesser fears; and I am applying that principle to this whole question of prayer. When you feel that you are in a kind of vortex, and you cannot forget yourself; when you are sorry for yourself and feeling that you are having an unusually hard time with everything against you and almost enough to drive you to despair, one of the best remedies is to sit down and say, 'What about so-and-so? What about this person, what about that person, what about Christians in other countries?' Get down on your knees and pray for them, and you will soon get up finding that you have forgotten yourself. So, apart from all the other reasons, it is a wise thing psychologically to make supplication for all saints. You will find that in praying for them you are solving your own problems and obtaining release.

The Apostle ends on the following note: '. . . and for me also'. This is still more remarkable. 'And for me!' He wants them to pray for him. What a staggering thought that this mighty man of God, this exceptional Apostle, this greatest preacher that the Church has ever known, this incomparable founder of churches, should be asking these people to pray for him! It was because he was such a great Christian. The greater the Christian the more he realizes his dependence upon the prayers of others. This is the man who went to Corinth 'in weakness, and in fear and much trembling'. There was no self-confidence in the Apostle Paul, none at all. He knew what he was doing, he knew whom he was representing, he knew the power that was against him. His one fear was that, at some point or other, he might fail his Lord and Commander, and the army of the living God. He was in a very prominent position and a mistake on his part would have terrible repercussions. So he trembles, and asks the Ephesian Christians to pray for him.

He does not leave them in any doubt about what they are to pray for him. He gives them instruction: 'And for me, that utterance may be given unto me, that I may open my mouth boldly, to make known the mystery of the gospel, for which I am an ambassador in bonds: that therein I may speak boldly, as I ought to speak'. When the Apostle wrote these words he was a prisoner, but he does not ask them to pray that he may be set free from prison. He was a sick man, but he does not ask them to pray that he might be healed. Paul was never merely subjective, and never considered himself primarily. He was always thinking of others. It is not a purely personal or human request that he makes of them. He is interested in one thing only, the thing that had always interested him since he had met Christ on the road to Damascus, namely, the preaching of the Gospel! This mystery of the Gospel! He has told them about it in his third chapter – 'How that by revelation he made known unto me the mystery; (as I wrote afore in a few words, whereby, when ye read, ye may understand my knowledge in the mystery of Christ) which in other ages was not made known unto the sons of men, as it is now revealed unto his holy apostles and prophets by the Spirit' (Ephesians 3:3ff). The mystery that had now been revealed! This message, this glorious Gospel of Christ! The 'unsearchable riches of Christ'! It is these matters that Paul is concerned about. And what he desires the Christians to pray for is the preaching of the Gospel and the spread of the kingdom of God.

But let us notice in more detail what he is concerned about. First, 'that utterance may be given unto me, that I may open my mouth boldly'. Pray for me, says the Apostle, that I may have power of speech and freedom of utterance when I have an opportunity of speaking. The fact is – and we tend to forget it – that the Apostle Paul was not a good natural speaker. Certain people at Corinth had taunted him, saying, 'his presence is weak, and his speech contemptible'. Apollos was the orator. Paul was not, and so he urged these Christians – Pray for me that utterance may be given to me, that when I get an opportunity of speaking I may have the words, that I may have the liberty, that I may be able to take advantage of the opportunity. Pray, he says, that my tongue may be unloosed, that my lips may be made mobile, that I may speak with freedom. It is most interesting to observe that this mighty man of God, realizing his own deficiencies and imperfections, pleads with these Ephesians to pray for him that he may be able to speak freely, fluently, without halting and without stumbling.

But Paul particularly emphasizes the word *boldly* – 'that I may open my mouth boldly'. He repeats it: 'that therein I may speak boldly, as I ought to speak'. This is most important at the present time. Do you pray for the preachers of the Gospel? Do you realize what happens every time a man enters a pulpit – frail, fallible, weak, and yet called of God to be His representative, and an exponent of His glorious truth? Do you pray for preachers of the Gospel? And do you pray in particular that they may 'speak boldly'? By 'boldly' the Apostle means freely, frankly, that nothing be kept back. Let me borrow the very words used by the Apostle to the elders of this church at Ephesus when he bade them farewell once, as recorded in Acts 20. He said that he had not failed to declare unto them 'the whole counsel of God'. Pray that I may keep nothing back, he said, that I may give it all, that I may give the Gospel in all its comprehensiveness. Pray, says Paul, that I may be delivered from qualifying the Gospel, and my statement of it, by carefulness and by endless modifications dictated by a concern for my own reputation or my own personal safety.

I emphasize this matter because it is a great problem at the present time. We are all so diplomatic, we are all so concerned about dignity, we are all so concerned about being 'scholarly' and not causing offence; we are all so afraid of fanaticism! We do not pray today that preachers may speak 'boldly', we prefer that they should speak ecumenically. We can read sermons which say, 'Though this is true, nevertheless . . .'! We are so afraid of being too extreme, of being too emphatic! 'While it is true to say this – nevertheless you must always remember . . .'!, and thus endless qualifications make the message indefinite and uncertain. The result is that the people do not know what the Gospel is. What is said at the beginning is often taken back at the end, and you do not know where you are, and the trumpet yields an uncertain sound. We are so much afraid of offending people that we tend to hold back the truth; and so the Christian faith is in jeopardy at this hour. 'Ah but', you say, 'we must not say anything to offend the Roman Church, we are going to have dialogue with her, so we must be very careful'. That is not what the Apostle asks people to pray for. 'Boldly', says Paul, that is, without qualification. Pray that I may be honest, pray that I may be true, pray that I may deliver the message that has been delivered to me, that I shall not be concerned about anything but to please God and to be faithful to His Word.

In other words he says, pray that I may be delivered from the fear of man, and of the learning of man and his supposed wisdom. The Apostle reminds us that he had become 'a fool for Christ's sake'. The philosophers in Corinth were laughing at him and jeering at him. Look at that man, they said, always saying the same thing, just that simple message about what he calls the 'Cross'. He does not argue, he does not reason out the great philosophies, he does not give us mighty disquisitions; the man is a fool. All right, says Paul, 'I am become a fool for Christ's sake'.

Any man today who preaches the simple Gospel will be criticized by the sophisticated and the learned. They say, Fancy still believing the Bible; fancy still believing in the Virgin Birth, and in miracles! Rubbish! All that is out of date, it is antiquated, the man is a fool! Pray, says Paul, that I may not listen to such criticisms, pray that I may go on preaching the Gospel boldly, say they what they will. Pray that I may have strength to preach it without qualifications, without fear. Take from me any desire to be considered learned, to be considered scholarly, to be considered a political orator. There may be people in the congregations who will be watching for what they call 'a beautiful turn of phrase'. Pray that I may be delivered from that snare, and that I may preach the Gospel boldly, not elegantly; that I may preach it in truth, not in a manner that appeals to the public palate. And that I may never be a man-pleaser, or afraid to face the scorn and the abuse of men.

We need to pray for preachers today that they may preach in that same manner. Pray that the preacher in his difficult position in some little country village, perhaps, may be delivered not only from the fear of men's intellects and their supposed knowledge, but that he may be delivered from a fear of their money. For a day may come when he will be told by someone who virtually can control the church financially, 'If you go on preaching that message I shall stop my subscription'. It has happened many a time, it is still happening. Pray, says the Apostle, that the Lord's servants may be enabled to go on preaching boldly, come what may, relying upon the living God, not upon any man. Pray for boldness, honesty, assurance, and certainty, in spite of men and their power, be it never so great.

But then Paul introduces a further thought – 'that therein I may speak boldly, as I ought to speak.' He has already told us in chapter 4, in verses 14 and 15, what he means: 'That we henceforth be no more children, tossed to and fro, and carried about with every wind of doctrine, by the sleight of men, and cunning craftiness, whereby they lie in wait to deceive; But speaking the truth in love' – that is the qualification! Pray for me, says the Apostle, that I may present this truth boldly, and yet pray that my spirit may be kept sweet, that I may not become partisan, that I may not become fanatical, that I may not become sectarian, or merely a party-man fighting for a label. Pray, says Paul, that I may be concerned only about God, about the Lord Jesus Christ, about the Holy Ghost, about the kingdom of God, the salvation of men and the advancement of the truth. 'As I ought to speak.'

Here is the mighty man of God, who because he knows his own weaknesses, his own tendencies, and the frailty of human nature, asks the Ephesians to pray for him. And men and women in the Christian Church should be praying for the preachers of the Gospel at the present time. Pray that we may be delivered from a spirit of compromise, pray that we may not be guided by diplomacy or expediency, pray that we may be delivered from fear for ourselves; but pray also that we may, on the contrary, be like the Apostles and the first martyrs and the Protestant Reformers and the Puritans, the Covenanters, and the mighty men of God of former days. Pray that the truth shall come first, that we may speak it with boldness, and yet have hearts full of love and mercy and compassion.

Why should we contend for the truth? Because it is the only thing that can save men! Let us therefore look beyond men to their lost souls, and let us be concerned about nothing but the glory of God and the salvation of men and women. So the Apostle exhorts us to pray with all perseverance and supplication in the Spirit for all saints, for all preachers of the Gospel whatever their circumstances and conditions, that they may speak the mystery of Christ boldly, as they ought to speak. And so he finishes.

Then look at Paul's purely personal postscript: 'But that ye also may know my affairs, and how I do, Tychicus, a beloved brother and faithful minister in the Lord, shall make known to you all things: whom I have sent unto you for the same purpose, that ye might know our affairs, and that he might comfort your hearts'. And then the final Benediction: 'Peace be to the brethren, and love with faith, from God the Father and the Lord Jesus Christ. Grace be with all them that love our Lord Jesus Christ in sincerity'. They are the people who matter, the people who love our Lord Jesus Christ in sincerity, with their whole heart, without any admixture, without any ulterior motives; only, always, all for Him. 'Grace', he says, 'be upon all such'. To which we can but say 'Amen and Amen'.